# ON THE EDGE

Richard Hammond is one of our most in-demand television presenters. On September 20, 2006, while filming for *Top Gear*, he suffered a serious brain injury following a high-speed car crash, and the nation held its breath.

*On the Edge* is his compelling account of life before and after the accident and of his year of recovery. It is also, perhaps, his explanation of why, as a married man and father of two young daughters, he was prepared to risk all by strapping himself to the front of a jet engine with the power of eleven Formula One cars.

His wife Mindy tells of the anxious hours and days of watching and waiting until he finally emerged from his coma. She and Richard then piece together the stages of his recovery as his shattered mind slowly reformed. The final chapter recounts his return home and his triumphant reappearance in front of the cameras.

# ON THE EDGE
# MY STORY

Richard Hammond
with Mindy Hammond

First published 2007
by Weidenfeld & Nicolson
This Large Print edition published 2008
by BBC Audiobooks Ltd
by arrangement with
Orion Publishing Group Ltd

Hardcover ISBN: 978 1 405 64921 6
Softcover ISBN: 978 1 405 64922 3



**British Library Cataloguing in Publication Data available**

Printed and bound in Great Britain by
Antony Rowe Ltd., Chippenham, Wiltshire

*For Izzy & Willow*

*. . . and everyone who has suffered brain injury in any form, with best wishes and hope for the future*

CONTENTS

# CONTENTS

CHAPTER 1

# PREPARING FOR THE NORTH POLE

Instinct told me that I was watching one of those things that looked very easy to do but that would, in reality, turn out to be very difficult. My instructor glided across the flat, frozen fields in an effortless sweep; her long, thin skis moving in a languid rhythm, until she seemed to ripple over the snow in a single movement. 'Bend the knees. You see? Bend, push, bend, push. You must get into a rhythm.' Even her voice, with its lilting, Swedish bounce, floated effortlessly across the open space. Her ski poles touched down gently with each stroke to add to the gentle forward propulsion from her skis, her legs worked slower than her progress across the ground, bringing the next ski up to the front to complete the cycle, and there was not a single break in her progress. The whole sequence looked like a piece of slowed-down film. She was demonstrating the classic cross-country-skiing style of her homeland and it looked as though she had spent her whole life doing it.

I knew that my efforts wouldn't look so good. And they didn't; I fell over, of course. I was discovering that cross-country skiing, or langlaufing, isn't just hard to perfect, it's almost impossible to get started.

It's mostly about grip, langlaufing, and I couldn't find any. And it's about rhythm—I didn't have any; poise—absolutely none; and grace—not a jot. Annoyingly, my first attempts didn't even amount to a hilarious, high-speed crash. I just slithered about for a few seconds, my skis slipping backwards and forwards on the snow-covered grass as I tried to waddle ahead, failing to gain even an inch towards my goal before gravity won and I flopped on to my side and lay there, feet clumsily crossed in their skis, my bedewed nose inches from the frozen ground. But I wasn't learning this just for fun. In three months I would set off to the Magnetic North Pole on these same skis. Yet I couldn't cross a frozen playing field—and this was my third day of trying. I closed my eyes.

It got frightening inside my mind and panic rose in my chest. I was struggling because of the brain-damage. It must be that. I'd always been good at things when I tried them for the first time. I mean, yes, after lesson one I'd get bored and fall to pieces. But I've always been good at the lesson one stage. A fast learner with a short attention span—pretty much every school report I have ever had said exactly that. I had a sudden, vivid memory of my first attempt at water-skiing behind a boat on Lake Windermere in the Lake District—when they used to allow such things. I had listened half-heartedly while the bloke droned on about the need to keep your knees together, the dangers of drawing your arms in too close to your body, the need to keep the rope tight, and a thousand other things that I had to know. Eventually I got to give it a go. I slipped into the freezing grey waters of Windermere and grabbed the plastic handle at the end of the blue nylon rope. The boat started to pull away and I was left bobbing around on my own in the green-fringed solitude of a quiet corner of the lake. I thought about old Donald Campbell and his *Bluebird* speedboat. Hadn't they gone down in Windermere when he tried to break the record for speed on the water? Actually no, that was Coniston. Or was it? And then there was a gentle but firm tug on the rope as the small boat reached the limit of the line extending behind it. I gripped hard, there was a lot of water and splashing, I gripped some more and eventually rose up from the foam like a small, straggly Neptune in a borrowed blue wetsuit. I was water-skiing; it was easy. I got cocky and waved at a boat going the other way. Logic told me that I could shift my weight across the skis to change direction and it worked. Crossing the wake, one of my skis was pulled off by the turbulent water. I shifted over to my right leg and carried on.

My wife, Mindy, can still hardly bear to talk about our first horse-riding trips together. She has been riding all her life. Usual sort of thing; spent half her childhood being shouted at by stern-faced women in polyester body-warmers about her leg position and posture in the saddle, and the other half shovelling out what those same horses she dreamed of riding had left in their stable overnight. Horse-riding is, for her, an art; something to be studied, learned and perfected. She approaches it with the same respect, consideration and, yes, fear, that a test pilot might approach each flight. By contrast, I wandered up to the first nag I was going to throw an inappropriately booted leg over, hopped on board, asked how you steered and braked it, and set off. There was no need to shout at me about leading legs or how I held the reins. I still ride horses in the same way as I did that first time; I get on, pull left to go left and right to go right and make sure I don't fall off. It drives Mindy mad. I have always been like this; I love trying anything new and can usually make a decent go of it the first time I try it. And then, if I have to learn how to do it properly, I get bored and want to do something I know I'm already good at.

Lying on the snowy ground, I grew slowly more convinced that my inability to just leap on to the skinny skis and dazzle my instructor by slithering across the surface on my first attempt must be down to the aftermath of the jet-car crash. On the way there, I had harboured a secret suspicion that she might watch my first, tentative tries at mastering the finer points of the classic Swedish cross-country-skiing style and suggest that I put in just a bit more practice and try a competition or two, just for fun. I might even have the makings of an international cross-country skier—if there are such things. Right now, she was more likely to suggest I took up something else. Like collecting Alpine horns or yodelling.

It might have been funny, but I knew that I was only struggling with this because I had damaged something important in my brain that would never fix. I must have dented my balancing gland or disconnected my coordination centre. Or something. Whatever it was, I wished I hadn't done it. The wet snow started to penetrate the damp fleece I had been issued with by the polar experts who had brought us here for our pre-expedition training. Somewhere, between the playing field I was lying on and Strasbourg airport, the rest of the guys were sharing a car, drinking petrol-station coffee from polystyrene cups and talking about home. They were flying back that morning; they'd no need to learn to ski; they were going to the Pole in a truck. Which meant right now, on this cold and suddenly rather lonely Austrian morning, they could go back home. I thought of Mindy, the kids, the dogs and our house. And I thought of that sodding crash and the pain it had caused.

CHAPTER 2

# THE EARLY YEARS OF AN ADRENALIN JUNKIE

I waited and silently weighed up the chances of actually becoming airborne. If the stunt went wrong and I hit the ramp too fast, there was a real chance that I might take off. I tightened my grip on the handlebars and swallowed hard. The crowd was a big one. I had better not look scared. Maybe I would leave the end of the ramp and really take to the air, zooming around the skies over our street, looking down into people's back gardens, at their sheds and their swings and peering on to their flat garage roofs at the collections of faded footballs and greying old tennis balls that had landed out of bounds. I shook my head in what I hoped was an heroic, preparing-yourself-to-do-something-really-dangerous sort of way. I didn't know it, or want to know it, but all the rest of the world could see was a spindly-legged eight-year-old sitting on a red bicycle.

The bike looked brilliant, I knew that for a fact. I had tied two school satchels to the back and draped them over the rack to hang down on either side like motorcycle panniers. There was a fresh piece of cardboard in place, ripped from an old Weetabix packet and fixed to the chainstay with a strip of electrical tape I had found stuck to the garage floor. When I set off for the ramp, the cardboard would rattle away in the spokes and I would sound and look exactly like a California Highway Patrol bike giving chase to a fleeing villain on the telly. At least in my eight-year-old imagination I would. I hoped I would to the eyes and ears of the assembled gang of neighbourhood kids watching now and all secretly hoping my attempt to leap over Action Man and into the history books would produce blood and possibly a sighting of actual bone protruding through flesh like that kid in the year above was rumoured to have done the previous year when he fell off a fence and broke his arm on an upended patio slab.

We often spoke about that, hunched in groups among the dustbins in the pressing spaces between the pairs of semis on our road. We loved talking about gore. And we loved our bikes. I once leant mine in the narrow gap between the two walls and used it as a booster step to set me on my way, climbing up, braced between our garage wall and the side of the house next door. I pushed off from the saddle, faced the ground, stretched my arms up over my head and pressed my hands into the wall as I forced my feet on to the wall opposite. I began shuffling upwards, feeling the rough texture of the red bricks surprisingly warm on my palms, hearing the nylon rasp of my jacket catching on the brickwork and scrabbling for traction with my smooth-soled plastic trainers. The next thing I knew, my bike had collapsed to the floor and I slid down the wall to join it in a tangled pile of wheels, legs and framework. It didn't really hurt; it looked great, loads of my friends saw it and I had started a new craze for wall climbing in the alleyways between our houses. Result for me.

Years later, I would be in at the start of a similar craze at school. We discovered that you could, just, make the climb from one balcony across to another in the big school hall where we would sit for assembly and the clever kids would gather for classical music recitals during lunch breaks. As they sawed at their violins and rasped through their clarinets, I would totter above them, stepping out from the heavy red velvet curtains that flanked what amounted to a sort of theatre box and feeling for the wooden edge of the next box with my foot. When I felt the time was right—hoping, for once, that no one was watching—I would throw my weight across to the extended leg and complete the manoeuvre to find myself standing on the edge of the neighbouring balcony. Boy, did that one catch on.

My regular stunt activities, public and private, were all just me showing off. It was a survival technique I had evolved. If you're a small guy and can't impose yourself on others physically, then think of something funny to say. When that fails, or you run out of funny things to say, hit yourself in the face with a bicycle pump. Goes down a storm every time; they'll love you.

Comedy is a great way of making up for other shortcomings in your life; ask any comedian. Hurting yourself for the amusement of others is even better. Ask any court jester, if you can find one. Don't ask a gladiator though; I imagine they'd be pretty touchy about that sort of thing. I learned my lesson pretty early on and now, by the age of eight, I was a master of the prat-fall, the mock-slip, the comedy trip and the pretend faint. It probably helped that I was small and light; when I dropped out of a tree, fell off a bike or walked into a lamp-post, there wasn't the kinetic energy generated by one of the big kids doing the same thing. When they fell, they broke bones and stuff. When I fell, I just bounced, laughed and checked someone was watching.

I would spend hours trying to impress the girl next door. She was several years older than me, tall, clever and blessed with intriguing creases to either side of her mouth. She would sit on her swing, bored, while I looned about on the other side of the fence, telling jokes, making up stories, telling the same jokes again and reciting lines from favourite cartoons. When I eventually ran out of jokes, stories and stolen swear words to share, I would resort to just throwing myself about in an attempt to fly or leap clear over the flower-beds. It worked every time; a few falls, a slip on the crazy paving, a madcap, headlong dive into the shrubbery and she would be riveted like a Bond girl watching her fella shin up a cliff and take out a legion of baddies armed with nothing but a bottle opener and his razor-sharp wit.

Other kids hung around after school and built models out of giant milk straws to try and impress the teachers; the really bad kids set fire to trees in the playing fields or broke into school buildings that they shouldn't have been in. I set up ramps and tried to jump over stuff on bikes, tried to climb walls using whatever grip I could find between bricks or on window frames, attempted clearly impossible leaps across giant chasms and climbed trees until I felt sure the air got thinner.

My first love, though, was my bike. I've always loved whatever two-wheeled transport I've owned at various stages in my life. I still do today, though now, of course, it has an engine. I sat down with my father when I was eight and worked out just how many days until I could drive a car. When I discovered that there were 365 days fewer to wait before I could ride a bike, doing so became an all-consuming passion that I would never lose. The walls of the bedroom I shared with my two brothers, Nick and Andy, were decorated with chopper bikes that I stared at until I fell asleep and dreamed of them. Stunt legend and motorcycling hero Evel Knievel was my idol, even though I had never really seen him in action. This was before sports channels on satellite TV put every crackpot and loony attempting something daft in the limelight for all to admire or laugh at. I may never have seen him do it, but I knew what he did and I adored him for it. It was, perhaps, the combination of showmanship, theatre and downright lunatic bravery that set my imagination on fire.

The bike I sat on now, nervous and secretly scared as the crowd grew impatient for the action to begin and my best mate picked his nose and flicked the resulting booty at his sister, was a Puch. I didn't know it at the time, but Puch was an Austrian manufacturer, usually of mopeds and ordinary pedal bicycles fitted with tiny engines to make it easier to wobble back from the wine shop. Mine was a small, red bicycle, styled to look like a racing bike, but sadly it didn't carry the look through into the technical department. The wheels were fairly narrow, but also small in diameter, so they never looked like the sleek, skinny ones on the real racers slotted into their spaces at the school bike shed by their bigger, older owners. I was proud of the glamorous yellow racing tape coiled around the dropped handlebars and fixed in place at the ends by blue plastic plugs, but the plugs were forever coming unstuck and I had tried to glue them in with a dab of rubber solution nicked from a puncture repair kit. It had congealed and made a bit of a mess, which picked up dust and muck until the bar-ends were permanently black and sticky. But perhaps the most pressing concern I had was the lack of gears. It looked like a racer, albeit a small one, but gears were the defining element of such things. Choppers and Grifters, with their fancy gear levers on the crossbar and their Sturmey Archer-style hub-gears could only manage three speeds, but a real racer, well, that had a dozen or so. Ten, at least. Or sometimes just five; but even that would have been enough to elevate me into a pretty select club on our street. Mine had none. Not a single gear. Well, it had one, but it was permanently in it. It was a fixed speed with a single cog at the back and not a hope of changing it. I used to ride everywhere at top speed, not to get there quicker but in the hope that anyone who didn't already know would not clock that my otherwise glamorous and good-looking steed had no gears. That didn't stop me loving it though. It was still the best, the most perfect, the handsomest and, of course, the fastest bike in the whole world. My parents bought it second-hand from the huge bicycle shop near Robin Hood Island on the outskirts of Birmingham. It was the most exciting purchase I had ever been involved in and the arrival of any new car or motorbike in my life since has struggled to eclipse that moment for excitement, pride and magic.

Right now, my pride and joy felt heavy, unsteady and infinitely precious. I didn't want to hit the deck hard and scuff it—or me—if things went wrong. Way ahead in the distance—probably twenty or thirty feet—waited the ramp. We had made it from a piece of thin, shiny wood, probably a melamine cast-off from someone's kitchen. A couple of house bricks pilfered from the pile at the side of our shed held it up. Beyond that was the pile of clobber I'd have to clear. And there was a crowd of people waiting for me to do it.

The ragtag band of kids from our suburban street in Shirley, West Midlands, had started that Saturday afternoon in the usual way; tearing around on bicycles, arguing over toy cars and spraying each other with machine-gun fire from behind the low-lying brick walls that surrounded our homes. When we'd grown bored of that, I had suggested we set up the jump. Along the way, I may have made a boast or two about how good I was at jumping over things. Someone claimed their dad had jumped over a bus, someone else said they could do that, easy, and so we'd ended up with the ramp. The goal started out as being to clear my mate's Action Man, lying prostrate at the end of the ramp in his Desert Combat kit. Another Action Man was added and then another, and then my Action Man, resplendent in a kit of my own devising which comprised mismatched boots, a camouflage jacket and one of those helmets the Horse Guards wear when they parade for the Queen. Of course, I decided that that wasn't enough; the jump had to be bigger, the spectacle more stomach-churning. The girls probably tried to add dolls, but Barbie wasn't going to get a look in on this one. We added a plastic helicopter with guns on it that fired little pellets of paper when you flicked a spring backwards with a plastic tag on the side, and the fabulous wooden Jeep my grandfather had built for Action Man to tear around imaginary war zones. It would take a big jump to clear the resulting heap. The confidence I had felt when swaggering around earlier faded as I sat summoning up the courage to go through with the plan. But the preparations had taken a long time and the spectators' interest was rapidly cooling. A scuffle broke out between a couple of boys. I was losing their attention. I tried not to cry.

So, rather than bear the pain of losing the admiration of the crowd, I decided to take the plunge and risk physical pain. Needless to say, it was pathetic. I got a bit of a wobble on midway through the run-up to the ramp. Correcting the wobble used up precious momentum, the ramp itself was too bendy to hold the weight of the bike and just bowed to touch the pavement beneath as the front wheel rolled on to it. The leading edge of the ramp, supported on two bricks, couldn't bend and so stood proud immediately in front of my wheel. It hit, I stopped quickly and flopped over the side and on to the ground. It wasn't an exciting fall, there was no damage to the bike, Action Man's head stayed on, the helicopter and the Jeep made it through to fight another day, there was no blood from me and no chance of a glimpse of real bone through ripped flesh like that kid in the year above in the patio-slab incident. By the time we had re-hidden the bricks behind the shed, slotted the piece of plastic wood down the side of a neighbour's garage and checked my knees for scabs one last time, the event was forgotten and we had moved on to talking about the kid from the year above who fell and chopped off both his arms and his head on an upended patio slab.

* * *

The big plus point about an early life spent performing low-rent stunts for the amusement of your mates is that you quickly find it is possible to get by with absolutely no acquired skills whatsoever. You don't have to be good at anything in order to hurt yourself for the amusement of others; in fact, it helps if you're not. I was a daredevil, sure, but all that meant at the age of ten was that I was prepared to fall over and didn't mind too much when I grazed the odd knee or elbow. There was little point in spending hours practising keepie-uppie with a football or solving a Rubik's Cube in under two minutes if you could earn much more admiration by leaping over a ditch full of stagnant water and imaginary alligators on to a bank full of very real stinging nettles. I took the leap, every time. So you would think that when new, exciting and seemingly dangerous crazes came along, I would be among the first to welcome them with open arms and without a safety net. But no, I never really welcomed the change.

My world revolved around my pedal cars when I was younger and, eventually, my bike. When skateboards became the rage my friends were all to be found slithering around the streets and alleyways where we lived, practising jumps, turns, and that really annoying manoeuvre where they leap in the air and flip the board underneath their feet before landing on it again. I just rode my bike up and down the street and fell off into a hedge every now and then in the hope someone was watching. Only once did I swap two wheels for those four very small ones: I borrowed a neighbour's skateboard, a stout, wooden affair, finished in woodgrain, with sensible wheels rather like the ones you might find under an office chair—nothing like the fancy, multi-coloured affairs with carbon fibre and titanium like you get today. After a brief blast up and down the pavement outside our front garden, I decided it wasn't for me and got back on my bike. As soon as I learned to wobble up and down the pavement standing on the board, I got an inkling of just how long it would take to learn how to do stunts on it, decided it was too long and gave up. I haven't been on a skateboard since.

Then BMX bikes arrived. Everyone around me, even adults, hurtled about on their brightly coloured little bikes and thought they were cool. I never had one. I didn't want one. While my friends practised their flips and turns on a home-made half-pipe, I hurtled about on a racing bike—one with ten gears by then—and got my kicks from going fast. There was always some muppet leaping about as a guest on *Blue Peter* and showing us how clever he was by riding his BMX while sitting on the handlebars or standing on the seat. I was happy enough hurtling down the hill between my house and the paper shop where I picked up my round, and seeing if I could keep up with cars.

But there was one area where I could be persuaded to settle down and apply myself to learn something. I didn't just love bikes for what they could do; I loved them for how they worked. I was fascinated by the mechanical processes going on and could, even as an eight-year-old, rebuild one pretty much with my eyes shut. By the time I was ten or eleven, I was confident enough to strip them down to the last nut and bolt and restore them to smooth-running perfection. In fact, I was never happier than when I was up to my neck in piles of cotter-pins, bearings, brake blocks and chainsets. I spent several weeks rebuilding my brother Andy's racer for him. It was a metallic red Peugeot and had been in need of a little attention. Andy was, I think, more interested in the bike as a means of transport; where it could take him and what he might do when he got there, rather than the mechanical process involved. But he was happy enough for me to take it off the road and mess about with it for a while. I was overjoyed at having another project to get stuck into, particularly one that involved fiddling about with someone else's bike, leaving mine intact for getting to school and showing off afterwards.

The work was done mostly on the area of patio immediately outside the garden shed. Sitting on the paving slabs, I would wrestle with stubborn bolts, often gouging holes in my palms with the sharp-edged multi-spanner and plastic-handled screwdriver that made up my tool kit. If heavy-duty weapons were needed, Dad was happy to let me raid his big metal toolbox inside the shed; as long as I put stuff back. Which I invariably failed to do.

After what seemed like months of work, but probably amounted to just a few days, the job was done. It was magnificent; a gleaming array of smooth-running, well-oiled, efficiency. Every moving part had been removed, fiddled with, lubricated and replaced. Andy was delighted, though I now suspect he may have been humouring me. It had to be test-ridden and that, categorically, was a job for me. Test-riding was, of course, the best bit about being a bike mechanic.

You learn a lot on the test ride, and not just about the bicycle you are testing, but about physics and life in general. I once fitted Chopper handlebars to a racing bike and test-rode it down the hill at the end of the road where we lived. When I dabbed the front brake, my weight was transferred to the handlebars. Because the Chopper bars were longer than the standard dropped ones, my weight was transferred to a point much further from the headstock of the bike. This, effectively, increased the leverage exerted on the headstock under braking; in this instance, it became the pivot. I learned a valuable lesson in levers and forces when I smashed my face into the headstock as the bars collapsed forward and failed to support me, throwing me off the saddle to mash my goolies into the crossbar as I hurtled towards the ground. The front wheel of the bike connected with a very low wall; the wheel, together with the low wall, then acted as yet another pivot, and the whole lot—me, the bike and my newly acquired appreciation for the basic principles of physics—crashed over the wall and into a bush. I had an opportunity to combine this science lesson with a horticultural one, for the bush had vicious, one-inch spikes all over it which had evolved, no doubt, to protect it from some predator or other in its natural habitat. But I had lost interest in learning by then and wanted to cry instead.

Andy's bike was up for testing next and I wheeled it carefully from the back garden, past the bins to the front, and got myself ready to put it through its paces. Several houses down from ours was a side road. It split off from the main road, made its way round a triangular patch of grass surrounded by houses to rejoin our street further up. This was known universally among us kids as 'the Triangle'. Some would use it for exploring, some for playing chase, others as the landscape on to which they could paint their imaginary military escapades. I used it for testing stuff. Residents along that stretch must have grown used to looking both ways twice as they left their front drives, because there was every likelihood that I might streak past at a scaled-down two hundred miles an hour while testing out a rebuilt bike, a scooter, a pedal car or a tea tray with wheels and string to steer it. Today though, I was planning to break all records.

The bike was working beautifully and I shifted through the gears to check I had adjusted the cables correctly. The chainset ticked smoothly when I freewheeled, but mostly I just kept pouring in the power with my frantically twirling trainers. It being a triangle, there were three corners in the road. I powered down the main straight, past the house with the dog and the one with the tarmac on the driveway that had little white flecks in it that I had always thought very sophisticated. I rounded the first corner, which was a gentle bend and took me past the opening to the alley that led to the school playing field behind the houses. (That alley was a source of mystery; as far as I know, it was the last place in Britain where you could see white dog poo.) And then I hit the second straight and speared into less familiar territory. If I turned left at the junction instead of right, things would get really complicated and I would probably never find my way home from the maze of streets and lanes. I turned right and sped towards the last corner.

There was never much traffic on the triangle, which was why we were allowed by our parents to play there. It also meant that it took a long time for the loose chippings left after recent works to be worn into the surface of the road. As I leaned the bike over to make the turn and shoved yet more power through the crank, I hit a deep patch of loose gravel. The front wheel started to slip away and that was it. I was into a crash. The first part of me to hit the deck was my right hand. I removed most of the skin on several fingers and a coin-shaped chunk of flesh from my right shoulder. In the hospital, they had to trim away the dead skin and tidy up the wounds. I swore blind you could see the white bone of my little finger's knuckle through the ripped and tortured flesh. It stung like hell when they painted it with iodine, but I couldn't wait to get back and show my mates at home. I had seen the bone.

* * *

Of course, when someone goes off the rails, even in a jet car like I did, it's all too easy to say 'blame the parents'. In fact, in this instance, I'm not so sure. My mum and dad never encouraged the daredevil in me, but neither did they try to suppress or crush it. With three sons to raise, they grew used to the fact that one of us would always have gravel rash on his knees, plasters on his elbows and a bruise on his face. It was usually me. They certainly never wrapped me in cotton wool. But they were dealing with the product of their genes and therein lay the problem. I say now, don't blame the parents, blame the grandparents. My father's father, my grandpa, George Hammond, was a tall, outwardly gentle man. For many years, I was convinced that he was, in fact, John Le Mesurier of *Dad's Army* fame, possessing as he did a gentle, soft-spoken, equable nature that was utterly compelling and soothing to his young grandchild. What I never appreciated in my childhood though, was that this calm, kind man was also capable of immense and almost reckless bravery. While serving in the RAF during the Second World War, he volunteered for bomb disposal duty. This meant sitting for hours down dark, damp holes or hastily improvised shafts, working on a bomb that could explode at any moment and kill you and your mates. While my father lay at home in Birmingham as a baby, Grandpa tinkered with German bombs and tried to stop them killing people. When the war ended, it must have been tricky for Grandpa to fill a considerable vacuum of excitement in his life. While he was as far as can be imagined from the baggy-trousered, thrill-seeking adrenalin junkie that snowboards down mountains today, this mild-mannered gentleman had tackled incomprehensibly dangerous situations with calmness, strength and dignity, and had done so voluntarily. He certainly didn't go off the rails, struggle with his family or get led astray. He seems to have come back to his family desperate for tranquillity and peace. But he did, occasionally, remind the world that danger was, for him, not something to be scared of. And, from what I understand, gleaned from tales of a time long before I was around, this was always done with action and never words. My father tells me now that not once did his father turn off the mains electricity when fixing a light switch or a plug socket. He would stand there, screwdriver held calmly in his strong hand, and carry out the task. Occasionally, he would accidentally complete the circuit with his screwdriver and get the full force of the mains electricity through his body. On one such occasion he was thrown backwards through the glass roof of the conservatory, on another he toppled off the banister he was balancing on and fell down the stairs. His response was to swear softly, stand up, dust himself off and get back on with the job. This was not deliberate thrill-seeking, I am sure, but there must have been a love of adrenalin deep inside my gentle, caring grandpa. And I am equally sure that I inherited a thin strand of it.

From the other side of our family, from my mother's father, I inherited my passion for machines, engineering and, in particular, cars. He had trained as a cabinet-maker and later worked as a coachbuilder at the Mulliner factory in Birmingham, using wood to build the frames that held the hand-built aluminium car bodies together. He went on to work at the Jensen factory, all the time expanding his considerable range of skills to the point where he must have been comfortable working with just about any material then in use. He could carve wood, turn metal, work leather and improvise a way of making anything out of anything. The attic at the home he shared in Birmingham with my grandmother and great-grandmother was a place of very real magic for a six-year-old boy. Grandad would lead the way through workshops crammed with vices, lathes and other tools I didn't understand. Huge pillar drills glistened in dark corners and racks of cleaned-out jam jars and tobacco tins contained screws, bolts, washers and fittings of every size and nature. Nothing was wasted. When finally something was beyond even his help it would be stripped for parts and those parts dropped into neatly labelled tins for use on another day. And that day always came. He could and did make everything: pedal cars, go-karts, sideboards, fancy-dress costumes, footstools, tables, bookends, cupboards and carvings emerged in a constant stream from his workshop. I stood in awe of his versatility, skill and engineering intelligence, and it would be a proud thing indeed if today I could say I had inherited a fraction of it along with the passion for cars that I undoubtedly owe to him. But there can be no denial; the evidence is clear. From these two gentlemen I inherited two things: a love of cars and engineering, and an almost equal passion for daredevilry and danger. So please, let's not blame my parents. Let's blame their parents.

CHAPTER 3

# FROM LOCAL RADIO TO *TOP GEAR*

Like any major road, the A40 into London has a great many landmarks along its length. But these are not in the same league as the Eiffel Tower, nor do they fall into the interesting-shaped-mountain category of landmark that makes it into the guide books. The rather humdrum features dotted along the A40 are the kind which tell bored commuters how far they are from work and how much longer they will be queuing to get there. Abandoned shopping trolleys, bent lamp-posts, old car wheels and mysteriously discarded training shoes all have their place and do their daily duty in reassuring the commuter that they are merely two miles from the office now and will be there in an hour or two.

Among the more major landmarks is a pale, concrete footbridge extending over the four lanes of carriageway. It connects the houses on one side of the A40 with the footpath on the other. Anyone queuing miserably along that stretch of road on the morning of 19 February 2002 with their nose pressed to the window and their eyes searching the grey day for something to distract them, might have made out a small figure in jeans and a leather jacket sloping across the bridge to stand at the end and stare out over the damp and dreary wastelands stretching alongside the road. With nothing to think about but the queue of traffic and the news coming round again on the radio, an idle commuter's mind might have constructed all manner of romantic motivations for this stranger's solitary amble. A lover spurned? A desperate man, contemplating something dreadful on this Wednesday morning? No, it was me and I was crapping myself. At eleven o'clock, I was due to audition for a job on the all-new *Top Gear* programme.

At the time, I was working for Granada as a presenter on car and bike shows on satellite TV, and this was my dream opportunity. I spent my time zipping around the country to film reviews of cars and bikes for shows that had smaller audiences than the film crew on most big-budget TV programmes. It may have been small, but it had been an excellent place to practise and I felt that now I was ready to move on and up. All I needed was the right opportunity—and this was it. It was like someone leaning over the fence at school as you played football with your mates to invite you to try out for Manchester United. With so much at stake, I felt the pressure bearing down on me.

I had gone for a walk to steady my nerves and try and kill the half-hour or so before I was due to arrive at the audition. Reaching the platform at the end of the bridge, I stood at the top of the concrete stairs and gripped the cold metal handrail. The scrubby fields of bushes and greying, roadside grass stretched out patchily until, in the distance, they managed to summon up a watery green. My efforts to calm myself with deep breathing left me light-headed. I tried to convince myself that it was no big deal, I would either get the job or I wouldn't, and then I would go back home to Cheltenham and life would carry on as normal. Maybe it would be better if I just drove home now and didn't put myself through the misery of cocking it up and failing. Maybe they had already made up their minds about whom they wanted anyway and I was wasting my time. This was not helping. Realising that standing there getting all soulful and miserable about it was hardly going to make me shine in the audition, I turned and walked snappily back over the bridge towards the car park. The hundreds of commuters trapped in the queue below rubbed their foreheads, lit cigarettes, tuned into the radio news and dreamed of going back home.

Looked at from the right angle, my life had been pretty much leading towards this moment. After a childhood dedicated almost entirely to fooling around in pedal cars and on bicycles and obsessing about cars and motorbikes, my adult life had seemed to plot a course for this point as inevitably as a well-steered ship heading for port. I went to art college in Harrogate and spent my time taking gloomy black-and-white photographs of scrapyards and painting pictures of American muscle cars. My photos and paintings can't have been very good; I finished art college and went straight to work in the least visual of all media: radio.

My first proper job was as a radio reporter at BBC Radio North Yorkshire. Based in a car park towards the middle of the city, the station was home to me for two years. For an eighteen-year-old lad, a career in broadcasting seemed almost impossibly exciting. Inside, the station boasted a sophisticated luxury beyond my wildest dreams. There was a full-time receptionist at the front desk to welcome visitors, a kitchen where we could heat our own pasties in the microwave, and a production office in which every horizontal surface supported stacks of papers and reel-to-reel tapes high enough to connect with the ceiling. It was hard to tell if the piles of stuff had grown up to meet the ceiling like stalagmites or grown down to touch the desks like stalactites. Or are those the other way around?

Best of all, there were the studios. On my first visit, I was taken to stand in hushed awe at the back of studio 1A and look through the glass to the neighbouring studio, which was live on air. A terrifying On Air light glowed red overhead as the presenter slid faders, pushed buttons and turned dials on a broadcast desk that stretched off into the distance, all the time talking smoothly into an enormous microphone suspended from a cradle of black elastic overhead. He laughed confidently, twisted a dial with his left hand, flicked a fader downwards and introduced another caller to the airwaves. I was mesmerised and swore that, one day, I would do that. In the meantime, there was coffee to be made for the production team upstairs and I had to go and learn how to use a Uher tape recorder to interview people.

I didn't know it then, but my first interview would be with the members of a local branch of the Hammond Organ Appreciation Society. They gathered at a village hall somewhere in North Yorkshire every week to swap stories, listen to organ music and pass the time. On the appointed day, trembling with nerves, I walked into the hall and introduced myself as 'Richard, erm, Hammond'. I interviewed old ladies who told me with moist eyes how, in their youth, they would 'travel miles for a good organ'. I bit my lip as they went on: 'Of course, we all liked the organs in church, but Hammonds were always the best.' I spoke with them for ages, the reels inside the massive German Uher tape recorder revolving slowly as the quarter-inch tape caught their words in all their analogue splendour. Later that night, I hunched over the huge broadcast desk in the off-air studio to edit the interviews together with sound effects, music and commentary, turning it into what the producer and presenter had explained to me was called a package, ready for broadcast the following day. I spoke into the microphone to record the script I'd written, explaining how they all enjoyed a good organ, but especially a Hammond one; their dedication in travelling miles to appreciate an extra special organ. The highlight was an interview with a chap who'd been sitting alongside me at an actual keyboard. 'So, is this your organ?' I asked. 'It's massive. Where do I put my hands?' It was brilliant. I loved it. Unfortunately, it was never played on air. I still had a great deal to learn.

And I spent the next ten years trying to learn it. Hopping from radio station to radio station, I lived in a series of bedsits and shared houses all over the North of England while honing my skills interviewing, editing, dodging news meetings and running away from angry farmers who didn't want to talk about subsidies for the evening news. I interviewed government ministers, authors, children's entertainers, celebrity chefs, adventurers and craftspeople. I spoke with people who had performed amazing feats, won incredible contests, battled terrible illness and started successful businesses. I learned that all of us, each and every one, lives a life that is, in its own right, an epic.

At this point, on 19 February 2002, my own epic had brought me to the car park outside B&Q, at the end of a footbridge over the A40. I bought a polystyrene cup of coffee from the burger van in the car park and settled in the car to wait. My stomach turned to water when I checked and saw I had ten minutes before I must head to the studios around the back of B&Q where the audition would take place. I was used to TV studios, but not ones where I had to audition for the job of my life. It was best, I decided, to sit back in the seat and let my eyelids droop and my mind wander until it was time to go and face the music.

I did eventually host a live show from that studio at BBC Radio North Yorkshire. It was a lunchtime slot on the Sunday—traditionally, the training ground for new presenters. My housemate, Andy Breare, now an established broadcaster on radio and television, had already taken the plunge and presented his first show. On the evening before he did it, we'd sheltered in the garage while the rain lashed the corrugated roof and I smoked a cigarette and lounged on the seat of my motorbike, perched on its centre stand. Andy was annoyingly confident, one of those guys who seemed to breeze through stuff that left me dissolved in a puddle of nerves and insecurity. He was looking forward to the show. The following day, he left breezily, put in a fantastic, confident performance in which he sounded like a seasoned presenter of a thousand shows, and afterwards made light of it in the station kitchen. I knew that I would be convulsed with fear when my turn came. I was.

On the morning of my first show, I rode to work, walked into the station almost blind with terror and sat in the production office trying to make plans and stop my hands from shaking. The show, *Last Week in North Yorkshire*, was a two-hour review of highlights from the week's broadcasting. In an hour's time I would be going it alone. There would be no producer as a comforting presence on the other side of the glass in the studio next door, ready to offer a guiding hand if things got tricky. Nobody to feed through suggestions before I opened the microphone and addressed the county, and nobody on air with me to bounce off and give me the chance to try and come up with a witty riposte or two. It didn't do to dwell on the terror of what was to come, so I kept myself busy. I read the papers, hoping to find funny stories, jokes or just something to talk about. There was nothing. I read and re-read the assortment of printed scripts, scribbled notes and handwritten jottings that would form the introductions to the various clips I would be playing. I checked and rechecked the box full of tapes I had to thread into the machines and play when the time came. Watery winter sunlight streamed in through the windows of the production office, which had suddenly changed from a comforting and friendly place to an antechamber leading to my certain doom. The clock moved on, I had no choice; I gathered up my sheaf of papers, box of tapes and official BBC record box, and limped downstairs to the studio—stopping off at the toilets on the way for what I can distinctly recall was the seventh visit of the morning. I didn't fall asleep in the lavatory or fall down the stairs on the way to the studio and drop all the tapes. I made it to the desk on time, settled in, shook like a leaf and when the time came, got started.

I still have a taped copy of the show. It wasn't brilliant. As the news ends and a station jingle is played, the tiny, thin voice of a young man clearly scared half out of his wits does its best to rise above the dying chords of the jingle. I welcome listeners to the show, introduce myself and mistime the introduction to Dusty Springfield's 'Son of a Preacher Man', and as my tremulous voice stomps all over the opening lyrics, my broadcasting career begins. There were more cock-ups as the show progressed; I left the microphone open while answering the telephone to a caller during a record. As the music plays, I can be heard in the background asking them to hold on until the record ends, fiddling with pieces of paper, drumming on the desk with a pencil and twirling knobs and flicking switches until, suddenly, I go silent and the noise behind the music disappears. I have noticed the mic fader is still open. You can almost hear me gulp. The record ends and I make a pathetic attempt to pretend I left it open on purpose by telling listeners, 'Well, that was the first caller, erm, you, erm, could be the next. Just call me on . . . oh, I've lost the number. Call me on the, er, the phone.'

Sitting in my car with a polystyrene cup of cold coffee and a stomach full of butterflies some thirteen years later, I still cringe at the memory of it. Shaking my head free of the recalled embarrassment, I glance around the car. It is a 1982 Porsche 911 SC. The steering wheel is on the wrong side because it was imported from Germany many years ago by a previous owner. The red paintwork is far from perfect, the headlining is green with mildew, the engine rattles ominously over three thousand revs, the rev counter doesn't count the revs, the oil gauge doesn't gauge the oil, and the huge, teatray spoiler on the back reminds other drivers of Thatcher and stockbrokers in red braces and inspires them to gesticulate at me accordingly. It's the best car I have ever owned and I adore it. The thing cost less than a used hatchback to buy, but probably needed twice as much spending on it to dry up the oil leaks and avoid disastrous failure in the very near future.

On the day that I collected it, I drove it over to my parents' house in Leatherhead, Surrey, and parked it on the street outside. It was autumn but the rain had stopped briefly and I climbed out and took in the lustrous red paintwork, admiring the way the raindrops formed round, silver pearls over the car's broad flanks. I was on the point of actually bursting with pride as I walked around the back of it, sniffing the warm, oil-saturated air as it escaped through the grilles over the engine, which was, of course, positioned at the back. I twirled the key-fob in my fingers and hit the button to lock the doors—the first car I had ever owned with central locking. I came as close as I have ever come to being unable to believe something I can actually see is real when I looked down at the Porsche legend on the boot-lid. My mother and father sensed immediately that I was there on a showing-off mission and they 'oohed' and 'aahed' accordingly. This, in fact, was a routine they had slipped into many times over the years—I would always turn up in whatever set of wheels I had ruined myself financially to own and they would always oblige by listening to my breathless demonstration of the car's finer points and my patient explanation of why this was the single best car ever produced by anyone, ever. They would even bite their tongues and endure my manic attempts to justify the expense of such a vehicle when I could hardly afford a new pair of jeans, and my even more crazed explanations of how just owning such a car would, in the long run, actually save me money. I would argue that I refused to be a coward and spend less on a more reliable, economical and discreet car simply because it might be better at getting me where I wanted to go, because I believed it would cause an almost dangerous downturn in my mental state by failing to effectively represent my much livelier and more daring spirit, thus reducing drastically the effectiveness of my brain and my creative abilities. How they did this, time after time, and how they resisted the urge to cuff me round the ear and tell me to try and learn a lesson from each and every other inappropriate vehicle I had chucked my cash into over the decades, I just don't know. But I thank them for it, and for playing along with my daft game, from the bottom of my heart. Of course, the fact that my father can recall going through almost the exact same process in his younger years may well have helped a little.

Even when work was trickling along nicely, there was always a far-too-large chunk of my mind dwelling on cars and motorbikes. Just as I'd gazed out of a classroom window at the playing fields beyond, I spent most of my young adult life looking over the bosses' shoulder at the car park beyond and dreaming which car I would go for if I had the choice and how I would set about improving it. It was that very car park though, that nearly finished my radio career before it began. Turning up for my first day's work at Radio York in 1988, I found it filled with dreary hatchbacks, rusty Ford Escorts and assorted family cars and old bicycles. I had assumed, naturally enough I think, that whatever time radio presenters and media types didn't spend hunched over a microphone holding the nation, or rather the county, spellbound with their silver tongue, they spent hooning about the place in sports cars. I had anticipated a car park resembling the pit lane at an exotic race-meet; packed full of Ferraris, Jaguars, Aston Martins and beautiful, sporty classics. What I saw was a car park like you'd find outside any supermarket. This came as a sizeable disappointment to my eighteen-year-old mind and one that very nearly had me turning on my heel and looking instead for a job in big city finance or gun-running. If I wasn't going to be able to afford at least a hot hatch if not a Ferrari, then did I really want to shackle myself to a life in the media?

But I soon found that there were small compensations to be had for the car fanatic working in radio. Whenever I reported for duty at yet another Northern radio station—and this was a common occurrence, thanks to the ebb and flow of life as a freelance radio reporter and presenter—I would secretly nip down to the garage to check out the radio car. Every station had one and using it was possibly the part of the job I liked best. It lived alone in a large garage, typically tended by a team of two or three sound engineers who guarded the vehicle and the associated piles of cables and outdoor broadcast equipment jealously. The car, or sometimes a van, would be equipped with a mast that could, at the flick of a switch, rise up pneumatically from the roof and extend ten metres or so into the sky to allow the aerial on top to connect with base and establish a broadcasting link. Every station had its legendary horror story concerning a rookie reporter who went out with the radio car to make a report. Inevitably, the reporter in the tale behaved like an extra on Scooby-Doo; happily flicking the switch to send the mast up while standing by holding on to the microphone at the end of a thick cable connected to the car as the metal mast rose gracefully up into the power cables suspended from a pylon immediately overhead. Depending on the station and, perhaps, the humour of the sound engineer telling you the story, it then became increasingly grisly, sometimes incorporating details such as the hapless reporter gripping the microphone ever tighter as the current increased until they resembled a fried snack stuck to the end of a melted boa constrictor. Needless to say, the important message in each station's salutary tale was one concerning the need to check overhead for cables and power lines before setting up the mast.

Once the mast was successfully erected and the wise operator not fried, they could then feed live reports into the station's output. I reported on road-blocks, farm animal breakouts, carol concerts, jumble sales, record-breaking attempts and sponsored swims. But for me, the job peaked when I turned the key in the ignition and pulled out of the garage. They were not, generally, glamorous cars. There isn't enough room for all the broadcast kit in a hot hatch and BBC budgetary constraints that I did not understand at the time ruled out a radio-Lamborghini. But after a lifetime spent coaxing a few more miles out of whatever wheezy, reluctant old banger I could afford on my reporter's pay, the opportunity to drive an almost brand-new car was too good to miss. Radio North Yorkshire had a rather fabulous new Ford Sierra Estate as a radio car and a fleet of brand-new Escorts for dashing out to record reports for the news bulletins. I would hover around the newsroom, hoping against hope that the editor would call for someone to dash out to record an interview and, finding no proper reporters available, would send me out instead. It only happened once, and it was to interview a bus driver within walking distance of the station.

I was, it must be said, slightly disappointed when I got to Radio Cleveland to find that the radio car was a rusty old Austin Montego estate with a tailgate rotten up to the rear window. I spent a lot of time editing and doing station-based jobs during my time there. On my first day at Radio Newcastle, they sent me out in the radio van to report from what I did not at the time realise was a famously rough estate. I found my way to the school I was due to report from, parked the van and set up the mast ready for action. I unwound the drum of thick, green cable and attached the microphone and headphones to the end, connected it to the van and threaded my way in through the gates, across the playground and into the school hall. I introduced myself to the teacher and the kids, popped the headphones on and prepared to hit the ground running when the presenter gave me the cue. Through the headphones I heard him announce my name and the location and I swung into action. As soon as I spoke, the headphones went dead. I put it down to a problem with the tired old bakelite 'cans' and carried on regardless, interviewing staff and pupils and hoping that the presenter wasn't interjecting with questions for me that I could not hear. I wound the piece up and signed off cheerily. When I went back out to the van, I discovered that I had left the door unlocked and the end of the cable had been torn out and the interior stripped and trashed. I didn't work there for very long.

On my first day at Radio Lancashire I crashed the radio van—it was a Ford Transit—into a wall while attempting to manoeuvre into place beside a small stately home and file a report on it opening to the public ready for summer. But it was also while working at Radio Lancashire that I experienced something of a revelation. I took over as producer and presenter of the weekend mid-morning shows.

With the shows I inherited a range of regular contributors who, together, brought to the programme a broad mix of subjects, expertise and personality. The editors of the local newspapers joined me to talk news, local politicians came in and talked politics and Bill Scott, a restaurateur, raconteur and hotel owner from Fleetwood, joined me every week to discuss food, drinking and the high-life. But when the mics were off our conversation turned to other matters. Mostly, that meant cars. Fifteen years on, I still count Bill among my closest friends today and often call him up to discuss the arrival of a new set of wheels in my life. His enthusiasm and reserves of boundless energy to enjoy life seem to grow stronger with every year.

There was another contributor who came with the show and opened my eyes to a whole new set of possibilities. Zog Ziegler, apart from boasting a fantastically unique name and, as I later discovered, bearing an uncanny resemblance to Jack Nicholson, fulfilled the role of motoring expert on the programme. He lived far away in Cheltenham, which was near London as far as I knew. Every week I would record a chat with Zog down the line from his local radio station in Gloucester. He reviewed cars and discussed motoring-related issues arising in the week. He was and still is exceptionally funny, witty and insightful when it came to pinpointing what it is about a car that makes it daft, useful or hilarious, what it is like to drive it, and just what it might mean to own one. This was the first time I had ever encountered a real live motoring journalist and I saw a whole new world open up. Maybe, just maybe, it would be possible for me to do that for a living too.

The idea of driving new cars, formulating opinions

on them based upon having driven everything else and then sharing those opinions with an audience struck me as about the most wonderful way possible in which to earn a crust. I live just three or four miles from Zog now and we can still reduce ourselves to tears of laughter or a lather of fury by talking about cars, car-makers and car stories. I had watched *Top Gear* every week for as long as I could remember, devoured the weekly and monthly car magazines and stalked the halls at every motor show I could visit. The idea of being involved in the world of cars and motoring as a journalist was like being told as a kid that you could get a job as a jelly-bean taster when you grow up. From the moment I first opened a microphone to talk to Zog, I had a far, far better idea of what I wanted to do for a living.

Fortunately, the love of cars and bikes that I inherited from my grandfathers didn't extend simply to a passion for posing in them. I'd also inherited a fascination for their innermost workings and a reasonable ability to fettle them when things dropped off or got broken. Which is a good thing to have if you are going to spend your entire life craving cars that are slightly too good for your budget. Inevitably, every car that I bought was a supremely tatty and ropey example of its type; it had to be in order for me to afford it. I quickly found that a childhood enjoyment of fiddling with Lego and Meccano was easily translated into an adulthood ability to prop up and nurse along whatever rusty, broken old nail was the current apple of my car-crazed eye. Sometimes this was just a case of topping up fluids and keeping a set of jump leads handy. Mostly though, I would find myself attempting to tackle jobs way beyond my wit and tool kit. I wrestled with changing my Mini's engine in a borrowed lock-up using a less sophisticated tool kit than I would expect to be delivered with a flat-pack chest of drawers. I lay in the mud to replace the gearbox under my Cortina-engined kit car through a winter so harsh I sometimes would lose all feeling in my back and have to roll on to my knees and crawl inside to get warm. Essentially, my life boiled down to two key activities: working as a radio reporter and presenter in order to pay for a procession of broken cars which I spent the rest of my time attempting to stick back together so that they could take me to work.

Even now, I get a huge buzz when I set off on a car journey that is slightly further than I can easily manage on a bicycle. Whenever I did that in my youth, my car would inevitably turn up its toes as I set off and I would be forced to make the journey under pedal power. That I own a car capable of reliably travelling tens and even hundreds of miles without incident is still a source of wonder to me.

The Porsche 911 to which I had aspired, and in which I now sheltered while waiting to go and audition for the new *Top Gear*, had never let me down. Though I often worried that, when it did—and I knew that, one day, it would—I would be ruined. But there was no more time for ruminating on the past and getting all soppy about the cars that had come and gone. Right now I had to fire up the 911, drive about half a mile around the corner and walk into a TV studio with all the confidence I could muster to audition for the biggest job opportunity of my life.

When I arrived outside the studio, I was greeted by Richard Porter, a car journalist who was joining the team as a researcher and is still with us today as the script editor. A tall, slender young bloke behind whose student-ish clothes and glasses lurks a sharp and agile mind containing an encyclopedic and occasionally embarrassingly broad catalogue of motoring facts. We talked cars, inevitably. He appreciated my 911 and I decided he was exactly the type of chap I would like to work with. I went inside and met with the crew who would be filming the audition. I was amazed how many people were involved. When we filmed stuff for Granada Men and Motors there was me and my mate Sid who did the camera work, sound work and directing. Suddenly, I was in a world of dedicated camera operators, sound technicians, lighting technicians, assistants and assistants to the assistants. I was terrified. And then I was introduced to another man. Not much taller than me, with a friendly, welcoming face that somehow immediately engenders trust and a sense that you are going to like this bloke; it turned out to be Andy Wilman. His title was and still is editor of the show, but perhaps co-creator would be a better one. Andy's the man who, along with Jeremy Clarkson, first came up with the idea for a whole new type of car show and persuaded the BBC that it was just what they wanted. He introduced himself with a handshake and an amiable grin. I had already spoken to him on the phone when he called to invite me to audition, but this was our first meeting.

We had got along instantly on the phone and our relaxed conversations seemed to continue seamlessly when we met face-to-face. He took me aside in the large and noisy studio and gave me a pep talk along the lines of: 'Try and keep your satellite-TV crap out of it, mate. Play it down a bit, not too bouncy. This is grown-up TV now, not your toytown stuff.' The fact that he had given me a few hints about what was wanted filled me with confidence. As far as I was concerned, it meant he was on my side; my wavering confidence soared. It was time to begin. Andy took a seat next to the camera operator, silence was called for and the studio lights rose and fell to the correct level. I had been asked to prepare a two-minute piece to present to camera, alone, about a car in the studio. It was a Skoda Superb. I rambled on and wandered around it, pointing out faults and flaws and possible good points, trying to be funny and informative and not to trip over the wires on the floor. The next phase of the audition involved presenting a sequence rather like what is now the news section of *Top Gear*. And for this I would be joined by a legend: Jeremy Clarkson.

To a guy like me, having served his time in local radio and worked hard to get to the point where he was presenting car programmes on satellite TV, meeting Jeremy was comparable with a rookie racer being invited to drive with Stirling Moss. And I had to meet him for the first time and immediately begin joshing and messing about for the camera. He was turning up for every audition with every candidate and so must have gone through the same process dozens of times. But he couldn't have made it easier or more fun. We argued about cars, discussed favourite motors from our past, took the piss out of motoring stories in the news that week and generally acted up in precisely the way we do on telly now. He laughed at me for being short, I laughed at him for being tall, we both laughed at people who drive electric cars and agreed that a V8 engine is the correct one for anything bigger than a fountain pen. It was like meeting up with an old mate. We could have conducted the entire conversation sitting on toolboxes with mugs of tea in our hands back at my lock-up. Eventually though, the audition ended. The next person called in to be tried out was waiting in the wings, so I had to leave and give them their chance.

Climbing into my car to begin the journey home, I felt no elation at how well it had all seemed to go, but rather a sense of disappointment. I had enjoyed my time with the people back there in that studio so much, had found so much to talk about, so many things to laugh about, that I just knew whoever eventually landed the job was going to have a truly fabulous time. Apart from working on what promised to be a brilliant show, they were going to be teamed with a great bunch of people. I just took it for granted that I was never going to be given the role, and so I was jealous of whoever eventually was.

I rang Mindy on the way home and explained my feelings to her. She wasn't surprised by my pessimism and commiserated with me for having done so well and enjoyed the audition so much despite being convinced I didn't stand a chance of getting the job. She's a patient woman, Mindy, and she understands me better sometimes than I understand myself.

In fact, it was largely due to my work in and around the media, combined with my obsessive love of cars, that Mindy and I first met. After about ten years living off credit cards and in bedsits all over the place, trying to support myself and my various daft cars and bikes as a freelance radio presenter, I had finally caved in and got a 'proper job' as a PR officer at a corporate headquarters on the outskirts of London. For a brief period, I enjoyed earning a reasonable wage, with healthcare cover, a pension and—best of all, without any doubt whatsoever—a company car. I even enjoyed the commute to work as it covered forty-two miles and I could rely on my brand-new company car to complete it every time without complaint, engine fire or oil leaks. In the end though, the call to return to my chosen career was too strong for me to carry on doing anything else. I returned to broadcasting. But not before I had found Mindy. She was working in the same office. I took one look at her curves and her long blonde hair, combined with her infectious enthusiasm, attitude and ever-present sense of humour, and I adored her but knew that I didn't stand a chance. She has told me since that she took one look at the long-haired, pale-faced, skinny wretch in a cheap suit that turned up in the office one day and was, miraculously, given a job, and decided that I was probably 'interesting'. In fact, we fancied each other from day one and it was just a case of when and how we got together and not 'if'.

We took to sneaking off together for fag breaks—we both still smoked back then—and spent the time chatting and standing about like teenagers at the back of the building while we both tried to think of excuses to spark up another smoke and perpetuate our time together. It was, with hindsight, pretty pathetic; we had both made it fairly obvious that we were interested in meeting outside of work, but we lacked the courage and confidence to say anything about it. The breakthrough finally came when I was given a couple of tickets to a motorsport-related ball. I determined to use them as an excuse to finally pluck up the courage and, like a lovelorn schoolboy, ask Mindy 'out'. Well, I didn't actually do the asking myself, if I'm honest. I recruited the help of the boss's chauffeur, Terry. He was duly despatched to go to Mindy's corner of the office and tell her that I had a couple of tickets to some party or other and wondered if she would like to come with me. It was nothing more than the equivalent of one of those 'my mate really fancies you' conversations from school. It worked though. Mindy said she would love to be my date for the evening and I picked her up from her flat in Northolt, London. She wore a skin-tight, figure-hugging blue dress and I nearly expired with desire when she answered the door. Away from work, our awkwardness disappeared and we spent the evening laughing, stealing cigarettes, talking about music and films and, eventually, snogging like a couple of sixth-formers.

Our follow-up date was spent walking her two beloved dogs around the common land near her flat. I remember being amazed that she managed to share a flat the size of a fag packet with a Border collie and a German shepherd, and being rather touched by the fact that she would sneak off from work every lunchtime to drive home and walk them rather than leave them alone all day. Our third date was spent at a local horse-riding centre where Mindy displayed the calm accomplishment of a lifelong horsewoman and I bounced around on top of a fat, black dobbin like a monkey riding a piano. For our fourth date, Mindy drove with her dogs out to where I lived on the edge of the Chiltern hills that roll across the landscape between London and Oxfordshire. We walked over the hills, threw sticks for the dogs, chatted about the countryside, and on the way back down the wooded slope we shared a hug. In an instant, I fell in love with her and realised I had met my soulmate and best friend for life.

Mindy's friendship and support would be sorely tested from the start though. She stayed with me when I gave up job security, pension and company car and went back to working in the media. I had secured an opportunity to present occasional car features on Granada TV's Men and Motors channel. I was once again broke, only this time too broke even to afford a car. Mindy would lend me hers or drop me off at a local garage where I could hire a purple Nissan Micra for a few quid for the day. She understood when I railed against the indignity of turning up at a film shoot in a hired Micra and when I raged about the difficulties of finding work. She helped me with cash and kind words whenever things got tricky and the bailiffs drew closer to the door, and she celebrated with me whenever something came good. We grew closer each year, eventually being blessed with our first daughter, Isabella, and getting married in May 2002. I still didn't have a 'proper job', and now was struggling to support us along with our first daughter and our first dog, Pablo, on whatever I could earn working freelance as a TV presenter, motoring journalist, radio presenter and occasional photographer. We had moved to Cheltenham, a beautiful spa town on the edge of the Cotswolds, because Mindy had family in the area and here was a place far enough from London to have its own sense of identity and independence, but not so far as to make travelling to the capital impossible. And now I was heading home with news of yet another audition for yet another job that I wanted more than anything else in the world.

It would be several months before the decision about who joined the team would be made. Having spoken to

Andy Wilman several times and been assured that things were in hand and they would be in a position to let us all know soon, I became more convinced than ever that I would be getting a call to say thanks but no thanks. In the event, I was sitting at my desk writing a script for a feature on Granada Men and Motors about a new Citroën when the call came. I had an office in the cellar of our townhouse in Cheltenham and it smelt of damp brickwork and paint. Mindy was down there with me and we had been chatting while I tapped away half-heartedly at the computer.

The phone rang loudly and interrupted our relaxed talk. It was an old-fashioned phone with a real, round dial and a set of bells inside loud enough to call out the coastguard. I leapt to my feet and we both looked at the phone. For no reason, we each declared excitedly that this was it, 'the call'. It was 'them'. We were convinced immediately that it was the long-awaited call about the *Top Gear* job. Quite why we should have decided this, I have no idea, because the phone rang ten or twenty times a day and usually turned out to be someone asking if we wanted to buy new windows or someone else asking if we wouldn't mind paying our credit-card bill before they had to send a man round to remove our telly. But we were right, it was 'them'. I lifted the handset, put my ear to it nervously and heard the quiet Scottish tones of Gary Hunter, the executive producer of the new *Top Gear*. He didn't mess about and got straight to the point:

*Hello, Richard. I was wondering—would you like to come and join our team?*

His tone was bright and happy, excited even. He was offering me the job I had dreamt of since I was a small child. But what I had heard him say was, *Look, I'm very sorry, but you haven't been lucky this time.*

*Thanks for trying though and good luck in the future.*

It was a mantra I had heard recited a million times; the gentle tone and the concerned manner as someone eases you down from a fever pitch of excitement and anticipation into the trough of despair and disappointment, and you find yourself wondering why, if they care so much about hurting your feelings, they can't just give you the bloody job.

It was such a familiar tune that it played in my head while, in the real world, the man was actually offering me the job. I drew breath, ready to go into my usual speech about being disappointed but hoping that it went all well for them and that whoever got the job enjoyed it and that perhaps we might work together one day, and all the other nice stuff you say while your world collapses around you and your precious hopes are pulled from your grasp and trampled on. And then I realised what I had heard. I had got the job. It had dominated our thoughts for the last few months. And now, finally, I had got the call and the news was unbelievably good.

'Wow, er, yes. Thank you. That's, er, brilliant. Thank you.'

'Right, well, good luck and we'll talk soon. Delighted you're joining us.'

* * *

I put the phone down and looked across at Mindy. She had guessed what he had said, but I told her anyway.

'He said yes. They want me. I got it.'

Mindy was crying. I was shaking.

'Bloody hell. I got it. I actually got it. What do I do now?'

I felt useless and stuck in limbo. And then I realised that I hadn't managed to ask a single intelligent question about what I would be doing, when I was starting or where I would be based.

'Christ, he must think I'm such an idiot. They'll change their minds.'

I called Gary back straight away and asked a few vague questions about what it all meant. Really, I just wanted reassurance that I hadn't got carried away and that he really had asked me to join the team. He reassured me, I hung up, relayed my findings to Mindy and called him back again to ask when I would actually start and where I should go. Mindy slipped upstairs while I was gabbling on the phone and then, after hanging up for the third time, I wandered off to find her standing in the kitchen. She had fished a bottle of champagne out from under the unit in the dining room and held it ready to open.

'Blimey. It's only eleven o'clock. Bit early.'

She looked at me and raised an eyebrow.

'Bugger it. Why not? You're right, let's celebrate. Let's actually bloody well celebrate.'

We sat in the tiny garden on a low wall, drank the champagne greedily and talked about what it might mean to us: if our lives might change; if this was the beginning of something amazing. We had, only a week earlier, agreed the sale of our Cheltenham house and the purchase of a crumbling little place in a remote corner of the Gloucestershire countryside nearby. Would this affect our plans to live in rural splendour with animals around us and space for our daughter—and maybe other children—to grow up? We had no idea yet. There was a lot to unfold with my new job. And most of it really would be brilliant.

## CHAPTER 4

# WHAT A JOB!

'I've got a great idea,' I announced.

No one looked up and I carried on fighting my way through the piles of papers, half-assembled bicycles, radio-controlled cars and assorted props that blocked every path through the *Top Gear* office on the fourth floor of the BBC White City building in London. I had burst into the office to find the production team working away in an unusually subdued silence, preparing for the ninth series of the show. It was four years since I'd got the call asking me to join *Top Gear* and we had been through a lot together. I knocked a pile of newspapers off the bosses' desk and hopped up and down like an eager child.

'It's a belter,' I panted. 'Really. Made for the new series. Perfect.'

Andy Wilman, slumped in his corner of the office, looked up from his crowded desk. He cleared his throat and harrumphed—his normally friendly and welcoming face creasing into a comically bad-tempered version of itself; an effect heightened by his mess of bristly hair in which the silver was rapidly outstripping the dark. He looked like the angry newspaper editor in *Spider Man*. In fact, as *Top Gear*'s editor, he is the man saddled with crafting the mish-mash of daft ideas, fragile egos, dangerous enthusiasms and crazy schemes that float around the *Top Gear* office into a television programme. He is also the man who has to spend a lot of his time keeping BBC executives, the board of complaints, the pro-politically correct lobby, the anti-car lobby and, occasionally, the police at a discreet distance.

It was not by accident that his desk was to be found in this cluttered corner of a noisy production office shared with twenty other team-members. He deliberately sited himself in the midst of the team of researchers, producers, assistant producers, production managers and runners. Management-guru types might claim it was because he felt it better to stay close to his team and to demonstrate his one-ness with them on the level playing field of a democratically run operation. I always suspected that it was really because he got bored sitting in an office on his own and he could never quite rid himself of the belief that, as soon as he turned his back, the entire team would leap on to their desks and start playing cricket or squander their time searching for bargains on eBay. He had worked his way through the ranks and could do the job of every person in the room if he had to. Which meant there was little they could get away with that he hadn't already tried. In fact, his many exploits over the years were so far ahead of anything his own team were ever likely to try and get away with that he could, to a degree, rest easy in the role of overseer. You can't kid a kidder and you can't trick a trickster. He was a past master and the team could learn a lot from him—not all of it connected with actually doing their jobs.

'Listen—' I tried to make it sound commanding but it came out like a plea '—I just want to go real fast. That's it.' I shrugged what I hoped was a dramatic shrug and added in a fake American drawl, 'Jus' real fuckin' fast.' I had rehearsed the speech and the sales pitch on the way down the motorway. It had gone better in the car. The show works best when people tip ideas into the mix and something comes out at the other end, so it's not a rare event for someone to stand in front of Andy and try to persuade him that their scheme has the potential to make a great piece of telly. I wasn't nervous about chucking a proposal in, but in this case it was something I really wanted to do and I didn't want the idea to vanish without trace. Andy continued to look up at me, but I could sense he might be about to concentrate on something else; perhaps the sandwich slowly curling next to his computer keyboard.

'Really, it's that simple. I don't want to enter a race or do anything complicated. I think we should just do a piece on going faster than we've ever gone before. Straight-line speed, that's the thing. I've driven at 200 mph in a car and on a bike. What does it feel like to go faster? And I mean a *lot* faster.' I ploughed on with the pitch, enjoying the rush as I warmed to my subject. 'Speed can make us feel good. Yes? There's just something exciting about it. It's a caveman thing. It's a basic, caveman desire: to go fast. If you can go really fast then you can outstrip a deer and catch your dinner and feed your family back in the cave.' I felt I was losing them with the caveman stuff. This was in danger of turning into an Open University lecture.

'So all we need to do,' trying to make it sound simple now, and therefore more tempting to the hapless band of researchers who would be setting this one up if the boss gave it the green light, 'is find something that can go real fast in a straight line. Anything will do. I don't want to set a record. Well, maybe just a record for a car show. We can be the fastest car show on earth. What about that?' I had caught him. Andy nodded; the team saw the nod and registered his approval and I knew it would happen. Probably.

In fairness, it wasn't that unusual for one of the team to champion an idea that came in from pretty far outfield. Someone had once suggested that we submerge a car in a tank of water to see how you really escape from a sinking car and if the old wives' tale about having to wait until it hits the bottom and the pressures inside the car and in the water outside equalise before you can open the doors had any truth in it. That idea got the go-ahead and, sure enough, one cold and damp winter's day, I found myself sitting in an old Vauxhall Carlton suspended from a crane over a special water tank that had been used in several feature films, probably including a James Bond movie or two. We were not making a Bond movie though, we were about to film a demonstration of just how terrifying and disorientating it actually is when you find yourself sitting in a car as it sinks and the water laps up and over the windows.

In a typically colourful moment of *Top Gear* genius, the director had, just before I climbed into the car to film my immersion, shown me a video clip of someone else doing exactly the same thing. Or rather, they had intended doing something similar, but the seasoned stuntman involved, faced with water rising in front of the windscreen and pouring in through the dashboard, had gone into a panic of such intensity that, watching the video, I feared he might die of stress before he got the opportunity to drown. He kicked the windscreen out and escaped to safety through the incoming flood of water. Snapping back to reality, I turned from the TV screen, grinned at the cameras, climbed into the old Vauxhall on the edge of the tank, tried to remember how to breathe through the diving regulator hidden in the back of the car, gave the thumbs up as cheerily as I could to the stunt crew, and hoped not to be meeting my maker any time soon. In the event, it was utterly terrifying.

Sitting in a car is such a familiar thing that it heightens the sense of strangeness when something out-of-the-ordinary occurs. I have sat in cars by roads, in car parks, up mountains and in TV studios. But to sit in a car and feel it float, bob about for a bit and then begin to sink, watching as the water rises up the doors and then the windows until everywhere you turn it's like looking into an aquarium is pretty frightening. Water rushed into the car with a threatening roar. It gushed in through the dash, pouring out through the hole where the radio was and spouting through the air vents. Looking down to my feet, it was even more disconcerting to see the water rising over them and rapidly covering my knees as the car sank.

The light from outside dimmed and turned green as the car sank beneath the surface and the sense of claustrophobia increased as I sat and waited, knowing that I must leave it until the car filled entirely before I opened the doors and scrambled out. The Vauxhall continued to sink, the water now covering the windows completely and rising up the inside to chest height as the car filled. The central-locking clicked over and over, the electrical systems shorting out with the influx of water sending the door locks in and out. I wondered if they would still open when the time came. I rehearsed again the moves needed to spin round and grab the ventilator and air tank hidden in the back if I needed it. I had never dived before and the regulator had felt uncomfortable and strange in my mouth in the practice session; it had taken a huge effort to persuade my reluctant lungs that they could suck in fresh air even though I was underwater. I hoped I wouldn't need it.

As the car filled, the water chased the last air pockets out of remote corners with sudden, explosive gurgles and hisses. The whole thing tipped forward as the car became neutrally buoyant in the water and the weight of the engine took the front down first. With a final hiss, the last air pockets were rooted out of the back and it sank faster. The levels rose quickly inside, my chest was soon completely submerged and the water rose up my neck and towards my face. I had rehearsed in my mind the moment when I must sit up straight and push my mouth up to the roof to get a last lungful of air before the car filled with water entirely, but the reality was more frightening than I thought it would be. The thing that really had me pinned down with terror was the fear of panicking. Panic stalked the submerged car like a shark. I was more worried about succumbing to panic and losing control than I was of anything else. If I passed out, if the locks wouldn't open, if the windows caved in under the pressure, we had taken emergency precautions and were ready for that. I had the air tank in the car and a team of emergency divers were on standby and could reach me before I so much as hiccuped or looked uncomfortable. All I had to do was not panic. If I lost it and flailed around like an idiot, then it would be harder to rescue me and I would endanger the people around me. I would also look like a complete and utter numpty, and the rest of the team back in the office would never, ever stop taking the piss.

In the event, I kept it together, pressed my mouth to the roof and sucked in a last breath of air, waited until the car was full and resting on the bottom of the tank, shoved the door—which opened smoothly—slipped out of the car and bobbed up to the surface like a cork. It was easy. Just don't drive your car into a canal.

The experts told me afterwards that it's all very well waiting until the car hits the bottom, but what if it ends up sitting next to an old fridge and the door won't open? Worse still, and perhaps most hauntingly of all, another told me that it's not uncommon for police divers to recover a vehicle from a lake and find the door open and the route to safety perfectly clear, but the driver still sitting there, dead, with their seatbelt still on, pinning them in place. That's how much of a problem panic can be.

In the four years I had worked on the programme, I had built a reputation for being happy to have a bash at the more risky-seeming stuff. I had absolute faith in the team around me and in their ability to foresee problems and be prepared if the worst happened. I guess that, really, I was just lucky to be getting paid for exactly the kind of showing off I had been doing all those years ago on my bicycle. And so we enjoyed racing a 2CV around Snetterton race track for twenty-four hours, joining the Norwegian Olympic bobsleigh team for a full-speed run down the bobsleigh track in Lillehammer, and running with the bulls in Pamplona. That actually came about when I was sent out to record a feature on the new Lamborghini Murcielago roadster in Spain. We decided that the car could provide a massive adrenalin rush and wanted to find something else that might give a comparable hit.

Running with the bulls was suggested, my hand shot up to volunteer, and the next thing I knew I was standing in a ridiculous pair of white trousers and a red sash in an absolutely crammed-full square in the town of Pamplona, waiting for the horns to sound that would indicate that several tons of really quite cross bulls had been released on to the streets and it was time to run like hell and try to avoid being trampled to death by the bulls or the rest of the crowd before I reached the bull-fighting arena and comparative safety. In the heavy silence that descended on the crowd as we waited for the bulls, nerves frayed and brows sweated. Half the people around me seemed to be over from Ireland in order to fulfil a lifelong ambition of running with the bulls. They also seemed still to be drunk from the night before, and the heady scent of strong spirits almost drowned out the deeper smell of sweat as we stood and waited.

The streets are cordoned off for the event, with hefty barriers running down each side. Walking the course earlier that morning I wasn't sure if the fencing was there to keep the bulls out of the watching crowd or us, the runners, in with the bulls to provide the spectacle that had drawn the crowds in the first place. But whatever the original purpose of the barriers, they mean that if you were to change your mind and decide that running with the bulls might not be for you after all, it would be a bit too late. Much of the route is flanked by shops and buildings a well as barriers; leaving no hope of an escape route that doesn't bring you into very close contact indeed with the horns of a bull.

The adrenalin rush was, indeed, massive as the klaxon went off and the crowd surged forwards. People screamed and just about everyone around me fell over for no discernible reason. The crowd lining the route on the other side of the barriers grew more frenetic as the bulls got closer and bore down upon those of us now trapped in the narrow confines of the Pamplona streets.

The bloke in front of me slipped on the strangely damp cobblestones and I leapt over his prostrate body. It probably would have been kinder to heft him over my shoulder and carry him to safety, but he was bigger than me and I was in sort of a rush. Another bloke ran towards me, which was strange because it meant he would be running at rather than away from the bulls. Maybe he was hoping to psych them out. Whatever his plan, he interrupted it to grab hold of me by my shirt and throw me into the road. I thought it annoying and rather rude at the time, but later when I watched the event replayed on film I saw that my back had been inches from the horn tip of one of the bulls. Needless to say, I made it to the safety of the arena where it was possible to clamber over the barriers to escape and meet with the film crew. We spent the rest of the day looning about to see if the Lamborghini could provide a thrill on a par with my recent bull-running experiences. It didn't.

Someone in the team once suggested we record an item for *Top Gear* on what happens when a car is struck by lightning. Obviously, it would be time-consuming and expensive for me to sit in a car in a field, next to a blasted oak, waiting for lighting to strike twice. We needed a way to guarantee the lightning. We found it in Germany at a hi-tech research lab where they can generate artificial lightning. Sure enough, I volunteered and was despatched, together with a film crew, to try and make lightning strike in the right place at least once if not two or three times.

There was a strangely oppressive atmosphere to

the place, on the day. The car sat in a compound surrounded by barbed-wire fences covered in warning signs indicating that trespassers would be fried with millions of volts of electricity before they were prosecuted. The film crew sat around the perimeter wire, the German boffins twirled knobs and inspected dials in the control room, and I sat in the car and wondered what being hit by lightning would feel like. We were about to demonstrate the Faraday cage effect, which dictates that the electricity from the lightning strike that this huge and complex set-up was about to send shooting into my car would travel not straight through the centre of the vehicle—frying everything inside, including me—but around the metal exterior, making the final leap to the earth from the wheels. The tyres would not be melted, the windscreen would not explode, my hair would not stand on end, and there would be no complicated forms for the director to fill in at the end of the day.

It was a scientific fact that this would happen; an absolute. It was as guaranteed as any other scientific law: if I dropped a brick on my head it would hurt, if I placed a ball at the top of a hill it would roll down; if you take water to 100 degrees, it boils. The lightning would behave in the way predicted because science said so. It couldn't suddenly decide to do something else just because it was a Tuesday, or to find out what would happen if it did. Nevertheless, sitting in the car as the machines outside hummed and cracked and the boffins read out the millions of volts being prepared especially for me, I felt the familiar grip of nerves. There's a big and completely illogical sense of 'what if?' when you're dealing with science like this. 'What if' the rules of science suddenly and briefly change that day? Just because they had never done so before did not rule out this being the first time . . . Then the boffins said 'fire', or something to that effect, there was a loud crack, an eerie blue light outside the car—and it was over.

Several million volts of Bavaria's best home-made lightning had leapt from the wires overhead, covering the two-metre air gap in a fraction of a second, drawn to the car's metallic body and to the earth waiting below. I said something to the camera to the effect of 'If I'm talking to you now without wings and a halo then we have demonstrated that the theory works'. It had, I wasn't dead, so we packed up and went home.

And now I was travelling home once more with news for Mindy of yet another stunt I might be attempting in the name of journalism, entertainment and paying the mortgage. I was pretty sure she would take it well enough. Every one of the stunt-based features I had made had been carefully researched and thoroughly planned, and Mindy knew this. No one in TV takes safety lightly because there is a policy of personal culpability, in principle if not in law. Essentially, if you cock-up and someone cops it badly, then as the responsible manager, the buck stops with you and you can find yourself in prison if it really is your fault. It's a good system and it gives reassurance to all of us, as well as to our partners and spouses.

I arrived home and was, as usual, mobbed by animals and children as soon as I prised the front door open. We had gone ahead and bought our little house in the country when I got the *Top Gear* job and we now shared it with two daughters; Isabella had been joined by her younger sister, Willow, now three years old, along with five dogs, four cats, four horses, a small flock of sheep and a handful of chickens. It was a long commute to and from London, but the reward was a chance to really escape when I finally got home and to live somewhere we wanted to be. Mindy could not believe that she lived in a place where she could have a horse of her own rather than travelling to a distant farm and paying to borrow someone else's. Early most mornings, even in winter, she could be found battling her way up the hills we lived among to take food to the sheep, to give the dogs a chance to stretch their legs, or to lead a horse out into the paddock.

Living in the country like that didn't leave much time for schmoozing around London at fancy parties, but we knew that, when were all home, we really were at home and away from everything else. We indulged our passion for horse-riding, dog-walking and taking the kids out for long rambles in the woods. Mindy had developed a passion for cars almost on a par with mine and we enjoyed trailing our Land Rovers around nearby Eastnor Castle, where the original Land Rovers were developed at the end of the 1940s. Also, when time and children permitted, we rode motorbikes. Mindy passed her bike test in 2005 and I had surprised her with a Harley of her own on her birthday the following July. I got one for myself too and we formed the world's smallest and least-intimidating motorcycle gang, riding around the lanes locally and laughing at each other until there was a real danger of us falling off and landing in a hedge.

Work made its presence felt, though. There had been times when Mindy found it difficult to watch the footage of me doing stunts on *Top Gear*. Even though she had known what I had been doing, actually seeing me do it was hard for her. When we watched the film of the car being dropped into the tank, I turned to see Mindy sitting with her eyes brimming with tears. She told me that she had been terrified, looking at me in the car with the water rising, even though I was sitting there next to her, weeks after the event, and very much not drowned. When the bull-running feature was broadcast she called me a daft sod and warned me about getting myself killed. She was, I think, only half joking.

We spoke briefly that evening about the 'real fxxxin fast' idea. But it was likely to be a long way off yet and might never become a reality. So it was filed away in our minds with the ever-growing list of things that may or may not be happening in an uncertain future.

CHAPTER 5

# THE JET CAR—JUST ANOTHER DAY AT THE OFFICE

Within twenty-four hours, I would be deep in a coma as my damaged brain expanded dangerously within my skull. But right now, I was in rural Bedfordshire, crouched in the lee of a Land Rover, picking grass burrs from my dog's coat. It was strangely soothing work, both for the dog and for me, and I let my mind wander back over the day's filming. It had gone well—for a *Top Gear* shoot.

We were working on a sequence in which all three of us decided to try and go green by making our own bio-fuel. To do this, we would need to grow a field full of wheat, which could eventually be processed and turned into something that worked very much like diesel. That meant doing a bit of agriculture, and we would start by ploughing. And that meant playing in tractors. James had managed to bury his in a boggy corner of the field; Jeremy had used explosives instead of a plough when he got bored with going slowly, and I had managed to tie my lengthy and, it must be said, very expensive plough in a knot behind my 26-tonne caterpillar-tracked tractor. Earlier in the day, I had parked the tractor outside a local newsagent while I nipped inside to buy a proper ploughman's lunch for the team. It was a very, very big tractor and when I dashed out of the shop with a carrier bag full of cheese spread, pickled onions and Dairy Milk to make a ploughman's, I discovered that my enormous machine had blocked the main street, in fact the only street, of the village. A man driving a bus was swearing under his breath. A lady in a BMW was swearing out loud at me, and every curtain at every window of every house in the street was twitching as the residents watched a red-faced man off the telly climb a ladder into an enormous tractor with tracks instead of wheels and trundle off down the narrow street, just missing the cars parked on either side.

Top Gear Dog—or TG as she is affectionately known at home where she lives with me, my family and our four other dogs—had enjoyed her day hugely. We had wheeled her out for duty as a sheepdog, clearing the sheep from the field before our ploughing attempts could begin. Me and the guys stood by the side of the field and wondered out loud how we were going to shift the sheep, and the other two pointed at me and the mutt and suggested that we make like *One Man and His Dog* and round them up. We were hoping she wouldn't be much good and it would provide a moment of light relief for the viewer before we got stuck in to the main business of the day. She didn't disappoint; she was spectacularly bad at being a sheepdog. In fact, I made a better sheepdog than she did. Half of the problem stemmed from the fact that with her pale, woolly coat, she looks rather like a sheep anyway and so our targets felt perfectly at home in her company. Instead of fleeing from her in terror and crowding through the open gate into the neighbouring field like we wanted them to, they were happy to nod at her in a friendly way before getting back to chewing the grass. We ran, slipped and fell over in the mud, ran some more, shouted, barked, fell over again and were laughed at for a good half-hour or so before a proper shepherd arrived to do the job for real. He turned out to be a Kiwi who comes over here regularly for work herding sheep about the place with his two Border collies. They made us look even more useless than we had already made ourselves look. The sheepdogs were great though; proper little working dogs that gave the impression they had better things to be doing than hanging around while I chatted and petted their ears.

When Jeremy's explosives were due to be detonated for his demonstration of a faster way of ploughing, I took TG off to a safe distance, installed her in the long grass under a Land Rover and sat with her, ready to offer comfort and calming words when the moment came. They went off with seven or eight dull thuds that you felt through the ground as much as heard. Every crow for about a thousand miles around lifted off from its branch and cawed at the pale grey autumn sky. A shower of dirt and small stones rained down after the blast and made the assembled mass of film crew yelp and shout as it pelted them. TG lifted one eyebrow, looked up at me, put her head down on her paws and went back to sleep. She's not easily flustered, that one. She was due to come with me to York after we finished filming that day; I'd thought it might add a rather jolly pilot-type flavour to the whole thing, having the dog standing on the airfield while I drove the jet car. We had rung ahead and the people at the hotel where we were staying that evening were looking forward to meeting her and were happy to let her kip in my room, even though they didn't usually allow dogs. I doubted TG would appreciate the benefits her new star status granted her, but was glad to have her along for company.

We had just finished filming the final sequence of the day and I was getting ready to leave for York.

The guys who had brought my tractor along were a top bunch and I thanked them profusely for trusting me with such a valuable piece of kit, then went over to collect TG from the people in whose care I had left her. I knew something was wrong as soon as I saw her. Clearly, she had spent the afternoon tearing up and down the fringes of the fields, where her long and woolly coat had picked up several million spiky grass burrs. These had so embedded themselves in her fur that they were causing her some discomfort as she wriggled around and tried to remove them. I sat down and picked as many from her as I could. But it was hopeless. I rang Mindy, she spoke to the vet and we agreed that there was only one alternative. A member of the production team would drive her back home, where an expert would make sure all the burrs were removed. She wasn't going to be coming to York and she would miss the jet car. I would miss her. A photograph of me sitting on the ground with her and picking those grass burrs from her coat would feature in several newspapers over the next few weeks as the story of what happened the following day unfolded. But I didn't know that yet. I rang Mindy and explained that she would shortly be visited by Pete, one of our researchers, bringing with him an even scruffier than usual TG who needed a visit to the dog-groomer. Mindy understood completely and was glad that we had done the sensible thing and sent her home for the attention she needed. I said goodbye to TG, who was by now looking pretty perky sitting in the back of Pete's car, ready to go home and be de-burred. When I ruffled the woolly fur on top of her head she looked up at me with her tongue hanging out and was, I knew, happy.

I packed my stuff in the car and made ready to set

off. The various crews were packing up their filming kit and readying themselves to head off to different locations for film shoots the next day. When we are getting ready for a new series, everyone is working hard to get as many of the films made as possible before we all get tied up with recording the studio element of the programme. That means one film day can run into another. Camera operators and sound recordists might be filming Jeremy hurtling around the *Top Gear* test track in a Lamborghini one day, a race between one of us in an off-roader and a guy on a mountain bike down a muddy hill the next day, and all three of us sinking in a lake while trying to make cars amphibious the next. It keeps them on their toes. James and Jeremy were heading off to their shoots and we all knew that we would talk on our phones the following day to moan about how the weather was ruining our filming or to boast about how brilliantly it was going. Jeremy asked me what I was going to do. I told him it was the jet-propelled car thing up at Elvington.

'Oh, you're actually driving it then?'

'Yes.'

'Goodbye.' He extended his hand with an air of absolute finality as one might extend a hand to a man walking to the gallows. It was a pretty standard joke really, the sort of thing we all do among ourselves on a daily basis. He was making out that I was sure to be 'killed to death' in a horrible crash.

'Yeah, whatever. It'll be fine. I'm looking forward to it. What are you doing?'

'New Jaguar XKR.'

'Well, enjoy it. See you soon. Talk on the phone tomorrow.'

We all set off in different directions, each with

their own thoughts about the day we had just shared and the one that was to come. I phoned home and spoke to Mindy. She had picked up Izzy from school and Willow from nursery and we spoke about their day. Izzy was breathless and excited as always, telling me about her swimming lesson, the fabulous lunch that she had eaten seconds of and how many times she had run round the field afterwards. When I spoke to Willow, she giggled, shouted at her big sister for pushing her, and said goodbye almost as soon as she had said hello. I felt a pang as I pictured them in the kitchen, helping Mindy tidy away the tea plates before a last-minute play and then bedtime. Sometimes, missing them becomes a real physical sensation in my chest that takes my breath away. On *Top Gear* shoots when we are all away from home, at about seven in the evening there comes a period when Jeremy, Andy Wilman, me and any other members of the crew with young families can be found on our own with a mobile phone glued to our ear wishing our kids goodnight. No matter how much fun we all have when we are away working, there are moments when we all, individually and privately, regret not being at home to tuck our kids in and give them a goodnight kiss. Of course, we would never normally share this feeling back at the shoot or in the hotel bar. But we all know it goes on. I said my goodnights to my two daughters, promised Mindy I would call her several times on the long journey north, and readied myself for a lengthy drive.

It was at least three hours from the field in Bedfordshire to the hotel in York. Obviously, because of my job, I drive a lot of different cars in order to write a script before filming them for *Top Gear* or to review them for my column in the *Mirror*.

On this occasion, I had borrowed a Honda S2000 two-seater roadster and, although not perhaps the best car for a long journey, I was glad of the distraction of a test car to drive and spent much of the journey planning what I would write about it when I got back after the following day's filming. Fortunately, the series producer of the programme, Pat Doyle, had been at the tractor shoot with us all day and was due to be at the jet-car shoot tomorrow. A calm Irishman with long hair and a relaxed, easy-going way about him, he was travelling the same way and had volunteered to go ahead in a hired Range Rover full of filming kit and tape stock for the next day's crew. I accepted his offer because this meant that I had the advantage of someone else to do all the navigation up front while I followed his tail-lights.

It was a long way, but the weather was kind, the roads weren't too badly clogged with evening traffic, and I had the radio for company. Settling into the driving seat, I relaxed my shoulders, rolled my neck, and turned my thoughts to the jet car I would be driving the following day. We had done a lot of research on it and prepared a great script for the shoot. It wasn't about the absolute speed so much as the sensation of driving a jet-powered car with 10,000 bhp. I tried to imagine unleashing the power of eleven Formula One cars in one huge hit of adrenalin-bursting speed and couldn't get anywhere near. I concentrated on the road ahead, illuminated by my headlights. I watched the trees and lamp-posts whizzing by to either side and tried to multiply their speed by a factor of three or four. I couldn't imagine it. This would be a whole new experience and would, I suspected, for ever change my idea of what it meant to go fast.

Over the past few weeks, we had talked a lot about how to make the best of this opportunity to drive a pretty special machine. We had all agreed that it would be best not to get too caught up on the numbers. This was, we decided, going to be a film about how it felt, rather than just about how fast it could go. As someone who has driven just about every performance car and supercar on the market, competed in a few races and hurtled up runways in some pretty special kit before, but never had a taste of jet-power, it would be an interesting experiment. If I spent too much time staring at the speedo and trying to squeeze an extra couple of miles an hour out of the car before I ran out of runway to drive on, there was a very real danger that I might get something wrong, and that could be disastrous. And anyway, driving a car with that kind of power and such an extensive track record, we knew it would be going plenty fast enough for our purposes. The best way to go about it, we decided, was for there to be no speedo in the car and for no one on the day to tell me how fast I had gone. We would know the figures from the on-board telemetry system, which would record the speed of the car, the acceleration, the g-forces recorded and every single input I made into the controls as I drove. But that information would be referred to in the studio, after I had driven the car and put it safely away again. I would be taught how to drive it by the man who had built it and drove it regularly at drag strips and events all over the country and beyond. I would progress slowly, increasing the power and, of course, the speed as the day progressed and at a pace that both the owner and I were happy with.

A mate of mine, Colin Goodwin, had already driven the exact same car. Of much the same age as me, he is a motoring journalist and had, some years earlier, been invited to take the Vampire for a blast up another runway and write about it for his magazine. By no means a gung-ho adventurer, but at the same time quite happy to race motorcycles or drive fast cars, Colin's down-to-earth explanation had been very useful in researching for the piece we were filming and, of course, in satisfying my pure curiosity about what lay ahead of me. It was, he had told me, mind blowing. He had hit over 270 mph and never again looked at speed in quite the same way. He assured me that the machine was actually simple enough to operate and reckoned I was in for a pretty fantastic time and would love my day in a jet car. A technical expert had been despatched from the BBC to go and give the car a thorough check and to make sure everything was in order. It was; the car looked great and I was looking forward to driving it in the way you look forward to an exciting and, of course, frightening experience that you know will make you feel good when you actually get down to it.

In the meantime, I was driving a borrowed Honda that I was supposed be writing about in a few days' time and about which I couldn't think of a single interesting thing to say. There were still a hundred or more miles to go to York and I was peckish. A motorway services snack killed off the hunger pangs and a phone chat with Mindy alleviated the boredom. Pat's Range Rover ploughed on ahead and I followed dutifully behind, the little Honda keeping up with the big 4x4's progress but making, I suspect, rather more noise about it on board. These road trips are an inevitable part of my job, and I guess you kind of get used to them. It becomes a chance to spend valuable time alone with your thoughts, to clear your mind of what you've just done and prepare yourself for what lies ahead. By seven o'clock we were rolling into York and getting horribly lost in the maze of one-way systems. I lived and worked in York for two or three years but can no more navigate my way around it today than I could find my way across Tokyo without a map. On a previous filming trip to the city, I had been asked by the crew to recommend a restaurant for that evening's nosh. After all, I had lived there for so long, I must have a few suggestions. I had to explain patiently that I had lived there while working in local radio for a truly minuscule pay packet. In the years I had been a resident, I had never visited a single restaurant and could only recommend the kitchen at my bedsit for a mean Pot Noodle and a tin of warm lager. They threw bread rolls at me when we finally found somewhere to eat that night. I don't think they believed my excuse, but it had come as a surprise to me to discover it. I look back fondly on my time in York and now realise how much I had been missing.

These thoughts and others had helped me cope with the frustration of trying to follow Pat's Rangie through the narrow streets of a city built to accommodate horses rather than massive twenty-first-century off-roaders. We eventually found our way to the hotel, parked downstairs and made our way to reception. The next day's film crew had arrived and eaten and were settled into the bar for a last pint before bed. Everyone long ago learned the lesson that overdoing it the night before a shoot can only make for an awful experience the next day, so it was not exactly shaping up to be a big session. We found them gathered around a couple of tables in a corner of the too brightly lit bar under a television on the wall showing Sky News and Sport. The team who had brought the car were also present. Colin Fallows, the guy who had built it, was in a corner of the blue Breakfast TV-style sofa and I sat next to him, eager to learn more about what was to come the following day.

I enjoyed our relaxed and friendly chat. As a technical man and a keen driver, Colin was someone I was bound to get on with. He had served extensively in the RAF, working with jet engines for decades, and was a fund of stories, anecdotes and technical insights on the subject of jets, planes and, of course, jet-propelled dragsters. I was surprised and charmed by his quiet manner. I had expected some gung-ho type full of bravado but found that Colin displayed the opposite traits. We quickly settled in to a friendly conversation about how he had built the car and why. I looked at him, a small, slightly portly chap who looked more like a pleasant bank manager or quantity surveyor than a man who habitually took the helm of a dragster that propelled him to speeds in excess of three hundred miles an hour. It goes to show that you really never can tell about people until you talk to them. When I nipped to the bar to replenish the drinks, ordering just a Coke for myself, the girl serving was surprised to see one of the blokes off *Top Gear* and asked me what we were doing. I explained about the dragster up at the airfield at Elvington and couldn't help but feel a little burst of pride as I told her matter-of-factly that it had a huge jet engine and could accelerate to three hundred miles an hour in just a few seconds. I was, of course, showing off and it didn't go unnoticed by the crew when I got back with the drinks.

I slipped away to bed early, although I suspected

that the rest of the group would be retiring soon anyway. In my room, I found a tartan dog bed and metal food bowl had been laid out ready for TG, who by now would be back with Mindy rather than lurking by my side. It made me sad to see this reminder that my dog couldn't be with me, but I was glad not to have to walk her around the hotel grounds until she performed her evening 'toilette'. I rang Mindy. TG was fine and was booked in to visit the groomer tomorrow morning. The children were sleeping soundly and soon she would be too. We wished each other goodnight. Another hotel room, another hotel bed, another night spent living out of a suitcase and padding into the bathroom carrying my bag full of toothpaste, razors and miniature bottles of shampoo purloined from hotels around the world. The following day was shaping up to be an exciting one and I was looking forward to it. Very soon, the jet-car drive would be behind me and I would be setting off home again. But first, sleep.

## CHAPTER 6

# 20 SEPTEMBER 2006

I fished an arm under the folds of the pleated valance thing around the bed base and stretched my fingers out, feeling for my quarry. The car keys could have dropped off the bedside table in the night and somehow rolled under the bed. But I couldn't find them. I had got to the room door, my bags hanging from my shoulder and my coat over my arm, ready to go, before I realised something was missing. And now, my face inches from the hotel carpet, I huffed and blew as I forced my shoulder under the bed, extending my reach further into the dusty recesses beyond, where my bare fingers would almost certainly encounter a huge and poisonous spider and I would never appear at breakfast that morning. There was nothing to be found. I pulled my arm out, gaining a slight carpet burn on my hand as I did so, and stood by the side of the bed. I am a fit bloke, but this strange and hurried exertion had left me breathless, though probably with tension as much as tiredness. Time was pressing. I had already decided to forgo the hotel breakfast; I knew that I could breakfast later on at the airfield while the crew rigged their kit and we made ready for the first shots of the day. All I had to do was find the flaming keys before dashing down to the garage underneath the hotel, where I was to meet up with Pat. I stamped over to the door and bent to pick up my canvas shoulder bag. I knew it was the action of an obsessive and nervous bloke, but I figured it was worth checking it just once more in case the keys lurked within the bag and had been missed on my first sweep of the pockets. Sure enough, I found them in the front pocket, jammed between my passport's brown leather case and my black Moleskine notebook. I felt that surge of relief and joy at finding something you had thought lost, closely followed by another surge, this time of anger at myself for being such a disorganised clot. Grabbing my overnight holdall, shouldering my canvas bag and sticking my brown leather coat over my arm, I hefted the door open and set off down the corridor. My feet fell silently on the garish blue conference carpet and the door shut behind me with a loud crash followed by a tinny rattle. Pat would be waiting in the garage. I ran.

It was not an easy feat of navigation, but somehow our tiny convoy made it to Elvington. A base had been set up at one end of the main runway and our collection of cars and crew vans were gathered on a concrete apron. Surrounding the airfield, I saw stretches of dark green coniferous forest in the distance. The land was flat and broad and a light wind blew across it under a pale blue sky. With the little Honda parked up, I leapt out and made my way towards the small crowd assembled round what was clearly some sort of catering van. I recognised Scott, the director, and said good morning.

'You all right?' he asked. In his fashionably crumpled clothes he looked, as always, as though he had just walked out of a nightclub or an advertising shoot.

'Yep. This is going to be a day then.'

'Seen the car yet?'

'Nope. Can't wait. Where's Colin?'

'Getting it ready. They'll bring it over in a sec.'

I ordered a cup of tea and a bacon sarnie. We've adopted a sort of military approach to eating on these shoot days, which amounts to nothing more complex than: if you see food, eat it now because you might not get any later. I chewed on the bacon sandwich and chatted to a couple of guys who were there with the support and emergency crew. They were firemen and this was going to be an interesting day for them. They were looking forward to seeing how we worked and what went on when we made a piece of *Top Gear* telly.

With a cup of hot tea in my hand, I sought out Scott again and we got our heads together for a brief planning session. There was much to do, but for once we had to do it at the natural pace at which events unfolded. We couldn't force anything today. I had to be introduced to the car, and taught how to drive it. This would take as long as it took. We had a few bits to film where I would talk to camera about the car and how it was made, but we decided to do that at the end of the day. We only had the runway until 5 p.m., after which time noise restrictions would end our chances of driving the car. By saving some of the links until after we had done all the driving stuff, we could make the best use of the day. I grabbed another cup of tea and sat in the Honda, reading through the script. There's only so much that you can really write before you make a feature like this one, but we could structure it pretty rigidly and knew the main points. The only bits to be sketched in on the day would be my responses to driving the car. We wanted to record how it felt, what went through my mind, and how it related to driving the other fast cars I have driven. I rang Andy Wilman, who was back in London trying, as always, to strike a balance between keeping the office running smoothly and spending time in the edit suite overseeing the assembly of the films that define so much of the look, feel and mood of *Top Gear*. We stay in constant touch when we're out filming, and it's useful to speak with someone away from the scene of the actual shooting, who can retain a sense of perspective and a useful overview. Andy reiterated the importance of not getting caught up in talking about specific speeds. We agreed that this was all about the noise, the acceleration and the sensation of driving the thing. I told him that I would call him back as soon as I had completed my first drive.

Before I even got to sit in the Vampire let alone interfere with the controls, Colin was going to take it for a shakedown blast up the runway. This was, I suspected, the only way that Colin's mind could be put at rest that everything was working OK. It was the sort of hands-on approach you would expect from him. The car appeared, being towed up to our end of the runway behind its support van, and I got my first look at it. I was surprised by how long it was. This was more like the top-fuel dragsters I had loved when I was a kid. I would sit in front of the telly and rummage about in my huge plastic tub of Lego to build drag racers that looked exactly like Vampire, with its long, skinny body, big chunky rear wheels and skinny little front ones. But my models had never had the strange, cylindrical, metallic addition that lay immediately behind the driver's head. This was the jet engine, the heart of the machine and the very reason for its existence. I had expected a smaller, more compact unit, but this was big, mechanical-looking and purposeful. Colin was in the driver's seat and steered the thing into position on the start line. We had gathered a couple of hundred metres away, along the edge of our concrete apron. The van was untied and manoeuvred alongside and slightly in front of the jet car. Colin's technical assistant hopped out and busied himself making adjustments and checks that I didn't understand but guessed were important. Our whole team stopped what they were doing and watched in silence. Knowing that one of us was going to be doing this next made the demonstration all the more interesting to us.

The technical checks went on for just long enough for my mind to wander and begin running over what lay ahead of me that day. This was a new world to me, with engines that worked differently to the ones I know and understand. Despite the distance, I could hear Colin and his assistant shouting instructions to one another and, eventually, I picked out the unmistakable whine of a jet engine starting up. The whine built to a shriek and the support guy got out of the way. We waited, our own tension growing with the noise from the engine. Hot air shimmered dizzyingly around the back of the car where the massive engine's thrust poured out into the crisp autumn morning. With no warning, the car leapt forward. There was a burst of flame from the engine's outlet at the back and a roar as the noise hit us. Colin was using the afterburners, so this would be a full-power run. I knew that much from our conversation the previous evening, and I tried to imagine what it must feel like, being hit in the back by a ten thousand horsepower engine and shooting up to 300 miles an hour in the time it takes a fast road car to hit sixty. Watching from the sidelines, the car's acceleration was endless. It gained speed with a relentless effortlessness that suggested it might keep getting faster and faster until it just disappeared. And then, only a few seconds after it set off, we could see in the distance the parachute mushrooming behind the car and then the noise from the engine dwindled and vanished. Silence descended on us as the parachute collapsed to the ground behind the now stationary car half a kilometre or so down the runway. I had seen Colin doing what he does for a hobby and now my turn was getting closer. This was showing off on a grand scale and I understood precisely why people do it. But I felt a twinge of nerves in the pit of my stomach. That had looked like a very great deal of power being unleashed in a very short space of time to catapult a suddenly very small car up a suddenly very short runway.

It took half an hour or so for the car to be made safe and towed back up to the launch point at the top of the runway. While Colin and his team did technical stuff, we loitered by the burger van and drank tea. The guys were asking how it felt, knowing that I was going to be driving the same car that day. I told them that I was nervous, but pretty sure we could manage it. I've spent too much of my life standing around waiting to do things that have made me nervous to be caught out by nerves now. It's best to be aware of the nerves, to feel them but not to let them take over and affect you. The nerves help by sending adrenalin flooding around your body, making you sharper and your responses faster; but if you let them take over your mind then you can lose focus. There's something strangely comforting about feeling nervous now; it's a familiar sensation and gives me a sense of consistency, taking me back to my first radio show all those years ago, or my first daft stunts on bicycles. I put the nerves to one side and ordered another cuppa.

Soon enough, the car was ready and towed back up to the start line. Colin and I walked towards it together, leaving the crew and support team behind. We would film a TV version of our briefing later on, but this was the real thing and best not interrupted by having TV cameras stuck in our faces. Close up, the Vampire looked smarter and neater than I had expected. So often, these super-specialised machines are engineered to work well but not necessarily to look good. Rally and race cars usually appear great from a distance, but when you get close up are a mess of exposed wiring, thin paint, gaffer tape and the tails of thousands of little cable-ties dangling from every surface like tadpoles trying to burrow their way in. This, though, was an altogether more polished creation. But then, to a large degree its purpose was to provide a spectacle and therefore looks mattered more than is usual in a race car. Colin snapped me out of my daydream and began to fill me in on what the car could do and how it went about doing it. We laughed and joked as he explained that the engine was mounted in such a way that the thrust it provided also pressed it down on to the tarmac. This was achieved, simply enough, by having the jet point up a couple of degrees at the back, so it shoved the car very slightly downwards as well as forwards. This put my mind at rest a little about the dangers of the engine suddenly trying to revert to its former life of sending an aeroplane hurtling around the skies. Then Colin indicated that it was time for me to climb in and I did.

The narrow aperture into the cockpit meant I had to slide myself in carefully, ducking my head beneath the protective bars of the rollover structure. I settled into the hard seat and felt the dense, wide webbing of the harness behind my back. I reached around and tugged the straps so that they fell in front of me, draping across my shoulders and chest. When I did this for real, the harness would be tightly fastened down to keep me firmly in place if anything went wrong. Colin talked me through the controls. There were surprisingly few. Essentially, the car consists of an engine, a parachute to stop, and the seat. Because the engine does not transmit the power to the road, there are no complicated systems for sending the power through the wheels. It just revs up and sends the thrust out of the hole at the back. Because it's bolted to the engine, the car is thrown forward with it. So there is a control for turning the engine up to the required level in much the same way that you set the volume on a radio. The metal dial, about the size of the base of a teacup, sat on the right-hand side of the rudimentary dashboard. It was unpainted and simple to look at, and the scale around the outside indicated the percentage of power being delivered by the engine—from zero up to 125 per cent, interestingly enough.

Just below the engine control was a large metal lever, hinged beneath the dash. Colin explained that this lever had two functions: it cut the engine and deployed the parachute simultaneously. This, then, was my main braking system. Once under way in earnest, the brakes on the wheels would be useless against the huge thrust from the engine and I would rely on the 'chute to bring everything to a halt. In the centre of the metal dash panel was the steering wheel. This was of the 'butterfly' type used in drag racers. It was made up of two small handles, each like the end of a garden spade, connected in the centre at a metal boss about four inches across. I had never seen one before but immediately liked it for its dramatic shape, tiny proportions and earnest, businesslike finish. This was not a wheel you'd find fitted to anything ordinary. I rested my hands on the two handles, feeling the bare metal beneath them cool and strangely sensual. Through this wheel would be transmitted the results of all the power unleashed by the massive engine just a couple of feet behind my head.

I looked around the cramped cockpit. These were all the controls I had to operate then. There was no clutch pedal because there was no clutch. There was no accelerator because I dialled the power in before I set off and then left the dial alone. My right foot rested next to the footbrake, which was used only to hold the car stationary as the engine got up to speed. My left foot would rest on a dead man's pedal, which cut the engine the moment your foot released it. This was a device that would come into action only in an emergency; if something went wrong, my foot would no longer hold the pedal down and the engine would be cut.

This was not the interior I'd imagined. I had envisaged rows of toggle switches controlling any number of intricate functions essential to the operation of such a huge and powerful machine. I had seen myself confidently flicking switches to operate complex systems to meet the Vampire's insatiable appetite for fuel and air. There were safety systems to be primed, monitoring systems to be watched and checked on. I expected to scan across and see every surface sprouting more switches, with the gaps between them filled by gauges with purposeful faces and important roles and dials set within the dials. But what I found in reality was a collection of controls as simple as the ones on the plastic dashboard I had stuck to the back of my dad's driving seat as a kid. There are more things to do, more systems to monitor on a family hatchback. I was, I admit, slightly disappointed. But also slightly reassured that if this was all I had to concentrate on, then there would be little to distract me from the business of steering and stopping at the right point.

I stared over the front of the car and down the runway stretching off to the tree-lined horizon. I imagined how it might feel. There would be a lot of noise as the engine speed rose. I would grip the wheel with both hands and hold the car still with my right foot on the brake. When Colin gave the signal, I would take my foot off the brake and feel the car surge forward with unimaginable force. I did not know how it would feel on my way up the runway. Would it be smooth and steady, or would my head be jostled around, making it hard to see ahead? Would the G-force snap my head back? Would I have to do much steering through the tiny, weird-shaped wheel to keep it going straight ahead? I asked Colin how I used the afterburner. He told me that we would not get round to using that until later in the day, but when I did, it was just a case of thumbing the innocuous metal switch on top of the left-hand grip on the steering wheel. When I hit the switch, a flame would be sent shooting down the centre of the engine behind me, igniting the unburnt fuel in the engine and turning it into something like a cross between a standard jet engine and a rocket. The power would instantly be doubled. The engine would already be running at full speed before I hit the button and I wondered about the timing of the actions.

'Do I hit the button as I take my foot off the brake,

or do I set off and then hit it?'

'You take your foot off the brake and then hit the button.'

'What if my foot is still on the brake?' I didn't want to get it wrong and damage the engine. Maybe it would stall, or whatever the jet engine equivalent is.

'Makes no difference. When you hit that button, you are going that way,' Colin pointed up the runway.

'Right.' I felt like a ten-year-old.

*   *   *

Before I did my first run, we would record a couple of bits of telly about the car and what I was there to do that day. Although we'd decided that most of this stuff would be done when I had finished driving the car, there were a few bits that required me to look fresh at the beginning of the day, before I got all hot and sweaty hurtling up and down a runway in a jet car. It would be no good speculating on camera about how it might feel to drive the Vampire if I was dripping with sweat from having already done it. I would get changed into my driving kit, knock off a couple of pieces to camera, and then get on with the serious business of the day; the driving.

Another member of the *Top Gear* production team, Grant Wardrop, had joined us for the day. Thirty-ish and an irritatingly handsome man with a concerned and genuine manner at work, Grant had joined the team only a year or so ago as an assistant producer and was making rapid progress towards becoming a producer. It was unusual for him to get out of the office and away from the phones and his computer, but he had been heavily involved in setting this one up and it was useful for him to be with us on the ground. We talked about the day and the fun still to come and he passed me one bag stuffed with a set of racing overalls, boots and gloves, and another containing a crash helmet. I protested that I had brought my own helmet with me, but he insisted that I use the one provided. It was, he assured me, the one for the job. He had realised early on in the planning stages that this was a pretty unique drive and had personally researched the best crash helmet for the job and got hold of one. And now he insisted that I wore it.

There was nowhere to get changed. I asked the paramedic guys if I could borrow their ambulance and turn it into a dressing room. They agreed that I could, as long as I didn't fill it full of flowers and blue M&Ms. It was quiet inside the ambulance. I laid the silver-coloured racing suit out on the trolley bed, put the boots at the end of the legs and the gloves at the end of the arms so that it looked like a deflated racing driver on a hospital bed. I inspected the kit more closely. The suit was made of thick, fire-retardant material and the label told me that it was four layers dense. I apologised to the figure lying prostrate on the bed and pulled its hands and feet off before throwing them on the ground and picking up the suit. I pulled it on over a T-shirt and underpants and knew, instantly, that I looked ridiculous. It did at least fit, but even without a mirror I could tell that it looked daft. The boots only made it worse. They were soft and a bit too clean and well-presented to be the boots of a jet-car veteran. They were more pixie than pole position.

At the bottom of the bag, I found the neck brace.

This is a circle of padding that opens on one side so that it can fasten around the neck with Velcro. It sits immediately below the opening of the crash helmet and limits how much your head can move in a crash, hopefully avoiding over-extending the neck and damaging delicate vertebrae. This one was blue and before I fitted it round my neck, I looped it round the top of my head so that it sat there and looked like an obscure hat with no middle and a padded brim. It's a gag I have pulled many times on track days until the crew are, I'm pretty sure, bored of it. They weren't in the ambulance with me now to see it and wouldn't have been impressed if they were. I pulled the ends apart and they separated with a loud, Velcro rip. I put it on properly. I doubted that the big blue circle just below my chin had improved an already shaky image.

The helmet, though, was a beauty. It was a plain white Arai, built specifically for car racing and there was an air of quality to it. I've ridden motorcycles for twenty-odd years and so a new crash helmet holds a particular appeal. I grabbed it by the chin-guard and hopped out of the ambulance's back doors. Predictably, the crew laughed when I came into view. I looked like an extra from an early episode of *Doctor Who*, with my spangly silver race suit, blue neck brace and racing bootees. I adopted a Superman flying pose and, declaring myself to be The Silver Flash, I asked if someone could sort me a cuppa before I set off to save a dog that was trapped down a well and put out a forest fire.

The car was waiting for me on the start line and it was time to get to work. The crew were despatched to their pre-appointed vantage points around the runway and busied themselves getting cameras and sound-recording equipment ready. There were cameras on board the car too, tiny digital ones mounted so that they could look back at my face and forward along the length of the car. They were set running and then left by the camera assistant, who dashed off to make sure the rest of the team were happy. Usually, the camera assistant would have been a bloke called Paul Bamford, but he had just been promoted to camera operator and this was his very first day working on the camera rather than looking after the other operators. The sound recordists, Russell and Barney, checked the microphone pinned into my race suit and made sure the battery pack was connected before getting into position with the camera operators to record the roar of the car when it went past.

As far as I was concerned though, this part of the day was not about the filming. My role now was not TV presenter but as a jet-car driver. I replayed Colin's patient and thorough explanation of what I must do and put one hand on the side of the car, ready to climb in. Colin was there to remind me of the routine and to check that I was OK to drive. We chatted briefly and I climbed over the side of the car, placing my foot on the seat, swinging my other leg in and lowering myself down. I made extra allowance for my head to clear the roll cage as I now had a crash helmet on and did not want to mark its shiny new paintwork on the metal bars. I settled into the seat, making sure that the harness straps were in front of me this time, ready to be fastened down. Colin glanced in, looked around to check that everything was OK, and stepped back to allow his technician to fasten the harnesses. They were pulled tight; so tight that I could barely breathe. These guys were not taking any chances. And then Colin leaned in again and began fastening straps that connected my upper arms to the harness.

'What are they for?' I asked.

'If you have a crash and go upside down, they stop your arms from flailing around and getting hurt.'

'I don't want to go upside down.'

I examined the straps closely as Colin fixed them in place. I could see how they would, in the event of a roll, stop my arms from flapping about as the car went over. I looked to the side at the massive roll bars and winced as I imagined trapping an arm between one of them and the ground.

Colin checked the harness and stooped to lean past the roll bars once more and ask me to run through the controls with him again. This time though, it was no dry run. When I asked for air and power, the engine would be started for real and I would be at the controls of a running jet engine for the first time in my life. Making a conscious effort to breathe steadily, I went through the motions one last time. I made no wisecracks now, there was no larking about. There was simply an atmosphere of calm and seriousness as we got ready. With Colin happy, we were ready to do it for real.

I called for air and power. Colin, hovering in the bottom of my vision as he crouched to tend to the front of the car, flicked the relevant switches on his technical gear and the engine was ready to start. On the signal, it did so. Immediately behind my head, an engine capable of delivering enough power to shove a jet fighter around the skies woke up and began to turn. Despite knowing exactly what was going on, how the engine worked and what would happen next, I felt a surge of excitement mixed with fear as my mind was invaded by the very real and very close presence of what was now, unmistakably, a jet engine. The sound rose to the shriek familiar to us all from airports across the world. But as I listened to it on this occasion, I wasn't settling into a seat and fastening my belt; there were no other passengers around me, chatting about take-off and the weather at the other end. And there was no one else to control the massive engine that was now increasing in volume and aggression as the noise rose to a howl. Colin gave the thumbs up and looked at me. I signalled that all was well and he walked backwards to the starting position, just ahead and to my right.

My foot now held the car in place and I could feel it straining against the brake. The car, which until now had been tended and ministered to like a delicate patient, had been transformed into a wild creature, held back just by my right foot. I could feel its essential desire to break away and hurtle off into oblivion. Colin signalled that I should go. This was it. I lifted my foot away from the brake. The car moved forward and I sensed its relief as the power from the engine was finally free, unfettered.

The acceleration was massive but did not feel how I'd thought it would. I had expected a mind-warping blur of speed as I exploded away from the line. But this was different. It didn't feel ferocious or violent; just that I was submitting to the inevitable. It was a firm and insistent shove, an absolute force that I had no choice but to go along with. But it increased in insistence and force. The speed increased too. Fast. Within 13.7 seconds of taking my foot off the brake, I had passed 205 miles an hour. But there was no way of knowing that inside the cockpit. And even if there had been a Speedo fitted, I would have hesitated to lower my eyes and glance at it. There was a lot to do.

Waiting to do this for real, I had begun to think of the steering wheel as pretty much an adornment, just somewhere to rest my hands while the engine decided which way we went. But in fact, I was making constant corrections, struggling to keep the car heading straight ahead. Because of the camber of the airfield and the crosswind, I had been told to apply a constant thirty degrees of steering input in order to keep the car going straight. I had not anticipated how much this was needed. Neither had I anticipated so much information coming back through the wheel. Perhaps because of the enormity of the engine, the power and the noise going on at the back of the car, I had not really thought about how busy it might get at the front. Far from being the brave but pointless passenger I had thought I would be, I found that the driver in this instance was a very, very busy individual.

I tried to keep my eyes focused on the track ahead. Very, very soon, I would pass the traffic cones that signalled the point at which I must shut down the engine and deploy the parachute to stop. It was hard to see. The runway surface communicated every bump and ripple through the wheel, tremors which in turn made their way through my hands and arms. The car itself shifted slightly and vibrated with the air going through the engine and round the vehicle. The runway, hurtling past underneath, sent vibrations through the car's chassis and into me. The noise now was all-pervading. It didn't vary or alter with the effort the car was making. My senses were swamped by a constant scream as the engine hurtled me towards the horizon and the air in front complained as I forced it out of the way at enormous speed.

As we charged forward, my crash helmet was

buffeted by that same air that now became a wind of unimaginable force. It buffeted my head about, adding to the disorientation. For a brief second, I wondered what would happen if I missed seeing the cones and hit one instead of passing between them. What would it do to the car? What would it do to me? To make matters worse, my visor was steaming up. This can happen in a crash helmet sometimes, and is usually due to air from your exhalations being unable to escape the confines of the helmet and condensing on the inside of the visor, fogging your visibility. Perhaps my neck brace was acting as a seal around the bottom of the helmet, stopping the exhaled air from escaping. Perhaps I was breathing too much, with the exertion of steering and the excitement. I tried to control my chest, pacing my breaths, feeling my throat shiver and contract as I tried to breathe out slowly and calmly. The visor misted more. I couldn't lift a hand from the wheel to fiddle for the latch and open it. And even if I could, I didn't fancy a face full of wind at whatever speed I was now travelling. And then, through the misted visor, I saw the cones, their fluorescent finish making them easier to spot on what was now, for me at least, a foggy day. They were just ahead but would, in a fraction of a second, be alongside. It was time.

I had wondered how I would release my right hand from the steering wheel to grab the lever that deployed the 'chute and cut the engine. This was the moment when I would find out. As the runway hurtled past at God knows what speed, as the jet engine behind me screamed and shook, as the car made tiny lurches left and right, I moved my hand away from the pistol grip of the wheel and found the lever to the right. My left hand felt rock-solid and reliable on the wheel. I trusted it. With my right, I felt for the lever. My fingers closed on the metal end. I pulled it and it moved smoothly backwards. The jet engine changed from a shrieking monster to a calmer, more docile beast as its furious howls relaxed into a lengthy sigh. I wondered if the parachute had worked. And then I was shoved forward in my seat and I knew that, yes, it had worked. The huge silk canopy had fired out of its tube at the back of the car and now grabbed at the air moving by at 206 mph.

Pulling the lever had felt like a satisfyingly mechanical and real operation. In an age when many significant processes are begun by flicking a switch or tapping a computer screen, it had been reassuring to pull on a big, metal lever that clearly moved other well-oiled bits of machinery about. The tug from the parachute was astonishing. At full acceleration, a car like this might manage to shove the driver into the seat with 1.8 g. That's 1.8 times the force of gravity, compared to the 0.5 g a road-going sports car might manage. Under braking, though, the huge parachute canopy can arrest the car so that the driver is thrown forward with 3.5 g compared to the most a normal car driver is ever likely to feel under braking of 1 g. It took my breath away as I strained forward against the tight harnesses. But it felt good. It was the finale; the last act in a drama lasting just a few seconds but taking in forces so incredible they seemed to belong to another world.

In 9.3 seconds, the car had slowed to a more pedestrian speed of 60 mph. I steered to the left and headed to the point where I knew the crew would be expecting me to stop. We had planned for the end of this first run. Having filmed the car as it hurtled up the runway, they would dash over to a pre-arranged spot where it would come to rest and I would deliver a few words about how it had felt. I didn't bother planning what I would say. This was one occasion when it is best to wait until it's time do it and then just open your mouth to allow whatever is in your mind to flood out. The results may not be neat, considered and eloquent, but they will be genuine, heart-felt and honest. And as a viewer, that gives you something more special and more personal than the most polished and considered pre-prepared speech. It's when TV really can take you somewhere with someone.

I used the footbrake for a second time now, to slow the car to a complete halt. The film crew dashed towards me, with the director, Scott at the head of the group. They were excited but professional as always, rolling the camera as they approached. As soon as the camera looked settled, I started talking. I blurted out words, trying to convey the exhilaration, the excitement. Trying to communicate how it had felt to be totally at the whim of something so incredibly powerful for a few brief seconds. My mate Colin Goodwin had told me how his drive in the same jet car had been a life-changing experience. I knew now what he meant by that. And I tried to convey just one tiny fraction of it to the dark, all-seeing eye of the TV camera in front of me as the slack parachute fluttered and settled behind the car and the jet engine cooled in the breeze. It was only 1 o'clock. I wanted to go faster, I wanted more speed. I knew that I would get it before the day was out.

It had been an enormous, overwhelming experience that turned out to be every bit as adrenalin-charged as I'd expected. But it was an experience that was due to be repeated several times that day and there was much work to be done. I was scheduled to make a further five or six runs. First, the car had to be returned to the top of the track and the tender ministrations of Colin and his assistant. The pair arrived on the scene in their ordinary-looking Transit van as the film crew were finishing off their sequence recording my reactions to the drive. I clambered out of the car, shook hands and patted backs among the crew, and then spent a moment or two with Colin. He had driven this car thousands of times and I looked into his eyes to try and catch a glint of recognition that we two had now shared an experience and visited a place not visited by many.

We hitched up the jet car with a rope attached to the back of the van. Colin would tow the car back to the top of the runway and I would steer it. He reminded me that it was pretty important to stay alert with the footbrake this time, as it would not do to run the jet car into the back of the van and damage the nose cone. Oddly, I found the drag back along the runway at twenty miles an hour being towed behind a Trannie van almost as stressful as going the other way under jet power. At slow speeds, I had time to remember that this car was a very special one indeed and belonged to someone who had invested a great deal of time and money building and driving it. We got it back to the start line without an embarrassing shunt and I left Colin and the team to their various preparations for the next run.

Over yet another cup of tea, I cornered Pat, the producer, and told him about the problems with the visor. We rang the production team and set them looking for a local shop where we could buy one of a number of products on the market that spray on to the inside of helmet visors and supposedly stop them from steaming up. Within minutes, the desk-bound researchers back at the office had found such a place and an on-site researcher was standing by to make the dash. But I knew of a simpler and faster solution. Smearing a tiny spot of washing-up liquid on to the surface of the visor has exactly the same effect. It's an old biker's trick and it works. While it might be cooler somehow to despatch a researcher who would return with a glitzy pot of spray-on demister, it was quicker and easier to pop over to the control tower and ask to borrow a bottle of Fairy.

I had recently taken up smoking again after several years of abstinence. It had happened on another *Top Gear* shoot when we had been chased across Alabama by angry rednecks after we painted slightly rude slogans down the sides of our cars. They were offended in a stubborn, stupid way and pursued us in pick-ups with shotguns. We fled across two states, only stopping when we reached the safety and relative civilisation of our pre-booked motel. I ended that day by sparking up my first cigarette in three years, and right now seemed like a good moment to indulge too. I slipped quietly into the peace and solitude of the waiting Honda press car, sparked up a smoke and sat back heavily. My hand looked steady as it raised the cigarette to my mouth and I relaxed a little and felt good. I had known all along that driving the jet car would be fine; that I would be nervous but then elated and in control. And that was exactly how it had turned out to be. With the first run out of the way, the rest would be more enjoyable.

There was much still to do. We had to film pieces to camera with me explaining how the car worked and we had to film more shots of the car in action. More to the point, I still had to progress to using the afterburner and do a full-bore run with all 10,000 bhp unleashed behind me. This would happen only when, and if, Colin judged I was ready. I was pretty sure that he would give me the go-ahead and I was looking forward to the experience. Driving the same car but with twice the power would be a huge buzz. I felt a twinge of nerves back again and reminded myself that the run I had completed had only been the first step on a bigger ladder. I knew that things had to get a lot faster and a lot more frantic before I could set off home to Mindy and the kids.

I rang home to speak to Mindy, mindful that I would have to try and disguise the fact that I was smoking. She knew full well that I was back on them, but I was aware that it upset her and I felt ashamed. We spoke about the day and the experience. I knew she was worried and tried my best to reassure her that it was no big deal and everything was under control. I rang off and then phoned Andy Wilman to let him know that the first run had gone well and I had not flashed past the waiting cameras as a flaming fireball and landed in the middle of York. We joked and messed about, but I could tell that he was genuinely relieved that things were going well and that we had everything very much under control. I told him about the visor and the solution we had agreed upon. He trusted me to make that particular call; crash helmets are something I do know about. And he recognised that. We spoke again about the decision not to bring the speed into the piece until after we had finished filming it. We both agreed that this made a lot of sense and would keep my natural competitive spirit under check.

My second fag finished on cue, just as the team were done prepping the car. The walkie-talkie lodged next to the passenger seat in the Honda yelped into life. I was wanted—duty called. I hauled myself out of the car and strode across the airfield; a man in his thirties, living the dream he'd had since childhood. I was walking confidently towards a jet-propelled car which I would be driving in front of not only an assembled TV crew but, thanks to the efforts of that crew, hundreds of millions of TV viewers the world over. It doesn't do to get too self-congratulatory in life—pride comes before a fall and all that—but as I walked across the smooth tarmac and slipped the neck brace on to the shoulders of my silver racing suit, the ten-year-old boy still living inside of me was giggling with excitement and bursting with pride.

After a pep talk with Colin, I made my second run. It went well and felt the same as the first. I thrilled to the sensation of the power and the speed, succumbed to the inevitability of the relentless acceleration of that seductive jet engine, and hopped about in front of a TV camera afterwards, trying to convey a sense of what I was experiencing. And then I did it again. By now, it was well past midday and the crew had been working hard all morning. So had Colin and his technician. We had filmed the beginning of the piece and several runs in the car. The next thing was for me to try a run with the afterburner lit. But first, lunch. Far from the lengthy, booze-fuelled nosh-ups at the Ivy that some seem to enjoy on a daily basis, lunch on the TV shoots I find myself on is more likely to consist of whatever we can grab from a petrol station and force into our faces between takes. It was a particular delight to us all to find that the same van that had fuelled us with bacon sarnies in the morning could now turn itself to knocking out burgers at a rate that even a hungry TV crew could not outstrip. It was genuinely heart-warming to see the guys getting to feast on real food for once. It was even more heart-warming to get to the front of the queue and put in my order for a burger with cheese, onions and anything else the lady behind the bare-metal counter could find and fry.

'We'll get soft if we get treated like this too often,' I muttered to no one in particular through a mouthful of burger bun.

I rang Andy Wilman yet again. He wanted to be kept in touch with every second of the day's events and was delighted to hear that we had done another run. I told him that I would be trying the afterburner next. He reminded me again that I had to go at my own pace. I reassured him that no one had told me anything about speeds achieved and that I would only do what I felt safe to do.

Back in the jet car, I studied the switch that operates the afterburner. It is a tiny, metal, unpainted thing; exactly the sort of hardware knick-knack that would happily lie at the back of a kitchen drawer for years before being slung out with the expired ballpoints, bulldog clips and plug adaptors that accumulate in odd corners. It was an inconsequential and frankly rather cheap means of instigating a procedure that would unleash quantities of power that, for millennia, were seen as the preserve of the gods. A small, metal toggle switch, perhaps a centimetre tall, it was fixed to the top of the left-hand side of the butterfly steering wheel. A simple flick of it would be enough to do the business.

Colin described the process, the results and the sensations that I could expect. A flame would shoot down the centre of the engine and ignite unburned fuel. The power output of the mighty jet engine would, effectively, be instantaneously doubled. I rehearsed the moment many times, going through the motions just as a bobsleigh pilot will stand at the top of the course and twist and turn on the spot as they rehearse in their imagination the turns and curves that lie ahead. In my case, though, the actions were much simpler: start the engine, look straight ahead, hit the button as my foot came off the brake and then, seconds later, pull the 'chute and celebrate being alive.

The procedure for starting the engine on this afterburner run remained exactly the same as on the previous runs. Until the moment I hit that innocent-looking little silver switch, everything would be as I had already experienced it. The jet engine whined into life and built to a screaming crescendo. I looked across at Colin, who gave me a confident smile. I took a deep breath, stared straight ahead and flicked the button as I lifted the brake pedal. I sensed, rather than heard, the roar. Something more than the engine kicked me in the back. The car jolted forward rather than beginning the inexorable building of speed that I had experienced a few times now. But then it settled again into something more familiar. I knew immediately that something had gone wrong with the afterburner. Perhaps it had gone out like a pilot light on a central-heating boiler?

At the end point, Colin was there ready to answer my questions. The afterburner had lit, briefly, but failed to catch and deliver the proper effect. What I had, in effect, experienced, was a sort of 'half afterburner' run. So it was back to the start line and a second chance to do it properly.

The same procedure, the same intense noise building behind me. I was overwhelmed yet again with the same sense of responsibility; I was in charge of a jet engine. Colin stepped back into position and gave me the thumbs up. I knew enough now to realise that this would be a very different experience from the runs I had completed so far. I took in a deep, measured breath, hit the button to fire the afterburner and lifted my right foot to release the brake. I was, suddenly, in a different car. I heard the roar and felt acceleration like I had never felt before. This time, the car didn't leave the line and gain speed slowly and inexorably. It exploded into action. Compared to what I had previously experienced in exactly the same car, this was like pulling up a chair at the very front of an explosion and then riding it towards the horizon. I realised now that the jet engine, without the afterburner, was a friendly, amiable beast that put a hand at my back and pushed me gently but firmly up the runway as an adult might push along a child's toy car. This though, was a manic, violent thing.

Perhaps not surprisingly, I found that my brain sped up to cope with the extra speed. My eyes could still see and register things, sending messages which my brain could then interpret and take what action was needed. I still functioned. But then we do; that's how we are made. People used to believe that we would be unable to cope mentally with travelling at the speeds reached by the very first steam locomotives a couple of hundred years ago. They worried that our senses might not be able to cope with travelling at speeds beyond anything we could hope to reach naturally, on foot or horseback. They coped, didn't go mad or transmutate into shrubs, and now, every single day, people happily cruise their family car up the motorway at five or ten times the speeds that so concerned the experts at the time of the

Grandad Leslie Dunsby on his bike in the 1930s.

BELOW: Nan Dunsby on her BSA with sidecar in the mid 1920s.

Grandad Leslie Dunsby (second from right) with his workmates at the Mulliner coachbuilding works in Birmingham in 1947. The rear of a razor-edge saloon is taking shape on the right.

Grandpa George Hammond in RAF uniform. He was in the Bomb Disposal Unit of the RAF. A calm (he would have to have been) and very brave man.

My father, aged about 5, ready to blast off on his turbo-charged tricycle.

Me, aged 2, at home behind the wheel of some heavy machinery (no change there, then). A similar look of determination to my dad (left).

Me (right) and brother Andy, probably considering a drag race up the drive for tea.

Me, aged 3½, and my first sports car—re-built by my Grandad, polished by me. I still love polishing them.

With my brothers—Andy, middle, and Nick, front, going nowhere fast.

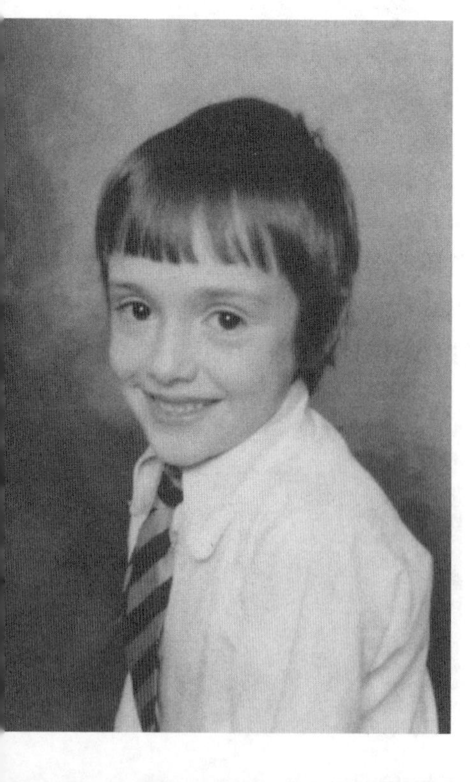

LEFT: Aged 8, grinning for a school photograph. And yes, I was a little s_d!

In Army cadet uniform and in trouble too probably—judging by the discarded hammers I have just broken something.

BELOW: With my cousin, Martin, and my bike, setting off on a touring trip across the Midlands. I dreamed of bikes with engines.

ABOVE: Adolescence begins and finally my bike has an engine. Quite a big, broken one, as it turned out later.
MIDDLE: Art student, long hair, leather jacket, roll-up. Of course, on the bottom half I'm wearing a floral skirt and roller skates.
BELOW: An early beginning to a lengthy bad shirt phase. And a moody look. Or it could be indigestion.

ABOVE: Camping in the Lake District with brother Nick. He's the one with a face full of Kendal Mint Cake, I'm sporting the enormous, bushy beard.
BELOW: Back to the Lakes, this time on the bike. The supermodel must have fallen off the back. Again.

Exposing white knobbly knees to breathtaking Lakeland scenery. Sometimes the picture you have in your head is not the one you are presenting to the world …

first steam locos. The answer, of course, is that our senses and reactions speed up in order to cope. And so it was in this instance. I can't say that it really felt any different from a fast drive in a supercar, but I was aware at the same time that it was, in reality, different. I could sense that my mind and my senses were operating at optimum speed to act fast enough to cope and stay alert to what was happening.

Within just 17.2 seconds, I drew level with the cones that signalled the end of the run. I pulled the lever to cut the engine and deploy the 'chute. Just 23 seconds after hitting that innocuous little button on top of the steering wheel, the run was finished. I had ridden a wave of power that ten Formula One cars together would struggle to achieve. I felt more alive, more vital than I could remember feeling in a very long time. Colin was happy, the crew were happy, the director was happy and I was ecstatic. On that run, I had hit 314.4 mph; faster than the official British Land Speed Record, though it would never be recognised as an official record because we had no official referees or monitors present from the record books. And anyway, no one was going to tell me how fast I had gone, just in case I suddenly decided to try and go a little faster. Of course, I would anyway.

Back at the tea van, there was lots of excited chatter about how it had looked from the outside and how weird it was for the guys watching to consider that the person in control of the long, yellow inferno streaking up the track was their mate Rich. And he had never done it before. We laughed, smoked, drank tea and spoke about the film we were making. Things were looking good; we had plenty of footage of Colin showing me around the car, plenty of shots of my first attempts without the afterburner and now, shots of my full-bore afterburner run, too. I rang Andy and we agreed that this was going to be a good, old-fashioned piece of family telly where a guy learns how to do something scary, and we all get to watch as he does it. It was now fast approaching 5 p.m. We only had permission to use the runway until 5.30, when local agreements meant the noise had to be cut. We talked it over. The car was running well, I was on top of controlling it, the weather was perfect. There was, we reckoned, just time for one more run.

While the guys prepped the car and the crew got into position, I chatted with the man in charge of the runway. He sat by the side of the track in a pick-up and I stood by the bonnet. From a distance, we could have been discussing anything in the early-evening warmth. The sun drifted towards the horizon enough to turn the light a gentle red and a soft peace fell over the pastoral scene. We agreed that the weather had been great all day and that the car was an amazing thing. He already knew that we wanted to do just one more run, but I wanted to make sure he was perfectly happy and assured him that we would get it over with and then cut the noise for the day. Back with the director, we reminded ourselves that we also had one more lengthy piece to camera to record, in which I had to walk around the car, describing it and how it worked. But that, we decided, could be done after the 5.30 p.m. noise curfew. Best use the noise-making time we had left to make noise.

**TIME: 17.25**

After the crash, some doctors felt that the degree of recollection I had of events running up to it were unrealistically clear. Perhaps, they reckoned, these memories were the product of an active imagination that had cobbled them together as I lay in a coma. But I remain convinced that they are real. And they tally perfectly with the records of the on-board telemetry system that can account for every millisecond and millimetre of the crash as it happened.

Walking towards the car for what I knew would be the final time, my mind wandered briefly back to a conversation with a race technician just a few weeks earlier. He had warned me never to race with a full bladder.

'You race when you need a piss, and there's a chance that, if you crash, your bladder could burst. And then you'll be dead before the medics get to you. Why do you think F1 drivers pee in their race suits if they need to go?'

Suddenly, just a few feet from the long yellow shape of the Vampire, I decided that actually, I could go after all. I turned round and hiked back to the blue plastic portaloo a hundred metres away. I do not believe that this was any sort of premonition or vision of what was about to unfold. I just needed a piss and so I took one before I did something that would, I knew, demand a clear head and full concentration.

With my bladder emptied and my conscience clear of doom and gloom, I walked back towards the car. It was waiting to the side of where we would actually start the run and would have to be towed back into position by the van. I looked at the car as I slotted my neck brace round my neck. The piece I would soon be delivering to camera dealt with some of the facts about its construction. It's not an off-the-shelf job, putting together a jet car. The brakes had originally been from a Transit van. Well they didn't have much to do as it was the parachute that really stopped it. The fuel pump came from a cement mixer and the steering box from a Robin Reliant. This was a long way from the over-funded and corporate world of modern-day motor sport. And I loved it all the more for that. A bloke in a shed who knew exactly what he was doing had put this thing together using experience and ingenuity.

I pulled my crash helmet on, climbed in past the roll bars and lowered myself into the seat. Colin was already in the van and he towed the car into position at the head of the runway. I was, once again, strapped down under the broad harness so tightly that my breath came in ragged gasps as my chest adjusted to what little space was left it. I looked at my blue race gloves as my hands gripped the wheel. One more crazy roar up the runway, a piece to camera about the car I had done it in, and then I would be back in the Honda heading for home.

With everything ready, Colin began the start procedure. I called for air and power to be sent to the engine. These essential needs were met and the engine breathed to life. It began its slow spin. The noise built to the signature song of the jet engine as Colin stepped back and gave me the all-clear. With the power dial set to 125 per cent, I knew that this would be a full-power run and one I would enjoy. There was no fear of the unknown now, but there was some fear of what I knew to expect and I readied myself for it.

**Run starts: 17.30 and 16.89 seconds**

On a particular moment within a particular second, feeling the time is right, I hit the button and release the brake. Inside the engine, a flame shoots through the middle of the spinning inferno and reaches the unburned fuel exiting out of the rear venturi. The already awesome power of the mighty jet engine is instantly doubled and it throws itself, the car and me forward.

**Time lapsed: 14.25 secs; 288.3 mph**
By the time my senses have sped up enough to keep pace with what is going on, I realise that something is wrong. This is not the usual push and pull of the steering as the front end scrabbles to keep the 1 tonne car and its passenger heading in a straight line.

**Time lapsed: 14.64 secs; 285.3 mph; cornering force: 2.1 g**
I am counter-steering now and battling something. My brain would later remember a sense of struggling to keep it going straight ahead, of having an elemental and basic fight to keep on going despite something trying to throw me off course and into disaster.

**Time lapsed: 14.64 secs; car drops 40 mm, possibly from a tyre blow-out**
The fight had just got a lot tougher. I registered that something terrible had happened and that I was in trouble. But I could not remember what.

In reality, the front right tyre has suffered a catastrophic and total failure. The resulting blow-out registers on the telemetry at 273 mph and the car drops 100 mm before leaping into the air. On video footage, the front of the car leaps high enough with the explosion to lift the other front wheel clear off the ground.

**Time lapsed: 15.00 secs; 279 mph; 3.9 g**
I am losing the battle. The car veers off to the right. My steering inputs and corrections, assessed later by

experts, have been well inside the speed of reaction expected of modern-day fighter pilots. The telemetry records tell that I am inputting only the degree of steering required to correct the car's slewing path. My foot hits the brake—a futile gesture as a car moving at 279 mph is not going to be stopped by a footbrake when just three wheels remain. It is instinctive but useless. I take my foot off the brake almost immediately after hitting it. I was not panicking, I am still fighting. But I am losing.

**Time lapsed: 15.71 seconds; 232 mph; deceleration 6 g**

My last memory now. As the car veers to the right, I know that my steering efforts have not saved the situation. I am going to crash. I remember the parachute lever. I pull it. The car does not stop and begins to roll over. I register that it is off the road entirely now and is going to roll on to the roof. I can do no more. The next thing to happen, I am quietly convinced, is that I die. There can be no other outcome. I am not scared, my life does not flash before my eyes, there is just a calm resignation. And also a strange relief at finally knowing the answer to a question that perhaps haunts many of us in the very background of our thoughts: *How will I die?*

Well at precisely 17.30 and 33.08 seconds on Wednesday 20 September 2006 I believed I knew exactly how and when my life would end. And I passed out as the g-forces generated by the crash exceeded those at which I could maintain consciousness.

**Time lapsed: 16.17 secs**

The car rolls upside down, still travelling at 191.1

mph. The roll bars protect my head from the impact, but they dig into the grass. This acts as a ground anchor, slowing the car from 232 mph to 191 mph in just 0.46 seconds. My brain is thrown forward; distorted; its shape elongated, hitting the front of my skull. The force my brain experiences overstretches some of the nerves and causes them to break. The resulting injuries could leave me paralysed, deaf, blind, or wipe out my personality, the person I recognise as me. But I am unconscious now and know nothing about it.

Part of the car touches down on the grass and digs in, sending the entire structure into another roll that turns into a flip. Were I conscious, I would briefly see a flash of blue sky before being plunged underground again as the car settles back on to its roof and begins its final stop. The avalanche of mud and stones kicked up by the roll bars ploughing into the field flips the helmet visor up, exposing my face. My left eye is damaged, the surrounding tissue pulverised. My mouth and nose fill with soil and mud as they are force-fed by the onslaught kicked up by the roll bar. As my head slews to the right, the side of the helmet is dented, cracked and caved in when it hits the crash structure. The right-hand side of my brain sustains more damage.

It ends. Just five seconds after the front right tyre blew and I began my ultimately hopeless battle to retain control, the crash is finished. The car lies upside down, the structure of the roll bars buried underneath and me with it. The wheels, exposed now to the sky, still turn as the engine cools. Inside, I am unconscious still, but changes are happening. My brain, thrown around inside my skull by the immense g-forces, is beginning to swell dangerously. My breathing is severely constricted by the soil in my mouth and nose. The arm-restraints have worked, keeping my limbs inside the relative safety of the cockpit, even upside down at 191 mph. The harnesses have done their job too; keeping me pinned in place despite the battering of the car rolling and pitching across the field. But I am in a critical state. As far as I am concerned, I have just met my own death and answered, once and for all, a big question about how and when it would happen.

## CHAPTER 7

# MINDY'S STORY

'OK, Ela, I'll be back in about an hour. Girls, be good and eat your tea and I'll be back before bath time.'

I ran out to my Land Rover. Damn—as usual, I'd forgotten something. This time, my riding hat. I threw open the heavy oak front door.

'Me again!'

Ela and Izzy laughed at me. Ela was standing with her arm outstretched, my riding hat in her hand.

'Erm . . . thanks! Byee.'

Ela was our Polish au pair. She'd arrived in June and had become such a friend to me and the girls. That summer we'd taught the children to swim in our tiny, previously frog-infested swimming pool. Every day after school the four of us—me, Ela, Izzy, our five-year-old, and Willow, three—would run to the pool with boogie-box and towels and splash about until the sun disappeared behind the trees and the chill of the night turned our lips blue, forcing us back down the slope to the house and supper.

Ela and I spent many, many nights in front of some great film which we would end up ignoring, and gossiping instead about her boyfriend, the events of the day, and the quality of the Indian or Chinese takeaway we were scoffing as we sipped a naff bottle of red wine or a couple of lagers.

Ela always helped with the animals, putting the

pony in her stable, or—her favourite task—feeding the dogs (five) or cats (three), which she did every night.

Ela was a pretty girl with dark, almost black shoulder-length hair and olive skin. She was always laughing, and taught the dogs dreadful habits like jumping up and sleeping on her bed, which also made me smile, although I'd tut at her occasionally.

The children simply adored her for the games she played with them and the love and caring she showed during that summer. She was with us during her break from university where she was studying physiotherapy.

So, riding hat in hand (one of those funky, pale blue ones), I leapt into my nine-seater Land Rover (Lollipop, as the kids had named him), a G4 110 defender long wheel base, and in a glorious, very bright yellow—love that car!—and set off for the stables to see my fabulous new horse.

I felt dizzy with excitement! All my life since memories began I dreamt of owning a horse. But it was just that—a dream. Then a few years ago Richard bought me a horse for Christmas. She was amazing, but when I took a break from riding her while she gave birth to a foal and weaned it, I lost my nerve, and by the time she was ready to be ridden again she knew my confidence had gone. So I'd sold her, which left me completely devastated until a friend of mine, Jenni, suggested I look at a fantastic horse who she said was absolutely reliable and would give me my confidence back.

I'd ridden him twice before this day, and on the last visit had decided to buy him. Today was to be my first 'lesson' on him. He was the most incredible-looking horse I'd ever seen. He'd competed at international level for many years and everyone in the show jumping world knew of him and his reputation, but the owners, Jenni told me, wanted him to go to a 'retirement' home as at sixteen they felt he'd done enough and needed a more relaxing life. I could buy him very cheaply because I wouldn't put him back into competition. Thomas was a Belgian warmblood (very posh); he stood sixteen hands three inches, and was chestnut with a white blaze down his face and three white socks. Just one look at him and you knew he was special. I'm five feet one inch short and to even get on him was a bit of a performance as the saddle was about a foot above the top of my head, but once on board I knew I was on the very best.

I parked the car behind the equestrian college offices (my future horse was on loan to one of the lecturers there who had retrained him to perform dressage, and she'd done very well competing with him). Thomas occupied a large stable in a U-shaped courtyard lined by about fifteen boxes. As I walked through the five-bar gate into the yard, I could see him in the far corner, standing quietly while white bandages were wrapped around his legs (a thing you do, I discovered, before exercising a dressage horse). The sun was glinting off his coat and again I was struck by the presence of this horse. He was like an oil painting, the very definition of power and beauty at rest. It was slightly unnerving and very exhilarating to know I was about to ride him. He was huge, and every inch the aristocrat.

Thomas is what's known in riding circles as a 'schoolmaster'; he knows precisely how you should ask him to do a particular movement or task. Ask incorrectly, and he'll simply ignore you. Or, worse still, stop dead. I, on the other hand, was a 'happy hacker'; every penny I could muster from various paper rounds had been spent on riding lessons, and I'd put in endless hours of mucking out at the riding school in exchange for ten-minute sessions on the back of a shaggy pony, but for all that effort my technique was rubbish and a million miles removed from this Ferrari of a horse. I approached him across the yard and couldn't suppress my giddy schoolgirl grin.

It was about 5.30 p.m. and the sun was still warm on my back as I crossed the grassy island in the middle of the yard. There were students and horses all around; but I didn't really notice them as I reached up and stroked Thomas's soft white nose.

'Hello, my boy.'

Wow! What a moment—he was finally mine. This incredible creature of impeccable breeding, whose passport was more well-travelled than mine, belonged to me! I fastened my hat and struggled to get my gloves on quick enough.

'Leg up?' a voice said.

'Erm . . . I think so, don't you?' I laughed. Then, 'One, two . . .'

'Mindy! Mindy! The phone—for you.'

'What?'

My mobile didn't work at the yard, so Ela had rung the equestrian college.

'Mindy, it's Richard. He's had an accident, you must ring Andy.'

'Oh God! No!' I hit the ground running and headed for the car. Nothing seemed to happen quickly enough. It was one hundred yards to my car, but it felt like a mile. The key in the door seemed to miss the lock. It took three attempts. When eventually the door opened, I threw my hat off, leapt in and stabbed the key in the ignition, jammed reverse, and my foot was to the floor. Phone! Phone! My mobile had no signal. Oh no! No! I was almost airborne driving over the speed humps on the way out of the college.

At last a signal reappeared on the mobile and with it voicemail and missed calls from Andy Wilman.

I called him immediately but the line was busy. He was trying to call me.

'Arrggh!' I yelled, tears streaming down my face. 'No! No! Not again, please God no!!'

As I turned into the main road, the phone rang—it was Andy.

'Mind, Richard's had an accident.'

'You mean he's crashed? How bad is it?'

'Yeah. Look, it's OK, he's moving his arms and legs. They're taking him to hospital in Leeds. I'll meet you there.'

I let out a despairing cry: 'No, it's not OK, Andy. Jesus! He's still got whiplash from the last one.'

Richard had suffered severe whiplash just six weeks before when a van he'd rolled during a stunt had bounced on landing. He'd been in incredible pain. I had absolutely no idea of the severity of this crash in comparison. It was only when Andy said, 'I'll meet you in Leeds,' that I knew it was serious. He was driving there from

London. He hadn't been at the shoot.

My mind was in turmoil, driving past the trees with tears blurring my vision. I remember focusing on a huge oak tree in the middle of a field. It looked peaceful and fresh and full of life—and it broke my heart. Perhaps my world, our world was ended . . . our beautiful tree was broken. I snapped myself back to reality and lifted the hem of my T-shirt to wipe my face. I took a deep breath and phoned Richard's mum, Eileen. It seemed to take for ever for her to answer. 'Please let her be home,' I thought. 'Don't let her be out, not now.' I couldn't bear the thought of breaking this terrible news to her on her mobile, in the street, or at work. She and Alan, Richard's dad, lived in Leatherhead, Surrey, in a well-kept bungalow which backed on to a small patch of woodland. They both worked as charity consultants and were always busy. If they weren't working they were doing DIY, remodelling the garden, or walking Callie, their beloved collie cross.

Thankfully, Eileen answered. She was her usual jolly self, but within seconds her world was changed too. Her first thought was for her grandchildren.

'We'll come and stay with the girls,' she offered.

Richard's dad volunteered to drive me to Leeds, but that would have meant waiting for him to drive three hours to Gloucestershire. I thanked them but said I just had to go, and they understood. We agreed to keep in touch.

After hanging up, I burst into tears again, screamed, yelled, wiped my face . . . and made the next call. I called my mum as I drove past the petrol station.

'Oh no. Oh darling, no!' She'd been worried about Richard doing 'all these mad things' for a while. Poor Mum has had enough tragedy in her life to know how things can go wrong.

Her own ten-year-old son was killed by a 'careless' driver. Tim was holding Mum's hand under the bus shelter in front of his school when the man ploughed into them. He was torn from Mum's grasp and slammed into a lamp-post. She witnessed the whole thing, and his last look across at her before he died. She's always said 'things happen, they just happen'. She's right.

This time she said simply, 'Drive careful now. Please, promise me. Let me know what I can do and ring me when you can, love.'

She said everything that needed to be said. Everything I needed to hear. So calmly, so gently, with such love. Another flood of tears exploded. I had little time left. I had to get myself under control.

As I turned off to the lane, I phoned Katrina, our PA. She was always at the end of the phone. She'd only been our PA for four months but during that time she'd proved to be a quick-witted, intelligent girl who helped with all the various logistical issues surrounding Richard's hectic work schedule. I knew she could be relied upon.

It was about 6 p.m. by now. I quickly told her what had happened and promised that I'd call again on my way to Leeds. She was upset, but instinctively knew I'd need her.

As I rounded the last corner, I pulled it

together, knowing I had about three minutes to make myself look as normal as possible for the children. I opened our gate and drove through. Shut the gate and parked in front of the door. I ran upstairs calling Ela as I went. She'd been waiting for me, keeping the girls occupied. She joined me in the bedroom as I threw a case on to the bed.

'Oh, Ela, I have to go to Leeds—I don't know what's happened. I don't know when I'll be back. Oh God!' Tears were running down my face as I threw ridiculous things into a suitcase. Ela watched me with silent tears running down her own cheeks.

'Oh, Mindy!' She hugged me and for a moment I slumped against her and wept. But there was no time for emotion, I had to get moving.

I had no idea what I was doing. What should I pack? Pants and socks, he always needed pants and socks; a dressing gown—in hospital you always need a dressing gown. My wash bag, a change of underwear for me and a spare top. The dressing gown almost filled the small suitcase, but I didn't take it out. It was him. It was comfortable. He'd like it.

I shut the case and ran from our bedroom to my office. The computer was on. I sent a one-line email to Richard's agent:

**Richard's had an accident. SERIOUS. I'm on my way to hospital. Call me.**

It seemed to take so long for the 'sent' sound to come through. I was shuffling on the spot. 'Come on, come on!'

The second it was sent I ran along the landing

to Ela, who was carrying my case downstairs. I looked at my watch—six thirty! Oh my God! I must go, I must go!

Izzy and Willow were in the playroom.

'Girls! Girls!' I called, trying not to sound hurried. They appeared in the hallway, both staring up at me with a look of curiosity and anticipation. I was sniffling, but smiling.

'Daddy's gone and bumped a car again.'

'Oh, not again!' said Izzy, rolling her eyes.

'Yes, I'm afraid so. And he's ripped some clothes, so I have to go and take him some new ones,' I explained.

'Oh, OK,' said Willow. 'He is silly.'

'Yes, darling, he is.' We hugged. Willow was easy. She was just three. But after she'd skipped off to the kitchen, Izzy looked at me. Really looked at me. Her eyes filled with tears and so did mine. I knelt down, cupped her tiny shoulders in my hands and looked her straight in the eyes.

'It'll be OK. It will. I love you. Come on, Iz.'

She nodded, thumb in her mouth, then threw her arms around me. 'I love you, Mummy.'

I gave that little girl such a hug as she stood on the dark wooden floor, her big brown eyes welling with tears, her brave face fighting them back. How often we would relive this moment I had no idea, and I will never know what went through her clever little head that day . . . but she knew something terrible had happened, and it had happened to her daddy. Her wonderful, wonderful daddy.

It was time to leave. As I reached for the car keys I noticed Richard's spare mobile was on the table. I grabbed it, along with my spare one and all the chargers I could see. I dashed outside and realised my Land Rover would be too slow and too obvious. As a motoring journalist, Richard regularly has cars on loan from manufacturers to review and a press car had arrived that day. I knew I was insured to drive it in extreme circumstances, so I ran back in and swapped over the keys then threw everything bar phones and handbag into the boot.

The girls were on the front step; both a little too quiet. I ran over and kissed them.

'See you soon. I'm sure I won't be long.'

'Will you be back tonight, Mummy?' asked Izzy.

'Well, maybe not tonight, but I'll let you know as soon as I can, and I'll phone you to say goodnight at bedtime—OK, baby?'

'Oh, OK.' She was trying so hard to be brave. Her lips were quivering and yet she managed to smile. We both knew she was being brave for her little sister's sake.

'Bye, Mummy,' said Willow, a bit confused by it all.

I had to turn away so they didn't see me crying. Then I ran to the car. I trusted Ela. I knew she'd look after them. In the meantime I had to get to Leeds. To Richard.

As I drove out of the gate something happened. The tears came again, but only briefly; this time I took hold. I had to focus. I had to think. There was no point in crying—I'd just lose sight of the road and then where would we all be? I remember taking a couple of deep breaths as I drove along, saying out loud, 'Come on, come on. Pull up, for God's sake.'

I had a can of Coke in the car and drank from it. I shoved the earpiece in and phoned Katrina. I had to organise things, make sure I'd sorted everything out.

'I've borrowed a press car. Can you call the manufacturer? *Top Gear* will have the number—explain what's happened. The pick-up address will need to be changed.'

Katrina told me one of the tabloids had already called Richard's agent. They knew he'd crashed. How? How does that happen?! I asked Katrina to check what was happening with all the other papers—I knew Richard would want me to keep control of the situation. He wrote for the *Daily Mirror*; I must make sure they knew what was going on. He was always adamant that, as his employer, the *Mirror* should always be kept in the loop.

While I was talking with Katrina, the phone was beeping; it was Jeremy and Francie Clarkson. They were on their way to a dinner party. At this stage all of us were still oblivious to the severity of the crash. Francie was being very sympathetic—she was one of the few people on the planet who could truly identify with exactly what I was going through.

'It's what we all dread; your worst nightmare,' she said, Jeremy joining in on their hands-free phone. They insisted I call them if there was anything they could do. I remembered our holiday with them on the Isle of Man: the girls adored their children, and we had all really relaxed—Richard had even painted for the first time in years. He'd enjoyed painting and was really very good, but there were few opportunities these days for him to spend time relaxing and submerging himself in his favourite pastime. During our brief stay he'd surprised Jeremy with a beautiful watercolour . . . I wondered whether he'd ever be able to paint again.

I snapped at myself to stop thinking like that. He'd had crashes in the past—plenty of them. He was the toughest man in the world. I'd get to the hospital and he'd be sitting up in bed with a few bumps and bruises and a sheepish look on his face, full of apologies. 'I'm sorry, I broke stuff . . .', and I'd give him a hug and a kiss and we'd carry on as usual.

Then suddenly reality hit. Katrina had just called back to tell me that every newspaper was following the story. The accident was big news. As I was talking to her, the BBC news came on the radio.

'*Top Gear* presenter Richard Hammond has had a serious crash in a jet car. The vehicle rolled and flipped at an airfield just outside York. He was transported by air ambulance to Leeds General Infirmary where he is in critical condition. His wife Mindy is travelling to the hospital to be with him.'

'Critical? *Critical*?!!' No one had used that word to me. And it flipped! It bloody flipped! 'Oh no! No!' I yelled so hard I could see stars. Katrina thought I was going to crash. The images in my head were dreadful. I'd never seen the jet car. The image in my head was of the *Bluebird* of the 1960s before it raced across the salt flats in Utah. I suppose it was the nearest thing my brain could come up with, and I imagined it going tail-over-tip and then rolling at high speed. I felt sick as I pictured Richard stuck in that thing, being cut out. I wondered what state he was in. I imagined so many scenarios all at once. Our house was up for sale. Well, maybe we would just have to stay there and change things. If he was paralysed, we'd have to put in ramps and have things altered for wheelchair access; you can get kitchens refitted; bathrooms altered . . . I'd get him a really fast wheelchair. It'd be OK. If he couldn't talk, I'd get him a great computer. Anything can be dealt with, everything can be overcome. Just be alive. Just, please God, I beg you, please, please keep him alive for me.

All the while phones were beeping with messages coming through. Both my phones were reading 'SMS full'. I couldn't respond—I couldn't even look at the messages. The phones rang constantly. I didn't answer them every time, I admit. There are certain friends you know you'll open up to. You'll crumble to. I couldn't afford that luxury. I had to get to Richard. If he could see me, he needed to see me looking positive and strong.

I called home quickly. I had to say goodnight to the girls. I remember being upbeat with them. Dear Ela had been playing games and keeping them entertained. They were fine.

I don't recall much of that drive. Memory is such a bizarre thing. I know I spoke with Richard's parents several times, although I can't recall in detail what was said. I remember checking Richard's phone to get a number for his editor at the *Mirror*. Katrina had heard nothing from them—they hadn't been in contact. I felt I had to call them. Richard would want me to.

When I got through they were amazing. They hadn't phoned me out of respect. They just wanted to give us space. I was so moved. 'Richard's a mate,' were his editor's words. 'If there's anything, absolutely anything we can do, call us, won't you?'

They just wished me all the best, and I promised to keep in touch.

Members of the team from *Top Gear* called me. Suzi from the production office asked if there was anything they could do. I thanked her, but no, there was nothing anyone could do unless they could turn back the clock a few hours.

That had to be the blackest night. I don't mean in terms of sadness or misery—although clearly it was a really dreadful journey—but I distinctly remember looking at the road in front of me, the sky all around, and it seemed blacker than black. All I could see were the lights of cars and lamp-posts. No scenery. No buildings. Just black. Nothing was important. Nothing worth seeing. Just objects to avoid and a path to follow. The slowest, longest path. The sat. nav. displayed an estimated arrival time and the number of miles left to travel. The miles just didn't seem to dwindle. It was like some cruel, twisted game. I felt like a mouse trying to escape while an evil cat stood on my tail, my legs desperately scrabbling to go forward in a vain attempt to reach my destination.

The bulletins on the radio repeated the news. I turned it off. I was shouting at the car in front to get out of my way. The traffic was slowing me up and Andy Wilman was calling periodically to see where I was. He was going to get there before me.

I didn't want to stop for a second, but my bladder was fit to burst. I pulled over at the dodgiest services I've ever seen. As I pulled up, I noticed a group of rough-looking lads in hoodies leaning against their various hot hatches. I parked the obviously very expensive and fast car as close to the building as I could and jogged in the direction of the loos, through the corner of an enclosed courtyard. The lights were out. Everything was closed except the public toilets in the far corner. At the door of the 'Ladies' there was a small, yellow, plastic A-frame that read 'cleaning in progress'. The lights flickered within. It looked to me like a scene from a cheap disaster movie. As I hastened towards that door every fibre of my being was screaming at me to turn around and go back to the car, but I had no time to look for another services, and my bladder couldn't wait. As I walked I said out loud, 'So, now I get mugged. Excellent.' But you know, as I reached the door, I knew. Even if every last scruffy, mangy one of them had tried to tackle me, I'd have knocked the lot of them to the ground. It was one of those times when a kind of radiation of intent surrounds you.

When I returned to my car, I got in slowly, determinedly, and drove steadily away. They watched me go. They craned their necks and followed the car out. My heart was beating hard. The second I was out of sight I put my foot down and breathed a sigh of relief as I rejoined the dark road. I still had a long way to go, and the phones were ringing and beeping one after the other.

I'd tried to call the hospital early on in my journey but they were naturally cautious about giving details. I left them both my numbers while they checked out my details with the BBC.

Trouble was that my phones were constantly busy. I stopped answering calls unless they were from Andy Wilman or Richard's parents, because I was desperate to hear from the hospital. Then 'unknown' came on to the phone. I answered it and a man's voice replied. 'Hello. Is that Mrs Hammond?'

'Yes, who's this?' I was suspicious at first—for all I knew it could be a reporter.

'Hello, Mrs Hammond—I'm one of the duty nurses from A & E at Leeds.'

'Oh, oh hello.' My voice broke. I wanted to speak to him, I wanted to know about Richard, but at the same time I was frightened to death.

'Are you driving, love?'

'Yes, yes, I am. Can you tell me how he is?'

'Not while you're driving. Can you pull over somewhere?'

'No I can't. I'm on a motorway.'

'Well, can you see if you can find somewhere to stop and I'll call back in five minutes?'

'Oh God, OK.' My voice choked with tears.

I drove on, scanning the road ahead for a turning, for anywhere to stop. I couldn't stop on the hard shoulder—that was dangerous. Richard had a thing about people doing that. I had to keep driving.

The voice called back. This happened three times, at which point I was close to a complete breakdown. The reason they wouldn't tell me was that they were worried I might have an accident if they gave me the news while I was driving. The fourth time, a woman called. I was screaming with frustration.

'Look, you'd better bloody well tell me or I'll crash anyway!'

'OK, love, OK. Your husband's had a blow to the head and he's sustained a serious brain injury.' Quickly followed by, 'Are you OK?'

*Serious Brain Injury*—three words you never imagine hearing in connection with someone you love. It echoes through your soul. Hits you like a lead weight. An injury to the brain. Not the head, the brain. And serious. It was as though everything was coming at once. My thoughts were spinning around: 'Flipped; Crashed; Critical; Brain injury.'

My husband, my Richard, broken? It just couldn't be true.

'Oh God! Oh God!'

'Where are you, love?' the soft Leeds accent asked.

I had no idea. I'd just kept driving. For hours. The miles never ending. It was the longest drive of my life. I looked about me for a clue to my location; I vaguely remembered seeing a road sign.

'Manchester. Manchester, I think—is that right?'

'Oh, you won't be too much longer. We'll call you again in fifteen minutes and see where you are. You sure you're OK?'

'Yeah, I'll be fine.' I was shaking. I loved that voice. I wanted to wrap myself up in the warmth and friendliness of that sound like a woollen shawl, and close my eyes against reality.

I was shaky and crying—no, weeping. My amazing, funny, brave, beautiful, lovely, adorable husband was ahead of me. But maybe it wasn't him any more. Maybe it would never be him again. We'd cope. It would be fine. Whatever happened, we'd get through it.

'Right. Enough now.' I remember saying out loud. Sniffing, I wiped my face and took a few huge gulps of air. I was getting close now, finally.

Andy Wilman called. 'Hiya, you all right?'

'Yeah. I'm OK.'

'Where are you?'

'About ten miles away.'

'Right, listen . . .' He spoke so softly, so gently, so carefully. 'There're a lot of TV crews and press and stuff here, so we need to get you in around the back, all right?'

'Yeah, OK.'

'Call me when you're a bit closer and I'll guide you in.'

'OK, speak to you in a bit.'

'All right, mate.'

We spoke gently and sombrely.

I was pulling myself together those last ten miles. I wiped my face, blew my nose, and pulled on my armour, ready for battle. It had to be good, that armour. I didn't know at the time, but it was to stay in place for many, many months.

As I turned the last corner to the back of the hospital and parked up, I remember thinking how bleak it looked, how dark and dismal. I sat in the car for a couple of minutes, then Andy came walking fast across the road towards the car. His appearance was shambolic as usual; overly baggy trousers and a grey T-shirt with a white shirt flying loose over the top. Dishevelled grey hair and a couple of days' beard growth on his chin. I opened the door and gave him a half-smile as he hugged me.

'What a day, eh?' I said to him.

He was relieved. He genuinely thought I was going to get out of the car and belt him, but all I cared about was getting to Richard.

Andy was closely followed by a lady security guard. They were both on edge. We were in a side road and the press were all over the place. Andy wanted to smuggle me in quickly without anyone noticing.

I had luggage. I had a case in the back of the car, but it didn't come with me into the hospital.

Did Andy park the car or did the security guard? I can't remember. Someone drove the car away to park it in a safe place. I was escorted into the hospital, towards that huge, dark building. I expected a shiny doorway with bright lights and lots of glass, but in front of me was a miserable-looking, dark, stone lump. I couldn't even see the door. I looked down at the road. It was covered with that knobbly, rough tarmac I remembered from childhood; the horrible kind that would take the skin off your hands and knees and leave lumps of grit embedded in the wound. I shuddered. I didn't like this place.

I don't remember how we got into the building, but inside it looked old. Then, as we walked, it grew brighter, newer. The floors changed from stone and woodblock to lino and tile. It looked more like a hospital, smelt more like a hospital.

I felt numb. Few words were said. The pace was hurried. We turned a corner to two rows of lifts facing one another. Standard hospital lifts. With brown metal doors. I think Andy was still with me. I know I felt secure, so he must've been there. I couldn't really hear anything. It was like being underwater. Whatever people were saying or doing around me was irrelevant. A siren could've sounded next to me—I wouldn't have noticed. I was on autopilot. I had no idea how to get to him or even where he was, but I was close. Every turn, every step, brought me closer.

The lift stopped. We walked down a corridor. There were signs hanging from the ceiling. Ward names. We stopped. Double doors. An intercom.

I could hear my heart beating in my ears. Andy came through the doors with me. It was like walking on the moon; everything was in slow motion.

We walked through the first set of doors. There were rooms on either side of an inner corridor. We turned a corner. Ahead was another pair of doors. The lights were dimmed inside. A nurse standing next to the doors was smiling at me. Andy quietly disappeared . . . I was alone.

The nurse said something. We walked. I saw a curtain drawn around a bed on my right. Was that him? No. We kept walking. Beeping noises. The sounds of machines. Intensive care. Past the curtains; the next bed. It was him. Banks of machines on either side. A ventilator pumping breath into his lungs; drips in both arms; monitors stuck to his chest and hand. His face yellowed with bruising, a bizarre lump the size of a fist on his forehead, and his left eyelid four times its normal size and deep crimson.

A ventilator tube was secured in his gaping mouth by a bandage wrapped around his head. He was still. Not a flicker of life. The only movement came from the ventilator as it deflated, then filled again. I went to him, fought back the tears and kissed his cheek.

'Hello, my darling.' The tears were dripping off my chin as I spoke, but I was half-smiling. Awful as it was, desperate as you may imagine it should be, I knew he was there. I knew with every ounce of my being, without doubt, he was there. Buried, tired, exhausted. But the spirit of this man who was as tough as any heroic warrior in a boys' storybook was dormant . . . not dead. I'd just have to wait for him.

* * *

The nurse insisted on getting me a cup of tea. She was Richard's nurse. She sat at the end of his bed, a desk in front of her like an enormous clipboard with records of all his tests and movements attached to it. She recorded everything regularly and plotted charts. Percentage of air in his blood; blood pressure; heart rate and 'obs'—observations. But mostly she just sat at the foot of his bed, looking over her 'desk'—watching him. Watching the machines. Like some guardian angel with the power to reinstate life should it falter, there she sat—a wonderful, warm, friendly woman with short, blonde hair and a kind face. I instantly felt reassured by her presence. She exuded calm. I trusted her.

I accepted the cup of tea, but refused the sandwiches everyone seemed intent on offering. The British—we're so predictable in a crisis—cup of tea and a sandwich.

I let my eyes examine Richard's face. I'd

expected a real mess. Cuts, bruises, blood and gore. But there was none of that. As I looked now I could see how swollen his face was; it was that horrible yellow-green colour which you usually get around the edge of a good blue bruise. Except for him the bruise wasn't visible on the outside. It was far more serious.

His left eye was really nasty. It seemed to swell more by the moment. There was a lot of dried blood around his nostrils, mixed with bits of earth. He looked exactly like Richard. But Richard himself I sensed was a very long way away. This was a husk, waiting for Richard's return.

It's very strange to live through a scene you've watched in TV dramas so many times. There's a sense that the magnitude of this situation just can't be real . . . it simply doesn't compute.

So I sat there, holding his unresponsive hand . . . a hand you could squeeze, stroke, manipulate, but which gave not a millimetre of movement in return. There—but not there. It was so bizarre, so unreal, so awful.

The machines reminded me of my father in his last few days. He'd been diagnosed with cancer some years earlier, and he'd lost his kidney, then his bladder. The surgeons had acted quickly and he'd been sent a letter confirming his tests were clear. Yet he'd felt ill, nauseous. In hospital, they opened him up to discover that his liver was so riddled with cancer it was inoperable. He was given six months to live. But that night in the hospital he fell out of bed. We suspect he thought he could get up; he wanted so desperately to go home. Had I realised what little time he had left, I would have taken him there. We think he may have broken his hip when he fell as he was certainly in great pain.

I've never been the 'nursing' type, but for the last three nights and two days of his life, I sat and mopped up the dreadful brown liquid which dripped from his nose, drooled from his mouth and eventually trickled from his eyes. I took turns with Mum, until she was exhausted. Her sister, my aunt Betty, was there too. The three of us in his little room; watching him die. My sister Sarah, who's a diabetic, found it all too much and felt she couldn't come to the hospital. She and Dad were extremely close, whereas I'd had a difficult relationship with my father until his last few years. As Dad's breathing became more laboured, Mum and Aunty Betty exchanged glances. It was 11 p.m.

'Oh no, Bert. Not today, not today,' Mum sobbed.

It was the anniversary of their son Tim's death.

'Come on, Bertie, just a bit longer,' said my aunt.

And he responded. He drew a monumental breath and restarted himself. He kept going 'til the following evening when, finally, my sister arrived.

She walked into his room and within moments of hearing her voice my father, who hadn't moved for days, whose eyes had been glued shut with this awful brown stuff which was seeping from everywhere, lifted his head from the pillow, opened his eyes, looked and smiled at each one of us in turn, dropped his head back on the pillow, and died. And my father, whose expression at rest was one of a mouth down-turned at the corners and general demeanour of anger, had a look I had never seen before on his face when he died. One of pure wonder and joy. I smiled through my tears as he died, because wherever he went, he looked thrilled to be going there. But the thing is, he could hear. The whole time he was unconscious, he was aware of what was going on in the room. It is true what the doctors say in these situations. Hearing still works. Which was why I was so blindingly aware of that with Richard. Just because he wasn't giving any indication of being even mildly aware of anything going on around him, I was going to be as positive as possible. Just in case.

Every thirty minutes the nurse would carry out observations, asking Richard to do various things. Open his eyes was the first task. Then say his name. She would place her index fingers in each of his hands, and ask him to squeeze her fingers, then wiggle his toes. He did nothing. She'd be talking sternly and loudly at him. Still nothing. Then . . .

'I'm going to have to cause you a little bit of pain, Richard.'

She explained to me that she had to gauge response from him, and to bring him out she'd use her penlight on a pressure point between his eyebrow and his nose, pushing and twisting the pen into it. It clearly hurt him, but his response was not great. He managed to flicker his eyes . . . little else. She'd hold open his eyelids and shine the light in each eye to check his responses . . . he didn't flinch. He didn't speak. And when she tried to get him to squeeze her fingers, there was nothing. It wasn't encouraging. The reality of a life with someone who doesn't improve from this stage is frightening. What on earth do you do? How do you cope? I wouldn't allow myself to think about it. I had no doubt this was simply the beginning of recovery for Richard. It was early days. I couldn't worry. He just needed time.

I know the nurse showed me his chart and explained everything to me. I put myself into a different mode when she did it. I concentrated, devoured the information, digested, understood, then filed it all away until I might need it. I didn't want to know his chances, I didn't want to know their prognosis. I knew him: he kicked, he fought. Because, by God, if anyone could heave himself through, it was Richard. And I'd be there when he made it back.

At the scene of the crash, when the paramedics reached him, they were surprised to find Richard breathing. The visor on his helmet had been pushed open and then filled with earth as his head ploughed into the ground. His mouth and nose were packed with soil and his eye was a mess.

On their arrival, Richard was completely unconscious. They removed as much mud from his mouth and nose as possible before using a measure called 'The Glasgow Coma Scale' to ascertain his condition.

It works like this: the GCS is scored between three and fifteen, three being the worst, and fifteen the best. It is composed of three parameters: best eye response, best verbal response, best motor response.

A coma score of thirteen or higher correlates with a mild brain injury, nine to twelve is a moderate injury and eight or less a severe brain injury.

Richard scored three.

Since the accident, we've spoken with the air ambulance crew who were on duty that day, I'll never forget what one member of the team told me.

'When you go to scenes like that and you see the patient, you can usually tell straight away whether or not they're going to survive.'

I was expecting him to say, 'Oh, of course we knew he'd be OK.'

Instead he told me, 'Y'know, he was really bad. I didn't think he was going to make it.'

Once he regained consciousness, Richard stayed in the jet car while he was given verbal instructions on how to help the team get him out without causing further injury. According to those at the scene, his eyes were pointing in opposite directions; he ignored everything the ambulance guys said, but when he heard a familiar voice, from a member of the *Top Gear* film crew, he obeyed. They worked out that the only way he'd cooperate was if a member of the *Top Gear* crew repeated whatever instruction the air ambulance guys gave.

Head injury is strangely predictable. The impact isn't felt immediately, which was why, once out of the jet car, Richard made protests that he needed to do a piece to camera, but then became steadily more aggressive on his way to A & E. His brain was swelling.

At A & E he was completely anaesthetised. This would prevent him damaging his brain further. The drugs were soon switched off and their sedative effect ceased, but by then the effect of the brain injury had taken over. There was no clear boundary between conscious and unconscious, and we would simply have to watch and wait to see how he would recover, and what permanent damage there might be.

Richard had haemorrhaging. His brain was bruised and there was some bleeding. A huge lump the size of my fist grew on his forehead, due to fluid draining forward from his injury.

He had suffered most damage to the right frontal lobe. This is the part of the brain that deals with recognition, the ability to judge distances, decision-making, problem-solving and personality.

He'd damaged nerve cells in his brain. The force of the accident had caused them to overstretch and break. These are injuries that aren't detected on CT scans; silent wounds which are extremely debilitating. Damage can range from paralysis, blindness, or deafness to depression, anger, or seizures.

We were told that he might never be the person he was before the crash. Some people no longer recognise their loved ones, or decide to change their whole way of life after such injuries, and simply abandon their family, their own personality changed for ever.

The future was, at the very best, uncertain.

## CHAPTER 8

# LEEDS GENERAL INFIRMARY

Memories of that night, and in fact the next couple of days, are very confused.

Perhaps it's shock. So many horrible experiences in such a short space of time.

It was really strange. I soon understood that when one of the machines went berserk and an alarm sounded, it was because the monitor had fallen off his finger, and I really didn't panic. I'd also grown accustomed to the routine. I'd familiarised myself with the coffee machine; knew who the nurses were and was quite relaxed in the surroundings. My husband was lying next to me on life support, still connected to all those machines, and as far as I was concerned this was my foreseeable future. I'd accepted it as you do when these situations present themselves, because to be unaccepting is madness and to panic is pointless.

Richard's younger brother Nick arrived at about 1.30 a.m. It was so good to see him. Odd though that I thought at the time how nice it was that he'd come all that way. This was his brother, for goodness sake; of course he was going to be there!

Nick had driven from Tunbridge Wells. He'd left his wife Amanda and his two young daughters, Lottie and Clemmie, and jumped straight into the car. Years ago, long before he was married, when Richard and I had been together just a few months, he was the first member of the family I was introduced to at Richard's house in Wendover. I'd been really nervous that evening, and when we met was surprised how little he resembled his brother. Nick was tall and slim with blond hair and sensible clothes . . . I worried he might be a bit stuffy, but as the afternoon passed into the evening I remember us all sitting on the floor drinking red wine, Nick with my collie's head on his lap as he told hysterical stories and recounted daft rhymes. Richard, Nick and I laughed 'til our sides ached. He could recall every rugby song he'd ever heard, and his repertoire was astounding. He and Richard had spent many years on penniless walking holidays in the Lake District. They'd irritated and annoyed one another, got drunk together and shared good and bad times. I quickly understood why Richard thought so fondly of him, and couldn't help but agree.

Nick now worked in the City, his free time as rare as Richard's. We used to joke about his 'very grown-up' job in banking and Richard would make fun of him . . . often calling him on his mobile in the middle of the day in the hope that Nick would be in an important meeting and be embarrassed by his brother's X-rated conversation.

We hadn't seen each other for a while. As he walked towards me, his face was pale, but he kept calm as he hugged me and came over to the bedside. I explained what was going on and Nick digested the news. I can't imagine how it must've felt for him. They were very close and had grown up being daredevils and pranksters. Suddenly there was no fun. No laughter; just fear.

We sat briefly with Richard before he peeled me away. We checked with the nurse when the next obs would be and, reassured that nothing would happen, went downstairs.

I needed a break, and I think Nick did too. I had my mobile phone with me just in case anything happened.

Leaving Richard was difficult; my mind was running away with itself. If he moved, flinched, or turned and I missed it, I'd feel dreadful. But I also needed to get a change of scenery and Nick was good company. He was amazing. He was very upset, but dealt with it by getting on with the practicalities. He made phone calls, spoke with everyone and was a kind of central liaison from the moment he arrived. I've no idea how many calls he made, but he ensured that everyone was kept up-to-date with Richard's progress.

He'd bought a packet of cigarettes on the way down. We stood in a back courtyard to smoke. I've no idea what we talked about. I remember the cigarette tasted vile but I still smoked it. I was trembling. I was scared, and I needed something to occupy me—smoking worked. I could be tougher if I smoked. After all, when we're young we start smoking to look cool, to be tough—I suppose I needed that crutch.

When we returned to Intensive Care, it was time for more obs. Richard had made little improvement from the last time.

*   *   *

At about 4.30 a.m., Richard's middle brother, Andy, arrived with his wife, Andrea. They'd driven from Devon, having organised for their three young children, Henry, Eleanor and Edward, to be cared for by Andrea's parents. Andrew was a teacher and educational author. He thoroughly enjoyed his job and both he and Andrea often worked long hours to help with school plays and trips with the pupils. Their move to Devon had been fairly recent and for them the journey to the hospital was the longest. The longer the journey, the worse it is. By the time they arrived they were exhausted. Nick and I greeted them, and I remember they were quite surprised at the absence of really severe external injuries when they first saw Richard. On a drive such as theirs, the imagination has time to run wild and I'm sure they'd expected to see him in a far more broken state. Andy and Andrea tried to encourage me to leave him for a while and get some rest or something to eat. I was reluctant. I still didn't want to leave him, but agreed to go downstairs with Nick.

Andy and Andrea spent an hour or so with Richard before leaving to get some rest at a local hotel. They were both shattered and I'm sure battling with their own emotions on seeing him. They'd return in the morning.

Richard's uncle Brian, a retired businessman who lives in Harrogate, came to the ward. He'd come to see his nephew, just very briefly so that he could report back to Richard's parents. They were all those miles away in Gloucestershire, and although we were all calling them whenever possible, conversations were brief. I'm sure Brian was there to act as their eyes.

During the night, James May and Jeremy Clarkson had both driven from London to Leeds. Jeremy had received a call while out at dinner explaining that Richard's condition had become extremely serious. Life-threatening.

He got up from the table and said he just had to leave for Leeds. Francie, his wife, was worried that he might be in the way, and pleaded with him that there was nothing he could do. He'd said, 'I want to be there for Mindy.' And he was.

James heard about the accident on the radio, then turned on the TV and heard it again in disbelief. He got into his car straight away too.

Brian Klein, the studio director on *Top Gear,* was in a restaurant having dinner when his daughter phoned him to tell him about the accident. Brian, who is one of the most genuine and lovable men I've ever met, left the table, walked to the nearest station and waited for a train to Leeds. Elaine Bedell, to whom the *Top Gear* team reported at the BBC, was already at the hospital. She'd been close on Andy's heels.

As I walked into the reception area of the hospital, near the café, I could see the whole gang had taken over a corner. They were all looking at the morning papers. It was ridiculous. Richard's crash was front-page news everywhere, and the TV stations had been showing bulletins through the night.

Meanwhile at our home in Gloucestershire, the press had been into the local pub. They'd received no help from the locals at all, but had soon discovered where we lived, and started camping outside.

*        *        *

I remember vividly the first time the nurse caused Richard some pain and he reacted. It was terrifying. His eyes rolled as he tried to open them, arms flailing wildly, grabbing at anything they came into contact with. He tore off monitors and grabbed at the drips, all the while so disorientated he could scarcely lift his head from the pillow. But the tough, scrappy Richard was there, ready to fight his corner with every last ounce of strength. The episode was brief but explosive. When he'd calmed a little, the nurse did the obs and made notes. He was trying to respond to commands, but it wasn't good. He couldn't open his eyelids; couldn't speak. The nurse felt an almost undetectable movement with his right hand; his feet didn't move. It was like watching a child learn to walk. You concentrate on the slightest improvement, you will them to succeed. I sat there and silently prayed. I felt desperate.

The next time she did obs it was worse. Again, he didn't respond, so she caused him more pain. This time he managed to tear a drip out of his arm and almost hit the nurse in the face. It was so disturbing—he was completely out of control. Not in that angry, measured, aggressive way you might describe as 'out of control', but in his case quite literally—there was no coordination. His brain wasn't quite getting the messages right, and there was something else . . . as the nurse shone the light into his eyes, I saw for the first time the awful mess which was once his left eye. The bruising externally had grown steadily darker until it was now shades of purple and black; each time the nurse touched the lid to shine her light into it I winced, but this time I kept my eyes open, and from my position seated next to his head, I saw beneath the lid. There was no white—it was all red. But worse than that, the pupil wasn't recognisable—just a dark lumpy mass in the middle. I'll never forget that. It seemed to happen in slow motion and what I saw burnt into my soul. I drank in the image, digested it, wanted to cry and then thought, 'It's an eye. Just an eye. He's got another one. He'll be fine. He can cope with one eye.'

In that moment, I suppose I accepted it was gone.

He wasn't speaking. He just grunted. He was still very bad at squeezing the nurse's fingers. But what was really worrying was the lack of response from his left-hand side. There were small improvements with all of his other responses, but the left side of his body was essentially paralysed, and I'd already been told that the impact had been mostly to the right side of his head, controlling left-hand-side motor skills.

Every minute at his bedside was an eternity. Time was suspended in Intensive Care. I'd no idea if it was night or day, and didn't really want to know. My world was in front of me, in that bed with tubes and monitors all over him. But although it was soul destroying to be there, I was determined to be as upbeat as possible. After all, I knew Richard. If he thought he was missing out, he'd be more inclined to come back and join the party. I settled down again next to him. His nurse came over, and beckoned me to go with her around the corner.

'Has anyone told you what's going on?'

'Sorry?' I was confused.

'In the bed next door.'

'Oh, um, no.'

She explained that the lad in the bed next to Richard's, with the curtain drawn, was dying. His family had all been called in and he was going to die that night.

'Oh God, how awful.'

I sat back down, took hold of Richard's left hand and spent the next few hours listening to the terrible sounds you hear as a body slowly leaves this life. That 'rattle' in the throat, the breathing getting steadily weaker, and finally the sad exchanges between mourning relatives just feet away.

I looked at Richard's vacant face, a face I knew so well. Every inch familiar and wonderful but now lacking in spirit, inanimate. There I sat, listening to someone die just feet away, and willing my husband to stay alive.

It was obvious when the terrible moment came, but when it did something very strange happened. As I sat there a cold chill brushed past me. It hovered as a ghost might, as if it were the spirit of the lad next door coming to have a look at Richard. It was suspended there for a second or two. Then left. I'd like to think he was joining with me, willing Richard to pull through; perhaps telling Richard it wasn't his time yet. But then it left, as did the poor lad's relatives—slowly filing out into the corridor united in their grief.

Back in the ward the nurses quietly, subtly asked all visitors to leave while they did what had to be done. When I returned, there was a fresh bed, and all the staff had moved on. It struck me then that death must be a common factor in their job. I wondered how they could be so upbeat when someone had just died, but I suppose that's the only way for them to continue; to do their job. They really are amazing, awe-inspiring people.

I resumed my post next to Richard. His monitors had quickly become familiar to me, and I was careful to position myself so that I didn't interfere with any of the tubes or wires. I felt so surplus to requirements. I'm usually so busy running around looking after him. I'd never been in such an alien situation. All I could do was sit and wait and pray. The hospital staff had warned us that the first forty-eight hours were vital. We'd know more about the damage to his brain after that. It's a little piece of knowledge you wish you hadn't been given, because while trying to be optimistic, a glint of stark reality is visible just around the corner.

His obs improved slightly. He managed to actually lift one of the fingers on his right hand. It was such a breakthrough! The relief was overwhelming. A message had reached its destination from his brain at last. I remember thinking, 'Something worked! If one thing works, then so will another.'

I was elated. The next few obs were showing slight improvement—as if he was on his way back. But then, about 4 a.m., he started to dip; to dip badly. He just wasn't interested—he wasn't trying. I looked at the nurse. Something unspoken passed between us.

'It's bad, isn't it?'

'It's not good,' she admitted.

She'd tried causing him pain, but on this occasion it hadn't worked. For the first time I really felt I was going to lose him.

'Richard! Richard!' She was really shouting at him.

'Can I shout at him? The way I do when he's drunk?'

'Try anything, love.'

I looked around me at the other beds. There were three other patients in the ward.

'I'll probably wake everyone up, though.'

'That doesn't matter. You go ahead.'

The way she spoke confirmed she was as worried as I was.

She had her index fingers inside his limp hands, but nothing was happening. Nothing.

I took a deep breath, got close to his face and yelled.

'Richard, you squeeze those fingers! Squeeze those bloody fingers—it's important!'

The tears were running down my face; both the nurse and I were hunched over him. We were both watching his hands, and as I finished yelling, he made a very tiny movement with his fingers. Both middle fingers! Oh! The relief was so great! I half thought I'd pass out. Never have I been so grateful that we don't shout at each other, because I'm sure the impact on him was quite shocking. The only time I ever shout at him is on very rare occasions when he's been on a boozy night out with the boys and decided to sleep on the sofa. He gets grumpy if I try to move him and it's the only way to bring him round and get him to bed. He has confided since that he remembers thinking he was tired, and there was a nice, easy route—he could just drift away there . . . relax—check out. That was what he'd decided to do. Check out. He said it was as though he was playing a game, but he'd decided the rules and was going to enjoy himself and drift over to the comfy place now. He remembers being jolted back. His mind suddenly, somehow recognised he was in trouble. He realised he'd upset me and he ought to stop playing the game now. He was a naughty schoolboy who'd been reprimanded and he had to pull himself back to face the music.

It is, I now believe, no coincidence that we refer to people as 'pulling through', because that's precisely what Richard did. He pulled himself back. Even so, he visited places that still haunt him to this day. He has referred to the incredible determination and strength it took to 'pull himself back' at that moment. It was, from his description, more akin to hauling yourself flat on the ground with only your fingernails able to provide any means of moving forward. Slipping back—or remaining stationary—meant certain death or disability. I'm so very grateful he made the effort, exhausted as he was.

After a few more sets of obs he was exhausted. I had time to make some calls.

CHAPTER 9

# HE IS NOT GOING TO DIE

As I left the ward and rang for the lift, I was thrilled and excited. When it arrived and the metal doors opened, Andy Wilman was facing me. His face was ashen.

I smiled at that sad, crumpled human being. 'He moved both his hands.'

'Oh God!' Andy burst into tears and threw his arms around me. He remained there for the journey down in the lift. He felt so responsible, but not only that, he loved Richard. They were mates.

He choked through his tears, and said, 'What am I doing? I'm supposed to be supporting you, not the other way round!'

It didn't matter. Richard had responded. Something magical had happened.

I called everyone. I'd spoken to Richard's parents a few times, and managed to speak to the girls daily, but suddenly needed to hear their voices. I missed them desperately.

I was outside in the smoking area when I called home and Richard's mum answered. I told her the good news and she was thrilled. We caught up on Richard's progress, and chatted about the girls. Richard's mum agreed that the TV and radio should be off while the children were around. We couldn't be sure how his condition would be reported, and that was something to keep under control for their sakes. At the same time, we both knew that the outcome was very uncertain. We were talking about the outlook as if it was all positive, but silently shared the nightmare of so many dreadful prognoses. We decided not to send them to school or nursery, for fear of miscommunication about Daddy's condition.

I had a quick chat with both Izzy and Willow. They each asked if I was coming home. It was hard to be jolly with them, but I tried to explain that Daddy needed me for a bit longer, and I'd be home soon. Besides, they had Grandy and Poppa with them, and that was fun.

It was tough, talking to Izzy. She was so bright, so perceptive. It was obvious she was being brave for Willow, but she knew there was too much fuss being made. I'd gone away—I never left them like that, and she could see straight through the façade. Izzy knew I was keeping things from her, and we both knew she'd made her mind up to humour me. I told her how wonderful she was, then said, 'Be good for Grandy and Poppa.' But when we said goodbye her voice, previously light-hearted, suddenly faltered. She checked herself, and said, 'Here's Ela.'

I spoke with Ela briefly, asked her to really watch over Izzy. I thanked her and asked her to keep them happy. She was their normality, their friend.

Richard's mum told me there were TV crews and reporters around the house. They'd seen them when they'd taken the girls on to the hill beside the back garden for a pretend picnic to keep them occupied. She reassured me that they were all fine and we agreed to talk again as soon as possible.

It was the first time we'd experienced big press attention. We lived quietly in our house in the valley. People knew where Richard lived, and the kids on the school bus craned their necks to try and spot him in the drive as they went past in the mornings, but nobody made a fuss.

Sadly, it was Richard's parents who were having to deal with it all, and this was an even more alien world to them. It wasn't as though the press were there to be difficult, they were simply reporting a story, doing their job. But for the parents of a man lying in hospital, bravely taking responsibility for his children, this was an added pressure which was hard to bear.

I called my mum to let her know that Richard had improved. She told me how she'd watched TV and listened to reports through the night. She wanted me to get some sleep.

'I couldn't, Mum. I'm not tired. Besides, I have to be there when he opens his eyes.'

'Oh, of course you do. Try and get an easy chair or something to doze in next to him, love, will you? We're all praying for him, darling, you know that, don't you? Oh, love, I hope he'll be all right. You take care now.'

'I will. Thanks, Mum. I love you. Bye.'

Mum was desperate to help in any way she could. She'd offered to join Richard's parents at our house to help with the girls, but dear Mum doesn't drive and she's in her mid seventies. The turmoil of a normal visit to our house with kids, dogs and lunacy is often exhausting for her, and she was already taking blood-pressure tablets. She understood her role as support at the end of the phone was vital and I needed her to be there for me. I wanted my mum as much as my girls wanted me. The tears came briefly and I wiped them away.

As I approached Richard's bedside someone from the hospital administration was waiting for me. She felt it would be difficult for the *Top Gear* team to have any privacy in the reception area of the hospital and volunteered the use of a boardroom in the old wing of the hospital for everyone to use as a meeting place. She was eager to show me where everyone was. So, reluctantly, I left Richard and accompanied her on the long walk to the old hospital.

She spoke the whole time, but it was all I could do to try to memorise the route. I'm sure people who work in hospitals forget that every floor looks the same unless you study the ward names as you go; and we took so many turns along different corridors. I was really concerned. I felt completely lost, and it was as if a piece of elastic connected me to Richard's bed; with each step it was being pulled to breaking point. The separation was almost physically painful, and yet I was powerless. This poor woman with her animated gestures and upbeat approach was unknowingly torturing me; I was accompanying her of my own free will, and yet all I wanted to do was stop and allow the elastic to pull me back. I seemed to be miles away from Richard. I hated it.

Eventually we reached the room. I vaguely remember walking in. It was unusually quiet, with people sitting around the edge facing a coffee table in the centre which was buried beneath an array of paper coffee cups in various stages of consumption: some half-empty and cold, others fresh and steaming hot. Half-eaten pastries and doughnuts were on the table. Everyone's appetite had disappeared. Andy Wilman was there; he was trying to sort out sending a BBC press woman to our home in Gloucestershire. Jeremy and James were there, along with the majority of the *Top Gear* crew.

I said my hellos and sat down in a spare chair. It was so strange. I was trying to smile and be positive as I told them about Richard and answered their questions. Everyone wanted to see him, particularly Jeremy and James. You see, apart from anything else, they're all very good mates.

The newspapers were strewn around. Richard's crash was front-page news. I didn't want to see the pictures of the jet car. Yet somehow I had to look.

I couldn't stay for long though, my mind was elsewhere. I wanted to be back with Richard. I hated being parted from him. It took every bit of composure I could muster to talk with them all, speak with the press officers, answer everyone's questions.

As soon as I could, I was running back down the stone stairs from the meeting room, glancing around me, seeking out a route back to the new hospital. I slowed to a quick walk, followed the flow of the people ahead of me who seemed to know where they were going, turned a corner and was relieved to see a familiar tunnel connecting old to new. I ran again down the tunnel, jogged past the reception area towards the lifts, and to Richard.

It was when I arrived back at the ward and sat

watching Richard's peaceful face while the nurse updated me on what had happened in my absence that I suddenly started shaking quite violently. I felt very light-headed, and really wobbly. I practically fell against the wall.

'Are you all right, love?' she asked.

'Erm, I think it's probably time I ate something.'

Although I had no desire to eat, it was time to take the nurses' advice. They'd all been encouraging me to visit one of the various restaurants or snack machines, warning me that I needed to eat, that it would all catch up with me. It had.

I resumed my seat next to Richard and a cup of sweet tea appeared next to me. I felt so guilty, so ridiculous. There I was, sitting next to my comatose husband, surrounded by a roomful of needy patients in intensive care, and the amazing nurses were diverting their attention to some daft tart who forgot to eat. Even with their ludicrous workloads, they were concerned about me. I suppose it's a kind of nursing instinct. They always say it's a calling, don't they? Maybe nurses are really born, not made. They just need a few years of fine-tuning to be perfect.

Richard was becoming a bit more responsive. He was grumbling, and really making an effort with his fingers and toes. The worst problem was untangling him whenever he moved. There were so many drips, tubes and monitors, and he'd heave himself about without any idea of the knots he was tying himself into.

* * *

At 8 a.m., Richard's nurse handed over to her replacement, Jim. It was really difficult watching her go. I felt quite apprehensive about this new nurse. I didn't know him at all, and he didn't know me. We didn't get off on a very good footing either when he asked me to move my chair further down the bed, and criticised me for putting the oxygen monitor back on Richard's finger when it dropped off. He was an older guy with glasses and slightly greying hair. He was very forthright and I instantly had the impression he'd stand no nonsense. His first obs with Richard were the most awful yet. Richard wasn't responding too well, so Jim did the 'I'm going to have to cause you pain' line.

'Oh, please don't,' I begged. 'He hates it.'

Within seconds of the pain registering, Richard was thrashing about. He threw himself into a sitting position and two other male nurses came running over. Richard grabbed the ventilator tube with his right hand and started yanking it from his lungs. He was gagging and fighting off the two male nurses as he kept pulling the inch-diameter tube from his throat.

The two nurses were desperately trying to restrain him. I was on my feet, tears running down my face, crying, 'No, Richard! No!'

But his instincts had taken over. There was a tube in him which he wanted out. No one was going to hold him. Jim shouted to the other nurses:

'Let him go! He'll hurt himself more if you try to stop him.'

They let go their hold, and Richard gagged like an animal regurgitating food. But each time he retched, he yanked another few inches of tube out of his mouth. It was so frightening. I felt as though I was watching my husband commit suicide. The tube had been keeping his lungs functioning and he was rejecting it.

I stood there with my hands over my mouth, completely horror-stricken. I looked from Richard to Jim, but there was nothing the nurse could do. That pipe took for ever to finally come free of Richard's mouth. It was about a foot long. Once out, he coughed and moaned, then collapsed back on to the bed and was out.

I asked Jim what would happen without the ventilator.

'We'll have to keep an eye on him and see if he can cope without it.'

Oh God! I sat there for I don't know how long, watching his chest, watching the monitors like never before. I didn't want to leave him, not for a second. His breathing was very weak; his chest barely moved with each breath. I sat there staring at him, sometimes jumping to my feet when I thought his breathing was failing. But then, unexpectedly, his right arm started to move. He fumbled around under the bedclothes and his hand found what it was seeking.

I looked at Jim and he was beaming. 'He's a scrabbler. That's what we want to see.'

I smiled back at him, thrilled that Richard had managed to direct his arm. 'Scrabbler?'

'Well,' he explained, 'it's a thing you see very often with men who've had this kind of injury. They regress. He's a little boy. He's back to basics and he's checking his most important part is still there.'

'It's a good sign then?'

'Oh yes, it's a good sign.'

I smiled at Richard's quiet, still expressionless face and kissed him on the cheek. It was easier to kiss him now the ventilator had gone; although odd because I was worried I was going to hurt him. His face was still yellow-green from the bruising; and of course there was no reaction.

The consultant appeared with a neurosurgeon. They were studying his X-rays, and were concerned about an 'air pocket' in his jaw. They wanted to do another MRI scan to examine the spotting on his brain as his temperature had gone up slightly.

I didn't want him to go. The porters came to take him, and it was like a scene from a film. I was told he'd be back in about forty minutes and that was it—gone! What if something happened in those forty minutes? What if he took a turn for the worse and I wasn't there? What if he woke up?

It was awful. But there was nothing I could do. I just had to accept it, calmly leave the ward, go downstairs and chainsmoke and drink strong coffee until his return, all the while being chatty and positive with everyone who asked how he was.

Richard's obs weren't improving dramatically, but he'd try to open his eyes for Jim, and make very small movements with his toes as well as his fingers. Admittedly, the left side was still weaker, but it was responding slightly. Jim had called the optometrist to come and look at Richard's left eye. The consultant was concerned that it looked pretty nasty. At this stage the lid was practically all black with deep purple and red around the edge. It was so swollen it was almost impossible for Jim to open when he shone the light into Richard's eyes during obs.

I liked Jim. He was different in character to the first nurse, but nevertheless a really good guy. He took what the doctors said with a pinch of salt sometimes; he'd been in the job for longer than many of them. When one of the young doctors suggested to him that one of Richard's drips could be removed, Jim acknowledged the advice. Then, after the doctor had left, he turned to me.

'I'm not going to do that,' he said. 'Bloomin' fool. And what? Put another one in the poor bugger tomorrow?'

He was absolutely right too, as it turned out. Trouble was, with Richard there was no telling how long anything would stay connected anyway.

Later that morning, when again he was brought out of his unconscious state, Richard decided to remove the catheter. It was his second attempt, actually. The first time I grabbed his hand and shouted at him: 'No, Richard, leave that alone!'

But the second time he was too quick. It was another foreign body inserted where he didn't want it. He grabbed at the tube and gave it a tug.

'Richard, no! Don't!'

I tried to catch his hand, but he pushed me away. As he did so I realised his good eye was slightly open.

'Hello,' I said gently to him.

He looked straight at me, but there was absolutely no recognition whatsoever. His look was one of total disinterest. I wasn't even registering. It was devastating. The tube which he'd removed was now leaking all over the bed and the floor. Jim told me to go and get a coffee while he sorted Richard out.

I walked to the toilets in the outer lobby of intensive care, closed the door, locked it; sat on the loo and cried.

'Where are you?' I was whispering as I held my head in my hands. 'Please come back, please.'

I could hear voices outside. I had to pull myself together, go downstairs—coffee, cigarette.

I took a deep breath, wiped my face and walked out, staring at the floor 'til I reached the lifts. Everyone seemed to know who I was, everyone stared.

* * *

The finger monitor which kept track of the percentage of air in his blood was always the first to go. I'm sure somewhere in the back of his mind it registered as an irritation which he had to rid himself of, and he made it his mission to free himself of its grip. Whenever he achieved this, it set off the most irritating alarm. I'd become very good at re-attaching that one. However, the drips were what really scared me. The nurses were all so accustomed to dealing with everything, they were quite relaxed about the whole thing, but I'd learnt early on that a broken needle is extremely dangerous; the last thing Richard needed was to break one of those in his arm. He proved pretty good at tugging them out, even with a ton of surgical tape securing each one to his arm.

Then there was the oxygen mask. This was a

new addition following his dramatic rejection of the ventilator. He needed more oxygen and so Jim and I spent most of the time chasing him around the bed trying to re-attach the mask. In the end, Jim decided that little tubes up his nostrils might work better. So he attached those. He was right, although we still had a battle to keep them on.

By this time, a great deal of positivity was building as Richard continued to make progress. He had started to move his limbs unprompted. Admittedly, it was either to grab a certain part of his anatomy or, his favourite pastime, to pick his nose. But it was fantastic progress.

I should mention, in Richard's defence, his nose was, at the time of the accident completely filled with mud, so he could be forgiven for wanting to sort it out. Earth and blood caked together up your nostrils must be really uncomfortable, and his instinct was to try and remove it.

He hated doing obs now. He was really irritable about being forced to wake up a bit, but Jim was quite stern with him. Richard managed to move both hands and feet slightly and he even mumbled a couple of times.

I'd switched to Richard's right-hand side as he'd turned over, and was stroking his forehead gently when he moved his head towards me slightly, and mumbled something. I was so surprised, I nearly burst into tears.

'Sorry, darling?'

He repeated, and I just made out the word 'Gearbox'.

I knew instantly what he was thinking about.

Just a few days earlier something had gone wrong with my yellow Land Rover. I was sure it was the clutch, and Richard had disagreed and said it was the gearbox. The local Land Rover dealer had taken it in for repair and told me the problem over the phone.

'No, it was the master cylinder,' I told him.

'Oh, OK.' He went back to sleep.

I was grinning like a Cheshire Cat. Tears rolling down my face. The box of tissues I had next to me was almost empty so I used my sleeves. It didn't matter. Nothing in the world mattered except him. He spoke, he was remembering a piece of life, recalling his world—our world.

Less than an hour passed and he spoke again.

'Where's the car?'

His eyes were still shut and I knew he was only semi-conscious, but again he was interacting and recalling things which were prominent in his daily life.

'What car?' I asked.

'The Morgan.'

'It's in the garage.'

'Where?'

'At home.'

He smiled slightly, nodded and was out. I wanted to tell the world! It was amazing—he spoke! We'd had a conversation. But it was so brief, so heartbreakingly brief. He had dropped back immediately afterwards. It must have been such a tremendous effort for him.

Sadly, his next obs showed just how exhausted he'd made himself. He wasn't responding at all.

CHAPTER 10

# HELLO, DARLING

I've no idea how the day passed, but I recall it was evening when Andy and Nick agreed it was time that James and Jeremy came to see him. They'd been waiting patiently downstairs for so long, and the nurses agreed that familiar voices might well help him. Nick went to fetch them, and Andy Wilman came too. We all instinctively tried to be jolly and Jeremy was doing his best to be his usual self. He sat next to Richard and told him he was a shit driver. He was acting as normal, and a corner of Richard's mouth flickered into a slight smile. Jeremy was elated. It encouraged the larking about to increase, and Andy, although in a really worried state, started to look slightly encouraged.

Everyone was tiring though. Andy Wilman and James were talking about going back to the hotel in Leeds which had been organised by the BBC, and I think Nick coincidentally had to attend something for work at a hotel in Harrogate. He'd wanted to stay too, but it seemed daft, and anyway there was nowhere for him to sleep in the hospital.

I was in the waiting room in the outer corridor with Andy and Andrea, trying to order some Chinese food, when the door flew open and Jeremy burst in.

'Mindy, quick! He's awake! He's sitting up!'

'What?'

'C'mon!'

We were both running down the corridor, Andy and Andrea close behind. Jeremy was visibly moved.

'It was amazing! He just opened his eyes!'

We dashed through the double doors, and there, incredibly, sitting on the side of his bed, his hair dishevelled, his face bruised and battered, was my wonderful husband. As I reached the bed, ecstatic but apprehensive, he looked straight at me, a great dopey grin on his face, his good eye half-open.

'Hello, baby.'

He knew me! He knew me! Oh thank God! Oh and how I loved to see that look. That cheeky, naughty, lovable look I'd wondered if I'd ever see again. He really resembled someone woken from deep sleep after consuming an awful lot of alcohol and winning a boxing match.

'Hello, darling.' I was so thrilled to look him in the eye as I said it.

He wanted to have a pee, and insisted he should stand up to do it. He was offered a bedpan, but decided that was an awful idea. He wanted to go properly. I took one elbow and a nurse took the other, with a second nurse wheeling the drip as we headed towards the loo. Richard was surprised at his lack of coordination, but kept looking at me and grinning.

'Ello!' and then a few moments later, 'Ello.'

I thought my face would explode, I was smiling so hard.

'Hello, you.'

It really was like dealing with a drunk. We had to stay with him in the cubicle, or he would have fallen, but he was very cross at the nurse being there, so she had to agree not to look. I remember warning him as he stood there.

'This is gonna hurt,' remembering that he'd ripped the catheter out.

'Oh shit!' His face was an explosion of unexpected pain. He blinked and looked quite shocked. It was as if he'd been on autopilot; taking a pee was a natural, easy function which, to his great surprise had suddenly become more complicated.

We all shuffled back to his bed. He smiled at everyone, said a couple of words to Jeremy, said 'Hello, cockface' to James, smiled and passed out.

Obviously, I phoned the world! I had a couple of cigarettes with the gang and we returned to the ward. We were in semi-darkness as Richard's nurse updated his notes, lit only by a small desk lamp at her lectern.

The others left and I encouraged Jeremy to go home. Francie had to go away the next day and I knew he needed to drive back to Oxfordshire to look after the children, but he sat there, arms folded.

'Thanks, Jeremy, you've been brilliant. But shouldn't you be getting back?' I asked.

'No, I'm not going anywhere until you agree to get some sleep.'

'I'll be fine.'

'Well, so will I.' He crossed his legs defiantly.

'Oh God, Jeremy, you've got to drive back to Oxfordshire. You'll fall asleep at the wheel.'

'I never fall asleep at the wheel. It's something I just don't do.'

I knew he'd sit there until I did something, so I agreed to sleep on the sofabed in one of the waiting rooms.

The nurses made the bed up and I thanked Jeremy for being so supportive before he set off home.

I spent about two hours sending texts to as many people as possible. The phones were so low on battery I was unable to respond to everyone, but I did as many as I could.

The sofabed almost filled the room. Through the slatted window set high in the door I could see figures moving past; nurses and visitors, all there to support and encourage the handful of patients desperately ill in the room down the hall. I sat on the bed with my bottle of mineral water, checking I'd turned my phones off. I felt so alone. I was accustomed to being by myself—Richard's work took him away from home a lot—but I always knew he was at the end of the phone if I needed him. He was a part of my world even when he wasn't physically nearby. This time the reverse was true. He was only fifty feet away, but he could've been on Mars. I missed his presence. I felt hollow.

We spoke to each other so often when he was away; it was a standing joke with regular members of the crew. We always called before going to sleep—very often each picking up the phone at the same time to dial the other. The last call was so important to us both. Even when Richard had been abroad, or filming late, and it meant calling in the early hours of the morning, he always did.

Perhaps that's why I sent so many texts that

night: to make some kind of contact with someone. I missed him so desperately and yet I knew I had to get some sleep. I turned my thoughts to the progress he'd achieved and tried to relax.

I spent a couple of hours dozing in the room before I escaped back to the ward. Everyone was satisfied that I'd had some rest, so the nagging eased up.

I'd already spoken to Richard's parents about coming to see him. A car would collect them and bring them to Leeds, where they could stay in the same hotel as other members of the family. They'd set off that morning, leaving Ela with the girls, our five dogs and three cats, their collie, and the pony to tend to, but she was happy to help.

Jim handed over to a new nurse at around 8 a.m., and, when doing the handover, he explained about Richard's condition, before thoroughly enjoying telling her, 'Estimated speed 200 miles per hour.'

Richard's obs were more encouraging now—his responses were incredibly improved.

She thought it would be a good idea to clean his teeth with a blue sponge, about an inch square, on the end of a plastic stick. She tried to get it into his mouth, but he clenched his teeth together.

'Shall I try?' I volunteered.

'Yes, of course, love.'

She handed me the strange sponge lollipop and I tried to get it into Richard's mouth.

'Come on, darling—open up.'

He parted his teeth slightly and I managed to wipe around his teeth for about a second or two.

'Gerroff!' he mumbled.

'I'm just cleaning your teeth,' I said softly.

He opened his eyes and gave me the most venomous look.

'Bugger off!'

I smiled at his nurse but inside I was heartbroken. He didn't recognise me. He'd looked straight through me. He'd forgotten again.

The consultants came and hurried about. They looked at his scans: X-rays of his brain clipped on to a huge rectangular light fixed to the wall opposite his bed. They mumbled and discussed various points; then came over to chat with me. They were concerned that Richard seemed to be suffering discomfort in his back and had been worried there might be some additional damage, but on examining the X-rays, he seemed to be free of other injuries.

Given his improvement over the past twenty-four hours it was decided he could be moved to HDU (high-dependency unit) later that day. It was great news; at last I felt he was really making progress.

Since his big lavatory expedition, Richard had been very quiet. He'd occasionally open his eyes but with no recognition. While he was semi-conscious, the nurse thought it might be a good time to remove one of the catheters in his left hand.

Everything attached to Richard had to be tied on or stuck down, and his drips were held on with very sticky surgical tape. His poor nurse was trying, very gently, to peel this off his hand as he slept. He seemed perfectly happy, until suddenly, eyes still closed, he snapped, 'Piss off!'

The nurse held his hand.

'I need to get the tape off, Richard,' she said softly.

'Fuck off!'

'Ooh! That's not nice.' She tried again.

'Fuck right off! Ow!' He pulled his hand away, briefly opened his one eye and gave us both an evil glare.

We looked at one another and pulled faces.

'He must be feeling better, then,' I said to the nurse with a smirk.

He was still cross when it came to the next set of obs. The nurse was trying to encourage Richard to squeeze her finger with the hand which had the catheter in.

'Ow,' he mumbled, his eyes firmly shut.

'Come on, Richard—squeeze my fingers.'

'No,' he replied stubbornly.

'Come on,' she coaxed.

He yelled angrily, 'Fuck's sake! Ow!' and yanked the hand with the catheter away from her.

'I think that's sore,' I said.

The nurse agreed. 'Sorry, Richard, I won't touch it again.'

He wasn't interested. He pulled a face, eyes still closed, and rolled over to turn his back towards us. We set about untangling the drips, monitors, wires and tubes, which had become entwined around him.

I left Richard briefly while the nurses prepared him for the move to HDU. It was great to be leaving the intensive-care machines behind, and to see Richard after his wash and brush-up. He was all clean and lovely. The bed had been changed, there were new, crisp white sheets, just one drip left in his arm, and a catheter in his hand which was blocked off temporarily. He was ready to travel.

His pillow was propped up a little and for a couple of minutes he must have come round. I know he did, because although I was at the coffee machine at the time, when I returned his clean, white sheets were splattered with deep crimson, as were the pillow cases, his chest, one of the nurses, and the wall opposite. He'd decided to see what would happen if he turned the funny little green screw embedded in the back of his hand. (It was blocking off the tube which accessed his vein.) I think we all found out what that thing did, quite memorably.

We arrived at HDU, me looking like a zombie and him my most recent victim. The nurse was apologising to all the staff for the shocking state of her patient.

I'd visited intensive-care wards in the past, so I was sort of prepared for what I would see there. But I'd never been to a high-dependency ward before. That was really quite a shock. It seems to be the place they put all the really ill people who can cope without having a nurse each, as they do in intensive care, but it's full of the broadest imaginable cross-section of ailments. I realised almost immediately that Richard's two closest neighbours were both breathing through holes in their throats, and subsequently discovered that one poor chap had been there, bedridden, for eighteen months. He was such a happy, upbeat character—I marvelled at his positive outlook.

The nurses were far more bustling and chatty in this ward. The hushed tones of intensive care weren't necessary here, and you instantly sensed you were with a gang of people who really enjoyed their work, and one another's company.

Richard was quite bewildered at his journey. He said a couple of things to the nurse along the lines of, 'I'm sorry, I've made a bit of a mess.'

He was very much acting the chastised schoolboy, but all the while trying to understand where he was. He looked at me regularly for reassurance.

Although I'm not sure whether he knew who I was, I think something told him I was someone to trust—after all, I'd been there constantly—so I suppose he sought comfort in familiarity.

The BBC had sent a car to our home to pick up Richard's parents and bring them to Leeds. They'd had a really scary car crash earlier in the year and, considering what they were going through, it was only right they let someone else concentrate on the driving for four hours.

I'd sent Nick a message to let him know of Richard's move. He returned from Harrogate and was going back and forth from the ward the whole time; talking with everyone and being highly efficient.

Richard still had no idea what was going on, or indeed where he was. His short-term memory was rubbish, and although he drifted in and out of consciousness, generally he looked at Nick or me, said hello, and drifted off again.

Andy and Andrea had left to fetch their children, but planned to return as soon as possible. Nick would leave later that day to fetch Amanda and his girls.

I seemed to spend the day going up and down

stairs. There were lots of flowers, cards and letters arriving from well-wishers. It was really overwhelming. So many flowers had arrived that I asked the hospital if they'd mind storing them all in a room. Richard couldn't have them with him, there were too many, but he should see them later if he could.

When I returned to the ward, the nurses were all of a kerfuffle. The sister bustled over to me.

'Just to let you know, we've locked this door.' She pointed to the door leading into Richard's bay.

'It's a bit too close to the entrance to the ward, and we're worried someone from the press might get in.'

'Oh, thank you. That's very kind, but I'm sure he'll be fine.' It was rather embarrassing, and I wasn't sure it was necessary.

Then she explained that the hospital security had alerted them, and they now had a security guard positioned at the entrance to the ward.

Richard had suddenly become big news, I realised, and no one really knew how he was doing. Fortunately, his consultant, Stuart Ross, came by later that day and suggested he make a statement to the press on our behalf which would update everyone on Richard's condition. He was a figure of calm authority. Very friendly, but clearly a man with a very important role to fulfil. He discussed how he would put the facts across, and it was reassuring to chat with him about Richard's improvement. It seemed the medical team were all delighted and astounded by his progress.

When he next regained consciousness, I told

Richard his mum and dad were on their way. He looked really crestfallen.

'Oh God, and I'm rubbish.'

I smiled at him. 'No you're not. You're really not.'

Every time he became lucid we were asking him if he knew where he was, or what had happened. He'd kind of understood that he was in Leeds, and when you asked him where, he'd respond 'hospital', but he had no idea why he was in hospital. I explained that he'd had an accident.

'Oooh shit,' he responded calmly, as if he was humouring me, and gave me a disbelieving look.

I told him about all the cards and flowers he'd received, but it didn't really register, and he was still looking blankly at me as he sat propped up against his pillows.

'You crashed, darling,' I whispered.

'Did I?' He lifted his eyebrows and looked vaguely interested. 'Was it good?'

'Mmmm. Pretty impressive,' I told him.

'Oh.' His attention was drawn to a passing nurse with a cup and saucer in her hand.

'Shall we have a cup of tea?' He smiled.

'Yeah. Let's have a cup of tea. I'll go and get it.'

He smiled at me. 'Thank you.' He was too polite. He was talking to me as he would to someone he didn't really know. The move had tired him. His expression was becoming very glazed.

The flowery plastic curtains around Richard's bed remained drawn at general visiting times to avoid too much attention; although, to be honest, anyone intent on finding his whereabouts wouldn't have had too much trouble, once they got through the entry system.

The ward seemed to have a lot of that hospital blue-green colour about it, the colour of hospital gowns and wipe-clean floors, and on every exit and entrance were the handwash sprays. Each time I saw one I was reminded of Richard's *Should I Worry About . . .?* series for the BBC a couple of years before. He'd covered MRSA on one of the programmes and it had been really shocking. Terrible as it is to find yourself seriously ill in hospital, imagine compounding that with contracting a life-threatening virus during recovery.

*  *  *

Richard's bed was close to a window, and the staff, bless them, were concerned lest photographers managed to get a shot of him in bed, so they closed the curtains, but this meant inflicting misery on others in the ward who were deprived of the view. I'm sure when you're bedridden the view becomes far more important than the portable TV which each patient was allocated.

Once again, the joviality of the staff was ever present. Whatever dreadful task they were about, their jokes and smiles shone through and was returned by their patients. I'm sure their positivity was a huge factor in the recovery of many patients, including Richard.

As I returned with cups of tea I was concerned that Richard's parents would be arriving at any moment and hoping he'd manage to stay awake for their arrival.

Andy Wilman had been in to assure me he was going to meet them at the door. He wanted Richard's mum and dad to get angry with him. He felt they should, that they were entitled to be angry with someone, and he was volunteering for the job. I chatted with Nick and we agreed that would be ridiculous. Nick would make sure he was there first. Andy had been to hell and back with the rest of us, and it wasn't as though he could be held responsible for Richard's accident, even if he felt it was his duty to take the blame.

When his parents arrived, Richard was making every effort to be the person they most wanted to see. He was smiling, sitting up in bed and making jokes. It was a heart-warming picture for his mum and dad; although they must have been dreadfully worried, at least their son, although obviously injured, was conscious. Sadly, it was clear after three minutes or so that his memory of the present was gone. He'd repeat himself again and again, and get stuck on a subject which would be quite strange. He'd ask his mum and dad, 'Did you drive here?' They'd explain that a driver had brought them, and Richard would impress upon me the importance of thanking people for their generosity. He'd take a sip of tea, then, 'So how did you get here?' We'd go round in circles. It was something I'd become accustomed to and I pre-warned everyone who visited that it would probably happen. Provided you drove the conversation and spoke about past experiences, or big plans for the future, Richard could stay pretty well focused and appear to be completely recovered. As he did when the

Director General of the BBC, Mark Thompson, sneaked in to see him.

Richard has absolutely no recollection of the visit, but it's one I shall never forget. I'd told him the DG was coming and, to be honest, he didn't believe me for a while, but eventually it sank in and he became excited.

Mark was being smuggled in through the back door. He was attending a conference elsewhere in Leeds and felt he simply couldn't be in the same city without checking in on Richard. Andy Wilman was running about like a headless chicken to make sure everything went smoothly, and when the DG arrived we'd all been well prepared. Richard was sitting up in bed grinning, and he became so animated, discussing programming and future plans with Mark, it was almost embarrassing. I wanted to interrupt, and say, 'He really is very ill. I know you wouldn't think it, but he has got brain-damage. He's just giving you a performance—honestly!'

Richard put on an incredible show, and as I walked him out of the ward, Mark even commented on how amazing Richard was. I agreed, although secretly I was very worried about him.

When I arrived back at the ward, Richard was much quieter. He was having a little chat with his parents and suddenly looked exhausted. They quickly noticed the signs, and made to leave and get sorted out in their hotel.

Richard fell asleep moments after they left. I went downstairs and turned the phones on, had a cigarette and spoke to everyone who needed news.

I'd called and asked Ela if she'd accompany Izzy and Willow to Leeds on the Sunday. Izzy's birthday had just passed and we'd planned a big party at home that weekend. Instead we'd get all of Izzy's cousins together at the hotel and organise a birthday party there after she'd visited her daddy in hospital. Not quite what she'd expected for her sixth birthday, but at least this way she'd know her daddy was close by.

*   *   *

The nurses had decided to move Richard into a side-room as soon as one came available, and luckily that happened very quickly. It took several trips to assemble all his bits and pieces in the room, but it was by far a better solution.

Richard's visitors were many and frequent during his last hours in the main ward. It felt as though everyone was there. At one point in the afternoon, just prior to the move, Richard's mum and dad were with me, chatting to him, when James May tumbled in and shuffled over to me.

'Erm, hello, sorry to disturb . . . erm . . . a newspaper has been on to the BBC to say that Richard was banned from driving for three months earlier this year.' He looked confused. 'What should they say? He wasn't, was he?'

'No, he wasn't, and you can tell them from me what utter bollocks—and how dare they?'

James grinned. 'Ah, yes, good. I thought you might say something like that. I'll pass it on. Ta-ta.'

'Thank you. Bye bye!'

*   *   *

At about 4 p.m. on Richard's first day in the little room, I was sitting on his bed talking to him, when he said, 'This is very nice. You're very lovely.'

'Thank you,' I said.

'But I have to go now,' he said sheepishly.

'What do you mean?'

'I really have to go now. I've got to go back to my wife.'

That was a shocker!

'No, darling. I'm your wife.'

'No, you're lovely, but my wife's French.'

Do you know, just for a moment, a million thoughts went through my head—Has he been having an affair with a French woman?' 'Is he a secret bigamist?'—I dismissed them quickly.

'Really, I am your wife.'

'But you can't be. I'm having too much fun with you. You're too lovely to be someone's wife.'

Phew.

'Well, aren't you the lucky one then?'

I smiled and kissed him as he grinned like a cheeky schoolboy. Then I left the room briefly to fetch coffee while the nurses checked his obs, a procedure which had developed a little and become more involved with questions, temperature, blood pressure, etc.

*   *   *

Alex, one of the *Top Gear* researchers, had

arrived upstairs with Andy Wilman. I came out into the corridor to talk to them.

'Alex is going to be your personal slave,' Andy said with a grin.

Alex was smiling too.

'Whatever you want, whatever you need, it's Alex's job to get it for you.'

I looked from Alex to Andy and back again.

'I can't do that.'

'No, you can,' insisted Andy. 'He's got nothing to do now *Top Gear*'s stalled. He needs a job, and you're it.'

'Anything you want,' Alex agreed, smiling.

'Great.' I grinned. 'Pants.'

They both raised their eyebrows and laughed. But it was true. I desperately needed more knickers! In the rush to pack, I'd put stuff in the suitcase for Richard but only minimal bits for me. Actually, poor Alex was sent out with quite a list: knickers, bras, T-shirts, a pair of jeans, socks, shower gel and shampoo. He also had to buy Richard some clothes, as they'd gone walkabout at the airfield, apart from his cowboy boots which I'd moved with us from intensive care.

Alex stood there with a pen and pad as we went through a list of items and sizes. Poor Alex—he'd joined *Top Gear* as a researcher to work on exciting and glamorous film shoots, and wound up buying underwear in a posh pants shop for the presenter's wife! Alex is a great bloke. He's in his twenties and has been working on *Top Gear* for a while. I'd spoken to him innumerable times on the phone about shoots and filming issues, but this was the first time we'd met, and here he was writing down my vital

The girl I fell in love with.

Blowing up a life-sized replica of the House of Lords for ITV in *The Gunpowder Plot: Exploding the Legend*. Yes, this is work. Sort of.

Grasping the PM’s knocker. We had tea. I didn’t spill anything.

THIS PAGE: On stage—*Top Gear*.
OPPOSITE (clockwise from top left): With two old men; a typical filming day; driving the Championship-winning Renault F1 car in early 2007. I had to come back in after 5 laps to have the tyres re-heated. They didn't sign me up; with Andy Wilman, *Top Gear* Series Editor and Executive Producer—and brains; Andy tells me what he wants me to do in the stretch-limo stunt; watching two of the worst parkers in the country attempt to park my hand-built Morgan Roadster on my ITV *Five O'Clock Show*.

Telefonica

sparco
NSK
W. Wright & Sons
IXEUROPE
NOS

Elvington Airfield, 20 September 2006.

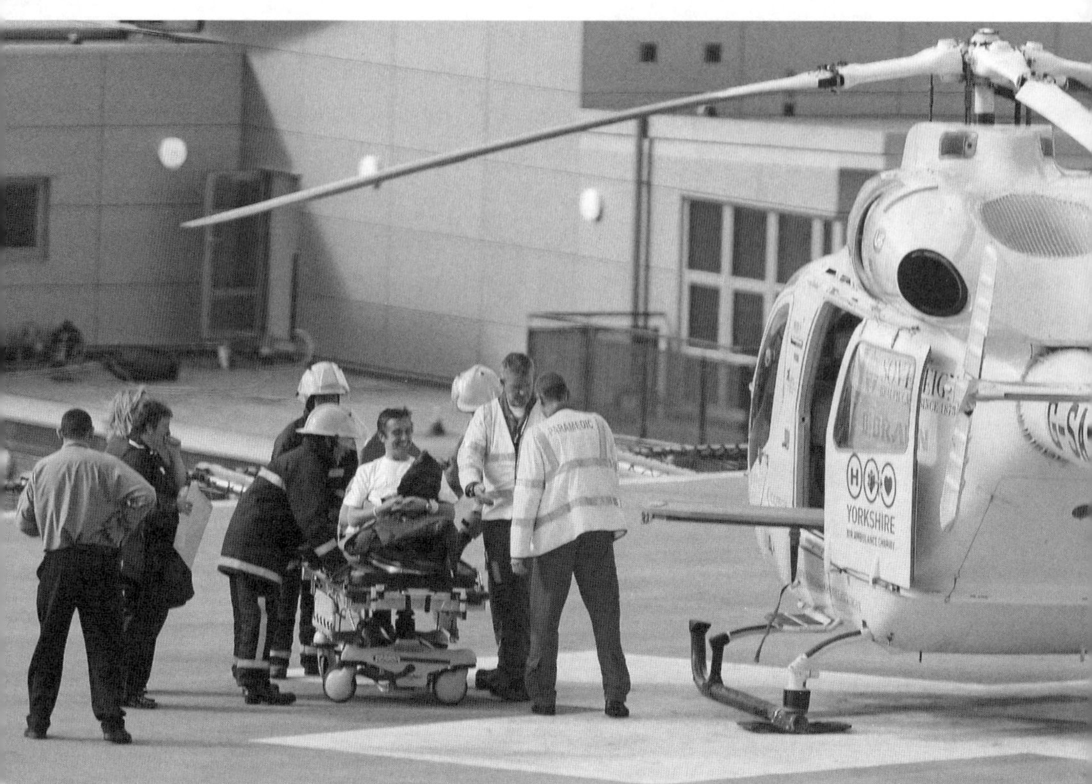

The airlift from the roof of Leeds General Infirmary to Bristol.

statistics.

We huddled together in a side doorway to avoid causing any disruption. The corridor along the side of the ward was a busy thoroughfare. There were always two or three nurses seated behind the desk at the middle section which faced the doors into the main ward. The traffic along the corridor was constant. Beds being pushed to and fro; orderlies and doctors; patients and visitors; nurses, sometimes walking and joking, sometimes running to answer an emergency call, but always busy. The doorway where we stood extended back a few feet and was the entrance to two storage cupboards. We shared it with three wheelchairs and some stacking plastic seats. As we talked, I saw her for the first time. A dear, sweet, elderly woman with a dreadful gash in the top of her head held together with some particularly serious-looking staples. The wound was about three and a half inches long. It looked as though someone had drawn a thick black-red curve across her head through the downy white hair. The enormous staples looked reminiscent of a macabre horror story. I don't know what happened to her, but clearly it was a nasty injury, and it was so sad watching her shuffle up and down with the aid of a nurse; slightly hunched over, her left arm outstretched and index finger and thumb rubbing together. All the while calling gently, 'Puss, puss. Puss, puss' and looking into every nook. I could only surmise that when she received the injury she'd been looking for her cat, so she continued to look for her cat, calling for it constantly. She had one of those delicate, friendly faces that are so rare. I imagined she was once very beautiful. Her skin seemed soft, though tired, and she was quite petite and slim. I had such an overwhelming urge to hug her, to take her home and look after her. She must have been in her late seventies at least, and as I watched her so many emotions rushed through my head—pity, anguish, sympathy and then concern . . . were her actions and demeanour a result of the head injury, or was some other underlying illness to blame?

Lovely as I thought her to be, would I cope with Richard if his grip on reality became so deeply affected by his injuries? How much further would he improve?

It was time for me to go back to Richard, and the guys to get on with their tasks: Andy handling *Top Gear*-related issues, the media and the BBC, and Alex buying pants in Leeds.

* * *

The following day was very busy. With Richard suddenly conscious and talking, understandably everyone wanted to see him. His brothers, Andy and Nick, had returned with their families, and of course Richard's parents were there too. But there was a real problem. Richard was giving everyone who walked up to his bed an excellent rendition of the Richard he thought they'd like to see. He was acting the role of the perfect host—chatty, inquiring after their health and personal lives. Then he'd falter. He'd repeat himself, become confused, or most often take the conversation round in circles. I could see that he was getting more muddled as the day progressed, and he was very tired.

I'd left him momentarily to deal with some matters the matron needed to clarify, and when I returned was horrified to find him on his knees, his hands cupped around the back of his head, his face buried into the pillows, rocking back and forth.

'Your head? Painful?'

'Yes! Oh God, help me! Arrgh!'

I ran out of his room and straight to the nurses' station.

'He's in pain. Really bad pain.'

Two nurses ran back to the room with me. It was dreadful. He was in such agony his face was unrecognisable. They fed some morphine into the catheter and I stayed with him until it took effect.

As he drifted off to sleep the nurses could see how worried I was.

'Is the doctor coming round soon?' I asked the sister.

'Yes, they'll just be doing rounds now. Would you like a word?'

'Yes. Yes please.'

I sat down heavily in the chair next to Richard, watching as the expression on his face, which he was trying to shield with his hands, slowly changed, and the pain and tension gradually dropped away as he drifted into a very welcome sleep.

It's strange how exhausting it is to watch someone you love in such misery. You go through every second with them, and you despise every uncomfortable moment, just willing it to be over. When eventually he fell asleep I really thought I was going to be sick. I was shaking and needed to get some air. The nurses were very good at reassuring me and spent a disproportionate amount of their time encouraging me to rest, or leave Richard briefly. But they knew very well how difficult it was. Whenever he was awake, I wanted him to know he hadn't been abandoned, to see a familiar face.

When he woke, the doctor came to see him. He asked Richard several questions and looked at his charts. He was very straightforward and businesslike and thanked Richard for his time. I followed him out of the room. He confirmed that Richard's condition had deteriorated, and suggested they reinstate the drip and keep him completely quiet for the foreseeable future. He'd been receiving far too much stimulus and from then on visits would be strictly monitored. He suggested I continue to be with Richard, but recommended only very close family be allowed visits, and then only for fifteen-minute periods.

Richard's determination to give everyone who visited him an enjoyable time had really taken its toll. Sadly, he was extremely good at acting; kidding everyone he was OK. He could fool just about anyone, and I knew he'd try to fool the nurses.

One conversation we had over and over again worried me, too. It went like this:

Richard: 'Do you know what I'd really like to do?'

Me: 'No, what's that?'

Richard: 'I'd like you and me to go out there'—pointing to the window ledge—'and sit together and have a beer and a cigarette.'

Me: 'We can't do that, Richard. This is a hospital and you're a patient. They don't allow smoking, and there's definitely no beer.'

Richard: 'Oh c'mon, you could get some, I know you could. And I've got some Marly Lights in my bag.'

He foraged in his Billingham camera bag.

Me: 'I can't get beer, it's a hospital. And you haven't got any cigarettes, honestly.'

Richard: 'Yes I have, I remember. They were here.'

Me: 'Well, it was my fault, to be honest—I was smoking them too.'

Richard: 'No, but I know they're in here. I've seen them.'

Me: 'No, Richard. Really, smoking isn't allowed anywhere.'

Richard: 'Oh, but I was just thinking. Do you know what I'd really like to do?'

Me: 'No. What would you really like to do?'

Richard: 'I'd like you and me to go out on to that balcony and have a beer and a cigarette.'

Me: 'No, darling, we can't. It's not allowed and we don't have any anyway . . .'

Richard (checking through his bag): 'I know I've got a packet of Marlboro Lights in here somewhere.'

Me: 'No, they're gone, I'm afraid. Why don't I get you a cup of tea?'

Richard: 'Yeah, OK. I tell you what, why don't we take our tea on to the balcony and have a cigarette with it?'

Me: 'Because there aren't any cigarettes and there isn't a balcony.'

Richard: 'Yes there is. It's just out there, and I've got a new packet of Marlboros in my bag somewhere.'

He picked up his bag again and started looking through the pockets.

Me: 'Richard. No balcony. No cigarettes. OK?'

Richard: 'Oh go and ask someone if we can just nip out for five minutes. Go on. Just for one cigarette.'

Me: 'I'll ask them when I get the tea.'

Whenever this conversation started I had to make sure it was brought to a satisfactory conclusion before I could leave him. Otherwise, left with the idea that the balcony was the ledge on the other side of the window, it could be rather dangerous to leave him. The other possibility was that he'd actually find some cigarettes and simply light up! He didn't have any, but I had some in my coat pocket. However, the first of these conversations, I made sure my cigarettes were hidden outside the room, and quickly decided to stop smoking as the smell of cigarettes on me would just remind him of his own craving.

The cigarette conversation could take ten minutes or more to peter out . . . and it was regularly revisited with small alterations. The best one was in the middle of the afternoon.

Richard: 'I was just thinking; you know what would be really lovely?'

Me: 'No, what?'

Richard: 'If we could walk out of here, go out to the country and sit under a big tree, just you and me.'

Me: 'Mmm. That would be nice.'

In my head was a romantic picture of the two of us . . . casually sitting leant up against the trunk of a large oak tree, smiling at each other through dappled sunshine; Richard in jeans with a casual shirt loose at the neck. Me with a long skirt pulled up over my knees. Laughing and smiling with tanned faces and windswept hair.

Richard: 'Mmmm. We could have a nice cold bottle of white wine resting in a stream.'

Me: 'Oh, how lovely.'

Richard: 'Mmm, and a packet of Marlboro Lights.'

*    *    *

Nick had a similarly odd experience. I'd left him and Richard alone for a bit to catch up. Poor Nick had been so busy organising everything he'd spent very little time with his brother in any state of consciousness.

Richard asked him, 'So, what are you doing next week? I'll be in London. Why don't we go out for a beer and a curry?'

Nick responded: 'No, no, mate, you need to stay here for a while and get better, but we'll catch up soon, when you're a bit brighter.'

Richard: 'Oh, how long am I supposed to be in here?'

Nick: 'Well, they're not sure. Weeks, maybe months.'

Richard nodded. 'Wow, really.' He looked around the room, seeming to be digesting the information, before looking back at Nick.

'So, next week. I'll be in London. D'you fancy meeting up for a beer?'

*    *    *

As you can imagine, with a severe head injury, balance is affected. For Richard this meant enduring the indignity of my assistance every time he went to the loo. He has always been very private when going about his lavatory visits. Even at home with no one around, he'd always shut the door, but suddenly I had to become quite strict with him—which is totally out of character in our relationship—and insist I accompany him to the loo otherwise he'd fall over. This point was very well proved one afternoon when Andy Hodgson, 'H', an old friend of Richard's from his radio days in the North, came to visit. He'd driven from London and been waiting in the visitors' room for over an hour before Richard was able to see him.

I'd left Richard in the care of 'H' and Alan, Richard's dad. I remember as I left the room to keep Richard's mum company and collect a change of clothes from the hotel, clearly saying to the three of them, 'Please be careful. If he needs to go to the loo, go with him or he'll fall over. And make sure you take the drip—he forgets it's in his arm.'

'Yes, yes, don't worry, he'll be fine.'

When I returned to the room, they had left, but I noticed the remains of a broken drip on the table near the bed. Some weeks later 'H' related what had occurred that afternoon . . .

He told me that initially, when in the room talking to Richard, he wondered just what all the fuss was about. He seemed completely normal. They were having quite a laugh . . . for the first five or six minutes. Then 'H' realised that the conversation had turned full circle and started all over again, but for Richard it was all new. His short-term memory had completely gone.

I imagine it was very unnerving for 'H', but not half as difficult as it might be trying to stop a grown man going for a pee on his own—even in hospital.

However, as 'H' described it to me, Richard swayed into the loo, shut the door, and seconds later there was a lot of banging and crashing and a little voice cried out:

'It's OK, I fell over, but I didn't pee on the floor.'

At this point a couple of nurses came dashing into the room (he'd grabbed the alarm cord on his way down), and went in to rescue him. I suspect he had a sheepish smile and was giggling naughtily.

* * *

One of the loveliest memories of this time with Richard was the overwhelming happiness that he had come back. He was childlike and forgetful and difficult, but he was undeniably Richard, and I think I probably loved him more then than I'd ever imagined possible. A part of me knew he could've been lost for ever. Yet he'd returned.

Throughout this period the pain in Richard's head was still very intense and he was given morphine regularly, together with a cocktail of other drugs. He tried to manage the pain and forgo the tablets, but the nurses told him he was being daft and should make life easier for himself. Unusually, he took their advice.

As Richard was so very exhausted, and in such pain, the nurses were quick to tell me he'd be asleep all night. They were desperate for me to get some proper rest and, to be honest, I was really starting to feel awful. So, at about 9.30 p.m., I left Richard and ordered a cab to take me to the hotel where the whole family were staying—visiting my room for the first time.

I joined Richard's parents for a bite to eat, and within about an hour Richard's brother Nick and his family arrived.

It was one of those strange situations you occasionally find yourself in. We should've all been happy to see one another, exchanging jolly hellos and hugs, but of course this was no happy occasion. There was some relief for us all: we knew he was still Richard. But we were all worried, and there was only one place in the world I wanted to be: with him. And yet I had to force myself to leave him. The mission was sleep, and I was soon on my way to bed.

I slept briefly and erratically, and by the time I turned my phone on at 6.30 a.m., I was dressed and ready to go. I was in the taxi when the hospital phoned. Richard had woken up and was distressed because he didn't know where I was. I told the nurse I was on my way.

This was to set the pattern for quite some time. I was his constant, his anchor. Knowing he'd become so distressed that they'd felt it necessary to call me, brought home to me how distraught he must have been. I would never sleep at the hotel again. I would never leave him alone again.

The taxi from the hotel seemed to take for ever. Although it was just a ten-minute journey, it was horrible. I was desperate. It's awful when control is taken away from you. I'm by no means a control freak, but I have, like anyone, a good idea how fast I can drive, how quickly I can manoeuvre, and how much speedier the journey could be. I had the money in my hand to give to the driver within minutes of taking my seat. My phone rang again.

'Hi, Mindy, it's the ward again. Richard's getting quite agitated. I was just wondering when you might get here?'

'I'm on my way,' I told the calm but obviously concerned voice. 'I'll be there within fifteen minutes. Please tell him I'm on my way.'

'I will, love, don't worry.'

But I did worry. I worried very much. To make him suffer any more than he was already suffering was just unforgivable. I felt as though I'd been completely selfish and stupid. How could I put him through this? Oh God! I was on the edge of my seat. Every traffic light was hell and when I finally saw the entrance to the hospital I put my left hand on the door handle; the cash clutched in my right hand. The second the car stopped, I was out like a flash—running before my feet hit the ground. The two armed security guards on the door smiled and waved me through. I ran on to the lifts. Pressed the buttons on every one. Fidgeted as I waited. 'Come on! Come on!' I said out loud. The second a door opened, I dashed in.

Why is it when you're in a rush the bloody door takes so long to close?! I paced the lift like a caged animal on the way up. It was on floor seven—it took an eternity.

I almost pushed the doors apart and ran like hell down the corridor, jabbing my finger on the button outside the ward door. They were clearly waiting for me. The door opened far too quickly.

I half ran, half walked down past the nurses' station.

'Morning!' I said as I passed with an out of breath, half-smile. It was acknowledged brightly, with huge understanding.

'He's expecting you,' someone said.

'You don't say?' I smiled as I jogged past.

I gently opened the door to his room.

'Hello.'

He beamed at me. 'Oh, hello. I'm so glad you're back.'

We shared an enormous hug. It lasted longer than any other embrace I've ever known. I wonder whether, as everything was so very confused and mixed up for him, perhaps Richard didn't believe I'd return. His memory was in such a dreadful state. Post-traumatic amnesia (PTA) is an alarming condition. For the majority of the time he had the memory of a goldfish (around five seconds). He could remember scraps of past history, just very little since the crash. I imagine he couldn't rely on his mind, which must be very frightening and confusing. He was described as being 'clinically confused'. The one thing he knew absolutely was that I was his ally. What he couldn't be sure of was whether I really existed or was simply a figment of his imagination. I can only think he lived out a dreadful series of acts in a frighteningly realistic sci-fi nightmare where no one can be relied upon. You're told of an accident you supposedly lived through, and yet by definition you should be dead. There are no serious injuries visible to support this 'crash' claim, yet you have a chronically black eye and your head feels weird, as though you've been drugged. You vaguely recognise people, but you don't recall an awful lot of information about them, and you seem to be held prisoner in a small room with an en-suite bathroom. Oh, and lots of people you recognise turn up all the time for some event that must be going on nearby to which you're not invited.

It's difficult to explain how our relationship emerged, and how scary the process was. It felt very much as though we were piecing together fragments of confused, emotional memories. Richard was stumbling through feelings and emotions and trying all the while to understand how they related to us. He'd accepted that I was his wife (I think), and I regularly held his face in my hands and told him:

'If you have any questions, any worries, ask me. I'll tell you the truth.'

I'd heard so many conversations with other visitors who hadn't realised the importance of talking straight with him. He'd ask a question they considered stupid, so instead of calmly setting him right, they made a joke out of it and answered in a flippant way. For instance, when he asked, 'Where's the party? Where's everyone going?' I once overheard someone answer, 'Oh, it's upstairs. We're all having a great time.'

I'd immediately cut in, telling Richard there was no party. But it was this sort of comment that just compounded his confusion. I spent so much time with him I was blindingly aware of the importance and credibility of every single word. I thought very carefully before answering his questions, and developed a huge amount of patience.

But it's impossible to expect everyone who comes into contact with a person suffering that type of injury to understand the complexities involved; particularly when, on the surface, the person they're talking to appears almost normal. He simply has a bit of a memory problem as far as they can see, and people act instinctively—if they speak to someone who appears coherent, they continue in their normal, everyday vein. It's only when the cracks show themselves as huge gullies that many of us will finally accept there really is something wrong. After all, it's far easier to believe everything is essentially OK, than it is to accept something has changed dramatically.

I'd quickly become the constant for Richard. After that morning I didn't leave his room unless he was either asleep or with someone. Whenever he slept and I left the room, I'd always leave him a large handwritten note sellotaped to the TV screen, telling him where I'd gone and that I'd be back soon.

I would go downstairs and buy anything I could find at the shop that he might like—Land Rover magazines, Curly Wurlys, Fry's Turkish Delight in the familiar purple wrapper, fruit-and-nut bars, liquorice, sweets and chocolates he'd always loved. James May had left him a copy of *Auto Trader*—their favourite game was fantasy car-shopping garage. They'd each have a copy and select their favourite cars (unlimited budget) and pretend they could go out and buy them. It saddened me that, although I kept putting the magazine in front of him, he hadn't found his usual enthusiasm to go leafing through the pages and turning over the corners of pages where there were 'possible purchases'.

There was a big hole in Richard Hammond, and I was very worried we'd never find all the pieces.

* * *

On my return from one of my trips to the hospital shop, I had quite a shock.

When I opened the door to Richard's room, he was on the phone! The little wotsit had rummaged in his bag and found his mobile (the battery from which I'd hidden). He'd taken the battery off my phone, which he'd found in my handbag (which he would never, ever have dreamed of dipping into before) and put it into his phone. He'd then—God help us!—called a newspaper!

As I walked in, he finished the call and blushed. He grinned at me.

'Er, hello.'

'Oh, who was that?' I tried to sound unconcerned.

'Oh, no one. Just a friend.'

'OK. Would you like to see what I've got?'

I showed him the contents of the bag and avoided the subject of the phone call. Soon afterwards, the nurses came in and gave him some medication. He was exhausted, and quickly fell asleep.

The second he was snoring, I grabbed the phone and quietly left the room. Telling the nurses I was just popping downstairs, I turned both phones on when I reached reception. My phone instantly rang. There was a message from

Richard's editor at the *Mirror*. We'd been in regular contact since the crash, but now he was calling because, as he put it, 'I've just had a chat with Richard, and wanted to check it out with you before we go to print.'

Richard had phoned him and chatted for some time—long enough for his editor to realise it wasn't quite right. He did the decent thing and checked it out with me. After a brief chat, he agreed not to write anything, and he promised that, should Richard call him again, it was to be kept between us. Thank goodness for honest newspapermen!

Having chatted with the *Mirror* guys and asked them to simply say a huge 'thank you' to everyone who'd sent flowers, cards, letters, gifts and messages to Richard, I made my way back up to the ward.

I handed Richard's mobile phone in at to the nurses' station.

'D'you think you could put this in a safe somewhere? Only, I just caught him calling a newspaper, and I think it might be best if he doesn't do that again.'

'Oh no! Yes, sure, we'll lock it away for you.'

Fortunately, when I returned to the room Richard was still asleep. I went to find Alex, our researcher/personal slave. He'd been shopping. He'd done very well. As Richard's clothes had been cut off him in A & E, he had only his hospital pyjamas. As he'd improved, I realised it was just as well that those pyjamas were all he had. I was beginning to feel more like a prison guard every day. Still, I'd asked Alex to buy him a pair of jeans, a couple of T-shirts, socks and pants, etc.

Alex handed over several carrier bags and as I returned to the room a sudden wave of panic crept over me. Where on earth could I hide the clothes? Richard was still hell-bent on escaping for a cigarette, and I'd had to take his cowboy boots to the hotel as I'd twice caught him putting them on over his pyjama trousers. He was stirring as I closed the door behind me as quietly as I could.

I crept into the bathroom and shut the door. There was a mattress leaning against the wall opposite the shower—it was to be my makeshift bed on the floor next to Richard. I decided to hide the bags behind that. I shoved them all behind it and quickly flushed the loo. As I walked back through the door, Richard was waking. He looked so unkempt. So lovable. His demeanour was one of someone just a little bit under the influence of a few sweet sherries. He was smiley and affectionate and very forgetful, but mostly he was still extremely tired. The nurses came in regularly to check his blood pressure, temperature, etc. and ask him questions. Did he know where he was? What day it was? What the date was? His name? By now, if they asked me those questions I had difficulty answering, so I wondered how on earth he could be expected to remember.

The nurses had been carefully monitoring the amount of fluid he was drinking. It wasn't good, and he'd grown gradually more confused from all of the visitors. The registrar decided he should have a drip put back in, which was upsetting as he'd been doing so well. By the time they'd finished, he was finding it difficult to stay awake.

I'd asked Ela to come to Leeds with the girls, and the BBC had kindly provided one of their drivers to fetch them, as Ela didn't drive. Alex, who was acting as liaison, came to the room to let me know they were getting close. So I left Richard and dashed downstairs to wait at a side door. I seemed to wait there for hours, although I'm sure it was only minutes. I'd missed the girls so badly. It had been Izzy's sixth birthday and her party should have been today. As a surprise, Nick and Amanda together with Andy and Andrea had spoken to the hotel and organised a birthday party for her there in the afternoon with all of her cousins. It was a good distraction, and would hopefully take the girls' minds off the distress of the hospital visit.

As they arrived, I nearly burst into tears. I gave them huge cuddles, and then hugged Ela. Roly, another of Richard's colleagues from *Top Gear*, had shown up just to be on hand, as had several others. Everyone just felt the need to do something. Anything. Someone organised for the kids' bags to be taken on to the hotel, and I asked the lady in charge of administration if there was a quiet room I could take the girls into for a chat before we went upstairs.

She showed us down one of the corridors along the gloomy but elaborate original wing of the hospital. The floors were mottled brown marble, and the walls and pillars a variation of the same theme. Finally, she opened the door to a large room with a boardroom table in the middle—there were probably twenty chairs around it. There she left us, Izzy, Willow, Ela and I. I picked up the girls and sat each of them on a chair facing me. I knelt in front of them.

'Now, you know where you are, don't you?'

Izzy, thumb in mouth: 'Yes, we're in a hospital.'

Willow nodded, straight faced.

I hadn't really prepared myself for this at all, but suddenly I realised it was my responsibility to reassure and prepare these two little souls for something quite distressing. I hoped I could swing it.

'Remember when I had to dash off because I needed to bring Daddy some new clothes?'

'Yes, because he broke his ones and they were all dirty,' Willow replied, very seriously.

'That's right, poppet.' I smiled at them both. 'Well, when he tore his clothes he also banged his head a bit.'

Izzy pulled a face and nodded. 'Was there blood?'

'Well, just a little bit, where he banged his eye.'

'Oh! Has he got a plaster?' asked Willow, excitedly.

'Sort of. More like a bandage.'

'Wow! That's really good.' She was impressed. She was three.

I looked again at Izzy. Her thumb was planted firmly in her mouth and her face was as serious as she could muster. I waited for a moment.

'Here's the thing. Because Daddy's banged his head, he doesn't really feel very well. He's really tired and a bit, well, a bit not like Daddy. But he'll get better, he just needs to get lots and lots of sleep, and then he'll be fine.'

'He probably needs a nap. He can have my

dummy if he wants.' Dear Willow. 'I'll give him a big cuddle.'

'You do that, that'll make him feel much better.'

Izzy's eyes were looking watery.

'Did you make Daddy some cards?'

They were each gripping cards and paintings they'd made. Izzy had written him a letter too.

'Oh, you are clever girls.'

'Can we go and see him?' Izzy asked.

'Yes, in a moment.'

It was nap time on the ward. Every day the staff turned the lights off for an hour or so in the afternoon. It encouraged rest and sleep. I had to explain a bit more about hospitals before we left the separate area.

'You know that hospitals are where people come when they're poorly, don't you?'

They both nodded.

'Well, because the people here are so poorly, they need lots of peace and quiet, so you must always whisper when you go in. OK?'

They agreed.

'Right then. Let's go and visit your daddy.'

Ela helped me with the girls as we went upstairs. She didn't want to come into Richard's room. She waited outside in the corridor. I'd already organised for the nurse to help Richard with his eyepatch before we came in. We'd explained to him that he should keep the piece of gauze over his eye as it looked quite gory and might scare the girls.

He was sitting on the bed when we entered the room. I'd prepped them just beforehand that we wouldn't be able to spend too much time with him, and they would be going to a party afterwards.

Richard was overjoyed when he saw them. But he'd completely forgotten why he had the eyepatch on and started trying to rip it off.

'Keep that on for a bit,' I gently pleaded with him. But he ignored me and tore it off.

Thank God I'd prepared the girls.

'Oh, Daddy, that looks sore,' Willow commented.

Izzy was very quiet. She was assessing the situation. She spoke intensely with Richard about the card she'd made him. He was over-excited. He got up from the bed and I dashed to grab the drip and follow him.

He took the bag from me. 'I'm fine. I'm fine.' He was going to the loo. He hadn't managed to go to the loo unaided before this. I always stood behind him to stop him from losing his balance. But I understood that in front of the girls he would hate me to go with him. My mouth was dry as he shuffled into the bathroom. Before he was halfway through, he fell forward and saved himself by grabbing the light pull with one hand, and the emergency cord with the other. Two nurses appeared like a shot, and helped me to rescue him. We brought him back to the bed where he sat, grinning sheepishly. Izzy was very subdued. She tried to talk to him about home and the games she'd been playing, but he wasn't able to concentrate. He was nodding but his eyes were heavy. The fall had exhausted him.

'Time to say goodbye,' I whispered to them.

Willow gave Richard a kiss.

'Bye bye, Daddy.'

Izzy's eyes really started to fill. I looked at her with an encouraging smile and a nod, and mouthed, 'Say goodbye.'

'Bye, Daddy.' Her voice was breaking, but he was half-asleep, and didn't notice.

'Bye bye, darling,' he said. His eyes shut, and I took Willow's hand, and lifted Izzy on to my hip. We walked out as quickly as we could to the waiting Ela. She picked up Willow as Izzy exploded into uncontrollable sobs and I hugged her to me, heading for the exit.

'Well done, Iz. Well done, baby. You did real good. You're a very, very brave girl. I'm proud of you.'

Poor Izzy. Daddy really wasn't Daddy, and if ever there was a little girl who worshipped her father it was this one. But she was also very clever and very trusting. I put her down and knelt in front of her.

'Iz, he will get better. OK? He will, he's just tired.'

She nodded, and wiped her tears on the back of her hand.

'OK, Mummy.' But I'm not sure she believed me.

'Hey! You've got a party to go to.'

Nick was waiting at the door with Amanda, who by now was cuddling Willow. They'd left their own girls back at the hotel with Richard's parents.

'Aren't you coming, Mummy?' Izzy was pleading.

'Well, I need to be here for Daddy.'

'Oh please, Mummy, please!'

'OK, I'll come a bit later. I'll come then.'

'Will you put us to bed? Will you be there for bedtime?'

'Yes, OK. I promise.'

It was really difficult, watching them walk away down the corridor to the lifts, but I knew Ela would look after them, and Nick and Amanda had really made a fantastic effort with the party.

I wasn't quite sure how I'd manage to get away later, as Richard really hated to be left on his own, but it was important to the girls and I'd promised. I couldn't let them down. Besides, I needed to see them. No, I *ached* to see them, to smell them, to play with them, to be their mummy again.

Richard was exhausted. When I checked on him he was very deeply asleep. It was one of those rare opportunities to get away for a few minutes. Straight away, I wished I'd gone downstairs with the girls, but then that would've drawn attention to them, and so far they'd avoided being recognised.

I wrote a note and taped it to the TV screen in front of Richard.

*Gone for coffee. Back in 15 mins. Love you lots. Mindy x*

Seeing the girls had really knocked the wind out of me. I'd been so caught up with looking after Richard and everything at the hospital; even though I'd just comforted myself by talking to Ela regularly, and the kids every morning and evening, it wasn't the same. Seeing them was heartbreaking.

I slumped against the wall of the huge metal lift as I went down to the ground floor.

Instead of grabbing a bottle of water or Coke

from the shop, I bought a coffee from the snack bar and sat down with my phone and a pen and pad in a quiet corner. Maybe I could make a couple of calls while I was there. I was just dialling a number when a plain, slim woman in her twenties with short, dark hair tapped me on the shoulder.

I looked at her quizzically.

'Excuse me, are you Mrs Hammond?'

'Yes, I am. Who are you?'

'I'm afraid I'm from the press.'

I couldn't believe it. The one time I had snatched a few moments for myself. To stop running around, to just be still for a moment and gather my thoughts.

'I'm sorry, I can't talk to you now.'

I scooped up my possessions, left the coffee on the table and half walked, half ran towards the safety of the lifts, but as I went I glanced around me, and suddenly realised how unusually full the reception area was. There were an awful lot of people sitting around with cups of coffee and by the time I reached the lifts, I understood why. The hospital was full of journalists.

I hurried back upstairs without my coffee, and went to the payphone near the lifts to call a few people before returning to the ward.

The old lady was going for a walk with one of the nurses. She'd stopped calling her cat, and the nurse was encouraging her to talk to people. But it transpired she wasn't keen to talk to women, although she was more than happy to grin and flirt with men. She was so lovely, but she'd obviously been trying to take her stitches out as she was wearing what looked like a pair of socks on her hands. I smiled at her as I passed, and she returned a weak smile. I'll never forget her face. She had one of those faces you'd just love for ever. I wondered where her family was, if she had visitors; if there were people at home who loved this dear, sweet soul. As I passed her, I whispered out loud, 'God bless you.' I don't do that sort of thing normally, but I really truly meant it. I hope she's OK, I hope she went home.

When I walked into Richard's room he was just waking. His head was aching, and I went back outside to ask the nurses if he could have more painkillers. They'd ask him, 'Morphine or Paracetamol?' He was very good at avoiding the morphine, but as one of the nurses told him: 'There's no point in being brave. You don't need to be in pain. If it's bad, you can have the morphine, OK?'

He asked for it straight away. She'd quickly learned how he worked. Richard's tough, to the very core, and sometimes it takes a voice of authority to break through. But he'd listened to her and accepted the help offered.

After he'd taken the pill, he looked about him, suddenly unnerved.

'Where are the girls? Where have they gone? They were here, weren't they? I didn't dream it?'

'No, you didn't dream it. There were here. They've gone back to the hotel.'

'Oh, can we go there? Let's go and see them.' He made to get out of bed.

'Oh you can't, darling, you have to stay here. Remember? You're in hospital. You had an accident.'

'Yes, but I'm fine. Come on. We'll sneak out.

No one will know.'

He threw his legs over the side of the bed and I leapt across and grabbed the drip bag before he pulled it out of him.

'Where are my clothes?'

'You haven't got any. You have to stay here, darling. Shall I see what's on TV?'

'Oh yeah, OK.'

He turned his head and relaxed a little. I put the drip bag back on its pole, and hurried to get the TV on.

Thirty seconds later:

Richard, sitting up and looking about the room: 'Where are the girls?'

Me: 'Oh, they had to go back to the hotel. But they're fine.'

Richard, horror stricken: 'Who's with them?'

Me: 'Ela's with them. It's OK, they're fine.'

Richard: 'Oh. Why don't we go and see them?'

Me: 'Darling, you have to stay here. You had an accident and you're still a bit wobbly.'

Richard: 'No one'll know. C'mon!'

He started to get up again, and I dashed round the bed to grab the drip.

Me: 'Darling, you really have to stay here. Shall I get a cup of tea?'

Richard: 'Mmmm? Yes. That'd be nice. Then we'll go and see the girls, shall we? I love my girls.'

Me: 'I know you do, and they love you too, darling. Shall I get the tea now?'

Richard, looking about him absent-mindedly: 'Yeah, OK.'

I was nervous about leaving him, and rushed to the tea urn. When I got back a few minutes later,

I couldn't believe what I saw: he'd found another mobile phone in his bag and was dismantling mine and putting the SIM card into the spare phone. I tried to act calmly as I put the two cups of tea down on the table next to his bed.

Me: 'What are you doing?'

Richard: 'My phone doesn't work so I'm just swapping the SIM card into this one.'

Me: 'Actually, I think that's my phone.'

Richard: 'No, I'm sure it's mine.'

He put his SIM card into the other phone and turned it on.

Richard: 'That's funny. Oh God, I think it is yours. Sorry, darling. Where's mine then?'

He started searching through his bag. I felt dreadful. I am probably the world's worst liar, and I'd taken his phone and put it in the safe. The doctors had impressed upon me that he shouldn't be making calls and he particularly wasn't allowed to even think about anything work-related. That was difficult. The majority of Richard's friends were also somehow involved in the industry, if not with *Top Gear,* then elsewhere. This was compounded by another problem. A great many journalists had Richard's mobile number, and he'd be only too happy to chat away with them, which could prove a bit tricky.

Me: 'Richard, you know you're not supposed to even turn the phone on in here, don't you? It messes with the monitors.'

Richard: 'Really? Oh, OK. You'd better turn yours off then.'

He handed my phone back to me and I reassembled it and replaced the SIM card.

He spied his tea and looked weary. His eyelids were heavy. His brow was knotted; headache again. The headache, he told me, didn't really ever leave, it was always there in varying degrees of severity. He looked miserable. He turned to me.

Richard: 'Can we go now?'

Me: 'What do you mean?'

Richard: 'Can we go home now?'

Me: 'No, darling, not yet. Not for a bit.'

Richard: 'Come on, let's just go, they won't mind.'

Me: 'Richard . . .' I sat on the bed in front of him and looked him straight in the eyes. 'You've had an accident. You banged your head and you absolutely have to stay here until you're better.'

Richard: 'Yes, yes. Now, let's go.'

I was debating what to say next when, fortunately, two nurses walked in. I explained to them that he wanted to leave. All of the nurses knew I needed to get away to see the girls and at this rate there was no way I'd be able to leave him for fear he'd try to escape. They explained to him that he had to stay there, and for some reason he was more inclined to believe them.

The nurses asked him if he was in pain and he was honest and asked for morphine. He really looked pretty dreadful. His whole demeanour was somehow deflated, and I suspected it was a mixture of fatigue and confusion. He clearly wasn't convinced he'd had an accident and seeing the girls had awakened all sorts of emotions. The nurses were concerned he hadn't been drinking enough water, and he'd eaten barely a thing. His drip was almost empty, and they decided to replace it to keep him going a while.

Shortly after they left the room, he asked me, 'Shall we have a cup of tea, then?'

'OK.' I left the room with two empty cups. His memory was so awful he'd eat breakfast and immediately after finishing the last spoonful of cereal he'd ask, 'Shall we have breakfast now?'

I didn't question him or correct him. To do either would be counterproductive. He had just emerged from an unconscious state. He was suffering post-traumatic amnesia. He was also, at this stage clinically confused. I wouldn't have dreamt of making life any more complicated. I went to fetch the tea, and when I walked back into his room, Richard had fallen asleep. Deeply asleep.

I poured the teas down the sink and wrote him a new note.

*Gone to put the girls to bed. Back soon. Love you, M x*

I sneaked out of the room and stopped at the nurses' station before leaving the ward. I explained I was going back to the hotel, but would return before 8 p.m. They assured me I shouldn't worry. He was very tired and they didn't expect him to wake.

I sped across Leeds in a cab to the hotel and I was so thrilled to walk into a roomful of happy children. Andy, Andrea, Nick and Amanda, together with Richard's parents, had gone to great lengths to make a really special birthday party for Izzy. But although I gave the girls huge hugs and kisses and treasured each moment with them, my mind was constantly drifting back to that bed in the hospital. Knowing how quickly Richard would become distressed if I wasn't there when he woke, I was suppressing a rising sense of urgency. Although smiling and chatting with everyone, inside the seed of panic had been planted and was steadily growing.

The girls had been so very wonderful. But Willow was just three and very, very tired. Ela and I took Izzy and Willow to the room. I'd been so worried about Richard I was considering saying goodnight to them and dashing back to the hospital. But they begged me to stay and put them to bed. They hadn't seen me for two days, which was a first for them, and although they had Ela, who was familiar and kept all the normal routines going, I felt overwhelmed by their love and desperately sorry to watch them having to cope, even though they were coping so well. I was proud of them. Of their resilience and their trust in me.

As I tucked them in, Izzy told me:

'I knew you'd come, Mummy. You said you would.'

I was so happy to hear those words. It's sort of my code of conduct. If I make a promise to the girls, I always keep it.

I gave her a huge hug, and felt her tears on my shoulder. She didn't want Willow to know how upset she was, and I held her there for a little while. I whispered to her:

'Are we OK now, baby?'

She nodded.

'Well done, darling. You're a very brave girl. I'm proud of you.'

She nodded again, and wiped her nose on her sleeve.

'Eew! Goopy sleeves!!' I pretended to be revolted and jumped off her bed—they both giggled.

I went over to Willow's bed.

'Mummy, where are you sleeping?' No flies on Willow!

'Oh, I'm going to go back to keep Daddy company.'

'At hospital?'

'Don't worry. I've got a bed to put together in the room.'

Willow was cross.

'But, Mummy, we won't see you!'

'Yes, you will.'

Now she became tearful.

'No, 'cos you'll be there and we're here, so we won't.'

I made a deal with them.

'You two are going to sleep now and you don't see me while you're asleep anyway. I promise I'll be back in the morning in time for breakfast, and we'll all have breakfast together. How about that?'

'Yeah! Yeah!'

'But you have to stay asleep all night and be good for Ela. OK?'

They agreed. I kissed them both, had a quick chat with Ela, filled in the breakfast cards, put them on the door handle, and headed out of the hotel. I'd phoned for a taxi before bathing the kids, and knew it was waiting.

Leeds was very busy and the journey took longer than normal. I was really starting to panic.

I didn't bother about going to the back entrance of the hospital—it would take too long.

We drove up to the front doors and I ran for it.

By the time I reached the familiar corridor which led to Richard's room, I was quite out of breath, but when I opened his door all my worries disappeared. He was just stirring.

The nurses came in and woke him for the usual tests and questions. He gave me some affectionate smiles and when the nurses left the room we snuggled up on the bed and chatted for a while. By that time we were both tired. I helped him to the loo; by now he had become quite accustomed to my help and wasn't embarrassed at all. In fact, we could even make jokes about it. He still had a hard time believing it was his bathroom next door. Convinced he was in a hotel, he would say:

'Don't go in there. It's someone else's room!'

His perception of time was completely bizarre too. After brushing his teeth and getting back into bed, he thought for a few moments and said:

'What're we having for lunch?'

I'd grown used to his strange questions, so I simply told him we'd had lunch, and tea, and now it was bedtime.

'Really? Oh. OK.' He was very sleepy, and by the time I'd returned to the room after brushing my teeth, he was fast asleep.

I dragged the mattress in from the bathroom and laid it on the floor beside his bed. The nurses had kindly left a neatly folded pile of bedding and a pillow for me.

It was about 9 p.m., and after switching off the lights I climbed into my bed and was soon asleep.

I woke to a most strange sensation. The hair near my ear felt uncomfortable. I rubbed it with my hand. It was sort of wet and a bit sticky. Still half awake, I was trying to work out what it was when something landed plop! on my head. I rubbed it with my other hand and opened my eyes. As I focused in the dim glow of the nightlight, I noticed Richard's head over my side of the bed, his mouth against the safety rail (I always made sure both rails were up while he was asleep), and drool slowly leaving his mouth, trickling over the bar then dripping off and landing on me.

'Ooh. That's nice,' I remember thinking. It did make me smile though as I went to the bathroom to wash off my damp hair and soggy ear. As I walked back into the room, I remember looking at him asleep and thinking, 'God, I love this man.' And in one of those brief, desperate moments, I whispered, 'Please God, help him.'

I kissed his forehead and eased him away from the bars. I checked that his drip was still OK and made sure his arm couldn't get tangled up in the tube, kissed him again on the cheek, and watched a smile flicker across his face. Then I went back to my mattress. I knew I couldn't sleep too long. I needed to wake by five to get back to the hotel for the girls.

* * *

I tiptoed out of Richard's room at about 5.30 a.m. and told the nurses I was having breakfast with the girls and would (hopefully) be back before he woke up. They knew I had my mobile on me if there was an emergency.

I called a taxi from just outside the ward and

didn't have long to wait before he arrived at the front of the building.

At the other end I dashed into the hotel, having sent a text to Ela to check they were awake. I'd ordered the breakfasts for 7 a.m. so we could have some time together.

We had a wonderful morning. To the girls this was more like an adventure. They'd stayed away from home, been to a party, and were having breakfast in their room. We tried not to talk about how poorly Daddy was, just how soon he'd get better and come home. Like most children, they're accustomed to time frames, and were very persistent with their questions about Daddy's going-home date. I had to be vague. Nobody knew how long it would take, and I couldn't lie to them.

We were very silly and jolly during their breakfast and Ela and I had a lovely chat. I couldn't thank her enough. She'd be returning home with the girls later that morning and we both knew it would be awfully difficult for them.

My phone rang. It was the hospital. Richard had called the nurse to ask where I was.

'He's a little agitated, so I thought I'd give you a call.'

'That's fine. I'm on my way. Tell him I'll be there in twenty minutes.'

The girls looked crestfallen.

'Oh, Mummy. You don't have to go again. Stay here with us. Please, Mummy. Please.'

Izzy was holding my arm and pulling me towards her on the sofa. 'I won't let you go. I won't.' She hugged my arm as I sat next to her. This was so unlike Izzy. She was usually quite independent, but this experience was unnerving her.

'Listen, Poppet, I need to go back and see Daddy because he's really not very well, and if I can help him to get better he can come home again, and that'd be good, wouldn't it?'

She gave a deep sigh, and the tears started.

'But I miss you, Mummy.'

'Oh, I miss you too, baby. So much.' I gave her a big cuddle, and Willow ran over and joined in.

Holding them both to me was wonderful and dreadful at the same time. We love our girls so much, and leaving them was just the most heart-wrenching experience, particularly when I knew they needed me. But this time Richard needed me more, and I explained to them very honestly why I had to stay at the hospital, and why they were needed at home—to look after the animals, and make sure everything was ready for when Daddy came home. They sort of accepted this, and Willow began chatting about everything she'd do when she arrived home, but Izzy was quite reserved. Her thumb in her mouth, she simply nodded in agreement.

I had to leave. Time was ticking by and reception called to say the car was waiting for me. I told the girls to hurry and get dressed and they could come to the hospital and say goodbye to Daddy before they started their journey home.

I was all smiles and hugs as I left them. But once in the car I cried till I was halfway to the hospital.

* * *

Richard was sitting up in bed when I arrived with a cup of tea. He was very pleased to see me. His face lit up. He was so excited about the girls coming to see him, but he tired easily and was soon dozing again.

The girls came later with Ela.

Willow held Richard's hand and looked earnestly into his eyes. She told him, very seriously, that he wasn't allowed to come home until his eye was better. OK?

Izzy was desperately upset but very brave. She smiled at him and then hid behind me. When we left his room, she burst into tears in the corridor. I carried her to the visitors' room and once again told her how marvellous she'd been. Ela followed us with Willow, and when the two girls met up with each other, they stood silently and cuddled. They're so very close, and each so supportive of the other. When they stepped apart, they both put on their bravest faces.

I was so overwhelmed by them. They behaved amazingly, careful to remember everything I'd told them, right till the end.

We went down to the waiting car and Ela and I helped them into their seats. It was hard to let them go. With all my heart I wanted to go home with them, bath them, lie on the floor and make up a silly bedtime story, all three of us on our backs with our feet in the air. Tucking Willow in, I'd ask her, 'What will you dream about?'

'Horses and ponies and everything.'

Then back to Izzy's room and try to end the long conversation by reminding her of the time, and checking none of the cats are hiding under her bed before closing the door.

My last words to each of them as I leave their rooms are always, 'I love you.' And when they respond with, 'I love you too, Mummy,' it never fails to tug at my heart.

I missed them so very much. Still, I couldn't let them see me upset, so we chatted about how they must look after the animals and thank our neighbours, Anne and Syd, who'd been back and forth at home to make sure everything was OK.

I promised them that, as soon as I could come home, I would, and we'd talk all the time. I hugged and kissed them both, and Ela, who was looking after them so well. I told her to take them somewhere on the way home—wherever they wanted to go, to eat whatever they liked. I'd been to the cashpoint in the hospital and handed her an envelope full of cash. I had no idea when I'd be back, and she needed to buy food and supplies.

The second she saw the amount of money, she knew I wasn't planning on being home soon.

'Oh, Mindy, you're so brave,' she said to me as she hugged me goodbye.

'Oh bollocks!' I whispered, but I hugged her close and swallowed my tears.

As the car doors closed, I remember smiling at them and saying, 'Be good for Ela, won't you? Make sure she remembers everything! Look after her. I love you.'

I stood and watched the car drive away until it disappeared. I wanted to drop to my knees and wail, but I knew by now Richard would be very fretful, and I had to get back to him. I took a deep breath. Straightened my back and breathed out slowly. Then I began the journey back to the ward. But I didn't run, I took my time. I needed some time.

## CHAPTER 11

# A WAITING GAME

For the rest of the day, apart from Richard's brothers saying their farewells, I was the only visitor. He relaxed and slept most of the time. Whenever he woke, he asked the same questions every five minutes.

'Where are the children?' He'd no memory of them leaving.

'Where do we go tomorrow?' He was convinced we were in a hotel.

'When are you meeting up with the others?'

He thought there was some kind of party going on, which was understandable, as it was pretty unusual for his entire family to be present at the same time unless it was a special occasion.

Other questons which quickly followed:

Where are my clothes? I have to get dressed. What time do we need to get to the restaurant (back to the hotel scenario)?

Then I'd explain (several times) that this wasn't a hotel, it was a hospital; there was no party; he couldn't get dressed because he had only pyjamas to wear; and no one was meeting at a restaurant. Eventually, he would accept what I'd told him, only to become animated again a few moments later.

Where's Nick? Where's Andy? Where's Mum and Dad? Where's James? Where's Jezza? Where's Wilman? I need to speak to the *Mirror*, my agent . . . When are we filming? What car did you come in?

The problem was, no sooner had you answered one question than it would be followed by another, then seconds later the first question would be asked again. It was quite exhausting, and sometimes very difficult.

The worse one was, 'Where are my clothes?'

He'd start looking around the room and I'd explain that his clothes were cut off him at the scene of the accident, so he didn't have any.

'Are you sure? Have you looked?' was his standard reply.

Once I'd satisfied his questioning on that one, his next move would be to grab his bag, or ask me to hand it to him. He'd start foraging through it, and I knew what for. It was the same every time:

I really want to go for a beer and a fag. Let's just go outside and find a local restaurant/stare at the sea/sit by a stream and have a drink and a fag.

When the sister appeared to check his blood pressure, I grabbed her and asked that she explain to Richard why he couldn't have a drink and a cigarette.

'The hospital is absolutely no smoking—anywhere on the grounds. And if you drank alcohol now you'd be at risk to fits and seizures. It's too dangerous.'

After she left the room, I spoke with him about why he was there.

'D'you know why you're here?'

'No, not really.'

'You had a crash, darling.'

'You keep saying that.'

'You still don't believe me, do you?'

'No, not really.'

'Do you remember the jet car?'

'Shit. I didn't crash that, did I? Oh God. I bet they're cross. Did I break it?'

He was half-joking, but there was a faint tone of belief in his voice I hadn't heard before, I knew I had to try and fish a little more out of him, but it was a scary moment. Up to this point I'd cared for him, watched and loved him and just concentrated on the practicalities. His memory of the crash hadn't seemed important. But sitting beside him on the bed, his eyes wide, tentatively seeking more information, I felt the time had arrived. But what to do? In a couple of seconds I considered the options. Should I tell him, yet again, my version of what had happened? No. He'd heard it before, and although his memory was practically non-existent, it hadn't worked before so why would it work now? The TV? I could turn on the news and he could watch it on TV. No—too dramatic. Get one of the nurses to come and tell him? No. By the time I interrupted one of them, explained and brought them to him, he would've lost interest.

Then it came to me. The newspapers. More particularly, Jeremy's piece in the previous day's edition of the *Sun*. He'd believe that, I was sure. It was written by Jezza, and there was a picture of the jet car, and him with TG.

I wasn't sure if it was the right thing to do. I had no one to consult, and must admit I was really worried that he might react badly, but at some point he'd have to digest it, and at least we were in a controlled environment.

I reached down behind the curtain and

retrieved the newspaper. He sat propped up in bed, one knee bent under the covers.

As I held the folded paper in my hand, our eyes met and held. I faltered.

'Are you sure you're ready for this?'

Why was I asking him? He had no idea whether he was ready. He'd absolutely no idea what had happened, and there he sat, blissfully unaware. Maybe this was cruel? Was it better he didn't know? No, of course not; it couldn't be. He trusted me. I promised him I'd only tell the truth. This was the truth.

'It's a bloody big deal, Richard.' I knew my eyes were filling as I looked at his face. His arm reached out to take the paper from me. His expression had changed. Suddenly he looked quite serious, and as he laid the paper on the bed, he was taken aback by the front-page headline.

*Hamster walks . . . and I watched, says Clarkson.*

'Fuck me! On the front page?!'

I'm not sure whether he was trying to make light of it, make me smile, or simply not digesting what he read. I felt like a jailer delivering his sentence.

I watched as he read. I knew the article well, and was feeling every emotion with him as he went through the text.

When he opened the paper to the double-page spread, his eyebrows lifted. He was really surprised. There was a picture of the jet car, and a huge picture of him and Top Gear Dog.

Before he read any further he looked at me, panic stricken.

'TG! Shit! Where's TG?'

'It's OK. She's at home. You sent her home the night before.'

'Oh. Oh yeah. Oh, thank God. So she's OK?'

'Yes. She's fine.'

'Who's looking after her and the other dogs?'

'Ela. Ela's at home.'

'Oh yes, with the girls.' He smiled. 'I love my girls. When can we go home? I wish we were home now. Can't we just go?'

His attention had been broken.

'No, darling, you're in hospital and you have to stay here for a bit.'

'No, I can't. We've got to get ready. What time do we need to be at the restaurant?'

'We're not going to a restaurant, we're eating here.'

'But the others'll be waiting.'

He was getting out of bed. I dashed over and grabbed the drip bag before it pulled out of his arm.

'Where are my clothes?'

He was reaching for his Billingham bag, becoming quite determined.

'Give me my bag.'

I knew we were about to get into the cigarette conversation yet again. I was trying to scramble across the bed with the drip bag before he stretched the tube any further. All the while my brain was desperately trying to come up with a change of subject.

But he was racing ahead of me as he foraged through the pockets of his bag again.

'Where are my fags? I really fancy a beer and a fag. Let's just go to a restaurant and have a beer and a fag.'

He was still looking. I was still holding the drip bag.

'Someone must have a fag. C'mon, let's go to the bar.'

Oh bugger! He was up and heading unsteadily for the door. I was close behind him.

'Richard, there's just a hospital corridor out there.' I spoke as gently and calmly as I could.

'No, there isn't. This is a hotel.' He looked at me as if I was some kind of fool. 'Let's nip out and ask Nick for a fag. Or Jezza. Who's next door?'

I wasn't going to stop him. What was the point? I hated trying to dissuade him all the time. He simply didn't understand why he couldn't join the party he firmly believed was going on without him.

It was heartbreaking to watch him stumble the few steps to the door, intent on joining the others. In his mind, he was convinced he was ready to meet them and have a good time.

He opened the door and stopped dead in his tracks, the conviction of what lay beyond that door lost in an instant.

He looked, recoiled, and retreated backward. A glimpse through the door revealed instantly the bustle of the ward; nurses rushing back and forth past his door; buzzers sounding, and patients wandering past wheeling their drips.

I caught him and helped him to sit back on the side of the bed.

It was so cruel. I hooked the drip bag back on the holder and knelt in front of him as he sat and stared at the door.

Quietly, he said, 'Shit.'

I held his hands and kissed them. 'I'm sorry.

I'm so sorry. It really is a hospital, you see?'

He nodded, but looked so very upset. I stood and hugged him. Not the way you'd normally hug your husband. Not a romantic embrace. I held his head to my heart and kissed him through his hair. Wiping the tears so he wouldn't feel them drop. Feeling so desperately, hopelessly sorry for him, and so very sad. He was lost and I didn't know how to help him to find his way back. Perhaps he never would.

He tugged at the newspaper he'd sat on. It was still lying opened to Jezza's piece about the crash. He turned and looked at the article.

'Bloody hell!'

It was a big surprise all over again, and I was grateful for the distraction. He turned, the experience at the door instantly forgotten, and started to read.

For most of that day, the newspaper remained open on the bed. He read about the crash over and over. And each time the news came as a surprise.

Eventually, when he took a nap, I removed the very crumpled and weary newspaper, closed the pages, and stored it back in its resting place behind the curtains. He'd glimpsed a piece of evidence; whether anything would stick in his confused mind, I didn't know, but enough was enough.

That evening poor Alex scoured the streets of Leeds for our dinner. A local restaurateur, hearing of Richard's love of spaghetti Bolognese, sent over a feast for him. It was incredible, and a meal Richard would've devoured under normal circumstances. But that evening he was too tired to eat. He had a couple of mouthfuls, and pushed the plate aside.

We had some wonderful chats that night. We didn't talk about where everyone was, whether he was in a hotel, or any of the usual concerns.

Several times, Richard asked me where TG was, which I found really encouraging. Clearly, somewhere in his mind, perhaps just seeing the picture in the newspaper, he had connected with a small piece of new memory.

He wanted to talk, and he kept apologising for being a prat.

I told him nothing mattered. He was alive and would get better and that was all I cared about.

He didn't want me to sleep on the floor any more. He wanted me to lie with him. It was so wonderful to be 'us'. I had been so frightened. There are so very many people who've been through a similar experience, who've sat by and watched as the person they love claws their way back to a life teetering on the brink of extinction. You watch and pray for the sparks of recognition, a flash of memory to bring the pieces back together so that what used to be can be rekindled, but there's no guarantee. No recipe for success. Just a passionate hope, a gentle, controlled yearning. We were lucky. We were strong before the accident, and in that amazing place in Leeds, that tiny room with boxes of cards and gifts strewn around us, pictures of cars drawn by children wishing 'The Hamster' better, emails and letters from all over the world from well-wishers aged six to ninety-six, we fell in love all over again. My Richard remembered me. Remembered our love, and came back running, as though embracing a lost emotion he'd been seeking for too long.

We were passionate and desperate for each other. Nothing else mattered. No one else existed.

We held each other all night, like our first time together. It was the start of the rest of our lives. He loved me without explanation, without doubt. I hadn't once mentioned or inquired how he felt about me. I'd felt he should make the discovery himself. Apart from explaining who I was and my feelings for him, there was never any reference to our relationship or life together. I knew it could disappear. I knew it was quite possible he'd dismiss his life prior to the accident and wipe away all knowledge of our past. He could choose to love me or not. I wouldn't have wanted to influence his emotions in any way. Rather I faced a life without him, than a life with him based on a lie.

Thankfully—and I am forever grateful—he fell in love with me all over again. Stronger, deeper, fuller. I knew then, whatever the future held, it embraced us together; we were one again.

I became an odd sight, padding up and down the HDU corridor in my nightie, back and forth to the tea machine.

The nurses all knew that I was sharing Richard's bed, but no one minded. They never commented or took any notice of me if I tried to apologise. All they cared about was the well-being of their patients. If having his wife with him made Richard feel better, then why not? We didn't need any more than his bed, and perhaps the odd extra cup of tea. I'm not sure whether we were unusual but I would imagine not. Anyone in my position would want to be with their husband, to help him with every fibre of their being, every ounce of strength.

I slept little, but was constantly able to untangle his drip, chase him to the loo with the drip bag when he forgot it was attached to his wrist, catch him before he stumbled through the loo door, and propping him up from behind as he took a pee; both of us always half asleep.

He'd changed from the private, slightly self-conscious man who hated me helping him to a smiling, affectionate husband who appreciated my help, enjoyed my presence, loved my love.

* * *

When the nurse from Occupational Therapy came to visit Richard, she told us about post-traumatic amnesia, explaining the reasons for the daily questions by nurses to gauge whether Richard's memory was returning. Essentially, we were playing a waiting game. There were no set timescales for anything. Every brain injury is unique. Every patient dictates their own recovery time, and her job was to help Richard through the next phase and towards recovery. To remain positive was everything, so she was careful not to voice what both she and I knew—there was no way of saying how well he would do; how much recovery would be achieved. The signs were good. He'd made amazing progress thus far, but brains are more complex than any of us truly understand. There are medical explanations for so many functions and results, but talking with the neurosurgeons and others dealing with brain injury, it quickly becomes apparent that the complexity, and to some degree, mystery of the brain is phenomenal, and very frightening. No one can tell you if or when your loved one will recover, or to what degree, but everyone without exception in that amazing environment would try their very utmost to achieve the best possible result. Not just for Richard, but for everyone in their care. There's a feeling of solidarity and hope when the brain injury coordinator enters the room. She's seen it all before many times, with many different outcomes, but her approach is firm and positive, like a sergeant major rousing the troops ready for battle—except this sergeant major sits next to her team, smiles, exudes warmth and caring and a wicked sense of humour. Her battle plan is clear, her passion to succeed unfaltering. To make it all better again is her raison d'être.

* * *

In the outside world, a storm was brewing over the future of *Top Gear,* with arguments for and against the series being cancelled. James and Jeremy, together with Andy Wilman, were adamant that the series was over if Richard wasn't able to return. In the media, some were vehemently opposed to the continuation of the show, accusing the BBC of being irresponsible and dangerous, and 'going too far'.

Richard himself was starting to ask about the show. He was eager to get back to work; concerned they'd have to start filming for the next series.

Reports in the newspapers that Richard had been trying to set a land speed record were untrue, but I guess it was an understandable assumption, if not the most positive spin. Jeremy was spending a great deal of time and effort defending the programme, emphasising the significance of keeping Richard's job waiting for him.

Imagine. You're critically injured. You've suffered brain-damage. You're fighting back to resume your life . . . only to discover your first day back at work isn't there for you any more, and it's your fault. You nearly died, you heroically fought your way back towards that huge goal—the first day back—and it doesn't matter, because no one's going to make the programme any more, and the job you loved, the programme you loved from childhood, has been abolished. And it's your fault. You killed it, because it didn't kill you. Had that been the outcome, had *Top Gear* been taken off air, I'm sure Richard's recovery would have been seriously affected. He would've felt guilty and miserable, and I daren't even imagine the depths to which his depression could've taken him.

*Top Gear* may seem a little gung-ho and dangerous, but it's very carefully put together, and the group of people who run around like headless chickens in the production office and obey ridiculous commands from Andy Wilman are some of the hardest-working people I've ever known. They're also intensely proud of the end product. Jeremy, James and Richard are mates; Andy Wilman refers to them as a band (himself included ). When Richard was in intensive care, with James, Jeremy, Nick and Andy around him, I remember Andy turning away from the bed where Richard lay motionless.

'C'mon, mate,' he said in a broken voice. 'We can't go on without the drummer.'

* * *

Richard's balance was slowly improving. He could walk the few steps around his bed unaided while keeping his hand on the rail for support, and could manage a trip to the loo if he remembered to lean one hand against the wall.

It was a complete joy to watch him take these small steps towards independence; sensing his frustration, and then pride at each small victory. But with strength came renewed determination. He was going completely stir crazy. He'd even resorted to watching a little television—a very rare occupation under normal circumstances.

I remember one night watching *Who Wants to Be a Millionaire?* with him. The whole way through, he was answering the questions with great enthusiasm. I was astounded that his interest was held so long. He hated quiz shows, would never dream of watching one normally, and yet he was completely absorbed.

Then it came to me. He was exercising his brain and, to his great delight, it was working and working well. He tired quickly, though. Immediately the show was over, he made ready for sleep. I raised the bars on either side of the bed, as was my habit, just in case one of us fell out, cuddled up to him, and thanked God he was moving forward.

The flowers continued to arrive in overwhelming numbers. Only a few could fit into Richard's room, in particular a bouquet of lilies from The Polar Challenge, which were beautiful, but very heavily scented. Unfortunately they made Richard sneeze—which was probably one of the most painful experiences for him post-crash—he'd hold his head and beg for painkillers. It was incredibly frightening, and heralded the end of flowers in his room.

All the flowers were gathered together in rooms downstairs in the bowels of the hospital, as I'd previously requested. I visited them with Richard's mum. It was a deeply moving experience. I still have the cards from each one. The messages were so sincere, so supportive. I took Polaroid photographs of them, as I knew Richard wouldn't be able to get there to see them himself, but it's an image I will never forget, and the goodwill contained in those cards was incredible. There were balloons and soft toys, too; a great many from children. Richard had always said he was just a bloke on a car show. He was. He is. But the love and hope contained in those messages were for a bloke on a car show who was held in deep affection by a great many people. I couldn't read many of the cards. I'd start to cry, and I couldn't do that; I needed to be strong and return upstairs. But it was one of those injections of love that really help you to carry on. There were huge bouquets; small posies; multi-coloured balloons; expensive, exotic flowers; simple bunches of wildflowers; planted arrangements; some in vases, some laid on the floor. There were so many they covered desks, chairs—everywhere. Their scent and colours overwhelmed the senses.

I was unsure what we should do with them. It was so hot in the room, and the ladies who had organised them so beautifully about their offices had an awful lot to water.

Richard's mum had a wonderful idea. She asked one of the women: 'Do you have an old people's ward?'

'Yes, of course.'

'What d'you think, Mind? Shall we send them there?'

'Oh yes, that's a fantastic idea.'

Richard's mum works as a fund-raising consultant for a broad range of charities, and knows from first-hand experience how distressing hospitalisation can be for many elderly people. Often it was made harder to bear by the absence of gifts and flowers. No one wants to be in hospital, but at least we could help improve the atmosphere a little by sharing Richard's good fortune.

A small army of porters descended upon the rooms where the flowers were being stored and set off with trolleys piled high. They were a glorious sight. Flowers went to as many departments as possible. Starting with the geriatric ward.

It was a heart-warming spectacle. Wonderful to know, if you were one of those incredibly generous and thoughtful people who sent flowers to the little bloke from the car show: not only did you make a difference to his recovery, you also helped so many others who appreciated the sentiment just as much.

I heard from one of the matrons that the elderly

patients were completely overwhelmed by the flowers when they arrived, and they brought smiles of appreciation throughout the hospital.

* * *

Richard's escape plans became even more complex. One night I found him trying to unhinge the bathroom window, determined to get to a pub or shop to buy his beloved Marly Lights.

I know it's cruel, but there was only one sure-fire way to stop him: I hid his pyjama bottoms while he was asleep. Even in his confused state, he wouldn't venture out naked from the waist down.

After showering the following morning, he began searching for fresh pyjamas. I could feel my face redden—I am useless at lying. He found the freshly laundered jacket, calmly buttoned it, then began looking about the room for the trousers.

'Oh, that's funny. No kecks!'

I knew I was puce! I shuffled into the bathroom so he couldn't see my face, and quickly jumped into the shower.

'Oh!' I called nonchalantly. 'Maybe they forgot.'

I winced as I said it, and thought what an evil woman I must be.

I awaited his response, but there was none. He'd climbed back into bed and was calmly looking at the kids' drawings.

When I left the room to fetch cups of tea, I explained to the nurses what I'd done. They smiled and completely understood.

Andy Wilman had contacted the F1 neuro-doctor, Professor Syd Watkins. A wonderfully supportive and informative man, it was Syd who'd designed the helmet that Richard had worn in the jet car. Undoubtedly it had saved his life. He'd also dealt with precisely the same injuries Richard had sustained many times before with Formula One drivers. He was on holiday in Scotland, but had given Andy both his home and mobile numbers and suggested I call him if I had the opportunity.

I had never met him or even spoken to Syd before, but by reputation I knew he was the best of the best. When we eventually spoke he was so matter-of-fact, so reassuring. After asking me a handful of questions, he calmly told me the future looked bright. Richard was doing very well. He was convinced he'd make a full recovery. He also told me that many patients in these situations think only of one thing: . . . escape and getting home. He recalled one man who'd managed to escape from his room. And the hospital. Syd inquired whether any vehicles were missing. It transpired that, yes, an ambulance had gone.

'Go to his house. He'll be there,' Syd told them.

They found the ambulance parked outside. Syd was right.

I couldn't risk Richard escaping. Knowing his determination and ingenuity, it would be the fastest car or bike in the car park he'd choose for his getaway, not an ambulance.

*   *   *

Some nights were very busy in HDU. Fortunately Richard was a very deep sleeper, but being accustomed to interrupted sleep, as every mother is, I was often aware of the drama beyond our door. Nurses had become friends, other patients now recognisable faces. Whenever I heard a commotion outside, footsteps running up and down the corridor, I felt a chill; a deep sadness. Who was it this time? How bad was it? I couldn't help. I couldn't move. I could only listen . . . and pray that whoever was in trouble would be OK tomorrow.

One night at about 3 a.m. there came hysterical giggling from the nurses' station. It filled the corridor outside. Uncontrollable, muffled chortles, giggles and guffaws. I lay in our bed squished against the bars and smiled. I'd no idea what the joke was, but it was wonderful to eavesdrop. Like a group of naughty schoolchildren behind the bike sheds sharing a rude story. The next morning, as I padded past the nurses' station towards the tea machine, one of them asked, 'Did we wake you last night?'

'What? With the giggles?' I smiled.

'Yes, sorry. It happens sometimes on night shift. You just can't stop.'

I grinned back. 'It was bloody lovely.'

I walked on to the tea machine and overheard their usual hand-over conversations as the morning shift came on. Lots of information about what had happened during the night went straight over my head, but there was one very odd exchange.

'So that's it really. Oh. Except all the lights went out at about four o'clock.'

'Oh, right. The ghost?'

'Yeah.'

It was said so matter-of-factly, and after my experience in intensive care I wasn't surprised. Whether you believe in them or not, if ghosts exist, surely hospitals must be rather well populated.

* * *

To help Richard's memory we'd bought him a large A4 page-to-a-day diary. He was to write in there what he'd done, notes to himself, etc. When I needed to leave the room I could add notes to remind him of my whereabouts and when I'd return, always adding extra time in case I was delayed. I quickly learnt how easily he panicked if I wasn't back exactly on time. If I returned early, it was always a pleasant surprise.

He was so very desperate to escape the confines of his room, but the nurses and doctors were concerned that a controlled environment was still essential.

After a long chat at the nurses' station, we came up with a plan to get Richard out into the fresh air . . .

A porter came to his room pushing a wheelchair for his use; a security guard alongside. Richard (with pyjama bottoms now 'found') took his seat grinning from ear to ear. He was laughing and very embarrassed at being forced to be a passenger; apologising to the porter, joking he was being bullied by all these women, but scared they'd turn on him if he tried to get out.

When he saw the security guard his first words were:

'Oh, come on, is this really necessary?'

The security guard laughed. 'I'm afraid so.'

We were all getting quite giggly. Richard's excitement was contagious.

The sister was coming with us, and she'd given Richard a pair of sunglasses and put a blanket over his head. By this time, we really were close to collapse. Richard looked like a criminal about to be bundled into the back of a police van . . . except perhaps he'd broken his legs on the way.

Once the giggles had subsided a little (after a 'stern' word from sister), we made our way out of the ward, sister marching ahead, and the ridiculous gang following—Richard making rude jokes, the porter chatting and laughing, the security guard trying to look tough but muffling giggles, and me, casting the occasional stern glance at Richard when he took the blanket off his head and held the sunglasses in the air with a sort of 'Ta Daa!' motion.

He was having a ball. Larking about and being naughty. Richard being Richard.

We soon reached the door of the memorial garden. It was a sort of roof garden and very concealed.

The security guard insisted on hanging around by the door 'just in case', and the sister took the porter over to the other side of the garden, leaving us alone.

It was a warm, sunny day. There were only a couple of others out on the roof.

Picnic tables were dotted around the decking, interspersed with planters whose contents grew along the walls with beautiful sprays of pink and red flowers.

Richard's chair was parked opposite me, across one of the tables. He closed his eyes and turned his face to the sun, smiling.

'Ahh. This is nice.'

'Good to be out?' I asked softly.

'Mmm. Sort of.'

He held my hands in his.

'I'm sorry, Mind.' He looked me straight in the eye.

'Don't be silly.' I smiled. But he wasn't ready to stop talking.

'No, I'm really sorry. I love you.'

He leant across the table and kissed me.

'I love you too.' Tears were dripping off my chin . . . I wiped them away.

We looked out at the view across the rooftops towards the centre of Leeds, in silence for a moment.

'So,' he interrupted, 'shall we have a sneaky fag?'

I rolled my eyes. 'I don't believe you!' I smiled.

'What? A boy's gotta try.'

He persisted for a few minutes with the usual argument, until I pointed out something on the horizon to distract him. Then his mood quite suddenly changed.

'I don't want to be here any more. Can we go back now?'

'Yes, of course, darling.'

The sister had been watching us from afar the whole time, and no sooner did I seek her out with my eyes, than she was approaching, the porter by her side.

'Had enough?' She smiled.

Richard was silent.

'Yeah, I think so.' I smiled back.

He made a few quips, but was far quieter on our return journey. I wondered whether this small interaction with the outside world had set him back a little. Perhaps he'd realised he really was unwell, and was in shock. He was certainly lost in thought when we got back to the room.

* * *

During Richard's recovery, routine was of great importance. Although the routine in Leeds was, by necessity, pretty boring, it was at least very simple. Regular mealtimes, magazines to read, visits from nurses, cups of tea, and nap times filled his days. Whenever he slept, I left a note fixed with surgical tape to the TV screen beside the bed, telling him where I was and when I'd be back.

As the days progressed, I had many discussions with the neurosurgeon, Stuart Ross. He was delighted with Richard's recovery, and aware that we were a very long way from home. He felt it would be better to move Richard to a special BUPA hospital in Bristol as soon as possible.

He was making calls to organise a room there, but we agreed to keep the plans from Richard until we had everything confirmed.

* * *

Richard's parents had been amazing throughout his stay in Leeds. They reacted as any parents would: rushing to our aid; dropping everything to help us in our hour of need.

I can't even begin to imagine the stress and fear they managed to hide. Ever positive, they were magnificently courageous throughout the whole ordeal.

As parents, they were always immensely proud of Richard's achievements. Although not necessarily comfortable with everything he did, they remained supportive. If it were Izzy or Willow in a similar situation, I'm not sure how I would have reacted.

Their son, their little boy was critically injured, yet they'd volunteered to care for their grandchildren to allow me to be with him. It was a colossal sacrifice.

Time in Leeds was difficult for all of us, but especially for them. Richard's confusion was dreadful the majority of the time, and I know, although she hid it well, his mum was deeply upset to see her beloved son in such a terrible state. He was an intelligent, articulate, witty young man; a man she'd raised from birth through boyhood, through adolescence to adulthood. Yet the lad she knew so well was so very broken; so very different, and no one could provide a definitive prognosis.

The doctors had decreed that visitors should be kept to a minimum. I was there constantly as I was living with Richard in his room. The only other visitors were his parents. His dear dad was always nearby, and took over whenever I left the room. It was a sort of tag team. More than one of us in the room became overwhelming, but individually Richard could cope.

The day before Richard was scheduled to leave Leeds, his parents set off on their long trek back.

Their car was still at our house in Gloucestershire, so it would be an incredibly long journey. Four hours there, then a further three hours to their home in Surrey.

They were both exhausted. It was a very emotional and difficult goodbye. Richard's mum put on her bravest face, but had to leave quickly. His dad was steadfast to the last with encouraging words and a positive air.

They must have felt so helpless. We all did. There was little we could do, except follow the doctor's instructions and hope for the best.

The penultimate day in Leeds was a bit odd. I started to assemble our worldly goods ready for departure; meanwhile Andy Wilman organised a fully equipped 'hospital plane' to take us from Leeds to Bristol, as the neurosurgeons were concerned it was too far to expect Richard to travel by road. The Yorkshire air ambulance would fly us from the hospital to the local airport, and we'd be met by ambulance on arrival in Bristol.

Andy Wilman was up and down the corridor all day sorting out travel arrangements. Sourcing the right type of plane hadn't been easy, but then Andy's probably the best man on the planet when it comes to delivering the impossible—just watch a few of the *Top Gear* challenges and you'll see what I mean. Harrier jump jets, army vehicles, aircraft carriers—nothing is beyond him.

When I'd explained to Richard the plans for the move to a rehab unit in Bristol he was very excited. But his elation soon clouded.

'So we're going home tomorrow?'

'No, darling, we're going to Bristol. To the

rehab unit.'

'Oh yeah. Right. What? For a couple of days?'

'Well, we're not sure. Just see how it goes, OK?'

'Can't we just go home?'

'No, darling. Not yet. Hey! Guess how you're getting there.'

'Dunno.'

'A helicopter is collecting you on the roof, then you're transferring to a little plane to fly you to Bristol.'

'You're coming too?' There was a slight air of panic in his voice.

'Obviously.'

'You won't leave me, will you, Mind?'

I knew straight away he wasn't referring to the journey. Richard had moments of great clarity when I believe he realised how unravelled, how different he'd become. For a man who simply doesn't feel fear, he was genuinely scared.

I smiled at him. Hugged him for a long while, feeling him relax into my shoulder, his head bent into the crook of my neck.

'Never,' I whispered.

He squeezed me tight.

I held him for a few moments more. I'd never seen him like this, and knew he'd be embarrassed if he had to face me. I felt physical pain as I held him. Fighting my own emotions. I couldn't collapse now.

'Cup of tea?' I asked softly.

'Yeah, that'd be good.'

I was careful not to look in his eyes as I made towards the door. As I reached it, I turned to him.

'You OK?'

He smiled. 'Yeah.'

As I closed the door behind me I drew a huge breath and exhaled slowly. One of the nurses was walking towards me along the corridor, and she gave me one of those inquiring looks which, in a glimpse, asks: *Are you OK? Do you need my help? Ask me now.*

I painted on a smile and as she passed I said to her in a high-pitched voice: 'Tea!'

She smiled and winked, and walked on.

I was returning with the cups of steaming tea when the sister stopped me briefly for a chat.

She explained that a nurse must accompany Richard on the flight, and she was thrilled to be coming with us. We joked that she'd have to hitch-hike back, or we'd pack a bicycle, so she'd better not bring too much stuff.

She followed me back to the room to take blood pressure etc. and check on Richard. He was sitting on the bed, smiling and joking with us, when another member of the team appeared with his medication.

'You won't believe what's been going on outside,' she reported.

A patient had arrived by air ambulance on the roof of the hospital, but the press had assumed it was Richard's lift, coming to transfer him. They'd caught wind of rumours about his imminent departure.

'The press are everywhere!' she told us. 'They're on the roofs, in other buildings—they all went rushing out of the reception area.'

'Blimey.' We were really shocked.

'It's as well they were flushed out today,' she continued. 'Security have been out and done a real sweep now. It'll make things easier tomorrow.'

'Oh God, I'm so sorry.' Richard shook his head. 'We've caused you so much extra work. I'm not only a crap patient but you have to deal with all this other stuff as well.'

They replied in unison:

'Nooooo!'

'It's nice to have a bit of excitement.'

'And you're lovely, so shut up and drink your tea.'

We all smiled, but after they left Richard continued to worry about it.

We had a long chat about the air ambulance; the money which had been raised in his name, and of course his popularity (which he didn't believe at all).

'Everyone just wants to see how you are. Don't forget, the last time anyone saw you, you were upside down. Like you always say, they're all "just doing their job".'

'But they can't be *that* interested in me, for God's sake. I'm just the little bloke off a car show.'

'Ahem!' I pointed to the sacks and boxes strewn around his room, brimful of cards, letters and gifts.

'You're the lovely little bloke off a car show. Don't underestimate how much people care about you.'

'But I'm just me.'

'Well, maybe that's why you're special.'

He gave me a quizzical look. 'Mmmm.'

* * *

During Richard's time in Leeds a brass-band competition was taking place. One of the bands taking part had approached the hospital to inquire whether they could play a special piece they'd composed for Richard, under his window.

The nurses asked if it would be OK, and we said that, as long as the other patients didn't mind, we thought it was a lovely idea. So it was arranged that the band would start playing after nap time, when all the lights came back on in the ward.

I'd told Richard and we sat expectantly in his room, awaiting the marvellous sounds of brass . . . but nothing happened.

We decided they were probably coming later, so Richard took his nap and I dashed about making the usual phone calls and tidying up a bit.

At teatime, when the shift changed, one of the nurses came into the room.

'Did you hear the band then?'

'Erm, no. I suppose they couldn't make it.'

'That's funny,' replied the nurse. 'I'm sure they came.'

She made some inquiries, and came back a little later. The band had been to the hospital and played their song for Richard, but unfortunately they'd been directed to the wrong side of the hospital.

We hoped the patients had enjoyed it, and prayed they weren't in a state of shock when the music started. Our lot were all ready to hear the band start up—the geriatric ward wouldn't have been.

It was a shame Richard didn't hear them, and they must know it was a very thoughtful gesture.

But he laughed and joked about the mix-up for hours; so even though he didn't manage to hear the music, they cheered him up immensely. Thank you.

CHAPTER 12

# THE MOVE TO BRISTOL

I don't remember what time we were leaving, but I recall waking early and foraging through the clothes Alex had kindly bought for Richard, which he was to try on for the first time. A pair of jeans, white T-shirt, pants and socks.

It was strange that morning, seeing Richard in real clothes for the first time since the accident; the first time he'd had to get dressed. The nurses were coming in regularly with breakfast and cups of tea, checking he was OK and keeping him calm.

I was putting essentials into bags and making small talk with him, but he was impatient. He just wanted to go.

'What time are they coming?' he asked every ten minutes.

'Don't worry, they'll let us know when the helicopter arrives.'

The plan was to get up to the roof as soon as possible after it landed, but there was no point in us leaving the room until the last minute. If the air ambulance received a call, we'd be kept waiting until they were free.

Andy Wilman and Alex were hovering in the corridor. Andy gave me a rundown on the plan of action. Alex had kindly volunteered to clear the contents of the hospital room and transport it all to Bristol by car after we'd left. It was a monumental task. And I was amazed he was prepared to take it on. I thanked him for all of his help. As I talked with them I felt quite choked . . . it was like saying goodbye to the last remnants of the support team, because that's what we'd all become. Richard's support team. I'd miss them.

Stuart Ross came in to say goodbye. He smiled and joked with us and told Richard how pleased he was at the progress made so far. Mr Ross was astounded at his rate of recovery, as were all the team, but he was anxious to reiterate his advice:

'No work. Your continued recovery depends upon it.'

Both Mr Ross and I knew that Richard's standard acceptance and promises to rest would be forgotten within minutes. I'd had endless battles, trying to prevent him from calling Andy Wilman, his colleagues at the *Daily Mirror* and, hardest of all, James and Jeremy.

As I explained to Mr Ross, although I completely understood the need to avoid work, and anything connected with work, Richard's best mates were also his colleagues. The people he associated with during his daily life, socially and privately, were very often involved in TV in some way. What we were asking him to do was effectively cut himself off from his life.

Fortunately, Mr Ross agreed a compromise: if I could ensure his conversations didn't turn to the subject of work, he could speak to his mates occasionally.

Andy Wilman, desperate to do everything in his power to help, was only too happy to follow the plan, as were James and Jeremy.

I'd asked everyone involved in Richard's professional life at the BBC and elsewhere to write to him, explaining that nothing would happen until his return. I could put the letters in front of him whenever he became worried about work. He needed physical evidence, rather than hearsay.

The evening before we were due to leave, Richard had been fretting about work, as he often did. He was sitting on the edge of the bed, a towel around his waist, having just returned from the shower.

'Can you get my phone? I need to call Wilman.'

I have to admit, I was exhausted. This exchange had been repeated on and off all day, and I'd taken three showers already, knowing Richard would leave the subject and move on while I was in the bathroom.

'It's OK, Wilman's fine.'

'And I need to call the *Mirror*.'

'I've spoken to them, everything's OK.'

I don't know whether it was the tone of my voice, but suddenly, for the first time, Richard's whole persona changed. His face turned to anger.

'Look, I know you think you know what you're doing, but this is my career! My life! Stop speaking to me like I'm an idiot!'

I was so surprised, so overjoyed, I started to cry. Perspective had suddenly arrived. He remembered a previous conversation. He remembered!!

'Oh, Richard, Richard—I'm sorry. I'm so sorry. Of course it's your career.'

But he still looked angry.

'Stop talking to me like that,' he snapped.

Oh God, suddenly he was so different; it was

fantastic, but at the same time quite shocking. I was up close to him. Speaking as softly as I could, taking care not to sound patronising, I said, 'I don't mean to talk down to you. I truly don't. But, darling, this is the first time you've remembered a conversation. You do remember us talking about this before?'

He looked at me like I was mad.

'Yeah, of course I do. Look. Just, just . . .' He paused, the memory gone again, but his anger still present.

'Just get on with what you're supposed to be doing.'

'OK. Sorry.' I rushed into the bathroom and took another shower. I was trembling. Exhilarated and nervous all at once. After five minutes under hot running water, my mind was in a frenzy. If his memory had returned, perhaps his anger would remain. Would I walk out to another stony evening? We'd had a few difficult nights when he'd refuse to leave a particular subject and get what the doctors referred to as 'stuck on point'. Moving the conversation on had become increasingly difficult, and he'd be very miserable at times.

Tentatively, I pushed open the adjoining door. He was in bed, gazing vacantly at the TV, which, thankfully I'd left on. As I walked through the door he shot me a loving smile.

'Ello! You were a long time. Have you shrunk?'

I beamed back at him and inside felt a huge sense of relief. His memory was working its way back, and although still muddled he'd taken another huge step.

*   *   *

From the roof, we were to go by helicopter to Leeds–Bradford airport. There, a small private plane equipped with stretcher, oxygen and all the medical equipment Richard might need, would fly Richard, the ward sister and me on to a small airport outside Bristol. Once we landed, an ambulance would be waiting to drive the final few miles to The Glen in Clifton, Bristol, which was the only private intensive-care hospital in the area. It boasted a physiotherapy team and gym, and most importantly was close to the brain rehabilitation centre in Frenchay. The team there would take over Richard's care during the difficult weeks ahead.

I was quiet, slightly nervous as Andy ran through the arrangements. Even though everyone assured me this was the best course of action—doctors, neurosurgeons, nurses, etc.—I was still worried. Richard was a master at fooling everyone. He couldn't get past medical fact—there was plenty of evidence to support the gravity of his condition—but nevertheless, his bright and breezy persona was a bit of an act, and it was all they saw.

However, with everyone else convinced, who was I to doubt them?

He'd improved so much in the now familiar surroundings of Leeds—although he was still confused, Richard had finally accepted that he was in hospital and, to some degree, that he'd had a crash and was injured—I was frightened this huge upheaval might set him back.

*   *   *

Inevitably, when the time came to leave it was a bit of a scramble. I can't even remember who told us, but someone appeared and said, 'Time to go.'

The sister came into Richard's room and made sure he was ready. Richard was being difficult as usual, insisting he could walk.

'Oh no you don't,' said the sister in her firmest tone.

A wheelchair was ready for him and, embarrassed or not, that was to be his mode of transport.

He was pushed by the porter; a security guard and matron in attendance. I'd grabbed a couple of important bags and was alongside. Andy Wilman came too. Richard kept trying to discuss work with him, but he was constantly reassuring and putting Richard off the subject.

Such a positive moment, to be moving to a rehabilitation unit, and yet . . . somehow I felt we were leaving everyone behind. There wasn't time to thank them all; I didn't have the words to tell them how much they all meant. We just had to go.

*   *   *

Of course, it wasn't that simple. Just before we went through the door, the sister and I had a battle to stop Richard walking to the helicopter. We both knew he wouldn't make it. Then he wanted to go by wheelchair—but here's the thing; I knew Richard, he'd want to mess about, or get out of it, or do something daft. In addition, I could see the helicopter. If he was in a wheelchair, he'd have to stand up and climb in. No way would he manage that. His confidence was high, which was fantastic, but I'd been warned that to step backwards while he was progressing so well could be catastrophic.

I didn't wait for the sister.

'Darling, you have to go on the stretcher.'

'Oh no I don't. Come on—'

The sister had cottoned on straight away.

'It's the only way they can carry you on the helicopter.'

'Oh, all right then.'

So, thankfully, he was stretchered to the helipad and lifted on to the air ambulance. It was then we discovered it was crewed by the same team who'd rescued him.

Richard thanked them for saving his life the previous week and once aboard quickly set about reviewing the interior of the helicopter.

He was joking and laughing with the crew, who were clearly delighted to see him so much better. I joined in, but was secretly petrified. He was putting on a show, and I'd back him up, but I was waiting to see what would happen as the trip progressed.

Also, I should mention that I'd only ever been in a helicopter once before. In bad weather. It put me off for life; I was petrified. I sat alongside Richard and held his hand. The inside of the helicopter was quite spacious, and Richard wasn't fazed by his second trip in the ambulance. As we took off, I was nervous he might react. But there was nothing, he simply admired the view.

His audience on board the helicopter was

captivated, and as he enjoyed their happy exchanges we noticed that down below us a crowd of photographers had flocked to the front lawn of the hospital and were aiming their cameras skywards, but it was too late.

The only photographer to get a shot of Richard leaving had been hiding on a roof opposite the hospital. No one knows how long he'd been there. When all the others had been discovered, he'd remained. We wondered later where on earth he'd hidden.

When we landed at Leeds–Bradford airport a small plane awaited us, together with a couple of members of the ground crew. They were very friendly and helpful and made sure the transfer went smoothly.

Richard was soon settled on the stretcher aboard the small plane. An oxygen monitor was clipped to his index finger. The sister and I sat opposite one another.

As the plane took off, I watched Richard's face. He was clearly exhausted and looked distant.

'Are you feeling OK?' I asked.

'Yeah, yeah.' He spoke quietly, nodding and half closing his eyes as he did so. It was his reassuring look. I knew he was trying to convince me everything was fine.

Even before the oxygen monitor registered any problems, I had already sensed he wasn't right. I hated every moment of that flight. He received oxygen several times during the forty minutes we were in the air. I checked my watch minute by minute. I even steeled myself to ask the pilot how much longer we would be on a couple of occasions.

Richard pretended to be asleep for part of the journey, but I knew him too well. He was trying to concentrate, dealing with his own demons.

Several times during the flight, I had to wrestle with my own sense of panic. If he was ill on the plane, how would we cope? What could be done? Jesus! We were stuck up there.

I was so grateful when we touched down. Richard insisted on walking to the waiting ambulance, and although it was a slow and difficult few steps, I was proud of his determination.

The journey across Bristol in the ambulance was quite brief, and Richard resumed his cheery banter with the ambulance crew. He'd relaxed again. Thank God.

* * *

I've no idea what time we arrived at the BUPA hospital. I remember Richard being exhausted; he fell asleep on contact with his bed. Bristol may have been another step towards recovery, but Stuart Ross warned me that the worst was yet to come. From a ludicrously quick recovery to date, it would all start to slow down now. This was where the hard work began, the frustration started, and the anger could really take hold.

But we'd arrived. Richard was safe. It was time to start the next phase.

CHAPTER 13

# DID YOU KNOW SWANS MATE FOR LIFE?

There is a scene in Stephen King's *Misery* where the main character—I can't remember his name—wakes to find that his ankles, which his less-than-friendly hostess has recently broken for him with a mallet, are hurting badly. I can't remember why his ankles had been broken, and I couldn't remember as I drifted between coma and consciousness in intensive care in Leeds General Infirmary. But that scene haunted me and fixed itself at the front of my bleary mind. I could see a woman. Clearly a nurse. She was holding a plastic cup. Her head fitted the frame of my vision above the white hospital sheets that I clutched in front of my face. I was in bed. The sheets smelled nice. The light shone through the weave of them and made a hazy, billowy outline around her. I didn't want to appear rude, but I couldn't understand who she was, why she was there, and why I was in bed. She offered me the cup. It was a dose of morphine. Did I want it?

In the Stephen King book, the character is offered morphine to dull the pain of his shattered ankles. This was why the memory of that particular scene had been tapping away at my mind like an insistent little bird at a window. The bloke with the ankles compares his pain to the jagged, blackened piles of wood sticking out of the sea bed on the coast. The morphine, he explains, is the sea and it washes over the pain, masking and hiding it. I thought what a beautiful metaphor this was as the nurse leaned closer with the drugs and I felt happy in the freshly laundered scent of the hospital sheets. The morphine must have swept over whatever pain was troubling me in my coma and I drifted back out of consciousness again. I don't remember the pain. There was only relief. And sleep.

The ground looked rough but friendly. Small rocks peppered the path which was dusty and warm. It twisted ahead, tempting me on. I walked towards a rise where the path turned to the left behind the hill. At the corner was a small plateau that a weathered old Hawthorn tree had made its home. On either side, the mountains rose to meet me and the valleys between lay cool and dark. I walked on and felt naughty. I was being bad by following this temptingly lovely path. But not bad in a terrible way; I was being cheeky, naughty like I was back at school, doing something the teachers didn't want me to. It felt like the Lake District, my favourite place in the world. I was somewhere familiar but made better, more fanciful. If the Lake District really did exist in my head, then this is how it would be: a heightened version of what it really is.

I sensed, but never saw, tiny flowers on long, velvet stems bobbing in the grass nearby. The sky beyond the plateau was pale and white and the rocks before it were outlined, their grey-brown hunches looked like sleeping bears. There was no noise but the soft, occasional gusts of a breeze that set the grass waving. I was happy to be there and didn't want to give in to all the people who were a bit cross about my journey. But the pressure of their disapproval mounted. I could sense that their mood was changing from indulgent and caring to genuine anger. I felt the humour drain away and knew that I was in trouble. I turned round. Mindy was cross, I knew it, and I didn't want her to be. So I stopped messing about and did as I was told. I came back.

Mindy was, indeed, cross. I didn't know it, but she had been standing over me in the intensive-care unit, bellowing my name and shouting at me. I have learned since that things had been looking very bad for a while and Mindy had asked the nurse if she could shout at me to see if I responded. I don't think the nurse knew what she was letting herself in for. She told Mindy that it might help, that she might reach me in my coma. That was all Mindy needed to hear and she launched into a barrage of shouting and yelling, urging me to respond and come back. I did. The medical observations made a turn for the better; I was safe, though still unconscious. The nurses and doctors satisfied themselves that my condition had stabilised once more and were happy for me to drift through my coma. With no more shouting.

I remember nothing clearly of being in Leeds General Infirmary. I owe my life to the people there, to their diligence in doing their jobs, the knowledge and judgement that they bring to bear on their patients every single working day. But I can remember nothing of being under their care. Time spent in a coma is time spent in an entirely different sort of consciousness. It's not sleep; sometimes people can communicate with the patient and sometimes the patient can respond. On many occasions, I am told, I woke, but I cannot distinguish those times from the distant memories of dreams and fantasy. Two worlds become blurred; the world in your head and the world that recently hurt you so badly. And so it was not a long, uninterrupted sleep, but a long time spent living between two worlds.

Bed was nice. I liked being there. But I had been in a crash, a bad one. It was easier, finally, to accept and believe it. Even though there was no evidence to support it. Apart from being in what, clearly, was a hospital, there was nothing else to back up Mindy's claims. I could move; there was no pain; everything worked. I felt sad. Something was wrong. I needed to sleep. So I did.

Distantly, in flashes, I remembered. The jet car had crashed. I had been fighting to save it. Something had gone wrong with the steering. I could feel the panic rising as I fought and recalled the sense that I was on the point of losing my fight. And then something else had gone wrong. Something worse—and I had to give up trying to stop it happening. I thought I was going to die. I hadn't been scared, just sad. There had been nothing more I could do but die; that was just the next thing on my list to do. Now I was in hospital. I hadn't died. But I had hurt my brain; damaged the very place where I lived. I was scared. I slept again.

It's the most intimate way to be hurt; the most personal attack imaginable. I was reduced to thoughts; to patterns and pictures but nothing solid. I had been forced back into the very cave that I came from and I had hidden at the back, lashing out at anything that came near. I didn't have a body any more and I didn't care. It didn't matter here, where my fight was going on. I felt like a monster; a grey, skulking, slimy thing that bit and hissed and scratched. I had been in a crash. My body had been hurt, but that didn't matter to me now. I wasn't a body, I was something else. I had to fight back. I needed to sleep. It was a dark battle and a bitter one. I needed strength. I needed to sleep. So I did.

Mindy was talking to me again. Slowly. I had been

If you wake up –
I have gone to get a
sandwich.
Back in a mo
love you very much.
Mindy x

Hospital is No Smoking
Have to rest – had a
head injury – SERIOUS
Must rest and sleep
to get better
No drinking
You have only pyjamas
Not allowed to go out
until you're better
Mindy loves you lots
XXX
You don't have to go
to work

Leeds General Infirmary: notes taped to the TV screen by Mindy whenever she left my bedside and one of Izzy's cards.

To mummy and
Daddy I Love
you so muchand
when you come
home I'm going to
give you a big
cudle because I
Love you so much
I carnt wait antill
you come home
home and Daddy
and me will clean the
cars and mummy will
help clean the cars to

Recovering in Scotland with some damage still visible to left eye

LEFT AND ABOVE: It felt good to be outside again. But a bit frightening

From the Health and Safety Investigation report:
'The immediate cause of the accident was a catastrophic failure of the Vampire's front offside tyre at 288 mph on the seventh high-speed run of the day. Examination of this tyre and video footage showed that the tyre was damaged, as a result of an object (or objects) having entered the sidewall immediately adjacent to the edge of the tread, during the latter part of the previous run. A blister was visible in the tyre's outer side but this appears to have subsided and was not apparent immediately before the final run commenced.'

The telemetry results from the Racelogic VBOX show:
**1**. The speed of the car during the successful 314 mph run. It had reached 200 mph in less than 8 seconds. The fastest production car in the world, the Bugatti Veyron, takes 24 seconds to reach 200 mph.
**2**. The longitudinal G-force attained over the crash run—during acceleration a force of over 1.5 times my body weight was sticking me into the back of my seat. Once the tyre disintegrated, 15.5 seconds into the run, the deceleration G-force was pushing me forward at 5G, peaking at 7G—or roughly half a ton sitting on my back.
**3**. The crash run with the lateral G-force attained. Initially there is none, as the car is going in a straight line. After the tyre burst the car slews sideways exerting a G-force of over 3G, peaking at 5G. The most a Formula 1 driver feels in cornering is up to 4G.

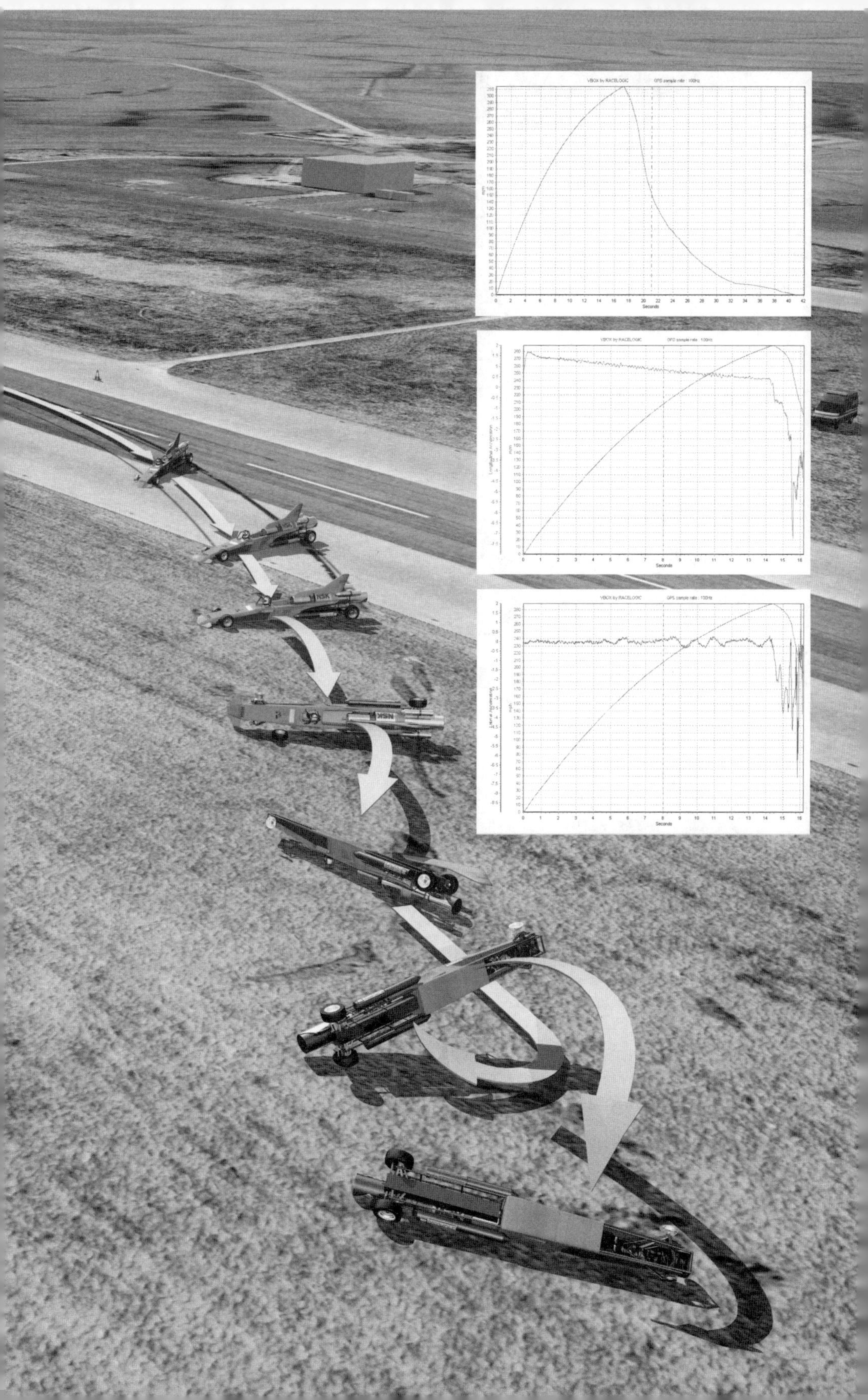

VBOX by RACELOGIC
GPS sample rate : 100Hz
mph
Seconds
VBOX by RACELOGIC
GPS sample rate : 100Hz
Longitudinal Acceleration
mph
Seconds
VBOX by RACELOGIC
GPS sample rate : 100Hz
Lateral Acceleration
mph
Seconds
NSK

Getting back to what we call normal. Izzy, me, Captain, Mindy and Willow on board our MPV.

Home and Away: Izzy and Willow with Hattie and, below, back to work and the normal day-to-day grind resumes—racing Jeremy and James to the North Pole with a dog sled.

in a crash. The jet car had crashed and I had banged my head really badly. I felt sad. I held her—or she held me—and I felt sad. But I believed her now, I understood. I was in hospital and I was here because of what I had done to my head. My brain. I was important, I was the patient. The world revolved around me. And it did. Meals came and went. I slept when I wanted. A nurse came round every now and then and stuck painful needles in me, but it was a small price to pay for being the centre of everyone's world.

A jet engine started up. I heard the distinct whine, rising to a scream. It was right by my head. I was sitting. Or standing. And then lying. There were many people around me, busy doing important stuff. Mindy was with me. I focused on her and her alone. It was exciting, whatever we were doing. We were with a group of people. I was in a gang again. This was good. The jet engine screamed more urgently.

'Last thing I remember hearing was a jet engine,' I said, pleased with the gag. Someone laughed; a pilot maybe. I was showing off. That felt great. I had been in a crash with a jet engine. That was why I was up here on the roof getting into a helicopter. And then nothing.

* * *

For two weeks, little flashes of consciousness meshed together out of time and sequence to make up a sort of thread that I lived along. I did not believe what had happened; that things could go wrong. We took care, we made sure, we mitigated against the risks. We weren't kids any more, we were grown-ups. So how could it go wrong? Finally, almost two weeks after getting into the jet car for the last time, I accepted that it had crashed. Mindy had explained it to me again and again and I had not believed her. Though I had no other theory to explain why I was in bed. But finally, in the hospital room in Bristol, holding Mindy's hand, I accepted it. I talked about my memories, of trying to stop something happening and failing. That made Mindy look sad. I felt guilty about the crash; maybe I had done something wrong? Was it my fault? Did I go too fast? But at least now I believed what Mindy said. And that made things a lot easier to connect together.

And for me, it was pretty easy to accept and understand in the end. If the last thing you recall is the sound of a jet engine starting up just inches behind your head before being fired up a runway at 300 mph in a dragster . . . well, your mind is hardly surprised if you come out of a coma in hospital a week or two later. How much harder must it be for patients who come out of a coma to find they no longer recognise the woman everyone tells them is their wife and the last thing they remember is riding a bicycle to the shops for bread, or climbing a ladder to clear a blocked gutter? When I was well enough to be able to process the thought and consider it, this would be the first of many, many lessons in the business of recovery from brain-damage. It's not just what you've done; it's important how you've done it. I had been almost primed for disaster. My mind had to cope with the aftermath of the accident, but at least it was spared the difficulty of trying to understand how a seemingly mundane act could change the way you look at the world. I was lucky; I had hurt myself in such an exceptional and unusual set of circumstances that it was easier to accept.

Mindy had been a constant presence and, without realising it, I had come to rely on her as I rely on air and water. She was more than sustenance; she was my refuge, shield and strength. She was my interpreter, the conduit of my difficult and confusing emotions. How these roles drained her, I can only ever try to imagine. When she left the room, even for minutes, I stopped coping. She was living for two of us.

I stirred in my bed. This was going to be OK. I've never been any good at the holiday thing and so a bit of enforced rest wouldn't do any harm, surely? No one could be convincingly specific about how long I might be there, but I quickly settled into a rhythm all the same. I would be a model patient; calm, relaxed, cooperative and, of course, patient. Maybe that's where the name comes from. I wanted to be good at it; to be the best patient they had ever had and one they would talk about for years to come as an exceptionally talented and understanding patient. I wanted to show off again.

I had been a patient only once before when, as a six-year-old, I had stayed in hospital for a few days for very minor surgery on my eardrums. The isolation, the loneliness and the home-sickness returned to me in waves. Some aspect of the hospital's plumbing had been particularly ancient or unreliable, and the pipes and boilers had moaned and mooed all night, like a herd of spectral cattle wandering the wards. Their cries had kept me pinned to the starched sheets with fear. They returned now to haunt the long nights in a hospital hundreds of miles and three decades away from the last one I stayed in. I dreaded their arrival at night, swivelling my eyes around in the dark as I drifted into sleep. I would sleep deeply and well until, for some unseen reason, I woke and lay silently, feeling once more the night-time dread of a scared six-year-old boy.

I slept in the day and, when I did, I dreamed of going home. I would devote every waking hour to trying to persuade the doctors that I was ready to go home. I knew that I was not being held here against my will; I understood that it was for my own good. But I wanted to escape more than anything else I could think of. I wanted to return to normality. To get back to a life in which I waved cheery goodbyes at the front door and went off to work, did daft stuff and came home again to Mindy and the kids with stories and tales. My memory was still badly damaged. This was not damage to my deeper memories; I knew who I was, I recognised my children, and I recognised my parents and brothers. But my day-to-day memory was still very much in the grip of post-traumatic amnesia. I wasn't aware of this, but it meant that my memory of immediate things only extended to a few minutes. A conversation would be forgotten within moments of having it, and I might ask the same question dozens of times; forgetting each time that I had already asked it and heard an answer. This only added to the state of deep confusion that nagged away at me and, I suspect, made me difficult to be around. For my family, it meant sitting for hours hearing me repeat the same things over and over, asking them the same questions time and time again. I grew irritated and frustrated when people reacted oddly to my questions and statements, unaware that it might be the tenth or hundredth time I had said it to them.

*　　*　　*

Richard's room was bigger than the hospital room in Leeds, and the floor was covered in close-pile carpet. It was decorated with wallpaper, and the furniture was more upmarket. Reminiscent, I thought, of a businessman's hotel room. A wooden desk with a chair against one wall, a DVD player beneath the TV. Everything else was as it had been in Leeds: the hospital bed, the emergency buttons—except of course there were new nurses. All very friendly and eager to make him comfortable.

He was very tired after his arrival. The journey had, not surprisingly, taken its toll. He was very argumentative, and as I was also tired it wasn't the easiest transition. Rick Nelson, the neurosurgeon taking over his care, came to visit.

Richard had noticed a lack of hearing in his left ear, and Mr Nelson was keen to test his hearing to check for permanent damage.

Rick had a wonderful manner. He was in his late forties, tall and of medium build. His expression was always receptive. In conversation we'd discovered he was a keen cyclist, as was Richard, which provided common ground in conversation. He was always very calm and softly spoken and would listen patiently to Richard's animated exchanges, but all the while glancing across at me. He was gauging the validity of the person in front of him, and guessed correctly this wasn't the true Richard. However, he also sensed I couldn't be honest in Richard's presence; he'd feel I was betraying him. At the end of the discussion, Rick asked Richard's permission to have a chat alone with me to discuss his progress as I saw it. He agreed. I felt I'd been given permission to disclose vital information.

I was Richard's ally. He depended on me and looked to me for support. I was also his protector. I'd stood alongside him as sword and shield; if I suddenly appeared to switch allegiance, all trust would dissipate. Rick had provided the ultimate solution.

He needed information on every development, positive and negative and I could be completely honest with him. However, sitting in a spare room discussing my husband's condition behind his back felt terrible. It was almost like sitting with a marriage-guidance counsellor. 'What's wrong with your husband?' could've been the opening remark. I felt disloyal. I felt I was failing him, but I knew it was vital the medical team were aware of all the facts.

Rick immediately recognised textbook characteristics in Richard. He was desperately trying to demonstrate how articulate, how well recovered he was, and yet . . . ask him what town he was in, there was instant confusion. What had he eaten for lunch? Again, no recall.

Deep, deep sadness overcame me whenever we discussed his mental state. Richard was a very intelligent man, but his mind remained jumbled. The doctors compared the state of his mental function to a filing cabinet that had been knocked to the floor; all the files were scattered about; all the various notes and papers contained within each file were spread all over the room. We were trying to help him put it all back together. It was a slow and difficult task. He would be frustrated; he'd become angry and despairing, but patience was the key. Patience and rest. The brain, as we often forget, is not simply a tool for thought and consideration, for mental calculation; it also drives every minuscule action. When you move your finger or twitch a toe, the brain is working. His brain was exhausted and the best therapy was sleep. The most dangerous factor was work. If he overtaxed his brain too soon, he would suffer a relapse. It would set him back dreadfully, and Rick spared no punches—it would be hard to claw back.

* * *

Post-traumatic amnesia helped alleviate the boredom. This, in turn, made life a little easier for people looking after me and for visitors, and compensated in some small way for the difficulties in dealing with a person so confused. I could happily settle down and read the same newspaper a dozen times; forgetting each time I picked it up that I had, only minutes earlier, read it, sighed at the news, folded it up and put it on my bedside table. It also meant that I was easy to cater for; I would read the hospital lunch menu, spot that cottage pie was available and exclaim that it was my favourite and ask for it. When it arrived, ten minutes or so later, I would forget that I had ordered it from the menu and be delighted that it was my favourite dish and ask how the staff could possibly have known it. When the dinner menu appeared, I would find that it had cottage pie on it and we would repeat the process. After several days of this, I learned later that Mindy asked the staff to tell me that sadly, the cottage pie was all gone. When they told me this for the second, fifth and tenth times, I had, of course, forgotten and was disappointed but not broken-hearted.

By the time I understood post-traumatic amnesia and that it might mean that a patient such as me could be left, temporarily with a memory that stretched back only a few minutes, I was getting over it. But the confusion that remained; the uncertainty, the fact that I could not trust my own perception of the world and my own thoughts, was a frightening state to be in. To know that I was in such a state made it worse. With every stage of gradually increasing awareness, I grew more scared. At this point in the long process of recovery, I knew enough to know that there was something wrong; that I had hurt my brain. But I didn't know how to fix it, or how it might be affecting me. I could have been dreaming the entire thing. But at least now I accepted that I was ill, that I had suffered an injury and that I was in a hospital so that I might get better. And I still wanted to go home. Badly.

* * *

There was little to compare with my role at Leeds to that at Bristol. Although some things remained in the now familiar pattern; I slept with Richard every night and was with him as much as possible but we were close to home, closer to the girls and clearly I should be with them, too.

At Bristol, there was a more relaxed atmosphere, mealtimes weren't set in stone, which allowed Richard to fit in naps whenever he wished. A routine was devised which allowed for a late afternoon nap for Richard. That was my time to rush home, see the girls and return before he became too distressed.

It wasn't terribly successful. Often the hospital would call my mobile before I'd even reached home. I'd run into the house, try to enjoy a calm, fun time with the girls, but all the while preoccupied with a nagging sense of urgency to get back to him. We'd chat about their day as they splashed in the bath; the bedtime story was shorter, and the 'goodnights' far more difficult. They'd phone Daddy to wish him 'goodnight' and then I was off again. The second I left their rooms, I ran down the stairs, and then continued running to the car. The keys were never removed from the ignition, no bags entered the house apart from Richard's washing, which I'd load on my way in.

Journey time was taken up by phone calls. I had two phones, which was useful. At least one was always charging. I listened to messages and returned as many as possible. Conversations were timed to fit the maximum in. So many dear friends were desperate to know how he really was, but naturally my first call was always to his parents. Their distress I cannot imagine, but throughout their patience and support was astounding. I'd update them on progress, and they'd filter the news to other members of the family. My mum was next. Her gentle comforting words overwhelmed me; gave me strength and perspective. Always positive, always loving.

I'd pull over to fill up with petrol on my return journey, grab a sandwich and several bottles of Coke. My main sustenance. Occasionally, I'd feel tired, but determination and sheer practicality drove me on, that and the desperate longing to be back with Richard; concern at the length of time I'd spent away from him, and subsequently the state of his coping mechanisms. It was like leaving a child in a strange place with kind but unfamiliar company. I sensed he was forever fighting panic; controlling himself. Being brave.

I was never sure what to expect on my return. He could be at the door, waiting for the lift doors to open, asleep in bed, or calmly assembling a Lego model.

The staff were very accommodating. They'd make sure we had a snack to share late in the evening. Richard often forgot to eat his meals if no one was with him, so our shared suppers were both enjoyable and necessary.

* * *

There is an expression that the doctors wear when they come into your room in a unit like the one at Bristol. It's a half-wary and half-defensive expression, and with good reason. As soon as they crossed the threshold, I would spring to attention and begin a torrent of talk as I tried to prove my return to health and sanity and regain my freedom.

'Morning, Richard, how are you?'

'Ah, yes, well, thank you. Much better. Bit worried about this weather though—looks like a spot of low pressure heading our way.'

I made a sweeping gesture to my right, meaning to encompass the window. Which was to my left.

'Or it could be an occluded front.' Anything—scraps of information and facts recalled from school or from the TV that now provided a link with the outside world. I found the window and looked out at the grey, autumn sky.

'Did you know that swans mate for life?'

‘No, Richard. Do you know what day it is?’
‘No.’
And I didn’t. I could recall stuff from years ago, random memories popped up with incredible clarity. Sometimes I could close my eyes and suddenly be in a place I last visited decades ago. And I would be there as the same thinking, feeling person I was at the time; the illusion was complete in time and context. But I could get no grip on the present, on what was going on around me. My sense of time and place was badly distorted. Facts, ideas, meanings slipped from my grasp and evaded my best attempts to pin them down. Eventually, I got used to the business of not being able to answer simple questions, but at first it was terrifying. I understood that the question was a simple one with a simple answer. I knew that I should know what that answer was, but I could not pin it down.

I became aware that there was something wrong with me that stopped me knowing or understanding. And I was scared. I had brain-damage. It affected the way I thought about things. It might be affecting the way I thought about brain-damage. And I didn’t know what day it was. Or where I was. Only why. And I was there because I had damaged my brain and these were the people who were going to help me make it better. The panic that rose whenever I failed to answer a question that I knew I should understand got in the way of my thoughts and made things worse. My mind would flail around desperately, I would be screaming inside my head because I knew that this should be easy. It was as much about my confidence failing as it was about my memory. Although my memory was still in a bad way.

I shall never forget the days of struggling in what

was a clinically confused state. I shall always try to hold on to the memory of how hard it was to make sense of the world, to interact, to process thoughts and to see myself in the context of the rest of the world. It made me horribly self-centred; childish, like a toddler who cannot comprehend that there can be a will in the world other than their own. My universe centred around me and so did that of everyone else around me. I shall try to keep these memories close, because it will for ever change the way I deal with other people who, for whatever reason, are likewise clinically confused. It was not always terrifying; I was not in a constant state of dejection or horror. Sometimes it was doubtless rather pleasant to bounce along, wondering what was for lunch when I had only ordered it five minutes earlier, and wondering if Mindy would come back and we could see everyone else at the party I thought we were at. The distress arising from my condition was, sadly, to be felt by the people closest to me. It is far harder, I am sure, to visit someone you know and love, and see them in such a confused state for weeks on end than it is to be the one happily asking where the bar is in a hospital ward. But in those flashes of insight and awareness, there were some deeply frightening moments and my heart goes out to anyone now similarly afflicted and for whom the prognosis might not, perhaps, be so bright as mine proved to be.

As my memory became better able to hold on to things and my mind relaxed into something closer to a normal state, there were some big emotions waiting to get hold of me. At some point early in my stay at Bristol, I was hit by a huge and overwhelming avalanche of guilt. I suddenly felt horribly aware of the worry and pain I had caused Mindy, my daughters, my brothers and, of course, my parents. The sense that I had done something very stupid and upset a lot of people by doing it hovered in the background of my jumbled thoughts.

I woke up, lying in a bed once more. But this time I knew that I was in hospital, that I was hurt. And I wanted to see my parents. I wanted to explain to them that it wasn't my fault, that I hadn't messed up, that something had gone wrong with the car and that I had not done anything wrong. I wanted to say that I was sorry and they mustn't worry. It was just like every time I had fallen off a bicycle or a garage roof as a child and felt both the pain of the accident and the guilt of knowing I would also be causing my parents pain, albeit of a different sort. I never worried that they would shout at me when I hurt myself as a child; they never would. But I knew, deep down, in the way that children do, that it would upset them. I remembered walking into the kitchen with my hand torn to pieces when I fell off my brother's bicycle. I remembered seeing the white bones and cartilage in my fingers and the red, ripped flesh. But I remembered, more clearly even than the pain, seeing my mother's face and her struggle to remain calm and help me when probably all she wanted to do was scream in horror that her baby was hurt.

Well, how would she feel now? This was worse than that, I knew that much. And I also now had a much better understanding of what a parent feels when they see their child hurt. I had children of my own and, once the switch of parenthood is thrown, it changes you for ever and you can never escape the extra pull of humanity it gives. I was lying in that hospital bed as both a ten-year-old child, holding up an injured hand to his mother and hoping she wouldn't cry, and as an adult, a father myself, who now had a much better idea about the pain a parent can feel but couldn't imagine how it must be to know your child is in an intensive-care unit surrounded by machines doing his breathing for him. I never managed to voice these feelings to my parents; somehow it just came out wrong when I tried. But I felt such a weight of guilt I thought it would crush me where I lay. And in my darkest moments, I hoped it would.

I don't know how they did it, but my mother and father never once gave me cause to succumb to that guilt, never once showed the anguish they must have felt to see one of their three sons broken in a hospital bed. Yet their concern and love made it through the barriers of pain, confusion and fear to comfort the child within me that had, temporarily, returned to seize control. I felt cared for and loved, and slowly lost the feeling that I had caused a lot of trouble by doing something very stupid. Although I had, of course, done just that. This guilt is a common thing among people recovering from head injuries such as mine, and from many bodily injuries too. Much later, when crawling further back towards health, I would be hit by a second avalanche of guilt, this time centred on how I had been so lucky when many people are not. I would lie awake, pinned down by the knowledge that I had been through such a massive accident and emerged alive and, eventually, well, when people are far more badly hurt falling down the stairs. That guilt is, perhaps, harder to fight against, and I still carry it today. But right now, as I lay in bed in Bristol, the only guilt I felt was for the worry I had caused my parents, brothers and wife. And they all worked unbelievably hard to protect me from it, and I thank them for that.

With my returning memory and confidence, the problem of filling my days became more pressing. But I was not lying in bed dreaming of getting back to work. I didn't want to go back and I couldn't really understand the concept of work anyway. Not in an adult way. I knew that work was something I did out there in the real world and that I had to be grown-up and that I had children and a wife and that my work paid for a house for us all to live in. But I couldn't imagine doing it, actually going to work. I wanted to fill my time, but I wanted to fill it with things I enjoyed. Work to me meant desks and pieces of paper and long, boring conversations with people in suits about stuff I didn't understand. I wanted to play. I had regressed until I felt and thought like a child, and was happy to do so.

It was raining outside and I watched the drops track their wiggly paths down the window of my hospital room. Outside, the roofs and walls slanted in the weak autumn light. All was divided into steely grey and harsh white as sunlight slanted through the low clouds and bounced off the wet planes of roads and buildings designed for function before form. I looked at the cars lined below, studied the colours and shapes of them, and wanted to walk among them. I wanted to touch their metal curves, feel the straining raindrops on their thick-painted panels gather under my hand and burst wetly like dense bubbles. I wanted to step out into the world and experience it for myself. I didn't crave an exotic or distant world; that didn't really exist for me. The world was what I could see from my window.

Above all else, I wanted to go to a shopping centre and buy something. I wanted to walk among familiar shop frontages, see their colourful signs, and know what they were without even reading them. I wanted to hear the voices of other people echoing off the big plate windows but not know what they were saying or to care. I wanted to see the hustle and bustle and be part of it all, be swept along, only to resist it when I saw something that caught my interest. In my mind, I drifted back to childhood trips to the Bull Ring shopping centre in Birmingham. We were buying school shoes or pencils for a new term. We turned a corner among the stalls and shops and we walked down some steps. There was another floor below and we walked to a stand on a corner selling bags. They were hung from the walls and the roof of the stall. These weren't for me though, these looked like handbags. Or bags for carrying grown-up stuff in. I didn't want one, but I admired their shiny surfaces and glistening buckles while my mum chatted to the man selling them.

At another stand further round the curving walkway, someone sold sweets. I knew it and I wanted to go there. Suddenly I was in front of another stall selling food. It was meat, or fish, or cheese; something sold in bags over a wooden counter by a grown-up who wore white and talked loudly. I wasn't interested and I thought about Batman. I listened to the grown-up voices echoing around the hall. The lights were harsh and bright, they were low down too, the ceiling was rough and echoey. I thought that, when I got home, I would make a model of Batman's car out of Lego. I would gather together as many black bricks as I could find, those big blocks that held wheels on would be useful, but they had holes in them where the wheels pushed in and wouldn't look right. I wished I could think of a way of making the blade that the real Batmobile had in the front to cut through any wires that got in the way during a chase. I wondered if I could borrow Dad's pipe knife and build that into the model. No, there would be no way of fixing it. I could use the green wire Dad used sometimes to hold plants up. But no, it wouldn't look right. It never did when you mixed real things in with Lego. It just looked silly. But the fins, the fins I would give this Batmobile would be fantastic. They would be huge and sleek and pointed.

Mum was calling me and my brother Andy. It was time to leave. I wanted some socks. Stripy ones. Andy wanted a brown briefcase. We had to go. We ran up a concrete ramp past the shop windows. In a flash, the scene changed. I was in Solihull now, closer to home. We ran down the ramp instead, into the big hall underneath. This was Mel Square, the centre of town, where the big fountains leapt from the square pool and splashed back into the shallow water. The ramp was cobbled with stones or ridges and we had to take lots of tiny steps. As we ran, we hummed and shouted, laughing as our voices wobbled. Mum thought it was funny too. Behind us, cars moved around the square and the fountains splashed and hissed in the blue pool where the pennies lay and grew green and mouldy. On the ramp, we all laughed and ran and hummed and laughed, and our voices echoed off the stony sides and filled the hall below.

I looked away from the window of my hospital room and I wanted to go outside. I wanted to visit a giant hall where the windows rose up into the sky, where there were smells and strangers talking loudly. I wanted to walk into a shop and treat myself to something special. I wanted to buy a new Lego set and savour the moment when the tiny bricks tumbled out of the crinkly plastic bag in a multi-coloured cascade, ready to form into the picture on the front of the box with the help of the shiny, crisp instructions that had yet to be unfolded. That was it. I wanted Lego. It had taken me through my childhood; I had spent nearly every waking hour trying to build the cars and bikes I dreamed of riding and driving for real. My gawky, hard-edged creations with their bobbly tops and mismatched colours would set off on huge adventures through jungles under the coffee table or into the dark and threatening canyon between Dad's chair and the wall. I craved that escape now, the ability to make huge, universe-spanning fantasy real within the confines of a single room. I knew I wasn't a ten-year-old boy any more, that I was a thirty-six-year-old man in a hospital. But I knew also that I was ill and allowed to do things if they made me feel better. I wanted to play.

With hindsight, of course, these long periods spent in solitary introspection might, in themselves, have been a factor in causing me to regress. Seldom do we have, as adults, the time to spend gazing out of windows wondering about ourselves and our own lives. I had returned to a stage when, perhaps as a young teenager, I could while away hours thinking about life and my place in it. But maybe also the process of recovery itself necessitated re-treading old ground to remember who I was.

I hauled myself up from where I had crouched by the window and shuffled back over to the bed. With a sigh somewhere between contented relaxation and wistful hopelessness, I climbed in and lay under the comforting sheets. In front of my bed, the door sounded quietly under a gentle knock and swung open. Dr John Holloway walked in and said hello. I recognised him now and could remember his name. A tall but gentle-looking man, I was happy to see his friendly, concerned face and to chat with him, enjoying his calm and easy yet authoritative manner. We spoke about how I felt. I said I was fine. While we spoke, I noticed him glancing down to the side of the bed. I looked down and saw what was capturing his attentive glance. He stooped to pick up a book of prayer that had been sent in by a kindly well-wisher.

'Are you reading this?' he asked gently.

'Er, well, yes, I glance at it.' I wanted to show that I had big, spiritual thoughts and was a kind man just like the doctor. I wanted, as always, to show off.

'I read through it sometimes.'

'Right. Good.'

He was sounding me out. Looking for something. I stayed silent. John waited quietly and thumbed the pages. I still said nothing. There was nothing really to say.

'Good. We just sometimes keep an eye out for sudden, you know, surges of enthusiasm for things at this point.'

'Oh. I see. No, I haven't suddenly found religion, if that's what you mean.'

'OK.' He remained calm but seemed slightly relieved.

We knew each other well enough now to talk about how accidents such as mine might affect people. I enjoyed these talks and, I suspect, John used them to gauge my recovery. He explained that sudden obsessions or compulsions can leap up, seemingly from nowhere. They might be to give away all your money, give up a stressful job, or to become fervently religious. It is, perhaps not surprisingly, common for people who have been near to death to return from that place with a new-found religious conviction. This is doubtless a fine thing, but to a mind in as delicate a state as mine, it might also become complicated. I assured John that no, I had not suddenly found God. I had been kind of aware of him all along and still clung to the same ill-formed and nebulous beliefs on the subject of God and the afterlife as I always had. It was a subject I would relish talking about further, but this, perhaps, was not the time. John seemed relieved. He asked how I was sleeping and I replied that, as always, I was sleeping well and long.

'Any dreams? Nightmares?'

'No, none.'

And after a few more comforting words, he left the room. I slipped into a deep sleep, eager to prove my prowess in at least this one aspect of life.

Mindy arrived. I came alive. We spoke about how I felt, how she felt, how the kids were and what was happening on the outside. By this stage, Mindy had begun to explain that my crash had caused a bit of a stir in the media. It was no longer in the news bulletins, so I never picked up on it during my long hours in front of the TV, but there had, she explained, been quite a splash. I don't remember her showing me the newspaper coverage and the doctors were still anxious that I should be protected from too many stimuli. Leafing through newspaper headlines about my imminent demise and subsequent narrow escape might prove to be just that. This was still, as far as I was concerned, an intensely private matter involving me, my family and the medical staff helping me back to health.

I knew that the *Top Gear* team had been to see me when I was still in Leeds General Infirmary, but I had no memory of the event. Andy Wilman, James, Jeremy and Brian Klein, the studio director, had arrived at Leeds within hours of hearing of the crash. We are a close-knit team and I wasn't surprised that they had each felt the need to be there and see me for themselves. We have joked many times that we all work in a playground for grown-ups. We all pretend to be working, but we mess about in cars and with TV cameras just as we mostly all did as kids. And one of us had fallen over in the playground badly. They all wanted to see how their friend was. It would be exactly the same if any of us were hurt. The fact that they had visited meant a lot to me then, but I was unable to access any details about their visit in my bruised and battered brain.

The newspapers were kept away, but what Mindy did allow was a gradual flow of the thousands of letters, cards and gifts from well-wishers. They arrived at the hospital in sack loads, and each day Mindy would bring in as much of the post as I could cope with and as the doctors would allow, until, gradually, we got to the point where I could happily plough through them alone. And it felt wonderful. I did not open them as a television personality, a celebrity tearing open fan mail and soaking up the adulation of people they had never met. I opened and read each card and letter as just a bloke, sitting in a hospital bed being wished well by thousands of kind friends who seemed to mean what they wrote with real sincerity.

Many of the letters were from people who had been similarly injured. Well, perhaps they had not suffered their injuries under the same circumstances, but they had faced similar battles to get well and were keen to share their experience with a fellow sufferer.

I read an account from a young teenage lad who suffered a head injury from falling off his motorcycle. He is, from his letter, clearly a young tough-nut who embraces life readily and enjoys action, adventure and the thrill of riding his dirt bike competitively. And yet he felt compelled to write and share the story of his accident, and to talk about how deeply it affected him and how hard it was to recover.

In doing so with such honesty and candour, he rendered himself vulnerable in a way that must have been uncomfortable to a teenager. He didn't write to the bloke off *Top Gear* to tell him about how fast he went on his bike; he wrote to tell him not to be scared that he had injured his brain, because he had done the same thing and got better. It was a source of comfort beyond words. His note, and the thousands of other similarly honest, sincere and thoughtful letters and cards written by people from all over the world were the most touching acts of kindness I could have imagined. Each contributed to the restoration of my shattered confidence. My heart went out then and does now to those who are far more deserving of such help and do not have the benefit of it. For me, the hours could be passed happily, lying on my bed reading these letters slowly and with care as you do a letter from a friend.

My world slowly narrowed in focus until it encompassed just the room I was in. Like a child, I could fill hours peering into corners, looking at things in a way I had not done for decades. There was never usually time to just sit and stare. Mindy arrived again. She had probably only been down a corridor to talk with the doctors or to make a phone call, but for me, like a dog, my sense of the passage of time was limited. When she wasn't in the room, she just wasn't there. It didn't make any difference if she was gone for minutes or hours, I just wanted her to come back. This time, she walked through the door carrying a box under her arm. It was large, brightly coloured, and I knew what it was more by instinct than by reading the familiar red-and-white logo. It was a box of Lego. Mindy explained that James May had bought it for me. He and I share a love of engineering and construction that can be enjoyed by examining and considering the inner workings of an F1 engine or just messing about with old motorbikes. He had guessed, rightly, that my tangled and confused mind would relish the prospect of the simple but involved process of building a child's toy. I just wanted to play.

It was a model of a tractor. A big green one. The bags of bricks and plastic cogs felt as temptingly lovely as I had dreamed. The instructions were colourful and, for me at that point, complex enough to demand my full attention. I can only imagine what Mindy must have felt and thought as she watched me throw myself into a project aimed at a child thirty years my junior. For me, the world came alive in a brightly coloured, technically demanding challenge. I built the tractor. People came into my room and went. Nurses visited to stick painful pins in my stomach that would, I was assured, do me good. Doctors visited and people brought food. I concentrated on the task and revelled in the achievement, the seriousness of it. Doctor Holloway agreed that, if I wanted to play with Lego, then I should. He went as far as to say that the process of translating two-dimensional instructions into three-dimensional models might even be beneficial. It would, he explained, help develop or rediscover my sense of spatial awareness and my concentration. This was all I needed to hear. I pleaded with Mindy to bring more Lego. She saw the good it was doing, saw the enthusiasm in my face, and ran to the shops.

* * *

Richard was becoming increasingly frustrated at his confinement.

'Why can't I go for a walk? I just need to get out.'

'I really want to go to a shopping centre and buy daft stuff, just rubbish to mess about with; just go shopping. Please? Why can't I go bloody shopping?'

Richard *hates* shopping. Loathes it. Avoids it at all costs. At Christmas he always calls several times from his annual shopping trip, when he has to buy my present:

'Oh God! I don't know what to get you. I've been everywhere. I'm giving up.'

Then, five minutes later:

'I'm going to have to do this. Bloody hell. What size are you again?'

Then . . .

'I can't do any more. Sorry, Mind. I hope you understand. I've got you something, but I can't take any more. I'm coming home.'

Every year I tell him to buy over the Internet, but he feels that's a cop-out, that he must suffer.

So why on earth would he now have this uncontrollable urge to go shopping? Escape. Instead, he agreed to give me a list. I'd go, and in the meantime, he could make a few phone calls.

The list read:

*Classic Bike* magazine
*Classic Car* magazine
Pen and paper for letter writing
Lego set

I dashed out to Cribbs Causeway, a large shopping complex just outside Bristol. The first three items were easy, and I bought myself a copy of *Horse & Hound* at the same time.

The Lego, ridiculously, was a nightmare! I was jogging from one end of the enormous mall to the other; and into every shop I vaguely imagined might stock it, but to no avail. In desperation, I went into Boots. In the children's department there were just a couple of models suitable. A boat and a remote-control car. I bought the boat and two of the cars, as I knew at some point Richard would enjoy a visit from one of his brothers and perhaps this would entertain them.

To compensate for my lack of Lego, I spent ten minutes in a sweet shop, buying all of Richard's favourites—sherbet fountains, jelly beans, liquorice and Turkish Delight in ridiculous quantities.

Constantly glancing at my watch, I knew time was passing far too quickly. I had an hour to get back to Richard, settle him and leave for home.

Shoppers wandering calmly, browsing the halls, stared at me as I ran at full tilt through the complex, down the stairs and out to my car. I was hot and sweaty, dishevelled with an air of slight madness. I yelled at slow-moving traffic and made swift progress when the road cleared. I managed a fairly relaxed cup of tea with Richard as we looked through his goodies before leaving again on the return trip home to Gloucestershire.

* * *

Within days, my room had been transformed; filled with brightly coloured boxes of Lego as I buried myself in my new-found work. The place looked like a toyshop. Or, better still, like my childhood fantasy of a Lego-testing facility. And I was chief tester. Mindy arrived once more, stepping into the chaos and smiling as I looked up from the floor where I was busily building a ship. She had brought the kids. I smiled at them and said hello. They advanced and said hello back. My heart leapt and then steadied. I asked them if they would like to join me and play. They said yes and crouched down next to me.

I might have felt daft, asking them to join in with the game that had kept me cheerfully occupied all morning. But I didn't. With Izzy and Willow around, I knew my place again. I was their father; I was in hospital because I had suffered a head injury and I had to try not to upset them. I loved them more than anything else in the world, but I couldn't go home with them.

We played and talked and my mind erased the memory of our time together as fast as it passed, because only this way could it block out the pain of being both in their world and, temporarily, outside of it. With no sense of the passage of time, I was unaware how long they had been with me when Mindy rose from her seat on the bed and announced that they must leave. I held the girls tightly; they clung to me and I to them. I walked with them to the door and, on a whim, followed them into the corridor beyond. I was still unsteady on my feet, but was not going to show it. We walked to the lift, the four of us. Mindy pressed the button and, too quickly, the lift arrived. The girls and their mother walked in. In the pause before the doors shut, I smiled at them as they stood, the three of them illuminated by the soft light inside the lift, making a warm picture framed by the metal doorway as I watched from the harsh, fluorescent light of the hospital corridor. They smiled back.

As the doors began to slide together, Izzy broke her gaze away from mine and turned her head to look up at Mindy. Her smile crumbled and her eyes filled with tears. She had held them back for as long as she could and now she could hold them back no longer. As she looked up to Mindy for support, her resolve not to cry failed and she succumbed. She was a six-year-old girl missing her daddy very much; scared and worried. I looked at Mindy as the doors shut with a soft click, ending the scene, and I stared for some time at the anonymous, blank space where my family had been. I wept too as I walked back to my room. My powerlessness only emphasised by the feel of the hospital floor under my bare feet as I trudged the few steps back up the corridor.

* * *

The second the lift doors closed, Izzy collapsed on to my legs and burst into uncontrollable sobs. I was on my knees with her in an instant. I swathed her in love, praised her bravery and was completely astounded by her. She instinctively knew how to help her beloved daddy. She was giving all her tiny body could muster for him, solely for him. At just six years old, she had been more thoughtful and caring than many adults would ever manage. She even composed herself, without any encouragement, so that by the time we reached the back door, some two minutes later, she would walk out and raise a hand to the windows high above, knowing that Daddy was watching and waving as she walked to the car, encouraging her little sister to do the same. Ela and I followed suit, the tears flowing down all our faces, save Willow, who thankfully didn't notice, 'til we all sat in the car.

'Oh, Izzy, baby. Well done,' I told her.

She simply nodded and smiled, and held out her little hand to me from the back seat, the tears dripping from her face, her thumb in her mouth.

'Are you OK, Izzy?' asked Willow.

Izzy nodded at Willow, and we drove out. We went home. Together, but without Daddy. For Izzy it was a truly dreadful act, but somewhere, somehow, she understood. This was the way it had to be—for a while. But as I told her again and again:

'He'll get better, Iz—I promise.'

She'd nod, and cry, and hug me. But she's from a tough stable, that little girl, nurtured by love and honesty. And she believed me, and believed in her father. She made Willow her responsibility, and I believe she determined to stay strong for her little sister, who didn't understand.

One day she'll know what she went through, marvel at her own journey, and perhaps understand how she became the person she became. I only know this: a little girl decided of her own volition to become more than a daughter—if there could ever be a greater gift—she became, as Richard described her, 'his mate'. She was understanding and strong, gentle and funny, mature yet childlike and, above all this, completely our Izzy.

It was wonderful to be home with them. As we drove through the gate, I could hear the dogs barking wildly from the kitchen, a sound I suddenly realised I'd missed. Home.

Pat, our neighbour, had kindly offered to look after the girls' pony, and was bringing her in from the field to an immaculate stable. Pat is one of those rare and wonderful people who offers help at the drop of a hat; she expects nothing in return, yet gives her precious time willingly. Even with three horses of her own to see to, she'd made the little pony her priority. We had a brief chat; she was careful not to dwell on Richard's condition, anxious to avoid upsetting me, and quick to allay any worries I might have about the pony's welfare. She'd be there for us as long as we needed her. Pat is a straightforward woman who just gets on and does the right thing. I thanked her, and hugged her before she left.

Ela and the girls opened the front door and we immediately set the dogs free from the kitchen. I was surrounded by bouncing, barking, tail-wagging excitement. TG grabbing my hand in her mouth, Captain leaping up at me, Pablo barking and Crusoe stretching forward and yowling; each of them desperate to impress their welcome upon me. Willow and Izzy laughed and giggled.

'I think they missed you, Mindy!' Ela smiled.

The girls and I ran outside with them all and watched them as they galloped off up the hill next to our house. Barking, scampering, happy to be free.

We went over to see Hattie, our enormous outdoor dog. She slobbered and harrumphed and lay on her back for her belly to be scratched.

'Ohhh! Hattie Pudding!' Willow gently stroked the dog's chest as she lay licking her lips in complete ecstasy. Hattie is a guard dog, and she'd spent a great deal of the past week barking at the many strangers at the gate. She was hoarse as a result, her usual deep bark a little husky and high-pitched. She was at least three times Willow's size, yet with the children she was gentle as a lamb. They were her babies and she took her role as protector very seriously. Apparently, when the children left the house she grew silent, uncaring, awaiting their return, her front paws resting on the top of the five-bar gate at the entrance to her kennel area, watching for a car.

We all returned to the house and Ela made a quick supper for the girls while I dashed around upstairs, grabbing clothes for Richard. The girls were in the playroom, lost in a game, and I just had time for a quick chat with Ela before Izzy joined us. She saw the suitcase in the hall. Her face fell.

'Oh, Mummy, do you have to go again?' She hugged my legs.

I looked across at Ela, and found it so difficult not to cry. Ela couldn't cope, she turned away. She was like their big sister; she loved them and felt for them.

I bent down and picked up Izzy, carried her into the hall where Willow might not find us. I put her down on the stairs and sat next to her. We had one of our 'grown-up chats'. It was something Richard often did with her. We talked about Daddy, how she felt, and why I needed to help him now. Just for a while, just until he was better.

'I miss Daddy,' she sobbed, but she understood. And we stayed there for a while.

'Daddy misses you, baby. He misses everything, but we'll help him get better, won't we?'

She nodded, and wiped her face dry with her sleeve, then ran her nose along her arm.

'Eeeew! Bogey slime!' I laughed, she giggled, we hugged.

'I love you, Mummy.'

I held on to her. I couldn't prevent my own tears. But she didn't notice. Or at least, she pretended not to.

We joined Ela and Willow at the table for supper, but before it was finished the hospital called. Richard was anxious. My time at home was fast running out.

* * *

Like many people, I guess, I am never happy in an institution. But here, in Bristol, the order and regularity of the days, the constant presence of caring professionals, and the sense that I was in the right place doing the right thing to get better, helped soothe away some of the fear and confusion. I adjusted to the new rhythm of life and became, perhaps for the first time, institutionalised. And I grew happier. I woke up naturally in the mornings, chatted with nurses and doctors who cared about me, ate breakfast and played with Lego. At lunchtime, food was brought; I ate it, slept for a few hours, woke and played with Lego again and wondered what was for tea.

In a sense, the transformation was complete; I was ten years old again, and quite happy to be so. And at this point, I began to miss my two brothers in a way I hadn't for decades. Because I missed them as playmates. I wanted them to be there with me, sitting cross-legged on the floor, trying to decide what model to build next or wondering what was coming up on the telly. They have wives and children of their own; jobs they work at to support their families and busy, complicated, rewarding adult lives. But I missed them as the kids I grew up with, who shared my childhood. I had now drifted back into that childhood and I wondered where my two best mates were.

Equally, I have spoken with them since and learned that, in many ways, they had been afflicted with similar emotions. Whatever happens to any of the three of us in our lives, part of us will always be the same three young tearaways who rode bicycles round 'the Triangle', made dens on 'the field' at the back of the house, and played with toy cars in 'the ditch'. And now one of us had been in a nasty accident. They had visited me many times in hospital over the past few weeks, of course. They were there within hours of my arrival in Leeds. But I held on to no memories of those early visits. On later occasions, they arrived to find me confused and bewildered. I guess I was wondering who these two grown men were and where my brothers had gone.

But these thoughts were childish and so, though intense, passed as quickly as they overcame me. I could happily distract myself in my simple, ordered days. The doctors would pop in regularly and I enjoyed our chats. I had, for a day or so, been building a model of the Batmobile. It was a big one, brought for me by Mindy. The familiarity of the character, if not the machine itself, made it a comforting and engaging prospect. I was sensible enough to know that Batman had moved on, that his car was far advanced from the ones I had built years before. But the style, the image, was familiar.

Dr Holloway arrived at the door, knocked and strode in softly. He asked how I was doing and I assured him that I was very well indeed. He asked how the Batmobile was going. And I began to explain that it was pretty tricky in places and you had to pay close attention to the instructions. I had taken his inquiry to mean that he too was in the process of assembling a Batmobile and was, perhaps, struggling. I felt sure that he would benefit from my many years of modelling experience and I was happy to share it with him. It was only after a good few minutes of giving patient and very comprehensive instruction in the finer points of assembling the Lego model that I realised he was humouring me. And I was embarrassed for the first time in a while. Which was probably a good sign.

At some point, someone had identified a need in me for physical exercise. I run nearly every day as a rule and benefit from it physically but also, perhaps more importantly, mentally. Maybe I had shown signs of stagnating in my tiny room full of Lego. Given that I had suffered pretty much no bodily injuries apart from those to my brain, I remained in reasonably good shape. But I had lost a lot of weight; a week or two of being fed through a needle in your arm will do that to you.

I was asked if I would like to go to the hospital gym and I bounced up and down like the ten-year-old I felt myself to be. Mindy brought in my running kit, ready for the big day. When the time came, a physiotherapist collected me from my room and took me along the narrow corridors and down the stairs to another floor. This was the furthest I could recall travelling for what felt like years, and I hungrily absorbed every new and strange feature. A fire extinguisher, a liquid-soap dispenser, a yellow bin all leapt out from corners to ignite my senses. I glanced through windows to see new and different scenes that both tempted and scared me. We arrived at a door and walked through to a small room.

Inside were a few bits and pieces of gym equipment and some pale green crash mats laid out on the floor. I was taken through some yoga moves. We stretched and talked and talked and stretched. The physiotherapist lady was very friendly and kind, and I tried to show off by being really good at yoga. I wasn't. And then she asked if I would like to use the rowing machine. I most certainly would, and I pounced on it eagerly. After four minutes of pulling I was pretty much exhausted. It doesn't take long for whatever physical fitness you have to drain away. Mine had disappeared down the plughole the moment I took to a hospital bed. But it felt wonderful to be exerting myself physically again. And the benefit was more mental than physical.

This was the first time I could really try at something, could pit myself against it and be allowed to struggle. It was as much about the realisation that the doctors felt I was well enough to work up a bit of a sweat as it was about the exercise itself. The rowing machine suffered from a piercing and very loud squeak which was emitted each time the plastic seat passed the halfway mark along the horizontal rail on its rollers. Over the next few days I would wonder if my frantic rowing and the accompanying regular squeak was keeping other patients awake on a floor above. I felt bad and hoped not, but I rowed on, slowly increasing my stamina. Mindy knew how much I would benefit from this gentle exercise and did everything she could to encourage it; listening patiently when I explained breathlessly and proudly that I was up to seven minutes' rowing and was now being allowed to use the running machine too.

I dreamed of being able to take off on my own and run outside in the real world. I dreamed of running along tree-lined paths scattered with big yellow leaves and clambering over fences to sprint across wide, muddy fields under skies with real weather in them, and to not care or worry. And in a small, anonymous room somewhere in a hospital in Bristol, I ran on with my eyes closed, my trainers slapping down on the treadmill, while in my mind, I crunched through golden leaves and breathed in the natural and vital smells of the real world.

* * *

I was going to leave. It had been discussed, people approved, I could leave the hospital. But I couldn't go home. By now, it had been explained to me that our house was ringed by reporters and TV crews, and the doctors were worried about how I might react. Dr Holloway explained that every single thing I saw or encountered, everything that caught my attention or happened around me, must be considered an episode, an event, a stimulus. Because of the fragile state of my mind still, and because of the fact that when it's a brain injury, there are few simple or obvious tests to see how everything is, we had to be careful. There was no dipstick to slot into my brain and tell the doctors if I was now liable to convulsions or mental complications. But there were statistics.

Thousands of cases are recorded and examined, as much for the benefit of subsequent patients as the one under examination. It's sad that there are so many cases of brain injury to record, but at least the resulting statistics can help predict problems that, history has shown, might arise as a patient goes through the recovery process and beyond. And these statistics told the doctors that, with a brain injury of the severity of mine, there were very real dangers associated with over-stimulation at this point. I had not been outside for weeks, not felt the air moving past me or been anywhere that wasn't a safe, controllable environment. Leaving the security and predictability of the hospital would be shocking enough, but to go home and be confronted with a horde of eager reporters, TV cameras and flashguns, could well provoke serious problems. But equally, Dr Holloway appreciated that I needed desperately to make the move out and to begin engaging once more with the world.

There was much that I wasn't yet ready for, but just as much that I needed urgently if I was to carry on recovering as quickly as I had been. And so a plan was hatched. We were going to slip away somewhere unnoticed and anonymously. We needed to be guaranteed privacy and a safe place from which I could walk slowly and carefully back into the world. Mindy had found such a place. And we were going in a couple of days.

I hated the secrecy.

No one must know where we were going, not even friends. This was because, if it did get out and we had to return to hospital to hide, it would be terrible to find ourselves looking for someone to blame. We didn't want anyone to be lumbered with the responsibility of keeping a secret that might well get out anyway. If people didn't know where we were, then they would never feel called upon to account for themselves if the secret got out.

I was told that I would be going to bed as usual on the evening of the great escape and would then be woken early in the morning. I had to have my bag packed with the few belongings I needed and be ready to leave. I packed and re-packed my bag every day to make sure I would be ready.

CHAPTER 14

# ESCAPE TO SCOTLAND

Richard's medication became less intense as the days passed. Steadily, his balance improved too. He could walk along a corridor without the occasional bounce off the wall; he spent less time in bed and his physiotherapy sessions were increased to two per day. Initially he could only cope with five or ten minutes, which would leave him exhausted. This depressed him. Richard was an excellent runner; he'd run almost daily and for many miles. Suddenly his body couldn't find the energy. The physios concentrated on Pilates and aerobic exercise, together with relaxation techniques. They were a great team, concentrating on small achievements, and helping him to regain his strength.

Massage sessions helped to relieve the stiffness in his back and shoulders, and a timetable was devised to monitor improvement in his overall fitness.

Once the sessions increased, and with them his core strength and stability, he regained not only physical strength, but also a more positive outlook. Richard had always waxed lyrical about the endorphin buzz he enjoyed when exercising. If ever he was down, I'd encourage him to visit the gym or go out for a run. He invariably returned recharged and happy. I sensed he wasn't yet experiencing the buzz, but at least his body was starting to perform again.

Because he was more mobile, the dreaded daily injections could cease. Anti-clotting jabs in his stomach had left a chain of painful bruises. He winced each time they were administered. They wouldn't be missed.

Discussions with Rick Nelson had demonstrated Richard's 'increased insight' into his condition. This better understanding of his situation, what had happened to him, and how he was improving, was a very positive sign.

Richard was introduced to Dr John Holloway, Medical Director of the local Brain Injury Rehabilitation Centre at Frenchay. He was a consultant neuropsychiatrist and would take over Richard's care.

John was very considered. Before a sentence left his lips you could sense the calculation, the thought involved in the order of words, how they were delivered, how they'd be received. He possessed an air of understanding and empathy, but whenever he spoke to Richard he was careful not to patronise or insult the latent intelligence hidden deep within the man in front of him. He was an expert.

Richard instantly warmed to him, and quickly turned off his usual act. John was very adept at gently cutting through the crap and discussing the real issues. His honesty was encouraging. He gave Richard enough information to convey the severity of his injury without causing alarm. Just enough so his advice would be taken seriously. I listened and watched the exchanges between them with enormous relief—Richard would listen to him, be guided by him.

John would help us for a great many months.

He was accessible night and day, and became an invaluable guide through the most difficult stages of recovery.

* * *

Every journey I took into or out of the hospital was met by a small group of photographers at the entrance. They were respectful, and didn't attempt to gain entry to the hospital; similarly, the photographers at home weren't intrusive, they were just waiting to see if Richard emerged.

However, I was becoming a little nervous about the press. We were really out of our depth with all the media coverage. Preoccupied as I was with keeping Richard happy, making sure everything was OK at home, and updating his work colleagues, friends and family on progress, and consulting with the medical team, I had no time left to make sure the press were correctly informed—and that worried me. Richard's agent had been approached by various publications who were very interested in his story, and I had no idea what to do. Luckily I was put in contact with someone who did.

Gary Farrow, a highly respected PR professional, became an important part of our lives. More so than we could ever have imagined. Initially, he was there to take care of media issues, but his role changed dramatically as Richard's condition improved.

Meanwhile, Richard was going stir crazy. The doctors had moved him to a different room in the hospital to try to appease him, but it wasn't working terribly well. He really wanted out, and was starting to get angry.

John Holloway and Rick Nelson had a meeting to discuss Richard's progress following their own individual assessments. The position was clear. Richard was at a point in his recovery where to keep him in hospital for much longer would become counter-productive. However, the issue was how to get him out of hospital without massive press attention. The flashing lights from a bank of press photographers could quite possibly put him at risk of a seizure or epileptic fit. Then there was the attention we'd be in for when word spread he was at home.

Our house abutted a country lane; the press could literally lean over the gate and at one point see straight into the house.

The two doctors were concerned he should enjoy freedom on his release from hospital; not feel like a prisoner in his own home. They suggested I try to get him away for a while, but the question was where? And how?

I called Gary. We discussed the problems, and at one point he suggested putting a twenty-foot-high temporary wall around the house, but that seemed a miserable way to see home.

The doctors were keen for Richard to go somewhere quiet where he could relax. Their one condition was that he shouldn't go on any long-haul flights. Gary and I discussed Ireland, but it was too complicated. The Lake District, but it was too busy. Nowhere had the privacy he needed. Then we hit upon the solution: Scotland. A cottage in the Highlands.

Perfect! But it had to be done very carefully. No one, not even Richard, could know the plan we were hatching. If anything reached the ears of the press, it would be all over. They'd know he was coming out and he'd never manage to hide away in secret.

Gary arranged for a group of highly trained, highly efficient ex special forces men to go into action on our behalf. They were great guys and professional to the last. I knew they'd make it happen.

Operation Joystick went into action. The brief we worked from went like this:

*A multi-phase operation to enable the subject and his family to go on holiday for a week without the press becoming aware of the plans or their location during that time.*

*To minimise the number of people involved and the chances of being seen by third parties, we plan to move the family and the subject independently to a rendezvous point from where they will be driven in a large Winnebago to the ultimate destination.*

*One person to fly ahead, hire a car to recce the location and act as a ferry vehicle in case the Winnebago cannot drive right to the final destination.*

*Constant radio communication to be maintained at all times.*

It was so difficult to keep the whole thing secret from Richard, but he was incredibly excitable and would absolutely tell everyone he was getting out if even a whiff of it reached him.

I had to be at home on Friday evening. Ela was leaving us. She'd extended her stay by two weeks to help us out, but had to return to University in Poland.

Richard understood that I needed to say my goodbyes to her, and naturally would have to remain with the girls once she'd gone. But I had a problem. He'd expected me to take the girls to visit him on Saturday, which was impossible, as the team had to come to our house to finalise plans for our departure on Sunday night. So, against all advice, I told him we were leaving in the early hours of Monday morning. I made him swear to keep the secret, and explained the reasons why. He was excited, but understood.

I called Richard's mum and told her we must 'disappear for a bit'. I asked her to buy a pay-as-you-go mobile phone and give me the number. I'd do the same. We would contact each other on the 'secret' phones to avoid any chance of a message being picked up by the wrong person, or any opportunity for eavesdropping. Clearly, if either phone rang we'd know who was calling.

Richard's brother Andy was due to visit him on Sunday afternoon. Poor Andy had missed Richard's really alert moments in Leeds. As a schoolteacher he was in demand back at work, and was terribly upset he hadn't had the opportunity to have a proper conversation with Richard. Although he'd been kept abreast of his brother's progress, he naturally was desperate to see him in the flesh. The visit would hopefully keep Richard's mind off imminent events, and make for an enjoyable afternoon.

**Saturday**

The two men in charge of the operation came to our house in Gloucestershire. They were accompanied by others in vehicles close by who were doing a sweep of the land surrounding the house. Some members of the press had been camping in the woods opposite in full camouflage gear with long lenses focused and ready for any interesting movement. There were plenty of hiding places, and these guys planned to identify their whereabouts in readiness for Sunday.

On their approach to our house in Gloucestershire they phoned me and I greeted them like friends at the door, as agreed. We chatted amiably in the kitchen over a couple of cups of tea and discussed the finer details of the plan.

**Sunday**

In the afternoon the daughter of one of the guys arrived. She was about eighteen years old, and was there to get to know the girls. She was to play an important role the following evening. She played with them for hours and, when she left, promised to see them again soon.

I visited our local agricultural feed store and stocked the house with dog, cat and pony food; wrote notes to neighbours who'd be looking after the place; and started to assemble luggage in my bedroom while the girls were playing in the garden.

I spoke to Richard many times on the phone and we were both careful not to mention anything about the plan. The hours were dragging for him. He'd spent two nights alone. He hadn't slept at all on Friday night, and Saturday was little better, but escape was imminent.

On Sunday night I put the girls to bed as usual, then started running up and down stairs collecting everything and packing bags and suitcases.

The team was already in position around the house; they'd ensured no one was watching. Simultaneously, other members of the team were sweeping the area surrounding the hospital in Bristol.

At 11 p.m. the guys returned and reversed their 4x4 so the back door of the vehicle practically opened into our hallway. There was a pile of luggage at the door.

Once the luggage was in, the young girl who'd visited earlier helped me to wake Izzy and Willow. 'Come on, we're going on holiday,' I told them.

They were sleepy, but happy. They were each secured in their child-seats before Captain, our Jack Russell, and Top Gear Dog joined them in the back of the car to giggles of delight. While we were gone the other dogs would be looked after by various house-sitters; trusted friends and neighbours who generously offered their help.

I explained to the girls that I was going to fetch Daddy and meet them in a bit. They didn't once worry or question anything. There was nothing but smiles and laughter as they set off on their adventure and great excitement at the prospect of getting Daddy back.

I jumped into the identical second car and followed them out of the drive and down to the motorway where we parted company. They headed north to a motorway services and a waiting Winnebago—we were going south to the hospital in Bristol.

Fifteen minutes before our arrival, the guys on site were contacted by radio to check all was clear; when we were given the OK, I called the duty nurse as prearranged, and told her our ETA.

'That's fine,' she said. 'I've just checked on him and he's fast asleep. D'you want me to go and wake him?'

'No thanks, it's OK, we'll get him up.'

Richard knew very well what time he was being sprung, and I was convinced there was no way he was asleep.

* * *

This was better than Christmas when I was five. In a few hours, I would leave the hospital and go out into the world for what felt like the very first time. Lying on my back in the hospital bed, I pulled the bedclothes up to my chin and gripped their soft edges. My bag was packed and lay tucked under the bed. I was quivering with excitement, trying to control my breathing. My brother Andy had been in to see me that day. I had rung him and begged him to come; the desire to spend time just knocking about with my brothers had grown to almost unbearable proportions.

I knew I would be going away very soon and wanted to see him before I went. The visit was fun; he indulged me by playing with Lego, and we spoke about what was to come. I told him, in secret, that we were going away tomorrow and that no one, not even most of the hospital staff, knew about it. I spoke conspiratorially about our plans, about how we didn't want to fly anywhere because I might be spotted in an airport and because the doctors didn't want me to leave the mainland.

I trust him and every one of my friends and family

entirely, and I knew that not one of them would even consider betraying a confidence at such a critical stage. In the end, it was enough for all of them to know that we would be safe, that we were going on the advice of the doctors and with their support, and that help was on hand if we needed it while we were away. All the same, the need for secrecy like this was very tough on my fragile mind. And I know that it was hard on Andy and all of my family.

I would later wish I had simply told them where we were going and explained that we wouldn't blame them if it ever got out and we had to dash back to the safety of the hospital. But the doctors had decreed that we absolutely must keep it secret and that I needed a safe, quiet place. So I told Andy that we would be staying on the mainland and that we would be travelling in secret by road. I told him that we would be leaving in the small hours of the following morning and I reassured him that, yes, the doctors knew everything we were doing and had given their approval. The secrecy and conspiracy didn't really help with my burgeoning paranoia. Andy left, I packed and re-packed my bag, and climbed into the bed in which I now lay, staring at the ceiling and counting the minutes like a child on Christmas Eve.

When the knock at the door finally came, it didn't have to rouse me from sleep. I lay awake, still clutching the sheets, tensed like a ski-jumper at the top of the ramp. Desperate not to appear too keen and childish, I resisted the temptation to leap from the bed and moved slowly to a sitting position. I stifled a massive, theatrical yawn as the figure entered the room.

'Is it time then?'

'Yes, let's go.'

The lights beyond the door were dimmed and the corridor wall opposite loomed dark and blank. I grabbed my bag filled with all the possessions I had gathered around me during the long weeks. I had stuffed my treasured Lego sets into the holdall along with as many clothes as I could fit in. My watch, the same that I had been wearing in the jet car when it crashed, was already on my wrist. There was nothing else to take. We stepped out into the corridor and I felt the grip of nerves on my stomach. The night-time silence of the hospital was deep and profound. This felt somewhere between a scene from an action movie and leaving early on a family holiday as a child. I half expected my father to arrive, point at the time and ask if we had packed everything in the car with the tents. We walked the length of the corridor and I tried to avoid peering into doors that stood slightly open to either side.

We spoke in dramatic, hushed whispers.

'You get here OK then?'

'Yes.'

'The car just outside is it?'

'Yes.'

'The kids OK?'

'Yes, they're waiting in the motorhome. We'll drive there in the car and transfer.'

I wanted to comment on how early in the morning it was, how exciting it was to be up and about and how cold it might be outside. Mindy held my hand. Somehow, I felt that the calm, dark-clad figure alongside me might not be so moved by it all. We walked down stairs and along more corridors, passing dimly lit drinks machines and rows of plastic chairs. We pushed confidently through doors and turned abrupt corners. My guide clearly knew the route exactly and precisely and he moved in a manner that suggested he was familiar with situations where taking a wrong turn down a corridor in a building at night might be more than a minor inconvenience. He had studied how we would get from my room to the car and the route had been committed to a memory that was not likely to forget it; whatever happened.

After more corridors and junctions, we crossed a carpeted lobby between plate-glass walls. And we walked outside. The air hit me, wrapped about my face and blew through me. I wanted to yell and scream and run about. I didn't. Behind me, the light shone through the hospital glass with a blue tint. A bird sang. The car waited by the entrance. The back door was held open for me. I looked at the sky, looked at the buildings outlined against it, breathed some more of the cool night air into my shivering chest and climbed in.

'The girls are all waiting for you, Richard. They're fine. And they've got a couple of the dogs with them too.'

I felt safe in the presence of the man who came to collect me, I knew instinctively that he was familiar with this strange, unearthly ritual. I felt exhilarated too; every moment that passed was a big, important one. I tried to collect them and preserve them. I would never do this again and I wanted to remember it. Nevertheless, I was asleep in seconds in the car and woke only when it pulled up alongside the motorhome. The kids were waiting inside. I climbed out and a man grabbed my bag, passing it up to the open door.

The girls were sitting inside on a sofa. TG and Captain, two of our dogs, were there too.

*   *   *

We arrived at the hospital just before 2 a.m. The night porter unlocked the side door and we made our way quickly into the lift, then out and along the corridor to Richard's room, passing the duty nurse on the way. She stood and smiled as we passed her.

I opened the door to Richard's room. It was in darkness apart from a dim reading lamp on the bedside table; a still form covered in blankets lay on the bed. For a second I wondered whether he had fallen asleep.

'Richard?' I called in a loud whisper.

He recognised my voice instantly and threw back the covers. He was dressed and ready, with an enormous grin on his face.

In a moment he was on his feet and hugging me.

'God I've missed you.'

I smiled back and shhhhhed him, before introducing him to his rescuer, who was already asking which bags to take. Richard was putting on his boots and pointing to various items of boxed Lego and his many jackets and jeans.

'No, darling, you need only take your Billingham bag. I've got everything else.'

'But we can't leave all this stuff.'

'Someone's coming tomorrow to pack it all up after you've gone.'

'Oh, OK.'

We filed out of the room and past the nurse again.

'Bye. Good luck,' she whispered.

'Thank you. Bye.'

I'd left a black hoodie and a pair of sunglasses in Richard's room on my last visit and, despite his protestations, he now wore them to leave the building. It was a few steps to the waiting car, then he had to keep his head well down as we drove out of Bristol. Once on the motorway he held me close and told me of his excitement and the game he'd played with the nurse who kept coming in to check on him. He hadn't slept a wink; he'd pretended to snore whenever she entered the room.

By 3 a.m. we were at the Winnebago. The girls were jumping around and playing, and so ecstatic to see their daddy.

* * *

Suddenly, the world was in colour once more; I was home with my girls. I clutched them all, held on to them. They were excited to show me around inside the van. They showed me a big bedroom at the back with a real bed in it. They showed me their bed, with its row of smart lockers overhead, and a place where TG insisted on sleeping. I felt Mindy watching us. She stood back and studied what happened as I re-engaged with my children. She had taken us through one phase of recovery and now we were entering another. My mouth had that early-in-the-morning dryness. I was tired but too alive to sleep. Mindy sat next to me on the sofa bed, we cradled the girls' heads as they slept. TG curled up by their feet, protecting her flock.

We talked softly of our lives together, of how our experiences might change things. The doctors had reassured us that, though it would be long and difficult, I would recover properly and fully. Right now, that felt like a very long way off. I was in too fragile a state ever to imagine feeling normal again. But we agreed on one thing; we could grab hold of what we had, make sure that, given a chance to carry on with our lives together when it had looked so much as though that would not be possible, we would do our level best to make the most of it.

I needed to sleep now, the excitement was taking its toll. As the van rumbled on through the night, I knew that I had to try and relax my mind, take the pressure off my brain. I grew worried that everything I was doing and seeing, the sudden rush of new experiences, might prove too much. I was scared again.

We thanked and said goodbye to the team who'd seen us this far, and were introduced to our two drivers. Again, both were highly overqualified special services men. They'd drive us from here to the Highlands of Scotland, and look after us the whole way.

The doctors had described how seeing too many different stimuli might trigger convulsions. I sat still, closed my eyes, and waited for something to happen. I had no idea what it would feel like, an epileptic fit, and with every rise in emotion or remote physical sensation, I imagined it was starting.

At the back of the van was a bedroom. The kids had been impressed with the full-size double bed and I surveyed it now from the sliding doors that led into the cabin. There were windows at the head and side of it, and through the blinds the lights of the motorway pulsed and flashed. I turned around to stare back into the main cabin and saw a similar pulsing as the overhead motorway lighting flashed by. Mindy looked up from where she sat, still cradling the girls as they slept.

'Go to sleep, darling. You'll be fine.'

I felt pale and thin. Being scared had become an almost constant state for me over the weeks, but was made no more pleasant by its familiarity.

'Mind, I'm worried to death. They tell you that flashing lights can trigger epilepsy even if they're on the telly. If they can do that to normal people sitting at home, what about me now?'

It sounded petulant and ungrateful. Mindy had coordinated this entire escape with the doctor's approval, and now I was rejecting it as too dangerous. What did I know anyway?

'And if I sleep in there'—pointing to the warm bedroom behind me—'the lights are flashing even more.'

'No, look—I'll close the curtains.'

Mindy rose carefully from her bunk so as not to disturb Izzy and Willow and squeezed past me into the bedroom. She reached across the bed and pulled the curtains together. I admired her shape as she leant across to do so, but felt too scared and nervous to give her my full appreciation.

'There, that'll be fine.'

'Thank you. I love you.'

The room was dim now and Mindy looked at me through the gloom.

'You'll be fine. The doctors know what you're doing and they said you'll be OK. What you need now is some sleep. Remember, they told you that the risks increased the more tired you get. So sleep is the best thing. Come on.'

She pulled the bedcover back and stepped to the side to make room for me to walk into the room and fall on to the bed.

'I'm sorry, I'm just scared. To come this far and then to . . .'

I tailed off. Exhaustion was taking over now. I understood the need for sleep, that it was about more than stopping me from feeling tired, that it could make all the difference in my recovery. I closed my eyes and Mindy padded out of the room. But sleep would not come. I lay and waited for a seizure to start, tried to access the remote extremities of my body to see if I could detect any tingle, any warning sensation that something momentous and unpleasant was about to occur.

The axle of the van thumped heavily as it dealt with a ripple in the motorway surface. I was actively trying to sleep, straining to do so, and I knew it would not work. I threw the covers off and got up just as the doors slid closed behind Mindy. I slid them open again and looked through. Mindy saw me and came back in.

'I can't sleep. Too scared. This is the worst . . . I just don't think I should be doing this.'

'Do you want to go back?'

'No. God no. But I just . . . Maybe we should go back. This is a stupid idea. For God's sake, they said no flashing lights, no sudden noises. Listen to it, when the camper goes over a bump there's a huge noise. You can hear it in here because you're right over the back wheels. I'm going to have a fucking fit and then I'll be stuck with them for life and I'll lose my driving licence and we won't be able to earn a living and we'll be fucking ruined. Why didn't you just book a flight? We could have snuck in somewhere and flown off somewhere warm. Who the hell would have spotted me anyway? Who cares if some bloke off a car show who banged his fucking head recently gets on a plane and goes off somewhere? This was the worst thing you could have done to me. Just leave me the fuck alone and I'll sit in here and stay awake. You go and get some sleep in there and I'll sit in here, awake.'

She stood, gripping the edge of the door. I was attacking her, blaming her for everything. The doctors had warned that patients recovering from head injuries can suffer problems with anger and rage. Maybe this was what was happening now. We both knew it and the knowledge made me angrier. I wasn't cross because of the bang on my head, I was cross because everyone wanted to kill me; to make me mad; to ruin all the hard work I had done in making myself better. It was all going to go wrong, and it was just because people didn't think.

'Darling, get some sleep. Please.' Her voice was soft and warm as she placated me quietly and confidently. I lay on the bed, pulled the cover over my head to block out the lights and waited to be gripped by a seizure. I wondered what it would feel like. Would Mindy know, or would I just seize up solid and die? The road rumbled past below the bed as we travelled further from one world and into another.

* * *

The girls had fallen asleep. They looked beautiful, cuddled up together on the enormous bed in the living area, a couple of blankets over them, and TG—who on every other car journey was sick—lying in front of their feet, edging them into the safest corner of the bed. She took on the role of a nanny dog from the moment the journey started, and whenever we turned a tight corner she pushed the girls further into their safety zone, their faithful Jack Russell, Captain, alongside.

My brief moment of peace was soon over, Richard couldn't settle in the bedroom, and he was petrified he might suffer a seizure. I was calm with him and tried to reassure him. There was very little light coming through the windows, it was one-way security glass covered by blinds, which were covered by curtains, but that didn't matter. I understood enough about Richard's condition to know reasoning with him was not the answer. Eventually he returned to the bed and pulled the covers over his head.

As I left the room, I realised he'd broken the sliding door off its runners. I tried to fix it back on, but it was quite heavy and he heard me and grew angry—'For fucksake!'

I wouldn't be able to fix it, and I needed to stay close to him to make sure I was there if he needed me. I couldn't join him in the bed; the door would slam. I had only one option. I put my hand between the door and its closing point and leant up against the wall at right angles to it, my right foot braced up against the opposite side of the Winnebago—actually the loo door—to avoid sliding down if I fell asleep. I stayed there through the night, sometimes grappling with the door when it escaped my grasp on a sharp bend, other times wincing as it trapped my fingers on a right-hand turn. When dawn came it offered no respite. I couldn't leave my post until Richard awoke, and I had no intention of waking him. At least the scenery became visible, with the promise of a sunny day.

We were all together. We were a family again. Richard had been nervous the previous night, but that was understandable. He'd been nowhere but hospital rooms for the past three weeks or so. The external stimuli had suddenly overwhelmed him, but he'd managed, he'd overcome it. He'd be OK. I yearned to climb into the bed next to him, to hold him and reassure him, but he needed as much rest as possible. The best I could do for him now was to remain there, with my crumpled fingers in the door.

*　　*　　*

I woke to find that the van was still ploughing on but the light of day had ended the flash of passing streetlamps. The terrors of the evening were gone. Izzy and Willow were still sleeping on their bunk with TG. Mindy was standing outside my door looking tired and strained, but she kissed me good morning when I slid the door open and peered into the main cabin.

'Morning, darling. You finally got some sleep then?' Despite last night, she sounded warm, caring and sincere. I knew how much she cared.

'Yes. Thank you. Sorry about shouting. I was scared.' I hung my head like a scolded schoolboy.

'I know. It's fine.'

'Where are we?' I looked along the length of the van and through the huge, flat windscreen to see tree-lined, sweeping roads and a warm, sunny day. Slowly I moved into the cabin to stand holding the small kitchen work surface as I stared ahead.

'We're in Scotland. The guys have done brilliantly.' She motioned to the two drivers up at the front.

'Oh yes. Morning, lads. All quiet then?'

They muttered that yes, all was good. On either side of the road ahead, the land swept back and grew to become gentle, rolling hills. Beyond, lining the edge of the horizon to our right, were mountains, huge and green against the pale blue sky.

'What time is it?' I asked, even though I still wore my watch on my wrist. Asking the time made me more involved in the day, more of a participant than a spectator. When I was told the time, I might make an important decision or comment on our progress.

'It's only nine, darling. You slept for four hours though. Well done.'

'Right. Good. What time will we get there?' I was feeling tired again now. And hungry.

'The guys reckon by four thirty, but we'll see. Depends on the traffic. You hungry?'

'Yes. What have we got?'

'Well, we can stop. We can get whatever you want.'

Suddenly, and for the first time, I felt gripped by a new paranoia, a new worry. I didn't want to see anyone. I didn't really understand why anyone would want to take photographs or call a newspaper and, right now, I wasn't worried about that. I just didn't want to see strangers; I was scared of them. The idea of meeting and talking with people I didn't know made my stomach churn and twist. I didn't even want to have two strange guys driving the truck. I had no fears that they might try and hurt me or do anything bad, I was just terrified of them. I was terrified of anyone I didn't know. Mindy must have seen the fear on my face.

'Darling, we can pull over at the services and park right at the back, out of the way. We've got to stop anyway to let the dogs have a pee. You can stay in here with the curtains closed and the guys will get us whatever you want. How would you like a bacon sandwich?'

I wasn't really hungry any more; the thought of meeting strangers had killed my appetite. But I wanted one anyway—mostly as a symbol of being back out in the world. I wanted a bacon sandwich at the service station because that's the sort of thing you did, out in the real world.

'Yes please. I'd love one. Let's do it, let's pull over.'

After a while, I felt the camper lurch to the right gently as it pulled off to the left. We drew up in a large car park and I retreated to the back, hiding in the bedroom. Peering under the curtain, I saw car wheels parked around the place. I shuddered and felt the tension through my shoulders. Mindy gave TG and Captain over to one of our chaperones and they took them outside. I couldn't imagine just striding down the steps like that, looking from side to side, taking it all in and being taken in by other people. By strangers. I pressed myself into the gloom at the back of the bedroom and waited. This was an important step; doing something because we had to. I had a job list again. And I ran away from it.

* * *

We all ate a 'full Scottish' breakfast, or at least we all ate a bit of it. Richard was visibly on edge and uncomfortable at being stationary. The girls were running about and getting restless and I noticed Richard closing his eyes against their high-pitched voices on a couple of occasions. This was so difficult for him. He adored the girls, but he'd been living in a different world since the crash and had been dropped back into the bedlam of a young family.

I asked him if he'd like to go back into the bedroom and lie down, but he was adamant: 'I've done enough lying down to last me a lifetime. I want to be here with you and the girls.'

'OK, but don't overdo it, will you?' I joined him on the sofa and put my arm around him where he sat with Willow on his lap. Izzy was happy with her colouring book, the dogs at peace on the floor, as if knowing instinctively the world needed to hush a while, to give him a rest, to take it all down a little, and give Richard time to acclimatise.

As we moved off on to the final leg of the journey, Richard was careful not to look out of the windows for longer than a few seconds at a time. His brain couldn't cope with the complexities of the view, and he struggled to digest what he saw. It was far easier for him to avoid looking, so that was what he did. Whenever the Winnebago slowed down or came to a standstill, he'd enjoy admiring the view again, and point out interesting things to the girls.

We saw streams babbling and chasing as they cut their way through mountainsides, powerful rivers flowing majestically through the valleys, the thickest of forests, standing tall and proud on the hillsides, and there in the distance our destination: the Highlands.

Just after 4.15 we arrived at a large five-bar gate. A young woman was there to greet us and lead the way in her car to the cottage we'd rented for three weeks. The Winnebago just made it along the narrow winding tracks; we turned a final tight corner and there it was, in a clearing surrounded by woodland: a quite remote, and staggeringly beautiful little house.

A Land Rover was standing to attention outside. I'd ordered it to use as our transport while we were there, and Richard was thrilled the second he saw it. We were escorted into the bright little house and Richard was instantly besotted. A roaring fire had been lit in the living room and mugs of steaming hot tea greeted us as we walked across the threshold. The lads carried our bags inside and dumped them in the hall. Richard excused himself and quickly disappeared into the master bedroom. He was exhausted. I was so proud of him. He was thrilled with the place, he was ready to relax. He just needed a bit of privacy.

CHAPTER 15

# THE COTTAGE IN THE HIGHLANDS

I had never been to the cottage before, I knew that. And I didn't for a second imagine that I had, in a previous life, worked in the Scottish Highlands as a stalker or a poacher. But there was an immense and comforting familiarity to the place. The rooms were large but not overwhelming. Heavy curtains dressed every window, but gave the impression they were there to keep the weather out more than impress visitors. Underfoot, warm, red carpets swirled contentedly as I padded about from room to room. On every wall hung watercolours capturing the textures, colours and pastimes of the hills and forests that surrounded the cottage. But it didn't feel like a gallery; the pictures were there to celebrate what went on and not to impress observers with how rich or clever the owners were. This was not an ostentatious house but a warm and friendly one, perfectly suited to a family wanting to spend time in a wonderful place and enjoy it to the full. I was happy as I roamed about, running my hand across polished wooden sideboards, smoothing the fabric on cheerily worn sofas and straightening bright cloths draped merrily across stout oak tables.

This place was the domestic equivalent of comfort food; warm, friendly, simple and honest. It was a giant cottage pie that I could walk into and curl up in for a snooze. We could be OK here, this felt like the safe place we needed in which to hide away and get better. And then I found the door. It was at the end of a corridor at the back of the cottage. It was not an inherently sinister door; it had no big, scary knocker on it, or sinister studs to suggest something the other side might want to break through. But it looked out of place. It sat square at the end of the corridor, covering the width of it from wall to wall. In the wall to the right of it was another door that opened on to the simple, plainly fitted bathroom. But where did this one go? I touched the cold, metal handle and whipped my hand away quickly. I studied the wood grain which I could see through the heavy stain on the door's surface. The door was out of place; it didn't lead to a room in the house and it didn't lead outside. It went somewhere else.

Mindy was in the kitchen, busily rooting through the provisions that we had arranged to have already in place in the plain, cream-painted wooden cupboards. Boxes of breakfast cereal, bags of apples and cartons of milk thronged the kitchen table. I asked her about the door. She explained patiently that we had been lucky enough to employ someone to come and cook for us once a day, so that we could have more time relaxing together as a family. The cook lived next door with her husband, and the door went through to her house. It wasn't going to be used and was locked, but it was a connecting door. I froze with fear. This safe, secure little place by the woods had a door in it that opened up into another house with strangers in. I walked slowly and carefully back down the corridor and stood a few feet away from the door. It stood, inert and blank. It didn't bulge out or fall down, but I didn't trust it.

I turned away to look through the window in the corridor wall. I looked past the heavy, dripping eaves of the cottage and into the cramped yard beyond. The walls around it were built of the same dark stone as the cottage and had grown darker still with the steady rain that puddled on the concrete floor. Rocks stood up from the puddle, like miniature icebergs in a sea made choppy by the falling rain. Out past the yard, the looming conifers braced themselves on the mountainside and dripped rain into the pine-needle carpet below. The window glass was old, with bubbles in it and imperfections that made the landscape ripple and roll when I moved my head. It was only a single pane and not double glazed, so through it I could hear the rain hissing and a slow wind shouldering through the trees. I looked back to the door. The friendly familiarity of the cottage had been replaced by my unfriendly but no less familiar companion: fear.

* * *

I'd called ahead a week before to order an enormous list of groceries. The kitchen cupboards were filled with goodies and I'd agreed a list of casseroles and pies which the cook would kindly prepare and store in the freezer. From bitter experience, I knew holiday arrangements rarely went to plan, but this time we'd struck gold. Everything was as promised. The house was comfortable, clean and welcoming, the children were outside with the dogs, running around and playing, all exhilarated to be free. I watched them from the kitchen window as they ran and laughed, then their obvious excitement as they discovered two Highland ponies in the paddock. They both came running in to find me.

'Mummy! Mummy! Quick, come and look!'

Willow cried, her cheeks flushed and eyes wide as she grabbed my hand and led me outside.

Izzy was beside her.

'Oh, Mummy, come and see, they're so beautiful!'

'What are?' I pretended not to know their secret.

'Just wait, you won't believe it,' Izzy continued.

We rounded the corner from the front door and walked towards the side of the cottage. 'Oh, girls, aren't they gorgeous!'

The two heavy-set grey ponies continued to graze as we approached. I clicked my tongue at them and they nonchalantly looked over, before slowly wandering towards us to say hello.

They were big softies and allowed the children to stroke them through the fence. I left them there, talking softly to the two ponies, as I returned to the kitchen to make a cup of tea. Watching the scene through the window I was moved to tears. To me, that was all we needed, two little girls lost in the joy of ponies. Simple pleasures. If only everything could be so simple.

Richard appeared at my shoulder, and put his arm around my waist.

'Well done, Mind.' He smiled. 'This place is fantastic.'

I sighed. 'Good. I'm glad you like it. I was worried you might not.'

'I know, I'm a difficult bugger to please, but you've done us proud on this one.' He sounded calm, but I sensed an air of unease; I didn't pursue it.

He sipped his tea and glanced out of the window.

'Oh, wow—look at the girls. Aah, look at them!'

They were still talking to the ponies, but now Willow was on her haunches, her hands between her knees, deep in conversation with her pony, while Izzy leaned against the fence, stroking the mane of the other. We stood there and watched them for a few minutes, until they noticed us and the biscuits we were eating and ran inside.

* * *

Breakfast would be enormous; it always was and I looked forward to it. Each morning, we were presented with thick bacon and short, chubby sausages with mushrooms, tomatoes and beans. I would wolf it down, my appetite returning fast. Now, I lay in bed, looked at the rough-textured ceiling and listened to the sizzles and splashes from the kitchen. Mindy must be in the kitchen too, because the bed beside me lay warm, but empty. I could hear that the girls were up; giggles and light voices came through the door, though the girls themselves did not. They were still cautious around me; aware that the usual rough and tumble of our lives together had to be put on hold for a while. Daddy was poorly. They understood this and were humouring me and giving me space.

The window at the end of the bed opened on to a green space that gave way to the darker, brooding avenues of dignified and silent forest. The curtains were drawn now though, and the light that shone through them bore a greenish tinge. I would get up and dress. I had a choice of clothes; Mindy had brought a few shirts and pairs of jeans and hung them in the wardrobe that stood next to the window. I looked at it and considered how much better it was to be in charge of my own life again. I could get up and dress myself now, even choosing the clothes I wore and what I did with my time afterwards. I pulled on jeans and a rough blue shirt and walked, barefoot, out of the bedroom and into the living room.

The girls were playing on the carpet in front of the fireplace. Coloured Lego pieces were scattered to every corner of the room. I had given them a set of their own to play with; the picture on the box depicted a garage with five cars to build and working ramps and stacks of spare tyres on trolleys. A man in a blue hat walked across the forecourt carrying a big spanner and there was a box standing near the front of the scene with the computer keyboard and screen of a modern diagnostics machine. The cars were customised with flames on them. I thought that I had had a similar set as a child, though not so sophisticated, of course. And I may have done, but if not, I had certainly spent many hours building a similar scene, even if I had improvised it with whatever limited selection of Lego bricks rattled around in the Tupperware box I kept in the living room at home. I was happy now that the girls wanted to do the same.

A fight broke out and interrupted my happy thoughts. Izzy was cross because Willow wanted to build the green car. She shouted and told her that she couldn't build it; that it was hers and Willow must build the white one. And why did she have to spoil everything? The noise of their shouts rose and my face grew tense. The argument turned into noisy bickering and the sound of it chattered and rattled about me.

'Girls, please. Come on, you can both play. Izzy, can you let Willow build the green one? She'll give it back to you afterwards. Go on, she's only small and she doesn't understand.'

Izzy pushed the green pieces towards her sister.

'Go on then, Willow. You build it.'

'Say thank you, Willow.'

'Thank you.' She muttered it but then looked up to her sister and smiled.

The moment had passed, the argument was over. But it had left me drained and troubled. This was hard; looking after the kids. I had felt closer to them than ever before, probably, but closer to them more as a contemporary than as a parent. I could happily have joined in and played their games all day, but to bear even a slight responsibility for them while they played and I stood and watched was very uncomfortable. I felt like I had when we first took Izzy home from hospital as a one-week old baby. We walked in and sat down on the sofa cradling her tiny, wrinkled form and waited for someone to come and tell us what to do. There were no instructions, no rulebook and we realised that, for the first time in our lives, we really were properly and fully in charge. That feeling came back to haunt me now and I felt dizzy with the pressure. I could hear Mindy moving about in the kitchen, putting out plates and glasses for breakfast, but I stood here alone, a solitary guard and sentinel over the actions and interactions in the living room. I didn't want to be in charge, I wanted to play.

'Girls, girls, let's all build it together. Here—I'll build the green one.'

*     *     *

The routine had established itself; it was the natural order into which our days fell. The ebb and flow of waking up, eating breakfast and hitting the major points of our day had defined the routine organically. After breakfast we went for a walk. And it was a 'whatever the weather' walk. This was a practice we had established years before in which, once a walk was elected upon, we would go whether it was raining or not. The kids loved it and were splashing along happily now as Mindy and I tailed them in our heavy Drizabones, rain slicking off them on to our boots and dripping from the brims of our wide hats on to our shoulders. It was wet but not too cold, and the girls played and ran happily in their waterproofs. Izzy wore a bright blue coat and Willow a pink one. Their wellies were a riot of multi-coloured bees, flowers and frogs as they leapt and danced.

Mindy shouted, 'Girls, don't jump in the really big puddles, please. You'll get your trousers soaked and maybe you'll fall in up to your chin and have to swim across.'

They giggled and laughed at their mother's crazy idea and grinned in the rain under their hoods, faces shiny with water and excitement. But they skirted around the big puddle that pooled across the broad, stony path leading away from the cottage and up into the hilly woods. The fringes of the puddle bore a muddy tide mark and were feathered with pine needles among the stones. The rain was soft but insistent and dense. It was, I declared, 'very wet' rain. Mindy laughed and we held hands and watched the girls play. Behind us, TG and Captain snouted along the edges of the patch, sniffing the hollows where sheep had slept and deer had chewed the grass.

'Where are we going?' Izzy's voice was strident

and confident over the rain.

'To the picnic place, of course.' Mindy answered the question as though she had been asked the most obvious thing in the world and Izzy giggled and then frowned.

'Ooh, that's too far. It's miles away.' Izzy stopped as she moaned and I saw Willow tense as she prepared to join in.

'Izzy, it's not too far. It's just up there, past the wooden bridge. Come on, the walk will make you hungry.'

'Yes, it's not far,' I chimed in, trying to help Mindy placate them. 'You've walked there before loads of times. Come on, race you.'

We set off, covering the last piece of open ground rising to the edge of the forest in short time. The girls ran as hard as they could and I splashed and staggered about in mock tiny steps to stay alongside them. We passed under the green, dripping canopy.

'Let's walk now,' Izzy said in the forest's silence and she slipped her hand into mine. It curled in my palm, damp and cold but with an essential warmth from within.

'Come on, Willow, let's hold hands for the last bit.'

Willow grasped the fingers of my right hand and I briefly slipped her grip to get a better chance to enclose her hand fully in mine and shelter it from the rain. The dogs came past, Captain trotting merrily, his tiny tail thrumming like a propeller on his broad, white back. TG barged into Willow as she overtook.

'Oh no. TG! She hurt me, she pushed me.'

'Willow, you're fine, sweetie. She's just clumsy, that's all. Silly clumsy dog.'

I made fun of TG, sticking out my tongue and

rolling my eyes and panting to make the girls laugh.

'She's really clumsy.' Willow giggled, the sorrow of a moment ago forgotten.

Our picnic place was a clearing on a bend of the path between the dark conifers. Logs lay on the ground and made perfect seats, tables and climbing frames. We sat with our backs to the hill and looked out over the tops of the trees sloping away to the valley and our cottage. On our right, the ground gave way to a steep-sided crevasse down which a mountain stream hissed and splashed among the granite. The trees behind us towered solemnly, their plain, dark trunks featureless and regular. We would eat sandwiches, drink coffee from a flask, play games, make up stories and fill our time laughing and talking. When the girls wandered off a few yards to study an interesting puddle or pretend to ride their horses, Mindy and I spoke about the future and the past.

* * *

Richard would confide his innermost feelings out there in the woods. The log where we sat at picnic times had become his talking place.

'I've been really ill, haven't I? I'm still bad.'

'Yes, you have, but you're getting better. You've improved so much in such a short time. You should be proud of yourself.'

He sat with his cup of coffee resting on his knee.

'I kept thinking there was nothing wrong with me, that I was a fraud, and everyone was being nice to me under false pretences. But they weren't. I know that now.'

He was so sad. It was heartbreaking. Surrounded by all this beauty, yet he still felt so awful.

I'd packed his watercolours and pastels, sketching materials and pads. As I looked about us I was bombarded with a thousand different hues of green, an amazing assortment stretching across the ground from a carpet of moss running through the trees, incredible dappled sunlight piercing through the forest canopy and dancing off every rock, every twisted tree root. The white foam of the river as it crashed its will against already smooth boulders, almost as white as the foam; scrubbed clean from years of abuse at the hands of such a torrent of water.

Richard refused to paint, he even refused to take a photograph. He confided in me: 'I'm scared I'll get stuck where I was when I was at college. You know I hated those years. I don't want to end up stuck as a miserable bloody teenager. I want to get past that.'

I nodded, I understood.

At times huge blocks of memory would just fall suddenly into his head. It was quite alarming for him each time it happened and he'd explain that within a second an enormous gap was filled with years of experience in amazing detail.

If he didn't want to explore his artistic talents yet, that was fine.

*  *  *

Today's picnic had been a good one. The girls had played happily and I lazed under the trees for a while thinking fondly of our family camping trips to the

Forest of Dean when I was young. We had used an old blue ridge tent and sat happily for hours inside, the five of us cramped around a small wooden table playing cards as the rain hammered on to the canvas and we strained our necks to avoid touching the sloping side with our heads and starting a leak. Looking up through the trees over our Scottish picnic place, I remembered the walk down through the woods to the river in the Forest of Dean and I smiled at the memory of the metal swing bridge that crossed it. The floor of the bridge was made of heavy wire mesh and you could look down past your feet to see the rush and swirl of the river as it passed beneath. As people made their way across, the bridge bucked and moved, which delighted my eight-year-old senses. Confident in my childish invincibility, I overcame the rush and thrill of the height and the exposure and tried to swing the bridge deliberately. My tiny weight could make no impression on the thick metal cables that fixed the structure at each end and ran across to span the river and support the bridge. But I wondered if it would be possible one day to swing it so much that it completed a full circle, like a swing going over the top in a playground.

Now, in Scotland, nearly thirty years later, we finished our picnic and gathered together our bags and our coats for the short walk down through the trees and back to the cottage. I looked at the girls in their tiny, colourful clothes and their sturdy little boots and I felt happy but strangely quiet. As we approached the squat, grey-stoned cottage, I saw something bright sitting next to it. It was a car. And it wasn't our green Land Rover. It was someone else's car. A small hatchback which, in my rising panic, I failed even to identify. I whirled into a state of paranoia and fear. I didn't worry that we were about to be attacked or robbed, I simply could not bear the idea of meeting with strangers. I felt the same about unfamiliar people as I do about spiders; I wasn't worried that they would kill me, I just shuddered at the thought of them. It had become a phobia.

*     *     *

Our walks through the forest were great for the girls, they picked up all sorts of treasure, from fossils to pine needles, and everything went into their pockets. They walked quite a distance too, but this served as a fantastic way to tire Willow enough for an afternoon nap, which I encouraged Richard to copy. He soon agreed and his nap became as much a part of the routine as Willow's.

It was an essential part of my day too. While Richard slept I made all the telephone calls. I updated his parents, spoke with the doctors and ensured everything at home and work was running smoothly. Every day there would be at least ten messages to be dealt with, most of which had to be out of Richard's earshot. He was too eager to get involved with work issues and in addition, I was regularly in conversation with the doctors. I had to be completely honest with them about his condition and they were always available to help if I had any concerns. Fortunately, there hadn't been any really dramatic episodes and I was delighted to receive a very long message from Rick Nelson, a week into our stay, congratulating us on the success of Richard's discharge and smooth transition out of Bristol. Not even Rick knew where we were, but I had assured him we wouldn't leave the British Isles. He understood completely, and was just happy that all was going well.

On our return from a walk one afternoon we noticed a strange car parked outside the house. It was a blue Vauxhall Corsa. Richard became agitated and nervous. He refused to walk further than the woods until I'd investigated. The girls came with me and we meandered into the house. Straight away the smell of cooking reached my nostrils. The housekeeper/cook had turned up and was preparing our food for the following week. It was her car outside. Although she lived in the cottage next door, she'd just returned from a trip to the shops to pick up extra ingredients, and unloading was easier from outside our house. I went back out and motioned for Richard to join us. He couldn't bear to be among strangers, and had an extreme reaction to anything unfamiliar. He was relieved when he heard who our visitor was, but his dislike of unpredictability was apparent. It occurred to me the doctors' advice about structure and routine had been wisely enforced. As long as we stuck to routine and he knew how his day would unfold, it was OK, but had we gone straight home, apart from other external forces, with the natural interruptions and opportunity for unexpected visitors, he would certainly have struggled to cope.

The following day it seemed ridiculously busy on our walk. We had to leave the track several times to let Land Rovers pass, and each time Richard would pull down his hat and walk with his back to them. There were many walkers on the footpaths too, which added pressure. It ruined the day for him, and he remained in a foul mood.

The only light relief came as we ate our supper, a casserole prepared by the cook, which I immediately noticed contained one ingredient Richard always detested—celery. I was very nervous about even offering the meal to him, but to my amazement, not only did he devour it with relish, he asked for seconds.

But that evening he was quiet. I watched his expression as he fought unknown battles in his mind; it was easy to read on his face the internal distress; all encompassing and so awful. He disappeared into a world I couldn't enter; I was powerless to help. Nothing could be done. All I could do was offer support in whatever way he would take it. Later he confided his hatred of the injury which afflicted him, we spoke long into the night and I reassured him all would be well, but as I lay awake, for the first time I felt really sorry for myself. I had no confidante; no one to share this with. There seemed to be no gentleness, no softness any more, just difficulty.

* * *

This was a moment to savour. I pulled the laces on my trainers and fastened them tightly, looking up from my crouched position to scan the leaden skies above the dense, green conifers. The rain had given up falling but still it felt as though it hung thinly in the air, suspended temporarily.

'You won't overdo it?'

'No, I learned a lot in hospital. That I shouldn't just throw myself in and overdo it. I shall be sensible and moderate. Honest.'

Mindy, standing behind me in the hallway with its heavy oak coat-stand half smiled and cocked her head.

'Really? You'll be sensible? How long are you going to be?'

'Er, about twenty minutes should do it.' I stretched my calf muscles, leaning forward with my palms stretched against the rough outer walls of the cottage as I spoke.

'I'll go up the hill towards the picnic place and see how far I get. Tell you what, best thing, I'll just run in that direction for ten minutes, turn round and run back. Better than trying to find a route that lasts twenty minutes.'

'Take care, baby.'

Turning round to face the open spaces in front of the cottage, I tugged my lightweight running jacket down a little, adjusted the zip and pinched the peak of my black baseball cap between finger and thumb to adjust it, pinning the back of the cap to my head with my other hand as I did so.

'All right, I will. I'll be careful, don't worry. I don't want anything to go wrong any more than you do. See ya.'

And I trotted off up the track towards the woods and the hills.

The sense of freedom was immense; I could go where I wanted. I was alone. My trainers slapped down on to the rough, broken path, made noisier by the stones, slick and wet from the recent rain. Ahead, the forest waited, and the bridge and the corner and any number of new things I was now allowed to wander among on my own. Running into the forest, it felt like an embrace as I passed under the thick-needled branches that formed its eaves. Inside, the air was tangy and heavy with the scent of pine needles, damp undergrowth and peat. I heard the stream running down from the hilltops, crashing over the stones it had slowly exposed as it carved its own route down the mountainside. In front of me, the path rose to meet another running across it and form a T junction. To the left, the newer, bigger path ran off across the mountainside and through the woods, following the contours to remain level. To the right, it passed over the river via a short, fat wooden bridge with flat-planked sides and thick, slippery sleepers as a base and then on to another junction. I turned right and ran up on my toes as my trainers hit the dark wood of the bridge's base. Underneath was the stream, by now a small river capable of rolling smaller stones around, and it made a broad base where the water was less than four inches deep and ran noisily across the cobbles. The noise faded behind me and I faced another choice; to turn left and follow the path another few hundred yards up to the picnic place or to drop down to the right, away from the hills. I turned left.

Running past the picnic place, I thrilled to the sensation of being somewhere familiar but on my own. I knew this spot now and could imagine the noises of our family playing there and eating our sandwiches every day. But I was here alone now, just a bloke out for a run passing a place he took the kids for a picnic. It was normal. My legs pulled and strained as I crested the hill, but not so badly I needed to slacken off the pace. In fact, the slight pain felt good; I was pushing a little, making myself work for the first time in what felt like years. With my heart now racing faster than the work demanded, spurred on by the thrill of what I was doing, I passed the clearing of the picnic site and pushed on to where the path rose again to another crest.

The thrill now was building to euphoria. I pressed on harder and ran past a tall fence to my left, where a small track vanished down to meet the stream that, further down, flowed under the bridge I had crossed. I measured my breathing against my paces and enjoyed the double beat as my chest reverberated to every footfall. I pushed my cap back and rolled my head on my shoulders without breaking the pace. The trees went past me faster. And I wondered what would happen if their flashing, flickering trunks acted as a sort of stroboscope and triggered a seizure. What would I do? Would I collapse and die immediately? Or would I fall to the ground, lying alone in the damp verge to die slowly of exposure before a birdwatcher or hillwalker stumbled across my damp and grizzly remains? But I didn't care now. I felt no fear at the prospect, but believed that what would happen would happen. Right now, I was running and it felt good. If it caused something bad, well, so be it.

As the endorphins released by the exercise flooded my system, my confidence rose. I laughed out loud, swung my arms wildly over my head and took a path that dropped off to the right into the muddy woods. This path was dark and deep with old needles and peat. It dipped down through the trees and there were broad puddles that gathered where it intersected the neatly planted rows of conifers. I splashed through them, laughing now and breathing deeply between laughs. Ahead lay a tall wooden fence in which, straddling the path, was a smart, well-made wooden gate. I kicked my legs forwards to slow gently as I reached it and shook my arms out, loosening my shoulders. There was no sign fixed to the gate and no padlock either, just a latch. The top rail stood at shoulder height and was stained dark brown. This gate and the fence were clearly in current use and not some remnant of a previous enterprise. But there was nothing to indicate that it stood there to keep people out; it looked rather more as though it was there to keep stock in. Well this was shooting ground; stags roamed wild and were farmed for the guns that visited in large numbers every season.

I could see no one beyond it and the path ran through, clear and well marked. I swung the gate open and closed it carefully behind me before I carried on, pumping my legs to take me over the rise where the fence line lay and then to follow the path that dropped down through the trees and narrowed until it was only a foot or two wide and muddy and broken. It continued to take me down towards a small valley floor on which the trees crowded and were joined by bushes and scraggy undergrowth. I swung round to the right and the path carried on down. As I ran, my thoughts levelled and grew calmer. This was what I needed, this would help more than anything else. Just one tiny thought floated in to disturb my new-found calm. Had I closed the gate? Well, yes, I remembered carefully latching the dull, light metal clasp. I had made sure it was properly closed, just as I have closed tens of thousands of other gates on other runs across other landscapes. But I didn't trust my memory. Had I really closed it, or was I imagining it?

And then another thought arrived like a late-comer to a motorway pile-up; was this paranoia? The doctors had warned that, among the many possible manifestations of neuro-chemical imbalance following an injury such as mine, paranoia might rear its head along with compulsive behaviour patterns. Was I being compulsive? Was this now burning desire to run back up a substantial and muddy hill to check a gate that I knew for a fact I had closed only minutes earlier compulsive behaviour? Was I being paranoid about my compulsion? That was it, I turned round and set off back up the hill. Bugger it, I thought, if it's going to send me mad worrying about it, I'll go and check the gate anyway, whether it's paranoia, compulsive behaviour or a latent desire to sleep with my bloody history teacher that compels me to do it. I ran back up the hill. The gate stood, firmly closed. I felt weak, broken and shamed and turned to run back down the hill to the shallow valley below.

* * *

Richard had been too long on his run. He'd promised to be back within twenty minutes. Thirty had passed and I was worried. I was sure he'd either overdone it and was lying in pain somewhere, revisited by shin splints, or had got lost, which was actually even more of a worry as it was starting to get dark.

I stayed calm and told the girls to get their coats and wellies on, we were going for a drive in the Land Rover. They were very pleased and had just started to argue over who would sit in the front, when the cottage door opened and a sweaty, muddy Richard stood in the doorway.

'Hello. Did you have a good run?' I started to take my coat off as I spoke.

'It was OK. Where are you off to?'

'I was about to come and look for you. You

were quite a while and I was getting a bit worried.'

'Oh God, I'm sorry.'

'Don't be daft, I'm just being over-extra. Where did you go?'

Richard recounted the episode with the gate, concerned he was chronically paranoid.

'Y'know, I couldn't begin to tell you the number of times I do stuff like that. Rechecking something I absolutely know I've already done. It's just like the lost key syndrome. Remember what John told you—people in recovery have to remember not to get caught up in that. Every time you've lost your keys in the past you haven't instantly assumed you've got permanent brain-damage, you've simply lost your keys. You just had to check the gate. Simple.'

He seemed a little appeased, and went off for a shower. Meanwhile I had to take the girls round the block because I'd promised them a ride in the Land Rover.

* * *

Sitting on a bench to take in a view and daydream is a deliberate act; it's not something I do by accident or without meaning to. As I lowered myself on to the wooden slats of the bench to the front of the cottage, I looked across to the forest-clad mountains under a grey, leaden sky and readied myself for a relaxing, thoughtful pause. I settled thankfully, my wax jacket crumpling comfortably to cushion me as I tucked my legs underneath the seat, feet crossed. Mindy and the girls were busy inside the cottage and I had stolen outside to take stock, relax on my own and let my mind wander.

Immediately in front of me stood a solitary tree, light and feathery, a rare and delicate deciduous thing in a realm of stubborn evergreens. At its base were grouped smooth rocks settled into shaggy grass punctured by the muddy mouths of holes dug out by rabbits. A single wooden post leaned crookedly to the right, a strand of wire hanging from it where a fence had once stretched. Behind stood the mountains and the forest, damp and mute in the mist. I breathed in slowly, let my chest subside in a long, slow exhalation and relaxed my mind, ready to let my thoughts wander where they would. And nothing happened. I gazed at the greens, blues and purples of the mountains and the forest. I let my eyes de-focus and blur the image to a tinted smudge. I looked back to the tree, its black trunk in sharp contrast to the hills behind it. I couldn't daydream. I thought about where we were, what we were doing, why we were there. I thought about what might be happening elsewhere in the world, who else might have sat on this bench and looked at the same scene. But my thoughts wouldn't wander. Like a faithful but irritating dog, they kept returning to my heel to look up and ask for direction.

I looked again at the scene in front of me. I examined what I saw. The tree dominated because it was closer and I could see it in more detail. I knew that it was a tree, that it had roots that ran into the ground and brought moisture and nutrients up into the trunk through the capillary action of the tiny vessels within their gnarled stretches. I knew that the leaves spread to capture the energy of the sun and that their greenness was to better facilitate the photosynthesis that brought the thing to life. But there was no poetry, nothing fantastic or mystical about the tree.

I could remember previous encounters with trees—my memory was working now. I recalled carving names into their sturdy hearts, perched high above a woodland floor. I could remember climbing until I thought I would fall through thin branches for ever. I remembered the huge, baleful arms of the beech trees in the Chiltern hills around my old home in Buckinghamshire. The beeches were the final stage of evolution for the forest, the grand, long-living and slow-growing patriarchs and matriarchs of the woodlands, and they grew relentlessly to dominate by starving all others of light. I remembered sitting on a beech branch as thick as a cow that reached to the floor and seemed to sweep away anything else that tried to thrive under its crown's selfish shade. And I remembered being moved by it. But I could not be now. I could grasp facts, remember fanciful thoughts and dreams, but I could make no more to add to those that had come and gone before. I could not daydream. And the thought of it took hold of my mind and, like the dominating beech trees, shaded every other thought out of existence. I felt thinner, made less, almost transparent because of the loss of this simple act. I could not daydream and maybe I never would be able to again.

* * *

The evenings in Scotland were often my most feared part of the day. I'm not sure whether it was fatigue or boredom, but often Richard would be in a bad mood.

He suffered a very real problem with confrontation and negativity, which angered him and would set the tone for the evening. He couldn't watch any television, because even the slightest hint of confrontation and he'd have to leave the room. Instead, we spent friendly evenings playing Top Trumps, or leafing through the many car magazines I'd packed.

Once the girls were in bed we whiled away about an hour before sharing a bath and climbing into bed ourselves. We were both exhausted; Richard could lie in late every morning, waking to the smell of bacon and eggs before he joined the girls and me in the kitchen. We were at the breakfast table one morning when he suddenly stopped eating and sat bolt upright. His face contorted into so many different expressions it was really very strange to watch.

'Oh . . . oh.' He looked like he'd just stepped off a fairground ride which had made him dizzy.

'You OK? What's up?'

I watched his face change involuntarily. He looked different. He didn't look like Richard. His face was ashen and instantly aged ten years. Had I seen this man in the street I wouldn't have recognised him. It was so frightening. I sat paralysed, hypnotised by this terrible, uncontrollable force; waiting for it to stop.

When it ceased, just moments later, he was bewildered and confused. All I could do was hug him. Richard explained that as he'd sat there, quietly eating a piece of toast, from nowhere about ten different emotions hit him all at once. He was bombarded by them from deep in his psyche.

I felt we were being reminded; it was going to be difficult. Very difficult, but we'd get through it.

*   *   *

Someone was out there. I was sure of it. My right hand rested on the wooden window ledge as I leaned round from behind the wall to look outside. The rain had stopped again and the expanse of grass in front of the cottage looked cold, damp and turbulent in the wind. The rough track that served as a road ran in front of the cottage and disappeared to my right where it turned. But I saw no one. Izzy and Willow played happily on the carpet behind me. They were colouring in; their pencils and felt-tip pens lay scattered in front of the fireplace. I had heard a car drawing up and leapt from the floor where I sat with them. My motivation had come from a desire to protect them and to hide from whoever was approaching. What would I do if they came to the door? What would I say? What did they want?

'It's OK, girls, I'm just looking at the fields. You carry on colouring in.'

'What is it, Daddy?'

'Oh, just the rain. Just looking at the rain.'

I saw the front of a van emerge from the bend in the track to the right and my shoulders froze. It was dark green and old. I slid further away from the window to hide behind the wall, leaving just enough room for my right eye to watch as the van rolled in front of the cottage. It stopped. The door was loud and creaky and it opened slowly. I crouched now, hiding below the window sill.

'What are you doing, Daddy?'

'I'm peeping. Just seeing what's out there.' My heart raced now. I suddenly felt angry. How could Mindy have left me alone? I didn't feel ready for the responsibility of looking after the kids on my own. I watched the shape of the driver moving around from the front of the van. I wasn't scared that he might come in and hurt us. Why would anyone do that? I was just terrified of him. It was like a phobia. I was too scared to look directly at him. He might see me. Through the blurry bottom edges of the window I could make out the shape of him in dark green clothes walking towards the front door. He wore some sort of waterproof jacket, old and lumpy. I thought I could make out a hat of some sort too. If I stayed hidden, if he thought there was nobody in, he would go away. And then the letterbox rattled and clattered. It felt like a direct invasion; a brutal, physical act. But then I reasoned, if he was leaving a letter or a note, it meant he was going away. I stayed hidden but breathed out and felt my shoulders sag. But I was angry still; angry that I was left alone, angry that I was scared, angry that I was hiding under the window sill. It made me feel trapped again, it reminded me of being trapped inside my head in that hospital bed, not sure of what was real and what was not. I had no distinct regrets, no specific hopes. I was just angry. Izzy and Willow were still playing by the fireplace. I slid down to the floor from my crouching position and shuffled over to them.

'How's it going, girls? Let's have a look.'

As the girls showed me their colouring and chatted about what they had done, my anger faded to sadness.

* * *

Our grocery stock began to dwindle midway through the second week, and there was only one way to get more supplies. I'd have to go out and buy them. I could take the girls with me; they'd enjoy it.

Richard disagreed.

'Don't be silly, I'll look after the girls, you go shopping, have a break.' He was trying to sound matter-of-fact, but it was very unconvincing. I knew the way to the nearby village, and calculated it would take twenty minutes to get there, the same on the return journey, and twenty minutes to shop. I could be back in an hour.

I was concerned about leaving Richard, but the girls are very sensible for their ages, and I was sure they'd try hard to be good for him. He wasn't taking no for an answer, and if I stayed and debated the issue, he'd just get very angry and the shops would be closed. He promised to go next door and call the cook if he had any problems.

I prepped the girls. 'You can have your favourite tea tonight if you're good for Daddy. That means no shouting or squealing, no arguing, and all toys away before teatime, OK?'

Izzy was considering a strop, I could tell. I took her by the hand and marched her into her room, sat on the bed and held her opposite me. Looking her straight in the eye I told her: 'Iz, you know Daddy's poorly?'

She nodded, thumb in mouth.

'Well, he needs your help to get better. He needs for you and Willow to be really extra specially good today. D'you think you can?'

She nodded.

'I'll see if I can find you a colouring book while I'm out, OK?'

She gave me a cuddle. 'Thank you, Mummy.' Then she followed me to the front door.

I picked up my bag and jumped into the Land Rover, waved goodbye to them all as I drove past the sitting-room window, and worried myself half to death over the next fifty-seven minutes.

On my return I was relieved to find them all happily playing with Lego in the living room. However Richard could bear no more and as soon as he saw me, escaped into the bedroom. I took him the customary cup of tea, and a bag of his favourite things.

'How was it?'

He was sitting on the edge of the bed and turned to me as I entered the room.

'Oh, Mind . . .' His voice was shaky as he cradled the mug in his hands; he seemed fragile. 'It's so different. It's scary being on my own with them now; being responsible.' He paused, sensing my concern.

'But it was fine, honestly. We had a lovely time. I'm just tired.'

'I shouldn't have gone.' The trip had caused him unnecessary stress, I felt terrible.

'No, Mind, I'm their father. For God's sake, if I was really worried I'd have called you. I just need to get used to it, that's all.'

He gave me a weary smile.

He was disappointed. He adored the girls, was always fantastic with them, but he'd been brutally reminded of his new limitations.

'Get into bed and have a nap. I'll wake you in a couple of hours. And, Richard . . .'

'Mmm?'

'You're doing really well, you know. I mean REALLY well.'

'Yeah, I know, but it doesn't feel like it. I hate

being like this.'

I cuddled up to him on the bed. 'You get better every day. We'll get through this, y'know?'

'We will, won't we?' There was doubt in his voice.

'Oh Christ, yes. We'll come back the new, improved, stronger us. The same as before, only more so.'

'God, I love you.'

'I love you too.' I kissed him. 'Now, get some bloody sleep.'

He smiled and snapped his eyes shut in mock obeisance.

I left Richard while I organised the shopping. Outside the light was fading, but just as dusk approached I saw something amazing: through the hall window, no more than eighty feet away, swathed in the evening mist and walking towards the house was a large stag. We'd heard them roar every night, and at one point TG came running in at such speed from her night-time wee I'm sure she was charged by one of them, but we'd seen nothing this close. The hunting season was over, and the stags were suddenly bold. I wanted to wake Richard, to share the moment with him, but he was asleep and to wake him would be selfish. I found the girls though, and the three of us sat by the window and watched that magnificent creature for some minutes before he disappeared back into the mist.

CHAPTER 16

# GOING HOME

We were going home tomorrow. Mindy had made the arrangements; a car would pick us up and drive us all home. We had packed our bags ready and they lay scattered about the cottage. I wanted to go out for one last run in the hills. Izzy and Willow were sprinting up and down the corridor by the kitchen and Mindy was preparing their tea. Crouched by the broad front door, I pushed my feet into my trainers, tying the laces quickly.

Leaning against the wall to stretch my legs, I looked across at the dark oak coat-stand. Still hanging from it were our long Drizabone waterproofs and the girls' brightly coloured coats. Gathered under it were our walking boots. This place had been everything we needed. We had enjoyed peace, tranquillity and a chance to regroup as a family. But I had also learned more about how I had damaged myself. As every day passed, I looked back over it and realised how unwell I had still been that day and how much better I now was. And then another day would pass, I would look back on that one and realise that I was still unwell. But now was not the time to slope about worrying and fretting. I was going for my final run through the beautiful, wooded Highlands and I was determined to enjoy it. This was yet another significant moment, I wanted to savour it.

The letterbox rattled as the door shut behind me. I turned right, ran the length of the rough road in front of the house and felt the surface soften and turn to broken stone as the road gave way to a track. To my left, the rough grass lay flat and still. Beyond it, a fringe of trees rose steeply up from the plateau and climbed the mountainsides in the distance. In front of me, the forest stood, familiar and inviting. My legs felt stronger now, I was running every day and feeling the benefit. I reached out in longer strides until I passed under the first few trees and into the forest. Crossing the footbridge, I smiled at the sound of the stream, now a small river, dashing underneath. I felt my own weight springing through my toes with each stride and felt my breathing syncopate with my pace naturally. I leaned to the left as I turned to run up and past the picnic place. I would miss it, we had spent many hours there, sitting, talking and playing. I would miss our time there together as a family and the hours that Mindy and I had spent, holding hands on an old log; two people who love each other talking over an experience that nearly parted them for ever and making plans for the future. We had sat there and looked forward as well as back across our time together and had become the stronger for it.

I pressed on, cresting the hill and running down again now, along a wide and muddy path bordered by elegant, tough conifers. The path reached the bottom of a shallow valley and curved to the right. I followed it round, enjoying the feeling that I was running well, all systems were functioning at optimum level. I had worked hard to get my fitness back, it mattered to me a lot. This was something I could do for myself, something I could be in control of. It was something I could be proud of achieving and that pride mattered more than the achievement itself.

I was running across the hillside now on a track that followed the contours roughly but dipped gently to descend through the trees. To my left, the forest fell away quickly and I could see the tops of the trees a few rows back. To my right, the forest stood dense and busy until it gave way to a clearing that opened back from the track for a hundred metres or so. I saw how the trees ended and a few straggly bits of undergrowth took advantage of the thin sunlight to form a fringe. And emerging from the edge of the trees to walk confidently into the clearing was a stag. It moved slowly but not from caution. Its antlered head turned to scan the ground in front and to either side.

It saw me, or caught my scent, and it stopped. I had blundered into the broad net of its senses and it stopped to see what I was. From where I stood I could see the curves of muscle stretching across its brown flanks and forming its shape. I could see the awkward joints of its hips and the strength of its legs tapering down to slender points. And I could see its deep brown eye swivelling below the woody turrets of its antler crown and around us the forest paused, frozen. The shooting season had ended several days ago and the local gamekeepers believed that the deer knew, to the day, when this happened and grew braver and less cautious. In front of me now, half a hundred metres away, the stag surveyed this interloper in his forest kingdom and I felt its confusion. I was smaller, slower and without the spiked antlers that weighed on its head to signify rank, status and potency. It turned away and then turned again to face me once more. I breathed slowly and steadily, a privileged observer not knowing quite what to do. It turned for a final time and walked slowly and deliberately back into the forest, breaking into a trot as it reached the trees, all the time balancing its antlers carefully to remain solemnly level as though carried by funeral bearers. I stayed where I was for some time. My moment had found me; a moment I couldn't understand or read, an encounter in which I was the one without language or purpose. And a moment I knew would stay with me for ever. I felt blessed and lucky as I broke into an easy trot back to the cottage and my family.

* * *

I took a five-minute drive in the Land Rover the day before we left Scotland; I needed to top up the fuel and it was an opportunity to savour my last memories of that amazing place. I drove across the hillside and through the forests, drinking in every last detail; the enormous pine trees which reached far into the sky, the colours of the heathers at their feet, the magic of the tiny red squirrels as they darted across the road in front of me, and the grace and majesty of those beautiful deer. I was suddenly overcome by a desperate longing to stay. I burst into tears and had to pull over. I didn't want to go back, didn't want to leave this wonderful place, didn't want to face the complications of our life at home. It was peaceful here; safe, friendly. I wished life were different, I wanted everything to fix; but I knew that was impossible. There was no point in running away; we had to face our demons and overcome them. Even so, the short drive back to the house, saying farewell to the place which had become our sanctuary, was one of the saddest journeys I've ever known.

The car arrived to take us home just after

lunch. We'd calculated to arrive home around midnight. There wouldn't be any press around at that time of night and we could hopefully walk straight in.

The girls said goodbye to the ponies and clambered into their seats. Richard and I thanked the cook and her husband for looking after us and joined them in the car.

It seemed to take an awful lot longer getting home, and we stopped for a burger at teatime. The driver parked in the corner of the motorway services car park, and I fetched a large selection of fast food. None of us was particularly thrilled at going home—even the dogs had acclimatised—but as we reached the outskirts of Gloucestershire we all started to pick up.

For the girls it was returning to their rooms and teddies, and their faithful pets. For me, it was the familiarity of my home, and knowing that when Richard crossed the threshold the picture, finally, after so many weeks could start to get back to normal.

I watched him as he sipped his tea, slumped on the oversized sofa in the sitting room, his hair dishevelled, and a strange beard-like thing on his chin. I loved him so very much. I was so grateful he was alive, so proud to be home together, shoulder to shoulder, ready to carry on.

* * *

This didn't feel the same as a homecoming after a long holiday. I had felt a gentle surge of warmth and excitement at crossing the threshold, but something was different. I had been away for just five weeks.

The house had not changed, everything looked the same. The dogs gave me their customary welcome, bounding around and barking happily. TG and Captain had melded straight back into the pack and assumed their places. I walked from room to room, standing in each one and taking it in.

I slept deeply. The next morning I stood at the top of the stairs and listened as Izzy and Willow dashed about, picking up favourite toys and saying hello to the cats. From the landing I could see the painting of a horse that I bought Mindy for Christmas two years ago. I looked down past the stairs and studied the wooden trunk we picked up from a junk shop to keep our boots tucked tidily away but which inevitably serves simply as a gathering point for footwear, piled randomly around it. Behind the trunk, wedged in a corner, stood the wooden staff I collected on a walking trip across the Lake District twenty years ago. I was surrounded by memories and artefacts. It should have been comforting.

Drifting back down the stairs, I stopped as Crusoe, our border collie, walked up to me and pressed her head against my hip. I stroked her neck and felt her bunched muscles, straining to contain the energy and excitement as she resisted leaping on me and barking. Crusoe ran off to reunite once more with TG and Captain, her clawed feet scrabbling noisily for grip on the wooden floor, and I walked into the dining room. Mindy was elsewhere in the house now and I knew that I should be helping unpack our bags. But something was still wrong. Why did this not feel like the joyous homecoming I had dreamed of nearly every waking hour in hospital? I rested my hand on the polished surface of the table and looked at the bookcase standing at the far wall. My eyes wandered across the titles. There were books from my childhood, art reference books from college, novels read and re-read over decades, and books bought recently, just before the crash.

The dogs were outside now and their happy barks and yelps came across the lawn beyond the windows. I remembered Sunday roasts with the girls, I remembered parties late into the night round this very table. And I realised that I felt sad. Finally, I had made it home, back to my own hearth. Despite the pain, the confusion, I was back. The doctors had said it might take me years to get home, but I had done it in just a few weeks. And now, standing here in my own house with my family and dogs around me, I felt sad.

I was, for the first time, in a familiar environment, one that was familiar to me from a time before the crash. I had lived in this house; laughed, shouted, argued and played. In flashes I remembered hundreds of little incidents with incredible clarity. I saw friends, heard laughter, remembered the quiet, private moments. And I knew why I felt sad. This was the first time I had been somewhere I could remember being before I damaged my brain. This was the first time I had met myself. And I knew that while the house was the same, I would never be the same again. Everything that had gone on in this house before, every episode, encounter and event, would feel different if I went through it again now. My reactions would be different, my interpretation of it. The home was familiar. But I was a stranger. There was a huge distance between me and this life that I had led. Everything was the same, yes—everything except me. The sameness in the things around me just served to illuminate the strangeness in me.

I found Mindy and we held each other. I didn't need to tell her that I was sad or why. She knew. We had made it this far and we were sure as hell going to carry on.

'You OK?' She spoke softly, her head on my shoulder.

'Yes. Just feels a bit . . . weird, that's all.'

'I know.'

'Where are the girls?'

'Putting their boots on, we're going outside to say hello to the pony.'

'Come on then. I'd like to do that too.'

'You sure you're OK?'

'Yeah. I'll be fine.'

# AFTERWORD

It's now eleven months since I sat on a bench in Scotland and wept when I realised I could not daydream any more. I can daydream now; my mind wanders and roams as freely as ever it did, maybe more so. I'm no longer terrified of strangers and I can get through a day without needing a nap. My emotions remained tricky for a while; I was still at the whim of whatever particular powerful emotion struck me at any time, often for no discernible reason. Sometimes though, I could recognise these phantom emotions for what they were and even trace their route into my head. I wandered across my garden some months ago and saw, from the corner of my eye, my old battered Land Rover. I must have thought to myself how much I loved that old thing. Because, seconds later, I was overwhelmed with a great flood of love, charging up through my chest to dominate everything, just as it does when I think about my daughters. I had, briefly, fallen in love with my Land Rover. It was a sincere, deep-rooted response, as real as any other feelings of love. But it was yet another phantom emotion. I was lucky, I could recognise it for what it was, understand how it had come about and untangle myself from it. This was pretty much the last time I had any such struggle. My emotional checks and balances are back now and I hope not to fall head over heels with a rusty 4x4 again.

As each week has gone by since I came out of hospital, I have looked back over it and realised how far I still have to go in recovery. I have sat and considered the things I found difficult and challenging in that week, things I would have breezed through before, and I have breathed a huge sigh of relief that I am better. And then another week has gone by, I look back over it in turn and realise once more that I was still in recovery, still had far to go. It is a long and sometimes tough process. The doctors, medics and nurses saved my life and gave me back my mind. But I then had to re-learn subtle lessons in how to use the fully functioning brain they had given back to me. It's still going on. I look back now on last week, think about the low points, the confusing moments and the difficult patches, and realise that even a year after I started out, I am still trudging along that road to recovery. And I thank every one of my lucky stars that I am able to make that trudge.

I did get out to the Arctic in the end. My skiing improved, though hardly to Olympic standards. I battled on through temperatures of minus forty, covering thirty or forty miles a day on foot and on skis. And yes, there were times when I battled also with demons inside that, perhaps, would not have been there before. But through every long, tough mile, I was overwhelmed with relief and a strange joy at being able to feel the pain, accept it and battle on. I had, by then, accepted that the damage to my brain would sometimes mean I struggle with things that were easier before, but it no longer scares me. It was no more frightening than feeling the occasional twinge from a once-broken arm.

I got back to the *Top Gear* studio too. The boys cooked up a few gags for my return to the show and we played it partly for laughs. But at the same time, we knew that we were dealing with something difficult and sensitive, not just for me and the team, but for anyone else affected in any way by the thousands of car crashes that happen every day. We did not want to make light of accidents and of brain injuries such as mine, but we could not gloss over the whole event and pretend to the world that, in the fantastic TV world of *Top Gear*, things don't go wrong. They do, they did and we all learned lessons as a result. Most of all, perhaps, we learned that you owe it to yourself and those around you to look very carefully at what you are doing, to consider the risks and to take whatever measures you can to prepare for them. Standing once more on the *Top Gear* stage, I silently thanked every member of the team for ensuring through their diligence and professionalism that when I did something dangerous and difficult and was hit by disaster, I stood a chance of making it through.

This is not a sad or miserable story, not by a million miles. Yes, there are things I still have to work through even now, but I am here to work on them. The lessons I have learned, about myself and the world around me, have far outweighed the personal discomfort and occasional misery. I do feel for my family though. Mindy, my daughters, my parents and brothers had to stand and watch and worry when they were told I might die or be changed for ever; that is not a lesson to be embraced and enjoyed, that is just a very hard thing to have to do. Perhaps though, by coming through it together, by weathering a considerable storm, we are closer and stronger than before.

Of course, there are thousands who are not so lucky. Visiting the Brain Rehabilitation Unit in Bristol for check-ups and chats with Dr Holloway, I saw many other brain-injury victims working through their problems. People for whom the last memory before their world was turned upside down really was of riding a bike to the shops for a loaf of bread or driving to work. The bravery, determination and sheer force of humanity of them, their doctors and nurses and their families watching on is difficult to contemplate but inspiring nonetheless.

I've learned too that it can be tricky for people recovering from an injury to their brain, if only because often there is no visible, external sign that anything might be wrong. You cannot see that someone has damaged their memory, their emotions, their personality. They may look perfectly well on the outside but be suffering all manner of turmoil in their minds. I wanted at one point in my own recovery to wear a T-shirt that, on one side, read *I'm OK, please stop asking* but on the back read, *I'm still bloody poorly, you know!* Both the best and the worst thing is when people would look at me, assume I was fine and carrying on as if nothing had ever happened. It was great to be able to forget about the accident and move on, but at the same time, I needed people to understand the trouble I might still be having doing ordinary stuff. I think by now, though, I could lose the panel on the back and just have *I'm fine, thanks* printed on both sides.

The one thing that has never been a pain though, is when people come up and ask how I am. They will often worry that perhaps I am tired of people asking or resent the inquiry. Why would I? Who wouldn't want people asking about their health? Every time a pleasant middle-aged lady I have never met before walks up to me, puts her hand on my arm, looks into my eyes and asks how I am, it's as though an aunt has given me a big hug and asked the same question. It's comforting and healing, if only because it's a reminder that it's rather good to be a human being after all. And so I will never be able to thank enough the people who wrote to me and thought about me when I was ill. It was a moving and powerful experience and contributed, I'm sure, to my recovery and to Mindy's ability to cope with almost unthinkable pressure.

And so life gets ever closer to returning to what was normal for us. Of course, as our 'normal' includes days when I call out goodbye to Mindy and the kids and set out to try and reach the North Pole by dog sled, cross the English Channel in a floating van or even drive a jet car up an airfield in Yorkshire, we can never entirely relax. My driving licence came back in good time, largely because the surgeons had managed to avoid opening my skull. When it did, I grabbed the keys to my trusty Morgan and, with Mindy by my side, cruised round the country lanes near our home. The doctors had been very worried about possible flashbacks and repercussions when first I drove. In fact, it never really crossed my mind. What happened to me happened in a jet car. If I had fired up my Morgan and heard a jet engine start immediately behind my head, I might have had a bit of a moment. But this was different, this was just driving, and I loved it. We laughed a lot. So did Izzy and Willow when I first took them for a drive a few days later.

'Daddy, are you driving?'

'Yes. Yes, I am, because the doctors said I can now.'

'Cool.' They sit in silence and exaggerated concentration.

‘Daddy?’ they both ask together in their sing-song voices.

‘Yes?’

‘Don’t go upside down and bang your head again, will you? We’ll all have to go to hospital then, and who will look after the horses?’ They laugh and laugh and laugh at their joke.

It’s a routine we still go through every time we all get into Mindy’s bright yellow Land Rover and set off on a family trip, even just to the shops. And in answer to their advice, I always say that, ‘No, no, I won’t go on the roof again.’ And if I can help it at all, I shan’t.

And sitting beside me when I say that, as she has been beside me now through the highest and lowest points in my life and the moments when it looked like it very well might end, is Mindy. The impact of any such accident is felt initially by the person at the front line, the one turned into a patient by it. But from that point on, it becomes a burden to be carried by those closest to them. And so I thank my parents, my brothers and my friends for being there when I needed them, and I am sorry for putting them through a tough time. My daughters were largely shielded from the hurt of it, but they missed their daddy and one day, I’ll be able to explain why and say sorry to them too. And to Mindy, I can only ever say a simple thank you. And dedicate the rest of my life to her.

# ACKNOWLEDGEMENTS

This is the story of how I came to be prepared to risk losing my life, and very nearly did, and then, with the help of many, many people, got it back again. It is also the story of how an event such as my crash in September 2006 affected not just me, but those around me. Picking up the phone to be told that your husband, son or brother has crashed a jet-powered car and has sustained serious brain injuries is not an easy thing to do. I have many people to thank, therefore; those who put me back together again, physically, mentally and emotionally.

Thanks to the teams at Leeds and Bristol who were instrumental in my recovery and who kept Mindy sane and focused. At Leeds General Infirmary: John Adams, Consultant Neuro Anaesthetist; Sister Susan Aitchison; Elaine Andrews, Matron/Head of Nursing for Neurosciences; Michelle Ayling, Nursing Assistant; Andy Bennett, Charge Nurse, Neuro High Dependency Unit (HDU); Mark Brocksom, Head of Portering; Sara Costie, Staff Nurse (NICU); Fiona Evans, Sister, Neuro HDU; Nicola Fenton, Sister, Neuro Intensive Care Unit (NICU); Nicki Gibbs, Occupational Therapist; Jim Jackson, Senior Charge Nurse, NICU; Steve King, Senior Charge Nurse, NICU; Charlie Lobley, Sister, Neurosurgery; Roberto Ramirez, Specialist Registrar Neurosurgery; Stuart Ross, Consultant Neurosurgeon; Louise Rymer, Senior Sister Neurosurgery; Kate Warner, Senior Physiotherapist; Karen Wilcock-Collins, Acquired Brain Injury Coordinator.

In A & E at Leeds General Infirmary: Shirley Wilson, Acting Matron Accident & Emergency

Services; day shift nurses Sister Laura Smith and Staff Nurse Cheryl Fenwick; night shift Charge Nurse Alan Sheward and Staff Nurse Asiscolo Prudenciado; Medical Staff Consultant Dr Peter Cutting and Specialist Registrar Dominic Hewitt.

All the housekeeping and domestic staff on Ward 23, Neurosurgery; and the Patient Relations and Communications departments.

At The Glen BUPA Hospital in Bristol: Onyx Brewin, Sister; Michelle Osborne, Sister; Louise Daniel, Clinical Services Manager; Brin Rees-Evans, Head of Clinical Services; Sandie Foxall-Smith, General Manager; Jamie Noble, Physio Manager; Catherine Garrett, Senior Physiotherapist; Sarah Wring-Nash, Hotel Services Coordinator; Alan Sheppard, Chief Engineer; Rick Nelson, Consultant Neurosurgeon; Pat Easterbrook, Sister; Andrew Martin, Reception Manager.

And at the Frenchay Centre for Brain Injury Rehabilitation, Bristol: Dr John Holloway and his team.

The Yorkshire Air Ambulance.

* * *

Mum, Mum and Dad, Andy and Andrea, Nick and Amanda. All friends and neighbours, especially Anne and Syd, Beano and Michelle, Pat and Steve, Fiona and Malcolm, Colin Goodwin, Andy Hodgson, Ela Turz, Jenni Schmit, Katrina Tanzer, Zog and Jill Ziegler and Bill Scott. Gary Farrow. The *Top Gear* team, especially Andy Wilman, Alex Renton and Grant Wardrop. Prof. Syd Watkins, Arai Helmets, Racelogic, the Operation Joystick team and all the people who looked after us in the Scottish Highlands.

And to my entire family: sorry, won't do it again.

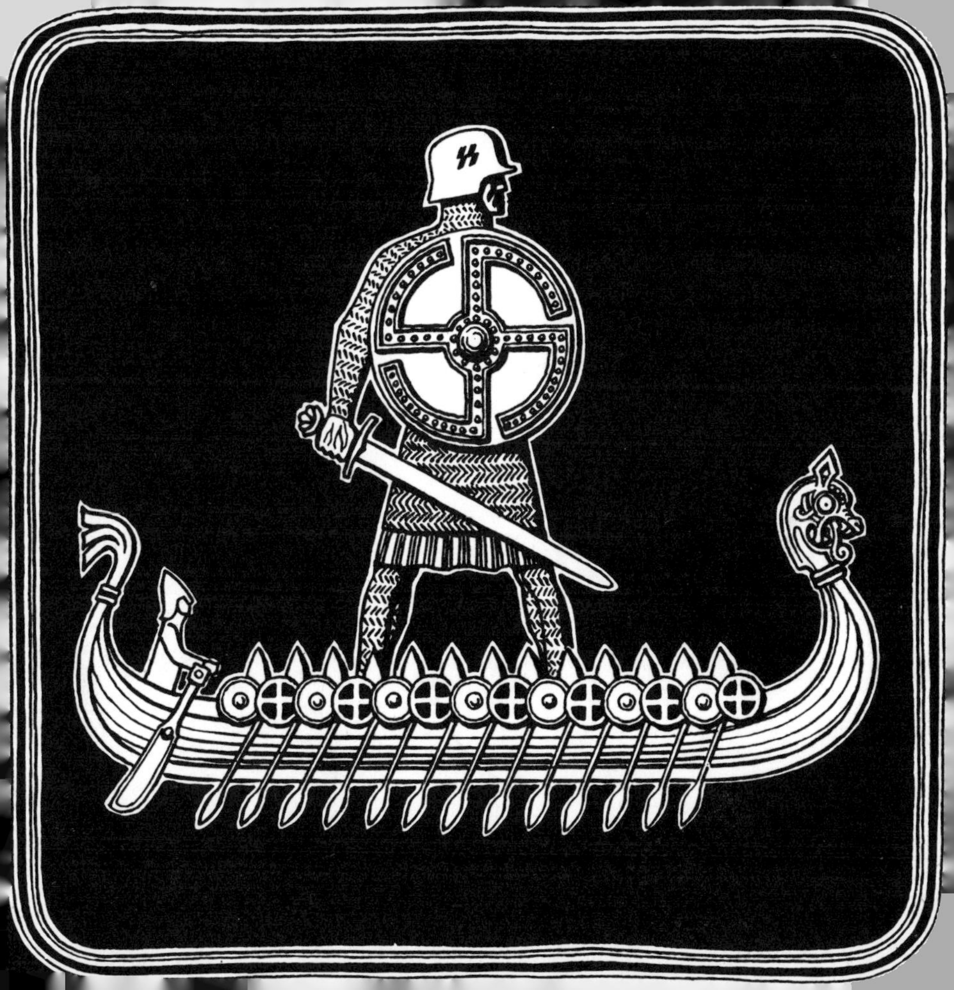

# Hitler's SS

PAGEANT OF HISTORY  EDITOR: JOHN GROSS

Richard Grunberger

# Hitler's SS

WEIDENFELD AND NICOLSON 5 WINSLEY STREET LONDON W1

SBN 297 00210 4

Printed in Great Britain by Ebenezer Baylis and Son Limited,
The Trinity Press, Worcester, and London

To I.G. (1883–1934)

# Contents

# Acknowledgements

The author and publishers would like to thank the people and institutions below for permission to reproduce the photographs on the pages mentioned after their names.

Archiv Gerstenberg, 17 (bottom), 18 (top), 73 (top), 74 (bottom), 75 (bottom), 90 (bottom), 92, 109; Comité International d'Auschwitz, 90 (top); Bavaria Verlag, 89 (top and bottom); Historical Research Unit, 20 (top), 38 (top), 57 (top and bottom), 58 (top and bottom right), 60 (top), 61, 64 (bottom right), 91; Novosti Press, 78 (top and bottom); Popperfoto, 38 110 (top); Sudverlag, 20 (bottom), 37 (bottom), 59, 60 (bottom), 63 (top and bottom), 73 (top), 80 (top); Ullstein, 17 (top), 18 (bottom), 37 (top) 38 (bottom), 40, 62, 64 (top), 74 (top), 79 (top), 80 (top), 110 (bottom), 111 (top), 112; Radio Times Hulton Picture Library, 10.

# 1

# From Beer Cellars to Power

ELEVENTH DAY OF THE ELEVENTH MONTH OF 1918: WHILE THE Great War expired all over Europe in Germany the Weimar Republic struggled towards birth. Amid revolutionary alarums and excursions German democracy – a slack balloon filling out in an airless jar – expanded to fill the vacuum created by the Kaiser and his generals absconding into exile (or retirement) one step ahead of unavoidable military defeat.

In the aftermath of a collapse so total and unexpected that it soon made many Germans say (with Field Marshal Hindenburg), 'We were not beaten in battle but stabbed in the back by traitors', the Republic's first Parliament met at Weimar to set up responsible government, introduce universal suffrage and establish civilian control over the Reichswehr, the hundred-thousand-man army permitted by the Versailles Treaty of 1919.

But the radical elements behind the strikes and mutinies that had accompanied military defeat judged piecemeal political reform an insufficient substitute for fundamental economic change and attempted – in Berlin, Bavaria and elsewhere – to transform postwar readjustment into social revolution.

Although in Berlin the Spartacists (forerunners of the German Communist Party) failed quickly and bloodily, a Soviet-style regime assumed power in Bavaria. It had a programme of workers' control, land reform and popular participation in government. However, it was soon crushed by a combined force of armed right-wing gangs derived from Reichswehr and Freikorps irregulars.

It was here at Munich, savagely purged of Red Revolution, that the story of the SS began. Heinrich Himmler (born in Munich in 1900), bespectacled, narrow-chested, a soldier *manqué*, had, to his chagrin, missed action in war, but had belonged briefly to one of the Freikorps that 'liberated' the Bavarian capital. Adolf Hitler, too, found himself at Munich in 1919 awaiting demobilization.

Before discharge he attended one of the soldiers' indoctrination classes with which the Reichswehr officer corps supplemented its armed combat of left-wing subversion. Hitler attracted the favourable attention of his instructors and was ordered to infiltrate, for counter-revolutionary ends, the suspiciously named National Socialist German Workers' Party – in reality no more than a conventicle of beer-parlour politicians.

By January 1920 Hitler, now a civilian, had made himself leader of the National Socialists and began to establish a reputation (and following) throughout Munich by his tirades against the 'Jew-ridden' Weimar Republic which he delivered before steadily increasing audiences of disoriented petty-bourgeois citizens.

At Nazi meetings the fury of Hitler's words fused with the activity of squads of strong-arm men to generate a noticeable aura of violence. Before one particular meeting in late 1921 Hitler informed his stewards: 'None of us will leave this hall unless we are carried out as corpses. If any coward shrinks back I will personally rip off his arm-band and cap-badge.'

Early on, a military bodyguard had been provided for him by Captain Röhm (a corpulent Reichswehr officer with contacts among the top brass), and this unit, soon reconstituted as the Party's private strong-arm squad, formed the original nucleus of the SS. Its leader was a stationery salesman, Josef Berchtold; Hitler's three initial personal bodyguards were Ulrich Graf, Emil Maurice and Christian Weber – the first a butcher and amateur wrestler, the second a watchmaker turned chauffeur, and the third a bloodstock-dealer who doubled as a beer-cellar bouncer.

By November 1923 when the Nazis made their first – and short-lived – impact on German postwar history, the so-called 'Stosstrupp Hitler' numbered fifty members, but in fact constituted no more than a special sub-unit of the *Sturmabteilungen* (SA, or storm-troops) – the two thousand-strong private army Röhm had built up for the Party since his discharge from the Reichswehr.

The abortive beer-cellar putsch in Munich on 9 November 1923 cost about a dozen fatal *Stosstrupp* or SA casualties and resulted in the short-term imprisonment of Hitler, as well as the temporary proscription of his party. Released in December 1924, Hitler reconstituted the Party, and in the following April set up a new 'staff guard', subsequently renamed *Schutzstaffeln*, or SS for short. Himmler, who since participating in the Munich Putsch had worked for the Party in various ways, as secretary to the Nazi Reichstag deputy Gregor Strasser, as a roving speaker, and as surveyor of secret arms dumps, now joined the SS and received membership number 168. In the following year, at the Party's annual para-military jamboree at Weimar (forerunner of the mammoth Nuremberg Rallies of the 1930s) the SS marched past Hitler, who awarded them the 'bloodflag' – allegedly stained with the gore of the Munich Putsch casualties – for services rendered on that heroic occasion. (The *Stosstrupp*'s actual exploit on the 'Day of National Uprising' had consisted of wrecking the Munich Social Democrat newspaper's printing presses; paradoxically the SS's primary non-combatant duties now also revolved around journalism: they were sent out to collect subscriptions and canvass advertisements for the Party-owned newspaper *Der Völkische Beobachter*.)

At the Weimar Rally Himmler had already acted as deputy leader of the SS, and in January 1929 Hitler appointed him Reichsführer SS. The twenty-nine-year-old 'eternal subaltern' had thus achieved the very height of ambition; but his new, grandiloquent title obscured the fact that the Munich-based SS headquarters only controlled three hundred men (the Berlin SS continued independently under Kurt Daluege, Goebbels' chief bully-boy) and that moreover the SS as such formed a mere sub-section of Röhm's much larger SA.

Yet at the same time, despite its theoretically subordinate position and small size, the black-uniformed SS could be said to outrank Röhm's brownshirts in the way a Roman Emperor's Praetorian Guard outranked the Roman legions. SA implied marching with the big battalions, SS meant membership of a select élite.

In Party parlance 'select' connoted hand-picked as well as thoroughbred – and since race formed the key dogma of the Nazi creed it was hardly surprising that some of its high priests had served apprenticeships in animal husbandry. The Nazi agricultural leader Walther Darré, who aimed at transforming Germany's farmers into a 'new nobility of blood and soil', was once a pig-breeder, while Himmler (a keen disciple of Darré's human bloodstock theories) had been engaged in chicken-farming outside Munich at the time of his appointment to the leadership of the SS.

Given the Nazi mystique of the soil, Himmler's earlier choice of a career would appear to have been quite apt, although it in fact represented something of a step down from his social background. His father, *Studienrat* (literally 'Study Counsellor') Gebhard Himmler, had in turn tutored one of Bavaria's royal princes (Heinrich of Wittelsbach, godfather to the SS leader), taught at a Munich grammar school and been headmaster of a provincial one. In other words, the sometime chicken-farmer had been born into the *Bildungsbürgertum* (the educated bourgeoisie), an esteemed, though not over-affluent, status group within Wilhelmine society.

The Himmlers' family life seems to have been close and harmonious, with the mother dutifully carrying out her prescribed role of *Hausfrau* and the *Herr Studienrat* self-importantly inculcating respect for the national past and established authority in his compliant children. In the 1920s occurred an episode highly revealing of the family ethos and young Himmler's cast of mind: on hearing that his elder brother Gebhard had become engaged, Heinrich commissioned a detective agency to investigate the fiancée's past, and when circumstantial evidence pointed to an earlier liaison, he prevailed upon Gebhard to break off the engagement.

At this time the twenty-four-year-old puritan was himself still a virgin. As far as his more conventional education was concerned, he had matriculated from his father's school and gone on to complete a three-year diploma course in agriculture at Munich University. At the university Himmler belonged to a duelling fraternity (wearing his rimless pince-nez even when duelling), did unpaid clerical jobs for the students' committee, kept a diary, attended Mass on Sundays and worked at self-improvement in two directions: to achieve great masculinity he practised shooting and subjected his unprepossessing body to athletic exercises, while in order to acquire greater social facility, he took dancing lessons and sought (platonic) contact with the opposite sex. Although immersion in political activity subsequently helped him to realize these aims to some extent, Himmler, the desk-bound progenitor of 'blond beasts', was never – not even at the height of his career – entirely to overcome his sense of social and physical inadequacy.

In 1928 he married Margarete Concerzowo, who was seven years his senior and owned a small nursing-home in Berlin, to which city Party business had taken him a year earlier. Though Marga Himmler had no strong political beliefs her nursing background led her to share Heinrich's interests in the pseudo-scientific folklore of homeopathy and herbal cures. The couple also shared a less esoteric interest in the economic viability of a smallholding they had bought with Marga's money at Waltrudering (ten miles from Munich) and on which they kept fifty hens. This joint absorption, however, did not long outlive the birth of Gudrun Himmler in 1929, after which the farm and the child became Marga's means of dealing with the life of a grass widow to which she was progressively reduced by Heinrich's other preoccupations – political as well as emotional.

The year of Gudrun's birth saw the world lose its fragile postwar equilibrium in the wake of the Wall Street Crash. While share values plunged crazily, the Nazis' political stock rose fast – at an even faster rate than Germany's unemployment figures. The September 1930 elections made the twelve-man Nazi *Fraktion* in the Reichstag mushroom into an ominous contingent of a hundred and seven that was to help nullify all attempts at parliamentary government.

SS membership began to reach four and eventually five figures during 1931, a year in which the 'Order of the Death's Head' (so-called after the insignia on the SS mens' peaked caps) took on ever more distinctive features. The blood-and-soil ideologue Darré set up the SS Race and Settlement Office (*Rasse-und Siedlungs-Hauptamt*, or RUSHA) which combined eugenic marriage-broking with researches into foreign Aryan stock potentially capable of 'Germanization' at a future date.

One of the Race and Settlement Office's first innovations was the SS marriage code under which official approbation of an SS man's marriage was made dependent on proof of the bride's Aryan descent – as far back as 1750 – and on her character, sanity, physical health and potential child-bearing capacity. RUSHA also kept stud records of the entire SS, and every individual member was issued with a *Sippenbuch* (clan book) containing the marriage code, in which the eugenic statistics of his wife and progeny had to be entered.

It was in 1931, too, that the Order of the Death's Head recruited the man who, more than any other, was to lend a chilling authenticity to that title: Reinhard Heydrich. Tall and fair, self-assured and intelligent, athletic and artistically gifted, Heydrich was in many ways the antithesis of the Reichsführer, whose deputy he soon became. The son of an opera singer turned music teacher, Heydrich started to train as a violinist, became caught up in the Freikorps movement at sixteen, and subsequently joined the Navy, in which he rose to the position of Signals Officer attached to Intelligence. Despite his Freikorps background his decision to join the SS in 1931 had not been politically motivated; it was in fact the rather indirect by-product of the sort of sexual peccadillo to which he remained addicted until his death.

A little earlier two strands of Heydrich's sex life had become awkwardly entangled: his engagement to the headstrong Lina von Osten had caused the father of Lina's more compliant predecessor to request that the *Herr Leutnant* make an honest woman of his daughter. On receipt of the classic reply 'No self-respecting officer could marry a girl who had given herself to him so readily', the father (who had influence with Heydrich's superior, Admiral Raeder) satisfied family honour by instigating the philanderer's dismissal from the service.

It was Lina von Osten, a dedicated Nazi, who advised her future husband to apply for a post in the expanding SS organization. The new recruit's personality and Naval Intelligence background impressed Himmler sufficiently to appoint Heydrich head of the newly created *Sicherheitsdienst* (SD for short), the intra-Party espionage service set up after the Stennes Affair when Kurt Daluege, the Berlin SS commander, had been hard put to crush an anti-Hitler rebellion among the capital's stormtroopers.

Daluege's action had earned a commendation from Hitler culminating in the phrase 'SS man, your honour is loyalty!', and in an amended form this became the motto of the Death's Head Order: hereafter SS belt buckles proclaimed *Unsere Ehre heisst Treue* – our honour is named loyalty – in (godless) imitation of the 'Gott mitt uns' legend engraved on army belt buckles under the Kaiser.

Also in 1931 Himmler was appointed as head of security at the *Braune Haus*, the newly acquired Party headquarters in Munich. The following year saw a further decline in the country's economic and political stability while the Nazi electoral advance assumed landslide proportions. By April 1932 SS strength stood at thirty thousand and the stormtroops disposed of ten times that number. The new brownshirt contingents were often unemployed, eager for soup-kitchen handouts, free uniforms and *camaraderie*; while the élitist SS attracted professional men, academics, ex-officers, and even such sprigs of the nobility as Prince Waldeck-Pyrmont and the Prince of Mecklenburg.

The flood tide of recruitment occurred during the opening months of 1933. On 30 January Hitler was appointed Chancellor and at a general election five weeks later – the last to be held in Germany during the Nazi era – he won a narrow majority which became a mandate to destroy democracy. The seizure of power inspired such a rich crop of Nazi recruits (derisively known as 'March violets') that in May the Party froze membership at the current level. With direct entry temporarily denied to them, thousands of young – and not-so-young –

The Munich *putsch* of 9 November 1923. Steel-helmeted storm troopers arrest city councillors

Storm troopers at machine-gun practice outside Munich (1923)

A Nazi orator addressing a crowd in the centre of Munich on 9 November 1923

Himmler as a standard bearer during the Munich *putsch*

On the road to power: Hitler and some top Nazis in 1932. Next to Himmler (front left) stands Frick; Goebbels is left behind Hitler and Goering on the far right

Hitler flanked by SS bodyguards (left to right: Schaub, Schreck, Maurer, Schneider) in 1925. Julius Schaub subsequently became his adjutant, and Julius Schreck his chauffeur. Notice the half erased figure of a fifth bodyguard

Ulrich Graf who had been wounded protecting Hitler on 9 November 1923 hopefuls streamed into the Party's auxiliary formations (the SA, SS, motorized NSKK), to be ahead of the field when the moratorium came to an end.

Reasserting the principle of selectivity at the heart of the SS ethos, Himmler, early in 1934, ordered that fifty thousand black-uniformed March violets be weeded out. This domestic clean-out, however, was an innocent interlude alongside the cannibalistic rite of purification the SS performed among German society at large and (after 1939) throughout most of Europe.

Two German terms, soon to enter every civilized language, became shorthand for this purification: KZ (short for *Konzentrationslager*, or concentration camp) and Gestapo (short for *Geheime Staatspolizei* or secret state police).

The seizure of power was accompanied by the rounding up, maltreatment and torture (often ending in death) of thousands of anti-Nazis. Arrested by the Gestapo, or police 'auxiliaries', these prisoners, for whom the existing police jails proved inadequate, were lodged in concentration camps. In 1933 neither the Gestapo nor the concentration camps were the streamlined institutions they subsequently became and their control was disputed between Nazi administrators, the SA and the SS. Local Gauleiters and SA leaders set up so-called 'wild' concentration camps, and on occasion – as at Papenburg camp near Osnabruck – rival agencies of the Nazi regime fought virtual pitched battles in disputes over the running of camps.

In March 1933 Himmler became Police President of Munich, with Heydrich as his assistant; June saw the creation of Dachau concentration camp – model for all subsequent Nazi hells on earth.

Camp routine, enforced by SS and SA men, whose only *alma mater* had been the drill-hall, was a sadistic perversion of military training. KZ inmates had to answer roll-calls, salute, stand to attention, report themselves present, and proceed at the double – and to endure the vilest forms of barrack-square abuse in the process. For breach of regulations they were liable, according to the official disciplinary code, to undergo any of the following: punitive labour, punitive drill, extended roll-calls, confiscation of mail, reduction of rations, solitary confinement, confinement in the dark, incarceration in a stand-up cell, twenty-five strokes on the posterior (covered or bare), suspension from a pole by the wrists, transfer to a punishment battalion, death by shooting or by hanging.

The first commandant of Dachau was Theodor Eicke, whom

Death's Head – symbol of the SS which was to become an emblem of terror throughout Germany and Europe.

Himmler had a little earlier sprung from Würzburg psychiatric clinic, to which Gauleiter Bürckel had consigned him – in a strait-jacket – as a lunatic constituting a public danger. Eicke, the son of a railway clerk, had seen war service in the Pay Corps and had subsequently joined the police, but failed to gain promotion. By contrast he managed to carve out a remarkable career in the SS, advancing within little over a year from command of the Third Reich's seminal KZ to control of the entire concentration-camp system, which in autumn 1934 comprised eight major institutions, ranging from Dachau to the dreaded Kolumbia Haus in Berlin.

The guards at Dachau – enrolled in the so-called Death's Head units – were largely drawn from the lowest stratum of Bavarian society: moronic and brutalized peasant types who in a period of reviving employment looked to SS service as a socially acceptable (not to say prestigious) means of avoiding honest labour. Irascibly primitive, these Dachau guards nursed a particular animus against intellectuals and Jews (two partly overlapping categories), and prisoners with academic titles or an offensively scholarly mien – such as wearers of spectacles – elicited even more vicious reactions from them than others. The camp personnel's native coarseness – thus the camp clerk's enquiry about the name of an inmate's mother might be phrased as 'Which Jew-whore shitted you out?' – was intensified by conditioning: during training, members of the Death's Head units would alternate three weeks of gruelling military drill with one week's concentration-camp guard duty, in the course of which they had to watch whippings and hangings alongside the prisoners.

As far as the outside world went, the SS arranged things so that the German public's knowledge about concentration camps was simultaneously – and paradoxically – both widespread and patchy. Though all Germans were vaguely aware of their existence, concentration camps remained taboo topics surrounded by secrecy and dread. But since total secrecy would have detracted from the value of the camps as deterrents, a minimal supply of information about what went on behind those electrified barbed-wire entanglements, searchlights and machine-gun towers was allowed to reach the outside world. Thus the stereotyped formula 'shot while trying to escape', behind which official announcements (on the inside pages of newspapers and in communications to next-of-kin) camouflaged the premeditated murder of camp inmates, soon passed into common usage as a universally understood cynical euphemism.

As time went on the unofficial grapevine which supplemented the official media as an essential source of information also spread knowledge of the SS practice whereby the next-of-kin of murdered prisoners would be informed of their bereavement by the postal delivery of an urn containing the deceased's ashes.

Even so, many citizens of the Third Reich remained fully persuaded that concentration camps subserved the professed Nazi aim – enshrined in the inscription '*Arbeit macht frei*' ('Work makes you free') above the camp gates at Dachau – of re-educating and salvaging prisoners for the German *Volksgemeinschaft* (folk community) through the educative agencies of hard work and discipline.

In tenuous corroboration of this myth, 'work-shy elements' – which in official Nazi terminology meant workers who had twice rejected employment offered them without good reason – would be consigned by the Gestapo to Dachau and similar institutions; but the 'work-shy' were in fact only one among many groups in the concentration-camp population.

The diversity of the camp inmates stemmed from Heydrich's and Himmler's adaptation of the Roman '*Divide et Impera*' to the conditions of their own slave state-within-a-state. The 'work-shy' belonged to the concentration-camp category *Asoziale*, alongside beggars, vagabonds, gypsies, prostitutes, alcoholics, brawlers, psychopaths, imbeciles and profiteers. These were intermingled with members of such other categories as professional and congenital criminals, homosexuals, Jehovah's Witnesses, anti-Nazis (ranging from Communists to Christians) and finally Jews.

To prevent stirrings of solidarity among these disparate groups, the SS furthermore created an internal camp hierarchy – such us block elders, or hut leaders – of congenital criminals whose power over their unfortunate subordinates, of whatever category, was almost as total and arbitrary as that of the guards. (KZ personnel exercised such unlimited dominion over the life and death of their shaven-headed, zebra-stripe-garbed prisoners that the Socialist poet Erich Mühsam, for instance, obediently hanged himself upon the expiry of a three-day time-limit the commandant of Sachsenhausen had set him.)

And yet these lords over life and death were themselves subject to the chill control and scrutiny of the Gestapo-staffed 'Political Departments' that functioned within the administration of each concentration camp as part of the command structure built up by Heydrich. The Gestapo itself had evolved according to Darwinian laws out of a tangle of warring institutions – old and new – whose vicious in-fighting continued for months after the seizure of power. Its relatively innocuous antecedents were the political police departments that had previously functioned in Weimar Germany's various constituent states – Prussia Bavaria, Saxony, and the rest.

The Gestapo's founding father was not Himmler – who was merely police chief of Bavaria in Spring 1933 – but Hermann Göring, who as Prime Minister of Prussia 'seconded' SA and SS killer squads to the Prussian political police during the reign of terror that followed the burning of the Reichstag (27 February 1933). This initial staffing of the new force by rival cliques turned its Prinz Albrechtstrasse headquarters into a small-scale battleground. Colleagues tried to arrest each other and alerted friends by phone before going to the toilet – in case they failed to return. Artur Nebe, head of the Criminal Police and a fast-rising member of the SS hierarchy, would slip the safety-catch of his revolver as he entered the building through the back door and would hug the walls as he climbed the staircase.

But these were no more than teething troubles, which in no way diminished the Gestapo's effectiveness as an instrument of totalitarian terror. Himmler and Heydrich, who during the interim had fused all the existing political police forces into one, took complete charge of this instrument in April 1934 and subsequently made it steadily more efficient by applying German thoroughness and ingenuity to techniques as old as Torquemada's or as contemporary as those of the OGPU.

The Germans and (after 1939) non-Germans who passed through the cellars of the Gestapo faced torture by a variety of means: flaying with cow-hide whips; alternate drowning in bathtubs filled with cold water and resuscitation; electric shocks through wires attached to feet, hands, ears, penis and anus; the smashing of testicles in a special press; hanging with wrists manacled behind one's back; the infliction of burns with matches or a soldering iron. (A particular refinement consisted of torturing a woman within a prisoner's hearing and informing him that she was his wife.)

The institution equipped with this sort of expertise was finally, under legislation passed in February 1936, given retroactive legal status and simultaneously placed above the law. (Since 1933 the only formality required to despatch a German citizen to a concentration camp had consisted of a Gestapo official's insertion of his name on the appropriate form.) Paragraph 7 of the February 1936 law stated that no appeals were possible against Gestapo directives and that courts were debarred from setting them aside or revising them. In October 1938 Hitler articulated the Nazi concept of legality: 'All means, even if they are not in conformity with existing laws and precedents, are legal if they subserve the will of the Führer.'

Illegal law is the equivalent of organized chaos, but the SS rose above such contradictions by synthesizing them. To Himmler the killers of his Death's Head units were also sperm-donors for a higher form of life; in the Third Reich reality and illusion soon became so inextricably enmeshed that non-Nazis – and even Jews – looked to the SS as a disciplined and therefore relatively reassuring counterweight to Röhm's dissolute stormtroop rowdies.

During the one major internal crisis the Nazi regime was ever to experience – in June 1934 – these two wings of the Party army, respectively black- and brown-uniformed, met in far from open combat; after this purge which later came to be known as 'the Night of the Long Knives' the SA declined into a stage army whilst the SS moved forward to challenge the primacy of the Reichswehr (subsequently the Wehrmacht) as 'sole arms-bearer of the German nation'.

# 2

# Knights of the Long Knives

TO UNDERSTAND THE PHILOSOPHY OF NAZISM ONE HAS TO appreciate that for all its pretensions to the status of an all-embracing ideology it boiled down to one single uncomplicated, though emotionally compelling idea: race-war to the death between German and Jew. This lack of an ideology or even a 'binding' programme left a gap which the regime filled with cynical exercises in opportunism: women, whose place – according to Hitler – was in the home, were forced into factories; the land (eulogized as the unsullied source of German folkdom) was slowly depopulated; and Russia was transformed overnight from arch-enemy to treaty-partner and back again.

Hitler showed comparable opportunism in his relations with the Reichswehr – the single semi-autonomous power that survived in Germany after February 1933. Though this takeover had been accomplished with totalitarian weapons of terror and *Gleichschaltung* (compulsory co-ordination), it was only after the death of the Reich President Hindenburg, who had enjoyed the support of the army, in August 1934 that Hitler's control of the state became complete – and even then it still needed the removal of War Minister von Blomberg and Chief of Staff Fritsch early in 1938 to make the subservience of the military as total as everyone else's.

Hitler's ascendancy over the Party had by contrast been total all along. It was based on personal charisma, the elimination of such potential rivals as the 'leftish' Gregor Strasser, and Olympian remoteness from the battle (for precedence, power and the spoils of office) which was fought in the wings by Ministers, Gauleiters, the Party's political organization, the German Labour Front, the Reich Food Estate, the SS and the SA.

The SA were the self-styled 'People's Army of Nazism' which meant that their strength lay in quantity of numbers rather than quality. However, their leaders, who were frequently ex-officers, were steeped in a military/mercenary ethos and saw themselves as cadres of

Germany's future fighting force. SA commander Röhm actually aimed to absorb the hundred-thousand-strong Reichswehr in his inflated Party army and entertained notions of himself as moulder of a new fighting machine freed from the trammels of caste and convention that had hamstrung the German armies in the Great War.

He therefore demonstrated – as well as improved – the effectiveness of his brownshirt battalions by exercises, manœuvres and the stockpiling of arms throughout the months following the seizure of power; and in December 1933 he prevailed upon Hitler to appoint him to the Reich Cabinet as Minister without Portfolio. Hitler valued Röhm as the Carnot of the Nazi revolution's *levée en masse* and as an invaluable contact-man with key military personalities (such as Ludendorff). Since their early postwar days at Munich the two men had in fact been on intimate 'Du' terms, whereas Hitler kept himself apart from all his other paladins by the formal 'Sie'. No secret of the Nazi 'court' had been as widely disseminated both before and after the seizure of power as Röhm's homosexual tastes – and yet despite adverse publicity and internal mutterings Hitler had persistently refused to 'conduct an inquisition' into the SA chief's (and quite a few of his sub-chiefs') deviant practices.

As any change in the Nazi pecking-order immediately threw all rival holders of fiefs into a state of injured rage, Röhm's elevation to Cabinet rank made Göring and Himmler – after months of vicious in-fighting for control of the Gestapo – swallow their differences and form an anti-SA alliance. As Prussian Prime Minister and Reich Air Minister, Göring was in close touch with the civil service and the armed forces and shared their common hostility to Röhm's 'revolutionary' schemes, whilst the SS – who incidentally entertained military ambitions of their own – could not but be alarmed by the expansionist plans of their closest rivals.

In February 1934 Röhm took the offensive by submitting a memorandum on military 'reform' to the Reichswehr chiefs – whereupon von Blomberg pressed Hitler to intervene in the threatening dispute. The latter imposed a fragile truce on terms under which the SA were given control over the pre-military and post-service training of army recruits.

This division of military labour produced understandable disgruntlement among the stormtroops' ranks. At a subsequent SA leaders' banquet, tongues loosened by alcohol gave utterance to wild if vague threats against the Führer. However to one Hitler-besotted regional

SA leader, Lutze of Hanover, these flushed outbursts sounded like evidence of treason, and he alerted Hess (Hitler's deputy), von Blomberg and Heydrich. Armed with Lutze's revelations, Heydrich persuaded Himmler of the necessity for an all-out pre-emptive strike against Röhm; and Friedrich Krüger, an ex-SS man in charge of SA training, was deputed to collect incriminating material from within the enemy camp.

While Heydrich was laying his plans with unerring clandestine precision, Röhm pressed the SA's cause in the full glare of publicity, voicing demands for a 'Second Revolution' – which alarmed the bourgeoisie – and enlarging the scope of SA manœuvres to that of army field exercises.

The anti-Röhm front stepped up its preparations in turn; the Reichswehr transferred heavy arms from its arsenals to the SS, and Dachau commandant Eicke's Death's Head units undertook war games with live ammunition. Heydrich, resident in Berlin (like Himmler) since the SS's assumption of full control over the Gestapo in April, spent May compiling a central 'death list'. Regional SS chiefs were asked for names of their own SA rivals, and it was while waiting for these addenda that Heydrich hit on the idea of broadening the projected SA purge into an all-purpose liquidation of key anti-Nazi personages, irrespective of affiliation.

On 17 June von Papen, the Conservative ex-Chancellor who had joined the Hitler cabinet to give it balance, spoke out against Röhm's revolutionary alarums and demanded 'normalization'; this appeal stirred a sufficiently widespread echo to make Hitler suspect a right-wing threat to his regime in addition to the one Röhm posed from the Left. He therefore determined to strike out simultaneously in both directions, albeit – since the Army's goodwill was essential until he finally took over from the near-moribund Hindenburg – under the guise of an alliance with the Conservatives.

After an emergency meeting with Hindenburg and von Blomberg – underscored by Heydrich's dissemination of faked SA plans for a coup – Hitler convoked a conference for 30 June at a Bavarian resort 'to resolve differences' with the SA leadership. Two companies of the crack *Leibstandarte* (Hitler's SS bodyguard) were despatched to Bavaria under their commander Sepp Dietrich, and during the early hours of the projected 'conference' day the assembled SA leaders were dragged from their beds – which some, incidentally, were sharing with male companions – and arrested on charges of high treason. Sepp Dietrich and Eicke supervised the subsequent executions at Munich's Stadelheim Prison; when the dying Röhm mumbled 'Oh my Führer', Eicke replied cynically, 'You should have thought of that before!'

From the early morning of 30 June motorized SS units roared through the streets of Berlin and liquidated – in conformity with Heydrich's directives for an all-purpose purge – the capital's upper SA echelons, together with Gregor Strasser, ex-Chancellor Schleicher, the Catholic leader Dr Klausener, von Papen's press secretary, and many others. Whilst the latter batch of victims were murdered in their homes, many SA executions took place at the Kolumbia Haus; it was there that one SS NCO told the doomed stormtroop leader he roused from his cell after midnight, 'Put your head under the tap so you look fresh and make a good impression in death!'

From Munich and Berlin the blood-letting spread to the provinces; in Silesia and the Grenzmark region manhunts of SA fugitives hiding in the forests went on for days.

In Nazi parlance (as well as, oddly enough, in that of later German historians) 30 June 1934 became known as the 'Röhm Putsch' – a misnomer echoing Hitler's lie that 'a clique of perverts around Röhm' had planned a coup in collusion with foreign powers. The man in the street, on the other hand, called it the 'Night of the Long Knives' and thereby hit on a phrase at once more accurate and more graphic.

As the vapours cleared from the slaughterhouse scenes at Stadelheim Prison and the Kolumbia Haus, it became apparent who had been the wielders of the longest knives: the SS was raised – by an order of the Führer dated 20 July 1934 – to the status of an autonomous organization within the Nazi Party and empowered to set up armoured units of its own.

The latter reward posed an ominous paradox for the Reichswehr, since it meant that no sooner had the challengers to its military monopoly been liquidated than the liquidators themselves presented the very same challenge.

As for the SS, the Night of the Long Knives can be said to have completed the chrysalis stage of its development. Hereafter the corporate personality of the Black Order remained fixed – despite the evolution of its sub-groups into intelligence service, political police, human bloodstock society, slave labour agency and Corps of Janissaries.

This protean role involved occasional mishaps – as when the murder of Chancellor Dollfuss in July 1934 failed to precipitate a Nazi takeover of Austria – but generally the progress of the SS was smooth and its scope limited only by Hitler's veto.

The first division of what ultimately became the wartime Waffen SS was raised – and accepted by a reluctant Reichswehr (now renamed Wehrmacht) – as part of conscription, which came into force in March 1935. This nucleus of the future SS army was given its own Sandhursts in the shape of the officer cadet schools at Bad Tölz and Brunswick, which were created by Paul Hausser, a retired Reichswehr Lieutenant-General and therefore the highest-ranking former regular officer ever to don the black uniform.

In April 1935 Himmler and Heydrich followed up their acquisition of an army with that of a newspaper, the *Schwarze Korps* (Black Guard) whose style – part-incantatory, part-prurient – soon attracted a mass readership. Besides adulation of Hitler and crudest Jew-baiting – the staples of Nazi journalism – the SS paper featured population-booster campaigns, attacks on wealth or privilege and directives for 'spontaneous' violence.

To boost the birth-rate it extolled motherhood irrespective of wedlock, campaigned for nappy services and served up visual aphrodisiacs in the form of photographs of sunkissed bodies among waving ears of corn.

These inducements to procreation dovetailed with attacks on 'life-denying' morality and religion: throughout the Nazi campaign against Political Catholicism the *Schwarze Korps* produced riveting exposures of sexual and financial malpractices in monastic institutions.

From thus shocking the bourgeoisie it was but a short step to scourging them; each week the paper held up some factory boss for providing inadequate toilet facilities, or a farmer whose tied cottages had leaking roofs, to public obloquy. (This was a profitable crusade from which the *Schwarze Korps* earned political dividends and its editors financial ones – in the shape of conscience money from employers who preferred blackmail to scandal.)

Most importantly the paper provided a free information service for amateur lynch mobs. It did this by publishing names, addresses and (occasionally) photographs of individuals up and down the country guilty of non-contribution to the Winter Help charity, breaching the boycott of Jewish shops or refusing to tender the Hitler salute.

A noteworthy feature of the *Schwarze Korps* was its total lack of self-consciousness: marriage and birth announcements on the inside pages carried the by-line Dachau as if it were the most natural thing in the world for a maternity home to be next to a torture chamber. (Dachau concentration camp, aptly illustrating the Nazi ethos, contained SS married quarters.)

Although few SS men were even of early middle age, the paper's personal columns also regularly carried black-edged death notices. Fatal training mishaps, riding accidents, motor-cycle crashes – all reflected that other aspect of the SS ethos whereby the general effusion of blood was the only circumstance distinguishing a field of battle from a field of exercise.

If the SS upper age-limit was early middle age, the lower one came close to adolescence: *Schwarze Korps* editor, Günther d'Alquen, was all of twenty-three years of age at the time of his appointment to this key post. But as well as enjoying unprecedented scope for advancement, young SS men were subject to minute surveillance: d'Alquen, for instance, was ordered to break off an affair with a brown-eyed young lady and given three months in which to affiance himself to a possessor of blue irises, thus guaranteeing the eventual procreation of 100 per cent Nordic stock.

Painstaking checks of this type on the eugenic dossiers of intending SS brides were a chore Himmler still liked to undertake in person, even though within two years of the seizure of power SS membership had shot up from 52,000 to 165,000. The Reichsführer's prodigious preoccupation with the Aryan myth made him lavish no less care on the past: he set up an *Ahnenerbe* ('Ancestral Heritage') institution to investigate Germanic prehistoric remains so as to establish the modern Germans' racial continuity with their forefathers. This institution, which operated under the aegis of a genuine professor of archaeology bearing the honorary rank of SS captain, with money donated by the big business 'Friendship Circle of the Reichsführer SS', sponsored large-scale excavations on sites in Germany, not to mention such bizarre adventures as an expedition to Tibet.

History – or to be more precise his own highly idiosyncratic version of it – gripped Himmler's imagination in an oddly personalized form. He was quite obsessed with the figure of Henry the Fowler, a tenth-century German king, on the anniversary of whose death he kept a yearly midnight tryst in the crypt of Quedlinburg Cathedral (the alleged site of the royal remains). At the millennium of Henry's death, 2 July 1936, Himmler vowed – before a band of Wehrmacht, Party and SS dignitaries bedecked with braid and medals – to continue and complete the anti-Slav crusade of the medieval monarch.

Einzelpreis 15 Rpf.

Berlin, 3. August 1944
31. Folge 10. Jahrgang

Das Schwarze Korps

ZEITUNG DER SCHUTZSTAFFELN DER NSDAP
Organ der Reichsführung SS

Verlag: Franz Eher Nachf. GmbH., Zweigniederlassung Berlin, Berlin SW 68, Zimmerstraße 88. Fernruf: 11 00 22. Postscheckkonto: Berlin 4454. Anschrift der Schriftleitung: Berlin SW 68. Zimmerstr. 88-91. Anzeigenpreise laut aufl. Preisliste

Bezugspreise: Durch die Post bei freier Zustellung ins Haus durch den Briefträger 65 Pf., durch Streifb. monatl. 85 Pf. Ausland mit ermäß. Porto 80 Pf., übriges Ausland RM. 1,05. In Groß-Berlin erf. Zustellung durch Austräger uns. Zweigstellen

Mast-head of *Das Schwarze Korps* (The Black Guard), the official SS newspaper.

In private he carried the identification with his royal namesake (Henry = Heinrich) to even greater lengths; he claimed to commune with the dead king in his sleep and eventually looked upon himself as his reincarnation.

As if this was not enough, Himmler also viewed his own personality as big enough to accommodate the shade of King Arthur of Round Table fame: he had the derelict Wewelsburg Castle in Westphalia refurbished at considerable cost, and periodically assembled the twelve highest-ranking Obergruppenführer of the SS round the oaken table of its lofty dining-room. (On Himmler's orders each of the twelve wore a coat-of-arms of his own, and during his stay at the castle occupied a period-furnished chamber dedicated to a specific hero from German history.) The Wewelsburg's holy of holies was a subterranean shrine: plinths for the Obergruppenführers' cremation urns encircled a sunken well; on the death of each Knight of the Round Table his escutcheon was burnt on top of a hollowed-out stone pillar, with the smoke – by means of a cunningly arranged ventilation system – forming a vertical column above the well.

Similar rituals, though naturally less expensive and involved, formed the basis of the religion all SS men were expected to practise. 'Religion' is actually a misnomer, however, since it implies something of an altogether higher order than the hotchpotch of Teutonic ancestor worship and nature-cult that catered for the spiritual needs of the Nazi élite. The most pronounced characteristic of this New Heathenism was a rejection of almost every aspect of Christianity, ranging from the virtues of humility and charity to the symbolism of the cross.

The mystery of the Resurrection yielded to the eternal renewal of the race, otherworldliness to hero myths, and Christmas (with its date brought forward to the winter solstice) to Yule-tide.

> 'On the day of the winter solstice,' according to an SS manual, 'the sun rises again from its wintry grave. This annual event was celebrated as the greatest festival of our forbears. They advanced towards the Yule-night with firebrands to liberate the sun from the bondage of wintry death, and thought of it as a young hero come to rouse and free them from their death-like sleep.... On Christmas Eve the main ingredients of the festive fare must be carp, roast goose and wild boar – drawn respectively from the sphere of water, air and earth. At the conclusion of the meal the father uses the Yule candleholder to kindle the lights on the Yule-tree, leaving three candles unlit. The other members of family and clan are summoned and the father kindles the remaining three candles, saying: "This light shall burn in memory of our ancestors who are with us today. This light shall burn for my dead comrades from the war and the time of struggle, and this light shall burn to remind us of all our German brethren across the globe celebrating Christmas with us today!" '

Yule-tide involved the use of such ritual objects as Yule-plates, wreaths and wheels. The plates, made of zinc, wood or earthenware and sometimes engraved with the tree-shaped life-rune, were actually all-purpose bowls, and as such could be filled with presents at Christmas, coloured eggs at Easter, apples at harvest thanksgiving, and bread and salt at weddings. Yule wreaths of riband-garlanded fir-twigs were either hung vertically as Advent wreaths or suspended horizontally from an upright wooden pole wedged into the hub of a Yule wheel (its six symmetrical spokes symbolized the intersection of the horizon with the diagonals formed by the terminal points of the sun's orbit at the winter and summer solstice in German latitudes).

The manual went on: 'After the exchange of the presents the family listens to the Christmas broadcast of the Deputy of the Führer. Thereafter – in view of the fact that Yule-tide is the greatest clan festival – it is becoming customary to look at old family photographs, recount old family stories and to exchange ideas about the success of the steadily deepening research into family genealogies.'

In its treatment of death the SS 'catechism' alternated mock-profundities with minute *pompes funèbres* regulations:

> 'Just as vernal resurrection belongs to life so does autumnal decease. Being born and dying are part of life. Because all life is sacred to us, birth and death too are indefeasible – hence funeral rites belong to the annual cycle of our festivals. . . . Conveyance to the cemetery

requires a horsedrawn flat carriage affording maximum view of the SS flag-draped coffin topped by the dagger and peaked cap of the deceased. (The carriage is to be adorned with fir-twigs and the horses are on no account to be caparisoned in black.) After speeches at the graveside the dead SS man's unit-commander exchanges the dagger on top of the coffin for that of one of the next-of-kin – symbol of the latter's assumption of his dead comrade's obligation to strive and struggle. When the coffin is lowered the SS men present form a circle round the grave and – in military posture – intone the SS *Treuelied* [hymn of loyalty].'

Himmler may have imagined himself to be King Arthur and Henry the Fowler incarnate; in reality he was Nazism's Duke of Alba crossed with Ignatius Loyola, and his SS doubled as a Council of Blood and as a monastic order defending the true faith. The analogy with the Jesuits even holds good in education – though with the difference that whereas Loyola had wanted to concentrate on a child's first seven years, the SS were directly involved in educating the ten-plus age group.

Since the German school system had shown strong traces of authoritarianism even under the Weimar Republic, the Nazis felt little need for drastic reform. Their main innovation consisted of the setting-up of two public (i.e. boarding) school networks: the 'Napolas' (*National Politische Erziehungsanstalten* or National Political Educational Institutions) for the training of officers and government functionaries, and the *Adolf Hitler Schulen* in which the next generation of Party and SS leaders was to be reared. (The *Hitler Schulen* were wholly, and the Napolas partly, controlled by the SS.)

The selection of pupils took place at ten, according to partly medical and partly aesthetic criteria: anyone below A1 fitness (such as spectacle wearers) or of insufficiently Nordic appearance was excluded. Applications for admission originated – independently of parents' wishes – from the Hitler Youth, which also tested candidates' 'leadership potential' at special selection-camps which they had to attend for a fortnight.

At the *Adolf Hitler Schulen* sport enjoyed virtual parity with academic subjects and occupied two-fifths of the timetable. Religious Instruction – still in the curriculum at ordinary schools – was replaced by 'Political Studies', i.e. the regurgitation of *Völkische Beobachter* editorials and news reports. The great watchword was 'Kameradschaft': pupils used the informal 'Du' when addressing teachers, whose desks stood at floor level instead of on the raised platform customary in German classrooms.

Even more novel was the absence of such standard means of evaluating pupils as tests and exams. In consequence no subject grades appeared on end-of-year reports; the only information conveyed related to the pupil's degree of leadership potential. Classes were called 'platoons', and outside the classroom the running of the schools largely devolved on Hitler Youth NCOs.

Each year a fixed quota of *Adolf Hitler Schulen* alumni graduated to the Party's 'finishing schools' or *Ordensburgen*, at which sport and military training of Spartan severity predominated (and produced a commensurate casualty rate). However, the *Ordensburgen* – not to be confused with the officer-training schools of the military SS – came under the control of the Party's Political Organization, which meant that the (non-military) future SS leadership would in fact have had a less than 100 per cent SS education.

This confusing overlap of Party and SS educational fiefs was paralleled in membership. To back his claim that the SS was synonymous with Nazi Germany's élite, Himmler awarded honorary *Ehrenführer* titles to highly-placed Party and government officials. These titles meant little but they did produce the bizarre situation whereby implacable personal enemies of Himmler like Martin Bormann and Foreign Minister Ribbentrop held nominal commissions in the SS.

Top-ranking scientists and academics were similarly honoured, though the *Bildungsbürgertum* (educated bourgeoisie) as such hardly required this sort of bait: no fewer than 12,000 representatives of the 'liberal professions' (half of them lawyers and doctors) enrolled voluntarily in the Black Order. In addition so many scions of the nobility donned the Death's Head uniform – modelled, incidentally, on the pages' livery at the Bavarian court – that in places the list of the SS officer establishment read like the German counterpart of *Burke's Peerage*.

Though only one German in 134 bore the aristocratic prefix *von*, the blue-blooded proportion among the SS Obergruppenführer (full generals) was one in five, among the SS Gruppenführer (lieutenant-generals) one in ten and among the SS Brigadeführer (major-generals) one in seven.

Some of these titled recruits conferred more than mere aristocratic glamour on their new knightly order – the 'SA hunters' von dem

Exemplary Nazi paterfamilias: Himmler with his daughter Gudrun at an indoor sports meeting in Berlin (1938)

S.S. top brass in full ceremonial panoply. Himmler (left), Heydrich (middle), Karl Wolff (front right)

A study in contrasts:
Himmler, the would-be sportsman

Heydrich, the champion fencer

The rivals: SA chief of staff Roehm and SS boss Himmler, four months before their lethal clash in 1934

The Burning of the Books in 1933. SA and SS men preparing for the auto-da-fe

Bach-Zelewski and von Woyrsch had both held army commissions and seen service in the Freikorps.

A key section of the SS leadership consisted of well-born desperadoes whom a combination of post-war circumstances and personal inadequacy had kept from their appointed station in life. The wartime Higher SS and Police leader in Poland, Friedrich Wilhelm Krüger, a colonel's son, was a failed businessman; Himmler's liaison officer with Hitler, Karl Wolff, a judge's son, had run an unsuccessful advertising agency; and the subsequent Higher SS and Police leader in Occupied France, Carl Albrecht Oberg, was a doctor's son whose banana import business had gone bankrupt.

Alongside *déclassé* aristocrats and bourgeois who had gone off the rails, the SS command accommodated selected well-publicized individuals risen from the lower depths of society. One such was the *Leibstandarte* commandant and subsequent Waffen SS general, Sepp Dietrich, a coarse-featured, squat man exuding peasant brutality. The illegitimate son of a Bavarian farmhand, Dietrich had been intended for the butcher's trade – a choice of career to which this Great War sergeant-major was to remain true for the rest of his life.

The social group most attuned to the spirit of the age were the unsentimental SD intellectuals enjoying unprecedented career opportunities as Himmler's social engineers and programmers of genocide.

Of these Otto Ohlendorf could well be described as first among equals. The career of this bright young economist with an – unfulfilled – postgraduate ambition to found an institute for the study of Nazism spanned the creation of SD Internal Intelligence, command of an *Einsatzgruppe* (killer commando unit) in Southern Russia and control of a department at the Foreign Trade Ministry.

Ohlendorf's colleague Dr Franz Six rose from being in charge of SD *Kultur* activities (at the age of twenty-seven) to the professorship of Politics at Berlin University and a top desk at the Foreign Ministry. *En route* Six held two 'shadow' appointments: SD chief designate for Occupied Britain and head of the SD task force detailed to secure occupied Moscow. (The main guidelines for his British posting were contained in a death list of two thousand names, headed by CHURCHILL, Winston Spencer.)

Then there was Walter Schellenberg, student of both law and medicine at Bonn University, who rose within seven years from apprentice spy to major-general and had by the age of thirty-two become head of SD Foreign Intelligence.

The SD – originally the Party's internal police and intelligence service – had by 1936 so enlarged its area of competence that the Wehrmacht was forced to negotiate a 'treaty' with it to demarcate their respective spheres of foreign espionage. This treaty (known as the 'Ten Commandments') allocated political intelligence work to the SD and its military counterpart to the Army's *Abwehr* under Admiral Canaris.

One of the SD's sensational though fortuitous espionage successes of this period related to the downfall of Marshal Tuchatschewsky, the Russian deputy Defence Commissar. Towards the end of 1936 Heydrich had heard – via foreign SD sources – of Red Army schemes for a *coup d'état* involving Marshal Tuchatschewsky, and he decided to forward forged documents to Stalin implicating the Marshal in treasonable contacts with Germany. Heydrich's design to precipitate a clash between Stalin and the Russian military leaders was facilitated by Tuchatschewsky's previous collaboration – under the terms of Russo-German agreements of the 1920s – with high-ranking Reichswehr officers.

When in June 1937 *Tass* reported the execution of Tuchatschewsky and seven Russian generals – prelude to a purge involving half the Red Army's officer corps – Heydrich claimed the credit for this auspicious *dénouement*. Though the claim was widely accepted among those privy to the affair, *Abwehr* chief Canaris dissented; a thorough analysis of the time-factors involved convinced him that the liquidation of Tuchatschewsky had been a long premeditated action on Stalin's part in which Heydrich's planted evidence was of no more than marginal importance.

This realization eventually led Canaris to the conclusion that the mendacity and amateurism of the expanding SD *Apparat* was endangering Germany's military security – a conclusion that brought in its train endemic friction between Wehrmacht and SS. But before the SD became involved in a straightforward contretemps with the military, there occurred a bizarre episode which illuminated the SS relationship with a much more powerful institution than the Army – namely the Party.

The economics expert Ohlendorf had built up an SD commercial intelligence network feeding data on business and labour trends to the government departments concerned. After a while he had switched from economic to political fact-finding with a particular emphasis on the state of public opinion in the Reich. In this the SS idealist - and subsequent mass-murderer – Ohlendorf was motivated by the reformist notion that the spotlighting of abuses might produce an improvement.

Early in 1938 the SD inflicted two consecutive – and cumulative – blows on the Army. In this, however, they acted less as initiators of policy than as executors, since essentially they only 'produced' the evidence which Hitler required to topple War Minister Blomberg and Army commander-in-chief Fritsch.

These two had been among half a dozen key figures to whom Hitler had in November 1937 divulged his plans for the forcible incorporation of Austria and Czechoslovakia and a premeditated collision with the West. Blomberg's and Fritsch's unenthusiastic response to this plan caused Hitler to cast around for a pretext on which they could be dismissed without alienating the rest of the military caste.

Heydrich was able to oblige almost instantly, since his unmatched weapon in the bitter infighting that passed for normalcy at the top level of the Nazi society consisted of incriminating dossiers – compiled with the aid of thousands of agents – on every person of any consequence in the Reich.

Blomberg, a widower in his sixties, had married a typist half his age. Within weeks of this *mésalliance* the SD produced documents implicating the second Frau Blomberg in modelling for blue photographs and her mother in running a call-girl service. The SD revelations caused the Field Marshal to lose caste among the military high-ups to whom they had been communicated and forced him into an early retirement.

The Fritsch affair was both more complex and more protracted. It hinged on an arrested blackmailer who claimed to have extorted money from the general by threatening to divulge his homosexuality. Fritsch denied the allegations on oath and was given indefinite leave while a military court of honour investigated them.

The deliberations of the court were interrupted by the invasion of Austria – which had been one of the main points at issue between Hitler and Blomberg and Fritsch. After the *Anschluss* (when it no longer mattered) the court established that the blackmailer had confused the general with a homosexual cavalry captain called von Frisch and had been forced to persist in his charge under threat of Gestapo torture. Though exonerated Fritsch was not reappointed – a slight he eventually expiated by his death in the Polish campaign of September 1939.

The purge of the army leadership in February 1938 had marked the beginning of the openly belligerent phase of Nazi policy. The subsequent twelve months saw – in breathtaking succession – the Austrian

*Anschluss* (March 1938), the incorporation of the Sudetenland (October 1938), the horrendous *Kristallnacht* pogrom (November 1938), and the annexation of rump-Czechoslovakia (March 1939); events which, besides giving the SS a greater share in foreign policy, drastically changed the scale and nature of the concentration camp system.

One of Himmler's pre-eminent concerns (as 'Commissioner for the Consolidation of German Folkdom') was safeguarding the *Deutschtum* of Germans outside the Reich, and the SS had had a stake in Austria since their abortive July 1934 putsch in which Chancellor Dollfuss had been killed. When Dollfuss' successor Dr Schuschnigg yielded to Hitler's ultimatum on 11 March 1938 and let the Wehrmacht march in, the German and Austrian SS dovetailed their activities with terrifying effectiveness.

Foolproof security arrangements operated during Hitler's triumphal 'homecoming'; within weeks 79,000 arrests took place in Vienna, whence freight trains crowded with human cargo departed regularly for Dachau and other concentration camps. A savage persecution of the Jews drove more than half of the two-hundred-thousand-strong community out of the country before the outbreak of war; in fact it is hardly an exaggeration to state that the Nazification of Austria – eagerly abetted by the local population – took the same number of months as that of Germany had taken years.

The chief local executors of SS policy were Ernst Kaltenbrunner, Odilo Globocnik and Adolf Eichmann – three men whose peers would be hard to find in the annals of inhumanity.

Kaltenbrunner, a hulking scar-faced lawyer with hands which reminded Schellenberg of a gorilla's, eventually succeeded Heydrich and became one of the chief accused at Nuremberg; the ex-convict Globocnik, notorious for dynamiting a Jewish jeweller's, lived in blood and corruption as his natural habitat; the Dachau trainee Eichmann was to reduce mankind by several million during the war – in the interim he terrorized Viennese and (after March 1939) Czech Jews into saving themselves by flight as best they could.

The material and labour resources thus appropriated during 1938–9 prompted a change in the scale as well as the nature of the concentration camps. With an influx of Austrians, Jews and Czechs swelling the camp population, the KZ network had proliferated into close on a hundred centres of varying size by mid-1939. Besides the prototype camp at Dachau – which with its ancillaries eventually accommodated a wartime maximum of anything between 25,000 and 60,000 inmates – there was

Sachsenhausen-Oranienburg with fifteen ancillary work-camps (20–35,000 inmates), Buchenwald with eighty (20–50,000), Flossenburg with fifteen (30–40,000), the *Frauenlager* ('women's camp'), at Ravensbruck, with twenty (15–30,000), and Mauthausen with fifteen (40–70,000).

Before the annexation of Austria, concentration-camp labour had been largely employed in the construction and enlargement of the camps themselves and of the adjacent SS buildings. After the *Anschluss* Himmler decided to use his unprecedented labour resources as a new source of enrichment and economic power. To the expropriation of the wealth of Jewish inmates (which the SS either confiscated outright or acquired through blackmail and the solicitation of bribes) he added a higher dimension of profitability by the impressment of prison labour in quarrying, road-building and other construction work, market gardening, handicrafts, and (later on) the manufacture of armaments.

Even though the guards would contrive to make the apparently most innocuous assignments lethal – emaciated 'market gardeners' manhandling heavy wheelbarrows would be beaten when they stumbled, and sometimes drowned in pits of liquid manure – a prisoner's chances of survival naturally varied according to the nature of his work. Assignment to quarrying and construction work was tantamount to a briefly suspended death sentence, whilst handicraft jobs – particularly those catering to the needs of SS camp personnel – might even procure privileges for individual prisoner craftsmen.

This informal grading of labour tasks according to the mortal hazards involved had its official counterpart on a different plane. Eicke's KZ administration classified all *Lager* under its control on a threefold scale of ascending severity – with I denoting 'soft', II 'medium' and III 'tough' camps. On Eicke's scale Dachau represented the soft end of the spectrum(!) while category III was exemplified by Mauthausen, the death camp in Upper Austria built after the *Anschluss* to accommodate Viennese Jews. (Despite this designation, Mauthausen differed from the rationalized death camps set up subsequently in occupied Poland because in it the infliction of death had not yet reached the level of industrial processing.)

Mauthausen had been a stone quarry on the edge of the picturesque Salzkammergut lake region near Salzburg; conversion into a KZ meant levelling a wooded hillside and building huge granite walls. Within the circle of megaliths, death was applied by pre-industrial means: SS guards would push human chains of prisoners over the precipitous edges of the quarry – a practice which so disconcerted the civilian quarry workers who had been kept on that they complained to the camp administration about the unsightliness of the human remains bespattering the rock face.

Having gained a virtual stranglehold on Czechoslovakia through the *Anschluss*, Hitler spent the spring and summer of 1938 exacerbating the conflict between the Czechs and their (largely Nazified) Sudeten-German minority. In these manœuvres the SS played a considerable part: the strings jerking the puppet-like Sudeten Gauleiter Henlein were pulled by the *Volksdeutsche Mittelstelle* (Volksdeutsche Liaison Office, VOMI for short), the SS special agency for Germans living outside the Reich.

Flashpoint had nearly been reached in September 1938, when the West appeased Hitler at Munich by agreeing to the partial dismemberment of Czechoslovakia. Under the Munich treaty the torso of the Czech state was further weakened by the granting of autonomy to a Slovak provincial government at Bratislava.

In early March 1939 the SD resumed its foreign policy initiative: a 'trouble-shooter' unit under Alfred Naujocks arranged a series of bomb explosions in the Slovak capital which provoked a rift between Prague and Bratislava and thus provided Hitler with a pretext for invading and obliterating the rest of Czechoslovakia.

Five months later an appreciative Führer cast his SD trouble-shooters in a leading role: the flames they kindled were to provide a farcical overture to world conflagration. On 31 August 1939 Naujocks's men, wearing Polish army uniforms, raided the German radio transmitter at Gleiwitz (Silesia), fired a few shots in the air, broadcast a Polish proclamation and departed – leaving behind a dead 'Pole' (actually the corpse of a German concentration-camp inmate in Polish battledress) to lend a touch of verisimilitude to the proceedings. Next morning Hitler, in a Reichstag speech, announced the invasion of Poland as a retaliatory move 'provoked' by the Gleiwitz raid and a host of similar fake attacks carried out by the SD.

The Naujocks type of operation had by then become standard SD practice, it would barely deserve mention but for Hitler's attempt to inflate it into the Sarajevo of the Second World War.

Rather less routine was the Venlo incident in neutral Holland which occurred some weeks after the end of the Polish campaign. An ostensibly anti-Nazi German émigré – who in fact worked for the SD – had inveigled Captain Payne-Best and Major Stevens of British Military Intelligence into a rendezvous with Schellenberg at the Dutch-German border town of Venlo, whence Schellenberg (with covering fire from Naujocks's unit) audaciously abducted them in broad daylight. This coup brought rewards for all concerned: Schellenberg was promoted to SS Major-General (and head of SD External Intelligence eighteen months later) and the SD acquired greater leverage in foreign policy through the elevation of the heads of its various foreign networks into – diplomatically immune – Police Attachés at German embassies.

Even so Himmler had good reason for viewing the Venlo incident with mixed feelings. Hitler, who later – in Spring 1940 – adduced Stevens's and Payne-Best's presence in Holland as proof of Dutch-Allied collusion justifying his invasion of the neutral Netherlands, had placed a different construction on it at the time of the actual kidnapping. The 'incident' happened to occur on the same day – 8 November 1939 – as an unsuccessful bomb attempt on his life (at the Munich beer cellar where the Party old guard assembled annually in commemoration of the 1923 Putsch) and this coincidence convinced Hitler of a connection between the British and the bomb.

The man solely responsible for the Munich explosion – as the police soon established – had in fact been a lone wolf German anti-Nazi by the name of Elser, who was caught trying to cross illegally into Switzerland a few hours later. Hitler, however, was so convinced that his would-be assassin was merely the man-of-straw of a widely ramified conspiracy involving Britain, the Jews, the Freemasons and the German Resistance, that he ordered the Gestapo to extract the truth from Elser (and also from Stevens and Payne-Best) by all the considerable means at its disposal.

After the veteran investigator, Kripa Chief Nebe, had failed to dislodge Elser from his claim to sole authorship of the bomb plot, it fell to the furiously embarrassed Himmler to extract the confession demanded by Hitler. Screaming abuse he hurled himself upon the trussed-up prisoner to kick him repeatedly in the chest, stomach and groin, and had him beaten into unconsciousness several times and thereafter brought round with jets of cold water – but to equally little avail.

The fruitlessness of this investigation markedly, if temporarily, lowered Himmler's standing in the eyes of Hitler – a fact that was not lost on Ribbentrop and sundry high-ranking enemies of the Reichsführer – but also paradoxically saved Elser's life since Himmler did not want to sever his only link with the supposed instigators of the conspiracy. Elser was accordingly transferred to Dachau, where he was given an assignment that saved him from exposure to the maltreatment and overwork general throughout the camp.

Even so, Elser may not have noticed that at Dachau nesting-birds were objects of the SS guards' special solicitude; just as it is doubtful whether any inmate concerned knew that the SS had made Goethe's favourite oak tree in the vicinity of Weimar their central point in the planning of Buchenwald concentration camp. One of Mauthausen's distinctive features were the curling roofs of the guardhouses on top of its granite walls – a deliberate pastiche of the guardhouses along the Great Wall of China.

These bizarre touches reflected the sentimental aestheticism which occasionally rose to the surface of the Nazi mind; among its best-known manifestations were the compulsory singing of (often specially commissioned) KZ songs by inmates and the creation of a camp orchestra whose music, broadcast over loudspeakers, provided a monstrous counterpoint to the camps' everyday sounds of toil, violence and pain.

Hitler bathed his emotions in the surging cadences of Wagner, Heydrich shone at private chamber music recitals, and Governor Hans Frank of Poland would make the Baroque spaces of Cracow's Wawel Palace echo with nocturnal piano-playing. But Himmler was a creature utterly devoid of artistic accomplishment. His aesthetic tastes were amply catered for by the commandant's house at Stuttof concentration camp (near the prewar Polish border) where he occasionally stayed after hunting trips on East Prussian estates. It was a sandstone house – white, clean and rectangular with wrought-iron grilles. At night, whilst the lethal current crackled in the barbed wire encircling the camp, the somnolent Reichsführer's ear would catch the rustling of the nearby pine forests and the distant murmur of the sea.

# 3

# Schoolmasters and Spies

A PHOTOGRAPH OF HIMMLER'S CLASS AT LANDSHUT GYMNASIUM shows a group of senior boys in multi-coloured caps and sashes who can be seen gripping the crooks of their walking-sticks like sabre hilts. The aura which these self-consciously haughty eighteen-year-olds exude compounds menace with *Romantik* – exalted romanticism being then very much in vogue among the educated young.

Himmler's lifelong penchant for *Romantik* – during the trial of General Fritsch before a military honour court he assembled twelve SS dignitaries in an adjacent room and bade them concentrate their minds to influence the general into telling the truth – accounted for the *Schutzstaffeln* exhibiting even wilder contradictions than other Party formations.

Thus the Black Order which ran a slave labour empire producing colossal profits forbade its members to acquire goods on hire purchase, which Himmler believed was a capitalistic vice. The barracks of the militarized SS were furnished with wardrobes and cupboards which could not be locked – to instil comradeship into recruits who were at the same time adjured to report each other's political (or sexual) deviations. Concentration camp guards were warned against wasteful use of firearms on the grounds that each bullet cost the Reich three pfennigs – the inference being that prisoners' lives were worth even less – yet they had to sign statements every three months to the effect that they knew they must not maltreat prisoners.

If during basic training SS recruits dropped the cartridges they were loading into chargers, they had to pick them off the ground with their teeth; for the most trifling slip they had to do fifty knee-bends with rifles held out at arm's length – yet, having been reduced to bundles of jerking limbs without a will of their own, they were subsequently raised to lords over death and creation.

And just like Olympian deities SS men exuded physical prowess and youth. Heydrich represented the Reich at international fencing contests and SS riders swept the board at German equestrian events. D'Alquen, the editor of the *Schwarze Korps* had not yet reached thirty when the circulation of his weekly (initial printing: seventy thousand) reached a peak of three-quarters of a million copies.

It took Heinz Reinefarth four years to rise to general of police; Kurt Meyer, nicknamed 'Panzer-Meyer' became – at the age of thirty-three – the youngest divisional commander in German military history. Himmler himself was only thirty-four when he took command of the combined German police forces and the Gestapo.

With his peering eyes, weak chin and sloping shoulders Himmler projected a rather unprepossessing image, but Heydrich – athlete, fencer, pilot, leader of military SS route marches – undeniably made up for the deficiencies of his superior. Nothing illustrated the two men's complementary qualities more clearly than the contribution each made to the sphere of Nazi fencing: while Heydrich garnered trophies, Himmler devised the SS duelling *reglement* which laid down, among other things, under what special circumstances the preliminaries to an *affaire d'honneur* could be conducted by registered post.

This not untypical attention to detail had a positive influence on the standing of the SS among a nation inclined to invest meticulousness with moral significance. While some Germans viewed Himmler's *Apparat* with unconcealed horror, others saw it as a repository of order and a deterrent against corruption. When during the war, in which corruption mushroomed, Himmler amassed ever more power, many Germans rationalized their apprehension at this development by interpreting it as a portent of the cleansing postwar purge to come.

The Black Order was well aware of the ambivalent feelings it aroused. As early as 1934 Himmler had stated with unusual candour: 'We know that some Germans feel ill at the sight of the black uniform and we don't expect to be loved.' The SS certainly never did anything to solicit love – but while disdaining to court popularity, they frequently earned the public's shuddering respect.

Thus during the *Kristallnacht* (the nation-wide orgy of anti-Jewish arson and vandalism in November 1938) the half-horrified, half-fascinated watching crowds could not but marvel at the efficiency with which the stage-managers of the SS pogrom prevented the destruction of Jewish property from affecting adjacent German property.

(Not only Germans came to marvel at the foresight of the SS. In April 1943 all Poles living within a mile radius of the Warsaw Ghetto

The wire-puller. Typical Nazi election poster depicting Jewish manipulation of the economy and public life.

were instructed to keep their windows open to prevent the panes shattering while Brigadeführer's Stroop's men dynamited the last crumbling Jewish dwellings.)

Beside meticulousness and foresight the Black Order placed considerable emphasis on smartness – both in the martial and the sartorial sense of the term. No state occasion in the Third Reich was complete without a steel-helmeted SS guard of honour with gleaming black jackboots and black dress uniforms with white insignia and piping. White-gloved and peak-capped SS subalterns also formed part of the décor at all Nazi social occasions, great or small. They would be found escorting screen starlets at Berlin's glittering annual *Filmball* (which Hitler took delight in honouring with his presence) or pouring the coffee and passing the pastries when the proletarian Frau Gauleiter Koch entertained the ladies of East Prussia's landed aristocracy.

True to its deep-seated ambivalence, the same Black Order that lent a touch of urbanity to Nazi social life also aimed to settle its members as farmers-in-arms (*Wehrbauern*) in Eastern Europe and promoted a cult of peasant simplicity in house and furniture design completely at variance with the décor of the *Filmball.*

The fittings and furnishings of the ideal SS house comprised heavy roof beams with metal mountings, unstained rustic furniture, hand-woven Frisian wool hangings, wrought-iron candelabra, earthenware jugs, pewter table utensils and, the centre of attraction, a rough-hewn wooden cradle – preferably hand-carved by the paterfamilias in person.

Equally rough-hewn was the Nazi approach to population growth – officially termed *Geburtenschlacht* (battle of births). As chief strategist of the battle of births Himmler deplored the low fertility of many German marriages and the widespread taboo, both social and religious, on illegitimate motherhood. The war eventually enabled him to by-pass these obstacles by the *Eindeutschung* or Germanization of Nordic-looking Slavs, i.e. by biological kidnapping; but even earlier his own SS had provided volunteer 'procreation assistants' for single women eager for motherhood.

All the pieces in Himmler's eugenic jigsaw – infertile couples, Germanized Slavs, 'procreation assistants', unmarried mothers – were moved into place by 'Lebensborn' (Fountain of Life), an SS foundling hospital-cum-adoption society established in 1936. According to the Lebensborn report for 1938, '832 valuable German women decided despite their single state and the sacrifice entailed, to eschew abortion and present the nation with a child'. Assessing each German's life contribution to the economy at one hundred thousand Reichsmark, Lebensborn claimed to have enriched the country by eighty-three million Reichsmark.

Eventually thousands of Lebensborn wards were placed with childless Nazi couples; more importantly, in wartime the original objective – delivering and fostering illegitimate German children – was superseded by the genetic spoliation of Eastern Europe.

During his first inspection tour of occupied Poland Himmler had been deeply stirred by the Nordic appearance of many Slav children and this may have started a train of thought culminating in his war aim 'to enlarge Germany's existing blood basis of 90 million to 120 million'. Kidnapped children – snatched from orphanages or alleged resistance families – were taken to Lebensborn homes dotted across occupied Europe; after a processing period during which the bewildered children were drilled in rudimentary German and denied any contact with their compatriots, they went off to the Reich already bearing the names of their designated foster parents.

Germanization was by no means confined to children nor were all Germanized Slavs necessarily outright victims of force. In Poland, where Poles and Germans had long intermarried, Polish nationals of part-German ancestry could apply for Reich citizenship which – given the situation of Poles under Nazi occupation – many were quite eager to do.

But volunteers could never meet Himmler's need for genetic reinforcements, and two special SS agencies – the Volkdeutsche Liaison Office and the Race and Settlement Office – scoured Europe to select human specimens considered suitable for Germanization. Besides abduction, the tasks of RUSHA, the Race and Settlement Office, ranged from conscription of slave labour, the infliction of (frequently capital) punishment on East Europeans guilty of intimacy with German women, to the clearance of Slavs from regions earmarked for German settlement.

One such region was the Warthegau in Western Poland. The Warthegau 'plantation' involved clearing one and a half million Poles and Jews out of a large area to make room for half a million *Volksdeutsche* from Eastern Poland, Rumania and the Baltic States. Himmler, newly styled 'Reich Commissioner for the consolidation of German folkdom', ordered the clearance during the Arctic winter of 1939–40, and thus caused a heavier death toll than resulted from Hitler's concurrent directive to decapitate the Polish nation by liquidating its intellectuals and priests.

These SS population transfers resembled nothing so much as the fourth-century Migration of the Peoples. Like their precursors in the Dark Ages, they were characterized in equal parts by barbarity and chaos: in 1942 Germans from Yugoslavia arrived in the East Polish areas whence *Volksdeutsche* had migrated to the Warthegau two years earlier.

The migrants, apart from having to give up ancient homesteads, frequently in exchange for makeshift accommodation in transit camps, were never asked whether or where they wanted to move; 'beneficiaries' and victims of the population transfers alike simply served the grand design of enlarging and consolidating the area of German settlement in Europe.

A related aim – that of purifying the gene pool of the German race – lay behind the Euthanasia Campaign of 1940–1. In September 1939 Hitler ordered the 'mercy-killing' of the feeble-minded and incurables throughout the Reich – on grounds both of eugenics and wartime economy in food, accommodation and medical personnel. The first liquidation centre became operational before the end of the year; another five, one of them situated at the well-known psychiatric clinic of Hadamar, came into operation early in 1940. The man placed in overall charge of the programme was Christian Wirth, the former superintendent of the Criminal Investigation Department in Stuttgart.

Wirth initially disposed of his victims by shooting them in the neck. After some time he switched over to gassing them in specially constructed chambers – and thus qualifies as co-originator of the mass-extermination methods subsequently used in the so-called 'Final Solution of the Jewish Question'.

In each euthanasia establishment a room camouflaged as a shower-room was hermetically sealed. This was connected by a system of pipes to cylinders of carbon monoxide. The patients, before being taken in groups of ten or fifteen into this gas chamber, were generally made drowsy with the aid of morphine (or scopolamine) injections or drugged with soporifics. Each centre housed a crematorium; families were informed of patients' deaths on pre-printed forms attributing death to heart failure or pneumonia.

The steep increase in fatalities, reported under conditions of ill-concealed secrecy – palls of smoke above the crematoria were visible for miles, and at Hadamar the village children would greet incoming hospital buses with cries of 'here come some more to be gassed' – prompted mounting disquiet in the country. Among many rumours in circulation

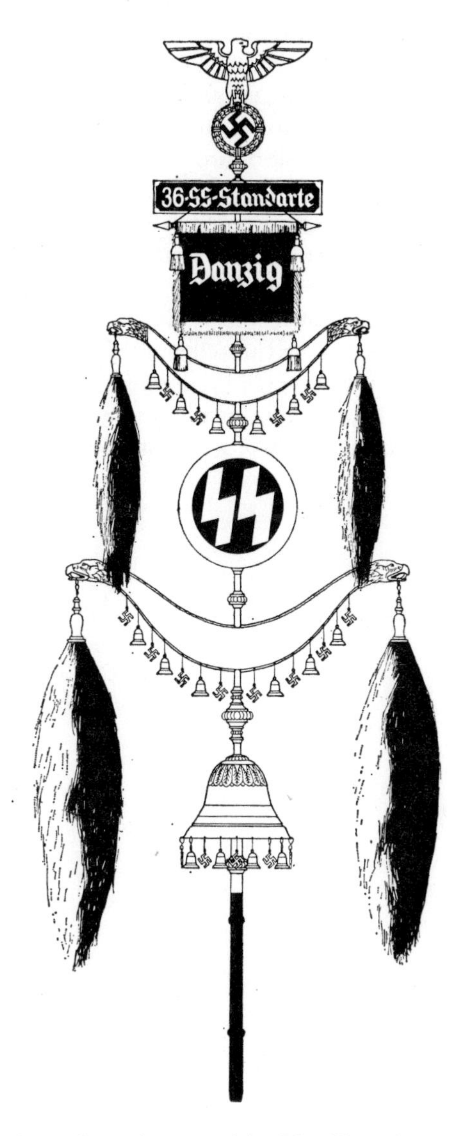


A Jingling Johnny used by SS military bands.

was one which alleged that even badly wounded soldiers were being 'mercy-killed' at military hospitals.

In August 1941 the Catholic Bishop Galen denounced the euthanasia killings in a sermon from the pulpit of his cathedral at Münster, Westphalia. This turned out to be the most successful single act of resistance ever undertaken in the Third Reich: the systematic killing of institution inmates (which had thus far cost approximately a hundred thousand lives) ceased almost immediately.

Nor was any retaliatory action taken against the bishop, although the Gestapo soon afterwards beheaded three parish priests who had distributed his sermon in leaflet form. Such glaring discrepancy of punishment was the fruit of Machiavellian calculation: while the death of anonymous parish priests would go unremarked in the surrounding welter of violence and confusion, persecution might have elevated the well-known prelate to the status of a national resistance figure.

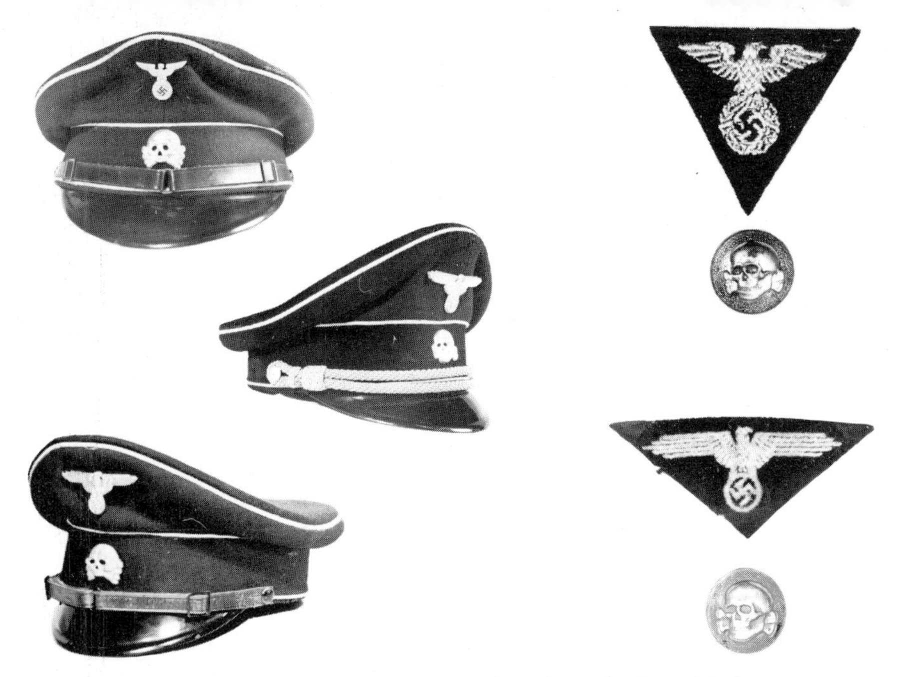

SS caps (*top*, other ranks 1934; *centre*, officers' standard model; *bottom*, other ranks 1935), and field cap badges (*top*, 1934; *bottom*, 1935)

SS uniforms (left, SS man in service dress; centre, SS man in winter service dress; right, SS officer in walking-out dress)

Formal evening dress for SS officers, 1938.

SS standard bearer's gorget (1938)

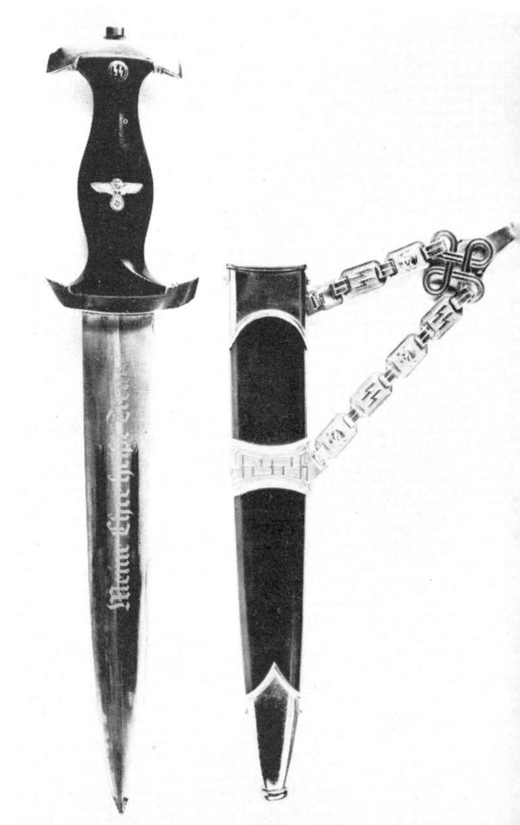

SS officer's dagger (1936)

SS drill: 'dressing from the right'

Changing the guard outside the old Reich chancellery (1935)

A medical for recruits of the SS *Verfügungstruppe* (1938)

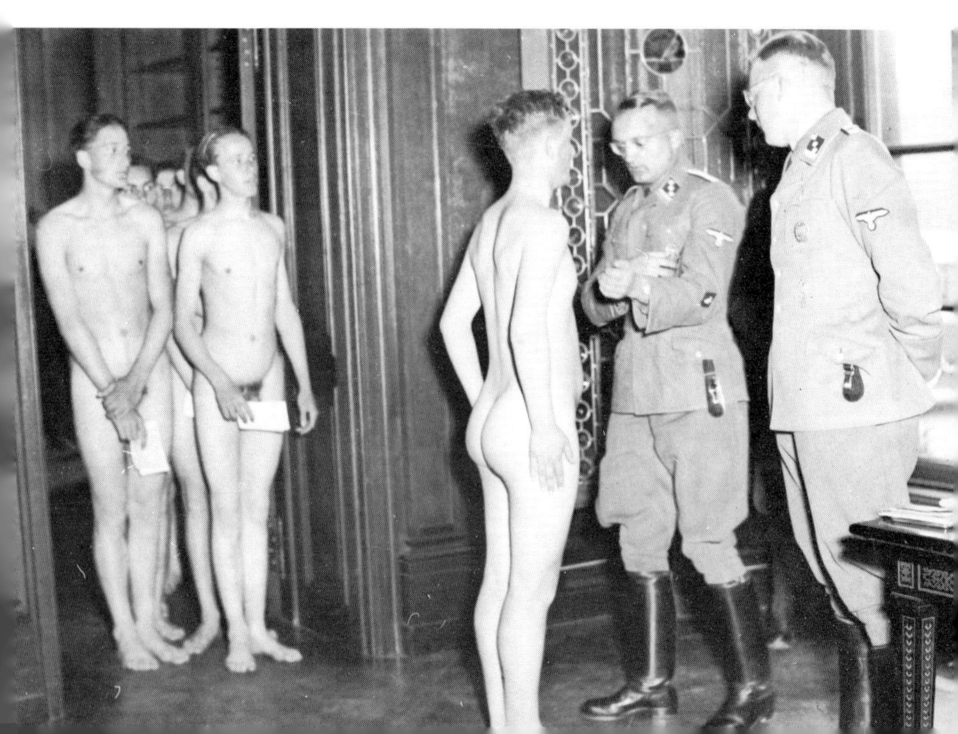

A meet in 1935. SS riders made a distinct contribution to 'high life' in the Third Reich

Hitler's 50th birthday

SS men partner Nazi maidens at a dancing display

Prescribed off-duty reading: *Das Schwarze Korps*

Nazi architecture: the refectory at *Ordensburg* Sonthofen, a finishing school for Nazi leaders

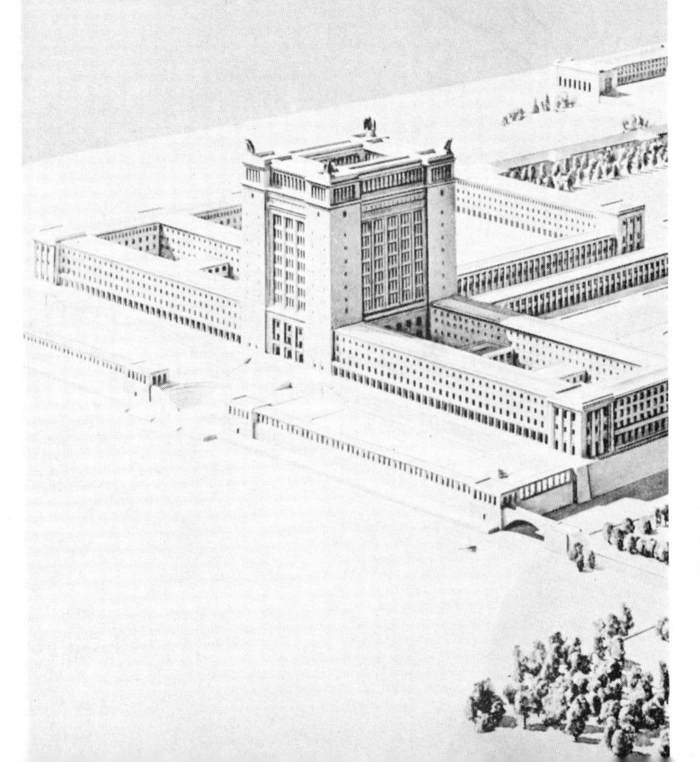

Nazi architecture: design for a High School

# 4

# The SS at War

CONSIDERATIONS OF 'IMAGE' ALSO PLAYED A PART IN PROMPTING changes in the role of the SS. Since Himmler's 'admission' that many Germans felt ill at the sight of the black uniform, though not for that reason, black had ceased to be exclusively associated with the SS in the public mind. The *Verfügungstruppe* (military SS) under their *Inspekteur* Paul Hausser wore field-grey uniforms only distinguishable from Wehrmacht issue by SS insignia and badges of rank. (It was this uniform, incidentally, which Hitler wore – and swore not to take off till victory – when he announced the invasion of Poland to the Reichstag on 1 September 1939.)

Though the Polish campaign had already seen some military participation by the *Verfügungstruppe*, in the early part of the war, Hitler still essentially ascribed security functions to the SS. In August 1940 he stated that a centralized militarized police force with an efficient listening service could have prevented Germany's collapse in 1918. Six months later he opined: 'to keep the trust of a soldierly nation the SS need to shed their blood'; by the winter of 1941–2 – when Germany suffered its first reverses of the war on the Eastern front – it had become 'necessary to send the SS to the front to maintain their prestige'.

These dicta of the Führer's reflected various pressures set up by the changing fortunes of war. While on the one hand mounting casualty figures increased popular resentment of deskbound Nazi warriors – Party and SS officials 'on special duty', and thus exempt from front-line service – on the other hand the SS leadership saw the escalation of the War as an opportunity for levering the Wehrmacht out of its position of military monopoly.

Thus Hitler eventually sanctioned (in the historian Gerald Reitlinger's apt phrase) 'the messy infiltration of the SS into the army'. As an initial pointer towards the transformation of the *Verfügungstruppe* into a thorough-going SS army, the title 'Waffen SS' was introduced in January 1940. When later that year the SS *Verfügungstruppe* Inspectorate became Waffen SS headquarters, the KZ Inspectorate was, confusingly, incorporated within it. In consequence the new force included *Totenkopf Wachsturmbanne* – KZ guard units formed from militarily non-employable members of the general SS after the transfer of Eicke's Death's Head units to the front. Himmler's characteristically imprecise nomenclature was to occasion a great deal of controversy after the war; we shall therefore restrict our use of the term 'Waffen SS' solely to the military formations of the *Schutzstaffeln*.

Their baptism of fire in the *Blitzkrieg* against Poland had been inordinately bloody – a fact duly noted by the 'senior service', Himmler was to complain a year later. 'After the Polish campaign the Wehrmacht said we had huge casualties because we were not trained for the job; after the French campaign they suppose we have not fought.' Though Waffen SS casualties in the West were proportionately lighter than in Poland, the underlying attitude had not changed. Thus when Eicke reported to his Wehrmacht superior, General Hoepner, that the SS *Totenkopf* division had carried out orders irrespective of losses, the latter commented 'This is the mentality of a butcher'.

Hopener spoke more truly than he knew. Transferring to the West the standard of barbarism which they had employed against Polish 'subhumanity', on 27 May 1940 *Totenkopf* men massacred a hundred men of the 2nd Royal Norfolks after their capture. (Private Pooley, the only prisoner not killed outright, had crawled out of the mound of corpses under cover of darkness and surrendered to another German unit; severely disabled, he was repatriated in 1943. No one in Britain would believe his story.)

In German eyes the Waffen SS had emerged from the war in the West like a breed of latter-day Siegfrieds. Whipped along by aggressive rage they stormed across the Low Countries and France with total disregard for casualties. The first Iron Cross of the entire campaign went to a soldier of the *Leibstandarte*, a unit whose divisional battle honours included Rotterdam and Boulogne.

Despite this added prestige, the Waffen SS remained strictly subordinate to the Wehrmacht – both in terms of command and of numbers. Hitler refused point-blank to amend a ruling under which the allocation of manpower to the fighting services devolved upon the General Officers commanding the Reich's various military districts. In October 1940 Himmler by-passed this limitation by extending SS recruitment to volunteers from Scandinavia, the Low Countries and France. It seemed an auspicious moment for enlisting 'reserves of blood of value to the struggle of the Nordic race' in a European anti-Communist force, because Russia had just annexed Finnish and Rumanian territory by force or threat of force.

Even so the European SS was more of a symbol than a real force capable of solving the Black Order's manpower problems. But a solution was at hand – thanks to Gottlob Berger, an ex-gym instructor in his forties who, after directing Henlein's Freikorps bullies in the Sudeten crisis of autumn 1938, had become head of the SS *Führungsamt* (Leadership Office).

The athletic, romantic Berger (he liked mountaineering and filming eagles and buzzards in flight) had a son-in-law who was leader of the German minority group in Rumania. It was this family link that inspired Berger's foolproof suggestion for overcoming the manpower deficiency of the Waffen SS: recruitment among the millions of *Volksdeutsche* whose residence outside the Reich rendered them ineligible for conscription by the Wehrmacht.

Berger's plan combined subtlety – Himmler could outmanœuvre the generals without being drawn into demarcation disputes over manpower – with the built-in ideological advantage that most Balkan Germans entertained a deep hatred for their Slav neighbours.

This point was amply illustrated by the *Volksdeutsche* Prinz Eugen division, who in the course of anti-partisan operations in Yugoslavia executed innumerable civilian hostages and perpetrated a series of massacres of entire village populations (for instance at Kosutica in August 1943).

Not that German-born Waffen SS men acted in a noticeably different manner. When, after their first winter setbacks in Southern Russia, advancing SS units discovered the mutilated corpses of six SS soldiers in the courtyard of the Taganrog OGPU (Soviet Secret Police) headquarters, *Leibstandarte* commander Sepp Dietrich ordered the massacre of four thousand Russian prisoners of war in a bloodbath lasting three days and nights.

Such barbarities did not prevent the Waffen SS performing prodigious feats of valour on the Eastern front. After Red Army units had infiltrated the rear of the Wehrmacht's Central Group, General Model ordered Obersturmbannführer Kumm of the SS regiment *Der Führer* to hold a line along the bend of the Volga in temperatures of well below zero, while the Ninth Army regrouped. Four weeks later Kumm personally reported to Model 'Mission accomplished'. Adding 'My regiment is drawn up outside', he pointed to thirty-five survivors out of an original complement of two thousand.

Locked in a pitiless struggle with the Red Army partisans, the weather, mud, vermin and disease, SS soldiers drew sustenance from both spiritual and material sources. Their greatest single source of spiritual strength lay in the fact that He who had made their honour synonymous with loyalty to Himself existed: 'And then we sat there,' wrote a combat-weary SS man at Vessoloye, 'on the clay floor and listened to the voice we love so dearly. All of us fastened eyes on the loudspeaker – as if he were standing there, the Führer. . . . Is there a finer reward after a day of battle than to hear him? Never!'

Though this diary entry carries absolute conviction, there were in fact other, equally fine, rewards awaiting the battle-stained Waffen SS man – as is attested by a note from the Chief SS Economic Administrator Oswald Pohl, headed 'Concerning the distribution of watches to members of the Waffen SS': 'Stored at Oranienburg concentration camp at present are 24,000 pocket watches, 5,000 fountain pens, 4,000 wrist watches, 3,000 alarm clocks and 80 stop-watches. These gifts are presented to the worthiest members of the division in your name.'

The sound of Hitler's voice and a gold watch taken from a Jew – these contrasting and yet complementary incentives indicate the poles of the spectrum of SS emotions; in between ranged fanaticism yoked to incontinence, self-denial laced with rapacity, rage fuelled by total non-feeling.

Despite their unique motivation the deeds of the Waffen SS for long barely stood out – in the world's awareness at any rate – from the global welter of violence, suffering and confusion. There was one exception, however: the punitive action against Lidice, a village near Prague, on 9 June 1942. Heydrich, the Reich protector of Bohemia and Moravia (since September 1941), had been assassinated in a Prague street by Czech patriots, said to have come from Lidice. In reprisal, the village was razed to the ground, all male inhabitants above the age of fifteen were shot, the women consigned to concentration camps and the children dragged off to Lebensborn homes (whence those unsuitable for Germanization were also despatched to KZs). This obliteration of a peaceful village received maximum exposure in the Nazi propaganda media so as to crush occupied Europe's will to resist.

Fearful retribution was also visited upon political suspects in Czechoslovakia and imprisoned Jews everywhere – as though a bloodbath (code-name 'Aktion Reinhardt') could expunge the fact that at the height of Nazi power Heydrich, the second highest leader of the SS, had fallen to a patriot's bullet.

His corpse was taken for a final display at the Reich Chancellery. Here the funeral orator Hitler touched the heads of the two little Heydrich boys (whom Himmler was holding by the hand) and then the Berlin Philharmonic Orchestra intoned Wagner's Funeral March.

In the black Valhalla to which Hitler had consigned him in his oration Heydrich was soon joined by another founding father of the SS. In February 1943 'Papa' Eicke, founder of the concentration camp system and subsequently commander of the Waffen SS *Totenkopf* division, was shot down by the Russians while on a reconnaissance flight over their lines.

Obergruppenführer Eicke, who a year earlier – at the Battle of Demjansk – had prevented a German *débâcle* of almost Stalingrad proportions, aroused such fanatical devotion among his men that a *Totenkopf* unit risked their lives to bring back his body from inside Russian-held terrain.

Before his death Eicke had on a number of occasions articulated a corporate SS suspicion that Wehrmacht commanders sent the Waffen SS to the most exposed sectors of the front in order to decimate the force by ensuring inevitable heavy losses.

Whatever the motive, SS divisions were in fact thrown into some of the most crucial battles of the Eastern Front. The resulting casualty rate – coupled with the natural propensities of SS men – accounted for Waffen SS cases outnumbering all others on the weekly (Oberkommando der Wehrmacht, or Armed Forces High Command) reports of grave misdemeanours (rape, etc.) in the armed forces, and this despite an average Wehrmacht : Waffen SS ratio of ten to one.

The early growth of the Waffen SS had been steady – one division in the Polish campaign, two in the French – and even the subsequent expansion (creation of the European SS and, more importantly, *Volksdeutsche* recruitment) had been kept within bounds acceptable to the Wehrmacht. In the winter of 1942–3 three newly armoured SS divisions were grouped into an army corps under Paul Hausser, who had won his spurs as a tank commander in 1940. Shortly afterwards the great tank battle of Kharkov gave Hausser the opportunity for achieving a unique distinction: he became (in March 1943) the last German general of the Second World War to win a victory in the East.

This notable feat invalidated all Wehrmacht objections to the expansion of the Waffen SS and made Hitler authorize the immediate enlargement of the force. A second SS armoured corps was formed under Sepp Dietrich, followed (in the winter of 1943–4) by a third under Felix Steiner – a former Reichswehr officer who had switched to the *Verfügungstruppe* because the military establishment frowned on his unconventional ideas.

But this upgrading of the Waffen SS in size and importance occurred only after the tide of battle had irreversibly turned. There had been too long a delay in equipping the Waffen SS with heavy armour – besides which a third of its cadre divisions lay buried in Russia by the end of 1943.

These losses were compounded with the deteriorating quality of the new intake into the force. The volunteers who had, up to the end of 1942, sufficed to meet all SS manpower requirements had to be supplanted by conscripts, some of whom – influenced by their families or priests – showed a marked aversion to joining.

At a time when the Reich had already forfeited victory, but seemed as yet insulated from defeat, some SS leaders began to show an unwonted degree of ideological independence. Strenuously casting round for a political solution to military stalemate – or worse – Waffen SS General Steiner, the former *Schwarze Korps* editor d'Alquen, who had become head of the Wehrmacht's propaganda company, and others suggested a drastic modification of Nazi policy towards the Russians.

Desperate situations call for desperate remedies. The SS ethos was the quintessence of Nazi racism; to guide SS soldiers in the East, Gottlob Berger's office in 1941 published an instructional pamphlet 'The Subhuman', which called the peoples of the Soviet Union 'the afterbirth of humanity existing on a lower level spiritually than animals'.

Now General Steiner told Himmler that the war could only be won by conceding sovereignty to national groups in occupied Russia, and SD reports from the Ukraine pointedly attributed increases in partisan activity to the repression practised by Gauleiter Koch. The *Schwarze Korps* and d'Alquen's Wehrmacht propagandists undertook a public relations operation on behalf of General Vlassov – the renegade former Red Army commander heading a Nazi-sponsored force of released Russian prisoners of war – with the object of elevating him to the figurehead of a semi-sovereign Russian state under German tutelage.

D'Alquen's maverick public relations exercise, SD exposures of Koch's misrule, Steiner's reappraisal of nationality problems – none of this helped. Although late in the war Himmler modified his own racial conceptions to the extent of setting up the Russian SS Kaminski

Brigade, Hitler remained obdurate. On the Führer's scale of sub-humanity, Slavdom ranked but one degree above Gypsies and Jews. While d'Alquen concocted the nickname 'hero-liberator' for the pathetic Vlassov, Hitler held fast to his vision of Slavs as helots fit only to serve their German masters and thus frustrated the belated attempt by a handful of high-ranking members of the SS to wriggle out of a racist straitjacket of their own making.

# 5

# The Final Solution

WHATEVER THE CONSEQUENCES OF HITLER'S SLAVOPHOBIA, ideologically it took second place to anti-Semitism. War to the death against the Jews was in fact the irreducible kernel of the Nazi creed – and in this war the SS manned the front line with frenzied dedication.

The Jews of the Reich had endured mounting persecution since 1933, to which growing numbers reacted by emigration. In a Reichstag speech on 30 January 1939 Hitler had openly avowed his intentions of genocide – 'a future war will see the destruction of the Jewish race in Europe' – but neither world opinion nor world Jewry could at that point in time fathom the awesome implications of his statement.

The coming of war and German conquests added new dimensions of scale and horror to the plight of the Jews. All emigration routes were blocked while the wartime black-out on communications freed Hitler from any vestigial inhibitions about implementing the so-called 'Final Solution'.

In September 1939 the head offices of the Gestapo, the SD and the Kriminalpolizei were merged into the *Reichssicherheitshauptamt* (RSHA or Reich Security Main Office) – keystone of an edifice of terror that soon spanned a continent. Heydrich became first head of the RSHA; his most important subordinate was Untersturmführer Adolf Eichmann, who in January 1940 took charge of the Jewish Department, the notorious subsection IV B 4, which functioned at a house in Berlin's select Kurfürstenstrasse crammed with filing cabinets, teleprinters and other office equipment.

At this very time the expulsion of Jews from the German-incorporated areas of Poland into rump-Poland (the so-called *Gouvernement-Général*) was taking a huge toll of lives through cold, hunger and disease. The winter clearance of the Warthegau was not the only foretaste of things to come for Polish Jewry: ever since their arrival in the country SS and police units had undertaken sporadic mass-shootings and burnings of synagogues.

Above the gates of Auschwitz: 'Work makes you free'

Concentration camp Dachau. The inscription states: 'There is only one road to freedom. Its milestones are obedience, industry, honesty, order, cleanliness, sobriety, truthfulness, readiness to sacrifice and love of country'

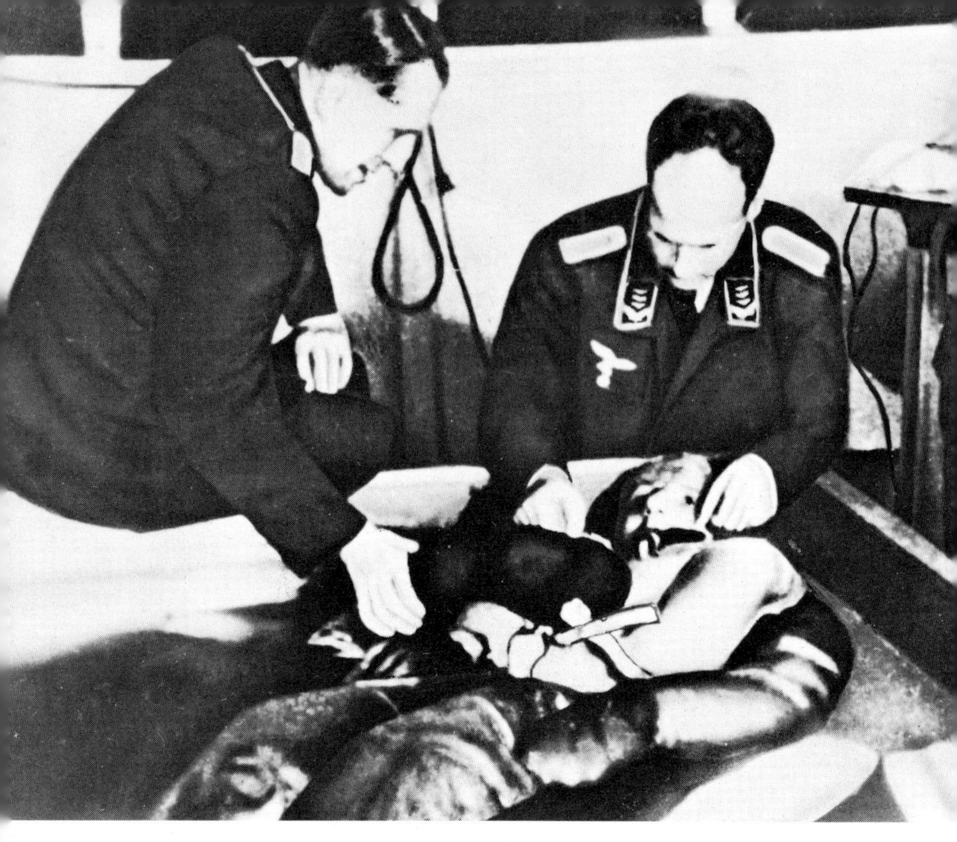

KZ medical 'research'. A super-cooling experiment during which Dr. Rascher immersed Dachau inmates in freezing water for up to three hours (1942)

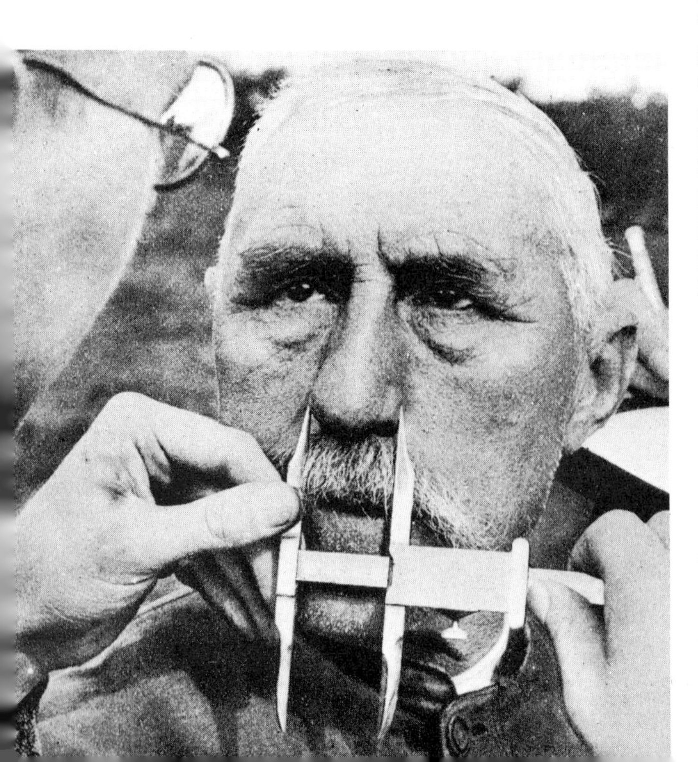

SS race research

Inmates working in the quarry at Mauthausen KZ (1938)

'Celebrating' the recapture of an escaped concentration camp inmate

Dutch recruiting poster for the *Waffen* SS

Norwegian recruiting poster for the *Waffen* SS

Title page of the SS periodical *'Die Schutzstaffel'*

Himmler, Heydrich and other SS high-ups in the crypt of the medieval *Quedlinburg* – the alleged burial place of Henry the Fowler

*Pour encourager les autres.* The inscription on the white board states (in Russian): 'I was a partisan'

Central Front 1943. Russian women take the mutilated remains of their menfolk back to their village for burial

‘SS home guard Danzig’ at the outbreak of the Second World War

Members of the Hitler jugend division of the Waffen SS in Normandy

SS leaders at war: Sepp Dietrich and Himmler on the Polish front (1939)

General Paul Hauser, father of the Waffen SS

'Papa' Eicke, father of the KZ system, walking pipe in mouth after the battle of Demjansk (1942)

The first winter of the war also saw the deportation of Jews from south-west Germany to camps in unoccupied France – in pursuance of Eichmann's nebulous 'Madagascar scheme' for turning the French island colony in the Indian Ocean into a Jewish reservation.

Huge *Judenreservate* were created during 1940–1, when Poland's three million Jews were inexorably herded into a few unimaginably overcrowded ghettoes – in Warsaw, Cracow, Lodz, Bialystock. 'Natural wastage' had already eliminated half a million ghetto dwellers before Hitler's final escalation of the war, the attack on Russia, created the setting for the climax of the Jewish catastrophe. Three months before Operation Barbarossa, the Führer instructed Himmler – in the notorious 'Commissars' Order' – to set up *Einsatzgruppen* (killer units) for the 'ruthless liquidation of all Bolshevik agitators, partisans, saboteurs and Jews found behind the Russian lines'.

Though Jews figured last in this order they provided the main quarry for the three-thousand-strong, highly mobile *Einsatz* commandos who scoured the vast area between the Gulf of Finland and the Black Sea on the heels of the advancing Wehrmacht. The Baltic States, White Russia and the Ukraine were areas of dense Jewish settlement; moreover, the lightning German advances during 1941 overran communities which Soviet censorship had – particularly since the Russo-German Pact of August 1939 – long kept in ignorance of the fate of their fellow-Jews under Nazi rule.

In these circumstances the tasks of the *Einsatzgruppen* were reduced to simple logistics: the round-up of the Jews in a village or town square, their transport to a secluded site traversed by a deep ditch, and, spaced correctly, their lining-up in the executioners' gun-sights. The ideal, rationalized solution was one whereby successive line-ups neatly produced layer upon layer of bodies in the ditch, which was then covered over with earth.

This economy of effort, though influenced by the smallness of the 'force', basically reflected the built-in economic orientation of the Nazi machinery of death: before stepping to the edge of the mass grave, victims had to undress and place their clothes, shoes, valuables and other belongings in separate files for subsequent – rational – utilization.

In all, the *Einsatzgruppen* liquidated an estimated 1,300,000 Jews, which, considering the 1 : 430 ratio of hunters to hunted, speaks volumes for their tireless dedication and efficiency. This score remains staggering even after allowances are made for the supporting role of

German soldiers or local volunteers – no less than for the competitive spirit which made *Einsatz* group commanders inflate their death tallies to outpace colleagues and impress superiors at RSHA, Berlin.

What manner of men were these latter-day Genghis Khans with a weakness for 'adjusting' the scorebook? Surprisingly enough few of them could be classified as outright thugs or psychopaths. Walter Stahlecker, leader of *Einsatzgruppe* A, which scored a 'first' by reporting Estonia clear of Jews in record time, had come straight from a top administrative post – Head of Foreign Intelligence – at the Reich Security Main Office. Dr Stahlecker was an intellectual of sorts – as was Otto Ohlendorf, his opposite number, both as leader of *Einsatzgruppe* D (Ukraine and Crimea) and as sometime Head of Internal Intelligence at the Reich Security Main Office.

University graduates were also strongly in evidence among middle-ranking *Einsatzgruppe* officers. Standartenführer Paul Blobel, responsible for the horrifying massacre of thirty thousand Jews at Babi Yar near Kiev, was an architect laid low by drink. Blobel's colleague, Bieberstein, was a theology graduate. When the Nuremberg judge asked this unfrocked ex-pastor in 1947 if it had ever occurred to him to offer spiritual comfort to his victims, Bieberstein replied, 'They were Bolsheviks – one should not cast pearls before swine. If I tell atheists the word of God I run the risk that they'll turn ironic. These things are too sacred for me to risk in such situations.'

At Nuremberg Blobel exuded self-pity – an attitude which, though superficially at odds with the prescribed SS image, could be dressed up as an expression of the Germans' much-vaunted capacity for inwardness. 'Human life was not as valuable to them, i.e. to the Russians and Jews, as to us. Our men who took part in these executions suffered more than those who had to be shot.'

The conscientious junior officer's concern for the well-being of his subordinates also shone through the Nuremberg reminiscences of another of the accused: 'In the mornings I would take my men to the lakeside for sports and in the evenings we had sing-songs around the camp fire.'

The only point on which the *Einsatzgruppen* officers in the dock significantly disagreed concerned the methodology of murder. Some considered execution by shooting 'more honourable' than by gas, while others, such as Bieberstein, expressed a preference for gassing as 'more pleasant for both parties concerned'.

Death by gassing, to which the Eastern *Einsatz* commandos had only resorted intermittently, became from Winter 1941–2 standard practice in the *Judenreservate* of the *Gouvernement-Général.* At Chelmo in Poland a pilot gas-chamber plant was already operational some weeks before the historic Wannsee Conference on the Final Solution (January 1942). This conference, chaired by Heydrich with Eichmann taking the minutes and attended by RSHA dignitaries and State Secretaries from a dozen Ministries, devised the master plan for the extermination of the Jews throughout the continent.

Within the next few months four gas-chamber complexes – Belcez, Sobibor, Majdanek and Treblinka – sprang up in the Lublin region, a vast reception area for deported Jews administered by Gruppenführer Odilo Globocnik. Globocnik's aide in charge of the actual death camp organization was Christian Wirth, who had supervised the euthanasia campaign. Like all who had risen high in the SS *Apparat*, Wirth was surrounded by powerful enemies, some of whom – unfortunately for him – were present at Belcez one August day on 1942 when the following scene occurred:

> 'At 7.20 a.m. a train arrived from Lemberg with 45 wagons holding more than 6,000 people. Of these 1,450 were already dead on arrival. Behind the small barbed-wire windows, children, young ones, frightened to death, women and men. As the train drew in 200 Ukrainians detailed for the task tore open the doors and laying about them with their leather whips drove the Jews out of the cars. Instructions boomed from a loudspeaker ordering them to remove all clothing, artificial limbs and spectacles. Using small pieces of string handed out by a little Jewish boy they were to tie their shoes together. All valuables and money were to be handed in at the valuables counter but no voucher or receipt was given. Women and girls were to have their hair cut off in the hairdresser's hut.
>
> 'At the corner stood a burly SS man with a loud, priest-like voice. "Nothing terrible is going to happen to you. All you have to do is to breathe in deeply. That strengthens the lungs. Inhaling is a means of preventing infectious diseases." They asked what was going to happen to them. "The men will have to work building houses and roads. But the women won't be obliged to do so; they'll do housework or help in the kitchen." For some this was a last small ray of hope, enough to carry them, unresisting, as far as the chambers of death. Most of them knew the truth. The odour told them what their fate was to be. They walked up a small flight of steps and into the death

chambers, most of them without a word, thrust forward by those behind them.

'Inside the chambers SS men were crushing the people together. "Fill them up well," Wirth had ordered, "700 or 800 of them to every 270 square feet." Now the doors were closed. Meanwhile the rest of the people from the train stood waiting, naked.

'An SS sergeant, the driver of the diesel truck whose exhaust gases were to be used, was making great efforts to get the engine running, but it refused to start. Fifty minutes, seventy minutes ticked away but the diesel would not work. Inside the gas chamber the people could be heard weeping. Furious at the delay Wirth lashed out with his whip at the Ukrainian assisting the SS sergeant.

'It was 2 hours and 49 minutes before the diesel started. At the end of another 32 minutes all were dead. Some Jewish workers on the far side opened the wooden doors. Inside the people were still standing erect like pillars of basalt, since there had not been an inch of space for them to fall in or even lean. The bodies were tossed out, blue, wet with sweat and urine, the legs soiled with faeces and menstrual blood. A couple of dozen workers checked the mouths of the dead, which they tore open with iron hooks. Other workers inspected anus and genital organs in search of money, diamonds, gold, dentists moved around hammering out gold teeth, bridges and crowns. In the midst of them stood Hauptsturmführer Wirth, in his element.'

But Wirth was not to stand in the middle much longer. During the 2 hours 49 minutes of lost killing time an internal SS controversy about the relative merits of carbon monoxide and *Zyklon B* (prussic acid) as asphyxiating agents had achieved resolution. This technical controversy marked, as frequently happens, a personal power-struggle – so that when, as a result of the diesel failure at Belcez, *Zyklon B* replaced carbon monoxide in all camps, and Wirth went down before Hauptsturmführer Karl Fritzsch, spokesman for the prussic acid lobby.

Fritzsch was on the staff of Auschwitz, the camp SS personnel dubbed – with characteristic self-pity – *anus mundi*. (Here the still-living envied the dead: hunger-crazed Russian prisoners expended their last ounce of strength hoisting themselves on to the carts which every evening conveyed the corpses of the day's dead to the burning pit.)

Auschwitz dominated the death-camp network both in size – four crematoria comprising forty-six ovens could handle five hundred corpses per hour, and still required supplementing by huge open incineration pits – and in diversity. Besides gas chambers and crematoria the camp accommodated (on fifteen square miles between the rivers Vistula and Sola) a huge industrial complex of arms workshops, chemical factories, synthetic petrol and rubber works, railway repair shops, quarries, forestry and farm enterprises – all staffed by slave labour.

Despite all this varied industry, its chief product was death: a commodity in which Auschwitz averaged an annual output of over a million throughout the three years of its existence.

On arrival at the camp whose gates bore the inscription *Arbeit Macht Frei* (Work Makes You Free), prisoners underwent selection either for instant despatch to the gas chambers or for more protracted extermination through work. During the few months (at most) which, except in the case of specially needed craftsmen, separated a worker's arrival from his final selection, he subsisted in a state of inconceivable degradation and helplessness. The trauma of being thrust into this inferno reduced him overnight from human individuality to animal reflexes; nameless, his identity diminished to the number tattooed on the right forearm, he became a speck of dust which existed for only so long as one of the SS men or *Kapos* (trusties) did not flick it off.

Slave labour on starvation rations was punctuated by endless roll-calls, debilitating parodies of military routine – prisoners were drilled for hours to take their caps off before SS men who had to be passed at the double at a distance of six paces with arms stiff and held tightly to the body – and by savage punishment.

Ex-police commissar Wilhelm Boger, the head of the camp's escape department, carried out his investigations by means of the 'Boger swing'. Two tables stood about three feet apart. The victim was made to sit down on the floor and fold his hands in front of his bent knees. Then his wrists were handcuffed, a heavy rod inserted between his elbows and knees, and the ends of the rods put on the tables. Thus he swung helplessly between the tables. The victim was then hit with a bullwhip on his backside and the soles of his feet so that he would turn an almost complete somersault. When his cries became too loud, a gas mask was pulled over his face; this was removed from time to time to see if he was ready to 'confess' or had lost consciousness.

The deputy camp commandant, Robert Mulka, a former businessman, liked to indulge in rabbit hunts: prisoners had their caps knocked off and when they stopped to pick them up they were shot – 'killed while trying to escape'.

Auschwitz's medical officer Dr Mengele demonstrated a less primitive sense of humour. On Yom Kippur (Day of Atonement) two thousand Jewish boys assembled on the camp's football ground and were made to pass under a plank nailed to the goalposts; all those whose heads did not touch the plank had to go to one side, and were subsequently gassed. (On the Day of Atonement the Jews recite a prayer describing the Lord as a shepherd who passes his flock under a rod.)

Every camp produced variations on the SS officers' favourite theme of mocking the Jewish religion in the very act of wiping it out. The commandant of Treblinka appointed a 'shitmaster' who, attired in rabbinical garb and armed with alarm-clock and whip, had to enforce time-limits among the dysentry-afflicted users of the camp latrines.

At Belcez the doors of the gas chamber were draped in synagogue curtains bearing the Hebrew inscription, 'This is the gate of the Lord through which the righteous shall enter'; and the way into the death compound from the guards' quarters was signposted 'Entrance to the Jewish State'.

At Auschwitz the guards whiled away their off-duty hours with sport naively untinged by religious allusions. They would order prisoners to put mice inside their trousers (which were tightly bound below) and to stand to motionless attention – on pain of being whipped – with the rodents crawling over their bodies. Prisoners had bottles placed on their heads and shot off; they were made to walk planks seven metres off the ground – an 'enemy parachutist' (anyone who fell off) received twenty-five lashes – or were savaged by huge dogs who on the order of 'Man, attack dog' literally tore their victims to pieces.

But it would be wrong to speak of all SS camp personnel as thorough-going embodiments of evil. One of the medical officers at Auschwitz, responsible for 'selecting' thousands, saved the life of a woman doctor who had attended the same university as himself and pretended to remember him as an habitué of the local student tavern.

When Sturmbannführer Höfle, an aide of Globocnik's with two hundred thousand deportations to his credit, lost a daughter in a diphtheria epidemic he sobbed at the grave: 'This is the punishment of heaven for all my misdeeds.'

Ohlendorf felt a need for dressing up the massacres perpetrated by his *Einsatzgruppe* D as military executions, and Himmler himself was taken ill watching a mass-shooting at Minsk in 1942 – whereupon Gruppenführer Wolff remarked to his escorts: 'Let him just see what he demands of others.'

Höfle's and Wolff's graveside *cris-de-cœur* showed the perversion of vestigial stirrings of conscience into self-pitying cliché – a feeling of being hard done by alternated with the euphoria of violence as a stock SS emotion. Thus Gendarmeriemeister Fritz Jacob complained bitterly at having to exterminate Jews while enduring separation from his family.

When Globocnik had 'dissolved' all the camps under his jurisdiction by late 1943, he querulously reminded Himmler of the iron crosses promised for 'this hard work' – it was unfair that the 'smaller Warsaw enterprise' (i.e., the crushing, in April 1943, of the heroic Ghetto rising by Waffen SS Brigadeführer Jürgen Stroop) should have brought Stroop's men greater rewards for less effort.

Globocnik's dissolution of the Lublin camp complex signified that another internal SS controversy – between advocates of the extermination of the Jews and advocates of their employment as slave labour – had been concluded; in the Jewish as in the Russian question, Nazi race dogma blotted out all considerations of German national self-interest.

The SS department most affected by this decision was Oswald Phol's *Wirtschafts und Verwaltungs Hauptamt* (WVHA, or Economic Administration Main Office). The ex-naval paymaster Pohl had been Himmler's economic overlord ever since the Reichsführer's decision to found an economic empire on concentration-camp labour in 1938. Under Pohl's aegis SS enterprises concerned with arms production, textile and leather manufacture, food processing and the distilling of non-alcoholic beverages had grown by the middle of the war to reach an annual turnover of fifty million Reichsmark.

The SS industry to show the fastest growth rate was armaments. Its director, Dr Hans Kammler, a technocrat of rambling ambition, also masterminded the construction of gas chambers, barracks, hangars and underground factories; in addition Kammler built launching sites for flying bombs and V2 rockets – top priority tasks for which he requisitioned a labour force of 175,000 prisoners of war and KZ inmates in 1942.

At this stage of the war Pohl's slave-driving senior executives became concerned about concentration camp labour being a diminishing asset: during December 1942 alone an overall KZ population increase (through continent-wide raids and manhunts) of 136,000 had to be offset against a 'natural' wastage rate of 70,000. Something clearly had to be done; the WVHA accordingly forbade the ill-treatment of KZ labourers and limited their working day to eleven hours.

To squeeze the last reserves of strength (and profitability) out of the surviving quarter of Polish Jewry, Pohl's men early in 1943 set up *Ostindustrie GmbH*, but as all its 'employees' were liquidated within that year the firm eventually went into liquidation, too.

Even then the supply of labour for the slave empire of the *Schutzstaffeln* did not dry up. One source of replenishment was the millions of foreign conscript workers in the Reich. By an arrangement between Himmler and Justice Minister Thierack of 1942, any foreign worker guilty of absenteeism, rationing offences or contact with German women was automatically sent to a concentration camp. During the first half of 1943 alone 200,000 suffered this form of punishment; a year later in 1944 Armament Minister Speer complained to Hitler that the SS were still bagging his labour force at the rate of 30–40,000 a month.

In the final twelve months of the war Pohl's slave-labour army numbered 600,000; 250,000 toiled in privately-owned arms factories (such as Krupps'), 170,000 in state-run 'Speer enterprises', 130,000 in agriculture and service industries and the remainder on construction sites.

Though by this time the situation of the Reich was growing increasingly abnormal, certain normal laws still applied – such as the ineluctable law of supply and demand. As shortages placed labour at a premium, SS 'entrepreneurs' able to supply the market with this scarce commodity – of whatever quality – stood to make a sizeable profit. The exact amount of profit involved, the ratio of yield to investment, emerges from this statement prepared by the cost-accounting department of the WVHA:

> 'The hiring out of concentration camp inmates to industrial enterprises yields an average daily return of 6 to 8 marks from which 70 pfennigs must be deducted for food and clothing. Assuming a camp inmate's life expectancy of 9 months we multiply this sum by 270; the total is 1,431 marks. This profit can be increased by rational utilization of the corpse, i.e. by means of gold fillings, clothing, valuables, etc., but on the other hand every corpse represents a loss of two marks which is the cost of cremation.'

In theory this profit accrued to the Reich; in practice it frequently went to one of the Reichsführer's minions, such as the commandant at Buchenwald, Hermann Pister, who amassed a personal fortune by supplying Ruhr industrialists with KZ labour. When negotiating with

Russian Jews begging for food (1941)

Access bridge to the Lodz ghetto (1941)

Auschwitz: arrival

Auschwitz: the ovens

Auschwitz: what remained

Belsen, April 1945. On British instructions camp guards bury their victims in mass graves

Krupp, Mannesmann, and the rest, Oberführer Pister could almost claim to be a fellow-tycoon since, in addition to his KZ post, he held lucrative directorships in the SS arms manufacturing company, the SS construction company and so forth.

Pister, though, still fell short of his predecessor, Buchenwald Lagerkommandant Koch who, after the *Kristallnacht* round-up of thousands of Jews in November 1938, had diverted vast wealth 'forfeit to the Reich' into his own pockets. Himmler, who held very strong views on the subject of corruption – though not totally averse to taking financial advantage of his position, he would deduct the cost of 'official' petrol used on family outings from his personal salary, told SS leaders at Posen in October 1943, 'We have taken the Jews' riches away from them; whoever touches a single Reichsmark forfeits his life.'

Himmler's draconian avowal rang both true and false. Harsh discipline and meagre pay invested the SS with an aura of austerity, but this was a smokescreen behind which Nazism – aptly defined as 'an appeal to the inner *Schweinehund* inside every German' by the Social Democrat leader Kurt Schuhmacher – acted as a goad to every base instinct.

# 6

# Collapse of the Third Reich

CORRUPT CONDUCT WITHIN THE 'SCHUTZSTAFFELN' ELICITED retribution in a highly selective manner. Each Nazi institution was a hierarchy in which punishment depended on the offender's place in the pecking order; thus after an investigation of the Warsaw-based Waffen SS Cavalry Division on charges of currency fraud and deals in confiscated Jewish property, two junior officers were executed while their heavily implicated commander Hermann Fegelein, show-jumper, founder of the (aristocratic) Reiter SS and Hitler's 'brother-in-law' – through his marriage to Gretel Braun – got off scot-free.

By the same token Koch's Buchenwald bonanza hinged on Eicke and Pohl, whose connivance the affluent Lagerkommandant purchased by regular gifts of 10,000 Reichsmark. Though the tax office responsible for Buchenwald, and the regional SS and Police leader Prince Waldeck-Pyrmont (a bitter adversary of Koch's), repeatedly pressed for an investigation of the camp's tangled finances, Koch's Midas touch even survived the front-line posting of chief KZ administrator Eicke in 1941. Some time later Himmler did, however, sanction an inquiry – either out of revived puritanical zeal or because he felt the need to curb his overmighty subject Pohl.

The SS investigator Dr Morgen encountered endless evasion – climaxed by Koch's evasive action in getting transferred to the Lublin camp command before Dr Morgen had even started on the case. At Lublin, where the new commandant relied on Globocnik's powerful protection, his corrupt rule soon resulted in a mass escape attempt after which – to deprive Dr Morgen of potential prosecution witnesses – Koch had thousands of prisoners slaughtered.

Nonetheless, particularly on account of the attempted mass breakout, Koch was eventually judicially executed – an extremely unusual ending to a corrupt (in the Nazi sense) SS career. Thus Rudolf Höss, the ex-Freikorps murderer who became first Lagerkommandant of Auschwitz, was charged with misappropriating gold from teeth in 1943; found 'guilty', he had to exchange his Auschwitz command for the

Deputy Inspectorate of concentration camps – a higher post with fewer bonuses!

Promotion as a result of blatant misconduct – a paradigm of SS judicial processes. Oskar Dirlewanger, a convicted child-rapist and head of a Waffen SS *Sonderkommando* staffed by discharged convicts, came to Dr Morgen's attention through reports of widespread looting and racketeering in the Cracow ghetto. When applying for a warrant for his arrest, the investigator discovered that Dirlewanger – whose officers' mess diversions included injecting Jewish girls with strychnine and watching their death agonies – was not subject to the jurisdiction of the regional SS and Police leader but to that of Gottlob Berger at SS Main Office, Berlin.

On receiving Dr Morgen's application Berger posted Dirlewanger to anti-partisan duties in White Russia and promoted him to Oberführer *en route*.

The *affaires* Koch, Höss and Dirlewanger are illustrations of the way in which inter-departmental rivalries – regional SS and Police leader versus Lagerkommandant, Waffen SS command versus regional SS and Police leader – determined SS judicial processes. Both within the Black Order and the Nazi state as a whole the combating of corruption was little more than a function of the rivalry between competing power cliques.

The first prerequisite for the cleaning-up of corruption is a visible distinction between right and wrong, which was totally absent from Nazi society. In the Third Reich it could happen that the medical officer of a concentration camp obtained a doctorate at the University of Freiburg on the strength of a dissertation written for him – in exchange for survival rations – by two Buchenwald inmates. More crucially, in the Third Reich it was possible for three hundred and fifty trained doctors (one in every three hundred of the medical profession) to take part in medical KZ experiments dressed up as research. Their experiments covered a wide spectrum of 'medical science' and inflicted indescribably agonizing deaths on countless camp inmates.

Research in sterilization techniques involved exposure to large doses of X-rays, straightforward castration, sterilization with drugs, and the injection of inflammatory liquid into the uterus. Other experiments entailed drinking sea-water, infection with gas, gangrenous wounds, bone transplants, exposure to phosgene and mustard gas, the artificial inducing of phlegmon, and so forth.

At KZ Neuengamme Dr Heisskeyer injected Jewish children with tuberculosis bacilli and watched their deaths. At KZ Dachau Dr Rascher conducted super-cooling experiments – for the alleged benefit of pilots forced to bale out into the sea – in which prisoners were immersed in near-freezing water for lengthy periods. Himmler, the dabbler in homeopathy, had picked up some old wives' tale according to which after sea-rescues the wives of North Sea fishermen took their half-frozen husbands to bed with them to warm them up; in consequence he ordered Dr Rascher to undertake resuscitation experiments with body heat and directed the women's KZ Ravensbruck to provide the doctor with four prostitutes as supplier's of 'animal warmth'. In his directive Himmler emphasized that the chosen four, who would come into physical contact with KZ inmates, must under no circumstances be German prostitutes.

The SS has often been described as a state within a state, but this is something of an over-simplification. The dynamics of power in the Third Reich are too complex for shorthand definitions, and unfortunately lack of space precludes further elaboration here. Perhaps both extremes can be avoided by an historical analogy, albeit tenuous, between the empires of Charlemagne and Hitler.

Both the First and the Third Reich were governed – under Holy Roman Emperor and Führer respectively – by powerful and mutually hostile feudatories: the Nazi counterparts of the Empire's warring dukes and margraves were the chiefs of the Party, the SS, the SA, the Propaganda Ministry, the Foreign Office, the Ministry of Eastern Territories, and the Labour Front. Combining abject deference to the Führer with venomous antipathy towards each other, Bormann, Himmler, Lutze, Goebbels, Ribbentrop, Rosenberg, Ley – not to mention the empire-builder *par excellence* Göring – were locked in civil strife with ever-changing fronts, allies, enemies and neutrals, and one constant factor: the struggle for power.

In this conflict Himmler managed to score over his rivals more often than they did over him. From his unassailable power base, he was ceaselessly encroaching on the sphere of competence of the Wehrmacht, the Ministry of the Interior, the Foreign Office, the Ministry of Eastern Territories and other institutions of the Nazi state. In August 1943 Himmler actually replaced Minister of the Interior Frick, whose purely nominal subordinate he had been since 1937.

The Himmler–Ribbentrop feud went back nearly as long and had been highlighted by SS forays into foreign affairs which ran counter to official Reich policy. Thus in Rumania in 1940 the Reich exerted pressure to install Marshal Antonescu as head of a pro-German administration while the SD produced a rival candidate: the Iron Guard leader Horia Sima. After Antonescu's assumption of power (with the aid of German troops who entered the country) the SD still supported an attempted Iron Guard coup – but to no avail. The discomfiture of the *Schutzstaffeln* was compounded by Ribbentrop's appointment of a whole batch of SA dignitaries as Reich ambassadors to Germany's Balkan satellites, where these survivors of the Röhm Putsch exercised vice-regal powers.

Not long afterwards the chance of a counter-stroke presented itself to the Black Order when Dr Luther, a departmental head at the Foreign Office, circulated among interested parties in Berlin a confidential memorandum about Ribbentrop's mental incapacity. Himmler, however, did not forward this document to Hitler since he was reluctant to provoke a showdown with Ribbentrop so soon after the 'Sima Affair'. More importantly, with Nazi victories rapidly reducing the area of Europe which was not German – and with it the scope for foreign policy-making – he may well have decided to concede to Ribbentrop the monopoly of an ever-shrinking field.

Henceforth Himmler concentrated on building up his power in Nazi-occupied Europe where, though up to 1943 heads of Army Groups outranked SS commanders on every front, in all rear areas the military were subordinate to the regional SS and Police leaders. Apart from exercising vast police powers, the SS contrived to infiltrate steadily into the administration of the occupied territories. In Poland they coerced Governor Hans Frank (an inveterate enemy of Himmler's) into appointing Higher SS and Police leader Krüger as his Secretary of State by the simple expedient of confronting him with evidence of his personal corruption unearthed by one of Dr Morgen's colleagues. In occupied Russia they gained additional leverage when the Reich Minister for Eastern Territories, Rosenberg, felt driven to enlist Gottlob Berger's aid against his own over-mighty subject, the uniquely refractory Reichskommissar Koch of the Ukraine.

But in the Nazi feudatories' war of all against all, fortune – or Hitler's countenance – hardly ever smiled on one of the belligerents consistently. While Himmler was enlarging his stake in the political administration of occupied Europe he met with a reverse in the economic sphere: his one-time accomplice (of Röhm Putsch days) Göring set up the *Haupttreuhandstelle Ost* (or Eastern Trustee Authority), which snatched

snatched up all confiscated industrial property in Poland and Russia.

At the height of the war Viktor Lutze, Röhm's colourless successor as SA Chief of Staff, joined Governor Hans Frank in an anti-Himmler *fronde* of considerable potential – Frau Lutze was related to the Wehrmacht Commander-in-Chief von Brauchitsch – but this threat evaporated when the stormtroop chief died soon afterwards in a car accident.

These intrigues and power struggles at Hitler's court had their counterpart within the narrower compass of the SS establishment. Although Himmler maintained no court in the accepted sense of the term, certain members of his immediate entourage had readier access to – and correspondingly greater influence over – the Reichsführer than senior officers outranking them. The key figure of this inner circle was Standartenführer Rudolf Brandt, the assiduous male typist promoted to Principal Aide, whose intercession was indispensable to anyone seeking audience with the Reichsführer. Less centrally placed was Dr Korherr, an academic who doubled as SS statistician and as Himmler's 'private eye' into the affairs of his top brass – an extramural activity which earned Korherr a nasty beating-up and eventual relegation to a provincial backwater. There was also the Finnish 'doctor' Felix Kersten, who owed his licence as political jester, and his ability to influence Himmler towards rare acts of mercy, to his skill in alleviating his exalted patient's chronic stomach cramps.

The death of Heydrich in June 1942 had left a vacuum at the apex of the SS power structure and Himmler prevaricated for eight months before filling it. The short list for the succession comprised three names: Dr Stuckart, Ernst Kaltenbrunner and Max Schellenberg, the head of SD Foreign Intelligence (whose suggestions for contacts with the chief of US Intelligence, Alan Dulles, in Switzerland during mid-1942 had been vetoed by Himmler in the aftermath of the Sima affair and the Luther Memorandum). Dr Stuckart was *Staatssekretät* at the Ministry of the Interior and Obergruppenführer Kaltenbrunner was Higher SS and Police leader of Vienna.

The eventual choice of Kaltenbrunner as head of the RSHA was influenced by Himmler's calculation that, as a newcomer to the capital and its cabals, the Austrian would prove a more pliable instrument in his hands than the others. The term 'pliable' may seem singularly inappropriate when applied to this scarfaced thug, but in fact Kaltenbrunner throughout fell short of establishing his predecessor's ascendancy over the six powerful departmental heads of the RSHA, who included Oswald Pohl and Gestapo Chief Heinrich Müller.

It was 'Gestapo-Müller' who in early 1944 issued the notorious 'cartridge directive' under which Soviet prisoners of war who had helped to identify captured political commissars for purposes of liquidation were themselves executed as *Geheimnisträger* ('bearers of secrets'). This blood purge was soon extended to all Russian prisoners charged with attempting escape, refusing work or inciting disaffection.

Müller's decimation of the Russian camp population occurred at the same time as the extension of the Final Solution to Hungary's three-quarters of a million Jews. Diverting badly needed military rolling stock, a small staff of experts from department IV B 4 of the RSHA headed by Obersturmbannführer Eichmann – and assisted by Hungarian officials and Fascists of the Arrow Cross Party – in three short months effected the round-up and deportation of close on half a million to the gas chambers of Auschwitz.

By summer the greater part of Hungary was *judenrein* (cleared of Jews); but with the Allies in Normandy and Germany's fortunes declining, the Hungarian head of state Admiral Horthy stealthily prepared to stop the deportations and take his country out of the war. To foil this move a Waffen SS unit under Otto Skorzeny (who had snatched Mussolini from Allied captivity in a daring airborne coup a year earlier) was despatched to Budapest, where Horthy was abducted and taken back to the Reich as a prisoner; his Arrow Cross successors in government kept Hungary in the war and continued the deportations of the Jews.

The overthrow of Horthy was one of a series of Waffen SS triumphs gained in the rear of the fighting front during the closing stages of the war.

In August the distant approach of the Russians had triggered off a mass uprising in Warsaw. German forces in the Polish capital were headed by Gruppenführer von dem Bach-Zelewski, who disposed of police and Waffen SS contingents stiffened with Dirlewanger's criminal rabble and the Pole-hating Russian Kaminski Brigade. As the Red Army regrouped beyond the Vistula, Warsaw became engulfed in a Walpurgisnacht of death, fire and looting. The atrocities perpetrated by the *Sonderkommando* Dirlewanger were such that they caused the Wehrmacht Chief of Staff, General Guderian, to petition Hitler for redress, while Kaminski's conduct reputedly caused Bach-Zelewski to have him liquidated shortly after the crushing of the Warsaw revolt in October 1944.

Since besides Hungary and Poland the *Schutzstaffeln*'s battle honours included Slovakia, where Obergruppenführer Gottlob Berger had established the peace of the graveyard after an autumn uprising, the SS star was now very much in the ascendant in the darkening sky of the Third Reich.

Every passing month brought an accretion of Hitler's power. After the failure of the July Plot, he supplanted General Fromm as Commander of the Replacement Army. He then took overall charge of the V-weapons programme, and in October he assumed virtual command of the *Volksturm*, an emergency militia of German males between sixteen and sixty (whose ideological training, however, remained Bormann's responsibility).

What amounted to the investiture of an heir-apparent occurred on 9 November 1944: Himmler addressed the Munich Old Guard reunion in place of the grateful Hitler – an unprecedented departure from hallowed Party routine.

This political accolade was followed by an ambiguous military preferment. At the prompting of Bormann, who wanted to discredit his militarily inexperienced rival, Himmler received command of the Army Group Upper Rhine at the onset of the last winter of the war.

Though the war now had barely half a year to run, the German people, the Wehrmacht and, above all, the SS were by and large still besotted with the Führer. The Black Order overwhelmingly remained faithful – the more so because non-Germans in the Waffen SS (who by early 1945 actually outnumbered Reich citizens) fought with the desperation of self-acknowledged traitors to their own countries.

The Waffen SS as a whole continued to perform prodigious military feats and even managed to repeat their horrendous performance at Lidice. Klissura in Northern Greece, for example, Oradour and Tulle in France, Putten in Holland and other towns elsewhere all shared the fate of the Czech mining village after equally little provocation. Hand in hand with the slaughter of helpless civilians went that of unarmed enemy soldiers: Waffen SS massacred their American prisoners at Malmedy and Canadian captives at Ancienne Abbaye in the Ardennes.

While the SS soldiery thus steadily added to their reputation for military prowess and bloody excesses, some SS generals began to entertain doubts about the Führer's infallibility in strategic matters. After D-Day, Sepp Dietrich demanded a free hand for field commanders in the event of a collapse of the front and both Hausser (promoted from the Second SS Armoured Corps to command of the

Seventh Army) and his successor Obergruppenführer Bittrich concurred in their Army Group commander Rommel's bitter criticism of Hitler's war strategy.

Rommel, who had been convinced of the impossibility of German victory by the Normandy landings, was also privy to the Officers' Plot of 20 July 1944, the failure of which led to his subsequent suicide at the behest of the Gestapo.

July 20 saw the climax of various schemes against Hitler which had been hatched by military and civilian resistance circles at least since the outbreak of war. The leading civilian plotter (and Chancellor-Designate of Free Germany) was Carl Goerdeler, the Conservative ex-Mayor of Leipzig. Among Goerdeler's closest associates was the former Prussian Finance Minister Dr Popitz. Popitz had an acquaintance, the lawyer Dr Langbehn, who happened to live next door to Himmler at Dahlem, a suburb of Berlin.

Early in 1943 Popitz asked Langbehn to sound out Himmler about putting out peace-feelers to the West, and the lawyer eventually succeeded in arranging for Popitz to meet the Reichsführer. The Resistance man told Himmler he was the one sufficiently powerful leader in Germany to extricate the country from a war which could not be won and urged him to depose Hitler and initiate talks with the British and Americans. Himmler – who thanks to Schellenberg was familiar with this line of reasoning – adopted a non-committal, though interested, attitude; however, when in September 1943 the Gestapo decoded messages implicating Langbehn in links with the Allies, he broke off all contact and ordered Langbehn's arrest.

All this time the Gestapo were maintaining a discreet surveillance of Goerdeler, Popitz and other figures in the Resistance. In January an entire provincial network of conspirators, the Kreisauer Circle, suffered detection and arrest, but the chief bomb-plotter Colonel Stauffenberg remained undetected because his post at the headquarters of the Replacement Army afforded a wide degree of immunity from police control.

After Stauffenberg's bomb had failed to kill Hitler on 20 July 1944 Himmler's terror machine went into top gear. All the chief conspirators were speedily arrested and sentenced to death by the notorious 'People's Court' – but the speed of the apprehension and the judicial process was in marked contrast to the tardy way in which some of the sentences were carried out. Goerdeler owed the repeated deferment of his execution to none other than Himmler himself. After first making the condemned man write out a detailed account of his peace plan, Himmler actually visited Goerdeler in his cell, where he asked him to act as an intermediary between Churchill and himself. Goerdeler indicated his agreement and asked to be allowed to travel to Sweden in furtherance of the plan, but at this point Himmler, probably thinking the Swedish trip too risky, altered course yet again and ordered Goerdeler's execution (February 1945).

Other SS dignitaries showed similar tergiversation on the eve of defeat. Dr Stuckart, the *Staatssekretar* at the Ministry of the Interior and contender for the succession to Heydrich, let a senior ministry official influence him into rephrasing and thereby virtually nullifying a directive extending the Final Solution to Jews living in mixed marriages and the offspring of all such marriages (the so-called *Mischlinge*).

The implementation of the Final Solution itself was being modified. A meeting between Himmler and the Swiss President Musi (on Austrian soil in October 1944) resulted in the saving of some thousand 'privileged' Jews for a payment of five million Swiss francs raised by Jewish organizations. (Eichmann had previously suggested similar deals to Hungarian Jewish communal leaders, but these had come to nothing.)

In October, too, Himmler ordered the blowing up of the crematoria at Auschwitz, which the Red Army was to reach three months later. This necessitated changing the nature of the deputations from Budapest: instead of being shipped off for gassing, Hungary's remaining Jews were to be force-marched to labour camps in the Reich.

The extermination programme was declared to be at an end and KZ commandants instructed accordingly. But this in no way improved the situation of camp inmates, since in order to remove tell-tale evidence Himmler had ordered the evacuation of all concentration camps in the path of the advancing Allied armies. At the same time he instructed the guards to shoot all prisoners who dropped behind; thus fully half a year after the crematoria had stopped belching smoke some approach roads into Germany were littered with corpses in zebra-striped rags.

Himmler's contradictory treatment of the Jews reflected his generally schizophrenic thinking in the last few months of the war. While one part of his mind continued to revolve around the taboo idea of approaches to the West (via such intermediaries as the Swedish consul at Budapest, Paul Wallenberg), Himmler applied all his remaining mental faculties to the prosecution of the war.

In this he showed distinct mediocrity, so that in March 1945 he was, on Guderian's urgent insistence, relieved of the command of the Army Group, Upper Rhine. The same month saw an additional erosion of the military reputation of the SS. The collapse of Sepp Dietrich's Sixth Panzer Army on the Hungarian front so enraged Hitler that he had the sleeve-bands with the names of the Sixth's constituent SS divisions – 'Das Reich', 'Adolf Hitler', 'Hohenstauffen' – ceremonially torn off the soldiers' uniforms.

Hitler's treatment of those whose 'honour meant loyalty' was soon to be reciprocated. Obergruppenführer Felix Steiner, who somewhat contentiously suggested to the Belgian SS leader Leon Degrelle that the British and Americans be greeted with banners inscribed 'Here is the anti-Soviet front', marked Hitler's fifty-sixth birthday (20 April 1945) by disobeying a directive of the Führer's to raise the siege of Berlin which would have entailed committing his 10,000-strong force to an attack on 100,000 Russians.

Yet at the same date 650 of Degrelle's Belgian Waffen SS men continued to fight the Russian crossing of the Oder until only thirty-five of their number were left alive. In fact all along the shrinking fronts SS units were still fighting doggedly – as well as executing would-be capitulators to ensure that directives for last-ditch resistance emanating from the marooned capital would be obeyed.

Now, as the Russian armies closed in on Berlin, Himmler, who saw himself as legitimate successor to the almost defunct Führer, moved towards treasonable negotiation with the enemies Germany had been fighting in her two separate, yet overlapping wars – the Jews and the Allies.

Because the Reich's Jewish War had been an encounter between total aggression and utter defencelessness without parallel in history, Himmler's parleying, though politically irrelevant, had an air of black comedy. Twenty-four hours after he had taken his final leave of Hitler and the latter's companions, who were busy celebrating the Führer's birthday in the bunker, Himmler met Norbert Masur of the World Jewish Congress at Hartzwalde in as yet unoccupied North Germany.

Masur was the first Jew Himmler had met in twelve years as an individual and not as an undifferentiated specimen of a genus doomed to extinction. Himmler opened the Hartzwalde meeting (prepared by Schellenberg and Kersten) by insisting that his emigration policy could have benefited the Jews, and blaming its failure on the obstruction of other countries. He even tried to argue that concentration camps were really retraining centres. Masur ignored this gibberish and asked that all

Jews in Nazi camps should be released and the evacuation death marches discontinued; but Himmler, still torn between fear of discovery by Hitler and the desire for an alibi for the West, would concede nothing beyond an already mooted transfer of one thousand Jewish women from Ravensbruck KZ to Sweden.

Three days later Himmler met his go-between with the West, the Swedish Count Bernadotte, at Lübeck. It was during this encounter that Himmler, who still considered himself German commander-in-chief, finally brought himself, at Schellenberg's prompting, to offer capitulation to the Western Powers, but not to the Russians. Bernadotte, who doubted the feasibility of this, asked the Reichsführer what he would do in the event of his offer being rejected. Himmler replied, 'Then I shall take command of the Eastern Front and be killed in battle.'

This statement was pure hyperbole – partly because in the short run Hitler, who heard of the Lübeck surrender offer through a BBC broadcast monitored in the bunker, posed a greater threat to Himmler's life than the Red Army. Immediately upon receiving the news Hitler had screamed out an order for Himmler's arrest and had gone on to vent his murderous rage by shooting the nearest SS man to hand, his 'brother-in-law' and liaison officer with Himmler, Hermann Fegelein.

The courier entrusted with the order for Himmler's arrest, Air Marshal von Greim (the last man to flee the besieged bunker by 'plane) caught up with the 'traitor' at the Baltic coast headquarters of Admiral Doenitz, Commander-in-Chief of the Northern Armies, but knew better than to press the matter. Doenitz remained unaware of Himmler's treachery and in fact – since news of Hitler's death was expected at any hour – looked upon the SS leader as virtually his Führer. In the event it was Doenitz himself on whom Hitler bestowed the succession in the political testament drawn up before his joint suicide with Eva Braun (30 April 1945). The sovereign period of office of the Doenitz government, from which Himmler – to his intense chagrin – found himself excluded, extended from May Day 1945 to VE Day, 8 May.

On this day Himmler shaved off his moustache and reduced his 150-strong retinue, which included Obergruppenführer Ohlendorf and von Woyrsch, to as many as could be transported in four cars. On 10 May the four cars set off in a south-westerly direction, but had to be abandoned on the right bank of the Elbe; the SS fugitives were ferried across the river by a fisherman.

Himmler, further disguised by an eye-patch, carried identity papers made out in the name of Heinrich Hitzinger (who had been executed after a 'People's Court' trial). On 23 May he was arrested at a British checkpoint and taken to 031 Interrogation Camp, where he was recognized and placed under armed guard. Later that evening an army doctor, convinced that the prisoner was concealing poison on his body, inspected Himmler's anus, hair and ears and finally order him to open his mouth. As the doctor was about to insert two fingers in his mouth Himmler suddenly bit down hard – thereby crushing a phial of poison between his teeth. Emetics and stomach pumps proved of no avail, and within minutes he was dead.

Two days later (25 May 1945) Himmler's corpse, wrapped in army blankets and camouflage netting, was interred at an unmarked spot near Lüneburg. In peacetime Sergeant-Major Edwin Austin, who performed this last office for the Reichsführer, had been a dustman.

# Postscript:
# Nuremberg and After

THUS HAD THE REICHSFUHRER FOLLOWED FUHRER AND REICH into limbo – into a sphere of history beyond myth or the involvement of posterity. Himmler had vanished; but what of his surviving followers – who were, incidentally, no less easily identifiable (through the bloodgroup number tattooed on their arms)?

Mowing down war-weary fellow-Germans in the process, they had fought to the last – or almost to the last. On the day of Hitler's suicide Gruppenführer Mohnke, whose *Leibstandarte* fanatics had been dragging wounded soldiers and schoolboys out of cellars and hanging them as a warning to the faint-hearted, tried to make his own escape and failed. Mohnke's case was far from unique. In this sort of conduct the upper echelons of the *Schutzstaffeln* were yet again – only this time unconsciously – aping their Reichsführer.

Had he not decreed a fight to the finish while himself engaged in surrender talks? Had he not – by the standard he had himself proclaimed – been guilty of even graver dereliction of duty when, instead of dying in battle or defiantly justifying his record before the victors' court, he had scurried away and died like a cornered rat?

The Neo-Nazi author Erich Kern* wrote in the aftermath of defeat:

> 'An SS officer and bearer of the Knight's Cross hanged himself in the camp latrine, leaving a note that declared he could no longer live since his Reichsführer had betrayed him. He who had denied SS suicides military burial swallowed cyanide instead of accepting responsibility and saving a hundred poor devils who had only carried out his orders from the gallows.'

The SS veteran Kern articulated a feeling common to many; Himmler, who had created the SS myth, was also instrumental in shattering it. After their liberation, news about the camps had spread, leaving an indelible stain on men's minds everywhere, but the postwar collapse of SS morale owed more to the unmarked grave near Lüneburg than to the pyramids of matchwood skeletons at Belsen.

* Erich Kern, *Der Grosse Rausch* (Zurich 1948), p. 184.

Belsen incidentally also provided a contrasting instance of the recovery of SS morale. By autumn 1945 local rumours were circulating according to which the British had deliberately fed Belsen inmates to death – besides inflating the camp's mortality figures by inscribing 'Here Lie Five Thousand' upon mass graves containing an uncounted, but allegedly smaller, number of corpses.

But there were also countervailing instances of contrition. Obergruppenführer Herbert Backe, the former Reich Minister of Food, before his suicide wrote to a Buchenwald survivor, Eugen Kogon, asking forgiveness for the starvation rations he had apportioned to concentration camp inmates.

In the aftermath of war, however, an outraged world was more concerned with the victors' retribution than with the contrition of the defeated. The Allies set up an International Military Tribunal at Nuremberg which (in September 1946) designated the SS as a criminal organization and indicted the top SS leader, Ernst Kaltenbrunner, head of the Reich Security Main Office, as a major war criminal alongside Göring, Ribbentrop, Sauckel, Ley, Streicher, Frick, Keitel and others.

These instigators of Nazi aggression and persecution duly ended on the gallows – preceded by some of the more notorious (though low-ranking) KZ guards, such as the SS maiden Irma Grese who had amassed a collection of lamp-shades made of camp-inmates' skin.

1947–8 saw the *Einsatzgruppen* officers' trial at Nuremberg – as well as the arraignment of the SS Economic Administration and of 'Death Doctors' charged with KZ medical experiments. The intensification of the Cold War at this time – the Berlin Blockade, the Communist coup in Czechoslovakia, the Korean War – hereafter prompted the Allies to temper justice with a degree of mercy conducive to the integration of Germany into the Western camp, and this led to widespread commutation of death penalties and drastic reductions of jail sentences.

The Allies' judicial appeal machinery became clogged with petitions for clemency; when the US High Commissioner John MacCloy in July 1951 finally dismissed appeals by seven SS officials sentenced to death in the 1947–8 trials, many Germans charged him with having played a sadistic three-year game of cat-and-mouse.

The fate of the 'Landsberg Seven' (so-named after their place of imprisonment) deeply stirred public opinion; a protest petition attracted hundreds of thousands of signatures.

* Göring actually cheated the hangman by taking poison.

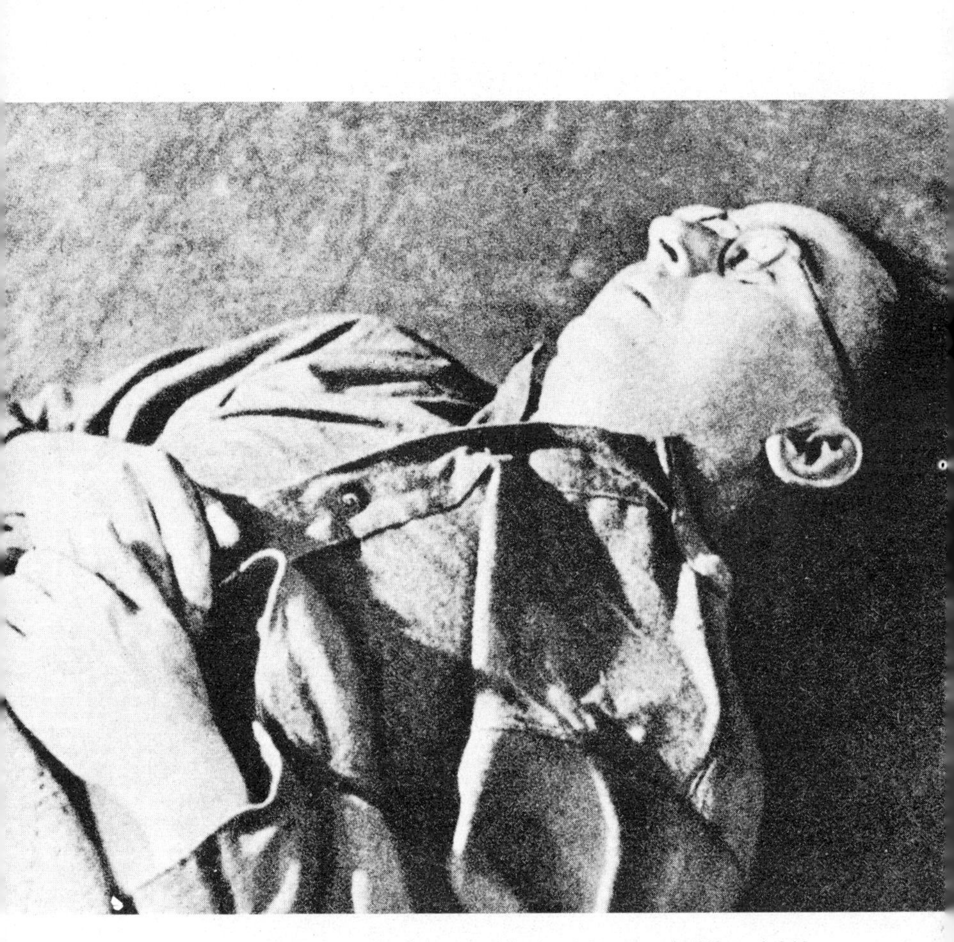

Himmler lies dead after swallowing cyanide (23 May 1945). His suicide, after a vain attempt to hide his identity, was the final blow to SS morale

The Nuremberg Trials: Ernst Kaltenbrunner, chief SS war criminal. Executed in 1946

The Nuremberg Trials: Einsatzgruppe commanders, who organised the atrocities behind the Eastern front. Otto Ohlendorf's (front row, left) appeal against his death sentence was not finally turned down until 1951

The Nuremberg Trials: Oswald Pohl, head of the SS economic administration, hears the announcement of his death sentence. (3 November 1947)

The SS rune – symbol of tyranny to the postwar generation. Protest at the Russian invasion of Czechoslovakia 1968

German townscape (Aachen), 1945

At the centre of this *cause célèbre* were Oswald Pohl and Otto Ohlendorf. Both men had given an extraordinary performance in the dock. The Jew-killer Pohl compared his trial to the notorious Dreyfus case – in which a Jew had been framed by anti-Semites – and described himself as a scapegoat for Obergruppenführer Wolff and other SS dignitaries still at liberty.

Ohlendorf's conduct had been even more bizarre. While awaiting trial on a charge of ninety thousand murders this trained economist pondered the workings of imperfect competition in the Nazi economy and berated his fellow-prisoner, ex-Arms Minister Albert Speer, for having favoured large firms against artisan enterprises in the award of government contracts. Cross-examined about his rationalization of gypsy executions as 'counter-espionage measures', Ohlendorf quoted the eighteenth-century dramatist Schiller on the role of gypsy spies in the Thirty Years' War.

When asked why the tally of *Einsatzgruppe* D – ninety thousand victims – was so much lower than that of the other units, Ohlendorf replied: 'I considered it beneath me to file returns which did not correspond to the truth!'

At the time of the Landsberg controversy some eminent Waffen SS veterans – such as Paul Hausser – launched a campaign to have their old force exempted from the International Military Tribunal's blanket designation of the SS as a criminal organization. Their campaign succeeded to a remarkable extent: Chancellor Adenauer, echoed by the Social Democrat leader Ollenhauer, attested the same soldierly qualities of courage and decency to the Waffen SS as to the Wehrmacht, and furthermore brought some SS personnel within the scope of the Bonn Government's Clause 131 (which gave Nazi civil servants pensionable status in the Federal Republic).

Even though 'Clause 131 pensioners' included – at least temporarily – the first Gestapo chief Rudolf Diels, the euthanasia expert Dr Clauberg, and the widows of Heydrich and Waffen SS General Turner – who had made Serbia *judenrein* – Bonn's solicitude for the welfare and respect of SS veterans did not turn out to have been entirely misplaced.*

* One alternative open to those charged with liquidating the heritage of the Third Reich was a massive onslaught on all culpable institutions and individuals. The 'pragmatist' Adenauer chose the other: he proselytized the large residue of unindictable Nazis left in the Federal Republic by concessions and by emphasizing the danger of the living Stalin – or Khrushchev – rather than that of the dead Hitler.

Many of West Germany's surviving 300,000 SS soldiers had grouped themselves together in the *Hilfsgemeinschaft auf Gegenseitigkeit* (HIAG, or Mutual Help Association), a potentially dangerous veterans' organization disingenuously camouflaged as a service for tracing missing *Kameraden*.

If HIAG slowly and reluctantly veered away from outright rejection of the Bonn state towards sullen co-existence with it, the credit was due – next to Chancellor Adenauer – to the war-hero-criminal Panzer Meyer. The famous SS tank commander, who had been sentenced for the Ancienne Abbaye massacre (see p. 72) and subsequently reprieved, denounced *Kameraden* who still dwelt in the past of nationalist dreams. He went on to describe the Federal Republic as 'our state' in which HIAG members could live with their wives and children.

Some SS men took acceptance of the new state to the extent of participating in its democratic processes at a variety of levels. Ex-Sturmführer Waldemar Kraft served as Minister without Portfolio in the Adenauer cabinet, ex-Gruppenführer Reinefarth, commander of SS police units in the Warsaw Rising, was a member of the Schleswig-Holstein *Land* parliament and ex-Hauptsturmführer Otto Hunsche (Eichmann's aide in Hungary) sat on a rural district council in Hesse.

Hunsche served in local government under an assumed name – a device also used by SS entrants into higher echelons of government service. Forged papers, and highly placed friends, eased Professor Heyde, ex-euthanasia expert and medical officer at Dachau, into a key post in Schleswig-Holstein's medical service, where he actually adjudicated on the pension claims of disabled concentration camp survivors.

Other – non-medical – SS *Doktoren* entered the private sector under their own names; the goodwill of certain Ruhr industrialists enabled ex-Obergruppenführer Werner Best (Reich Plenipotentiary in Occupied Denmark) and ex-Brigadeführer Franz Six (would-be SD Plenipotentiary in Occupied Britain) to participate in the German economic miracle at middle-management level.

Reintegration into postwar life took many forms. Prior to their respective arrests in the 1960s ex-SS *Sonderkommando* officer Friedrich Meyer trained police cadets at a *Polizeischule* near Münster and ex-Sturmbannführer Helmut Bischoff (who used to punish recalcitrant slave workers in a Harz Mountain underground rocket plant by personally stringing them up) worked in the tracing service of the Red Cross.

In this climate of apparent amnesia – only apparent, because the mills of justice continued to grind slowly – some SS veterans were overcome with nostalgia. Former Obergruppenführer Wolff serialized his reminiscences in an illustrated magazine and thus unwittingly provided pointers to previously undocumented wartime atrocities; this bizarre example of 'publish and be damned' earned Wolff a fifteen year sentence.

Hotel porter Kurt Bolender's nostalgia assumed a more private form. When arrested the former assistant Lagerführer at Sobibor death camp was found to have kept the metal clasp of his horsewhip (engraved with his initials) as a memento for twenty years. Soon after, Bolender killed himself while awaiting trial at Hagen, Westphalia. A Gallup-poll taken at Hagen near the end of this trial established that the word Sobibor carried no association for nine out of ten townspeople; some thought it the name of a new detergent.

Public indifference, bureaucratic sclerosis and a dearth of surviving witnesses all combined to enfeeble the due processes of Federal law concerning war crimes. Thus the largest single murder operation of the Third Reich – that of the *Einsatzgruppen* – escaped the comprehensive attention of the judicial authorities until 1958 and might have remained unexpiated *sine die* but for the initiative of one resolute policeman. The ex-police chief of Memel, Bernhard Fischer-Schweder, filed a suit against the Federal authorities for refusing him re-employment in the police force – thereby triggering off inquiries which revealed his own part, as an SS Oberführer, in *Einsatz* massacres of Lithuanian Jews and initiating a series of *Einsatzgruppen* trials which lasted until the 1960s.

These trials helped to clarify a crucial point in all post-war controversies about the *Schutzstaffeln*: did SS men have to kill on pain of being killed themselves? Controverting the standard defence argument of indicted war criminals former Brigadeführer Six declared that *Einsatzgruppe* service could be avoided by volunteering for front-line (or other) service, and ex-Oberscharführer Matthias Graf testified that refusal of an *Einsatzgruppe* commission cost him no more than 'social disgrace' and short-term imprisonment.

The most publicized German war crimes investigation was the mammoth Auschwitz trial held at Frankfurt in 1964–5, some of the twenty-three accused bearing names that carried intimations of immortality. All had readjusted to civilian existence with remarkable facility: Oswald Kaduk as a male nurse whose Berlin patients had nicknamed him

'Papa Kaduk', and Dr Viktor Capesius (the self-styled 'Satan incarnate' of Auschwitz) as a wealthy and publicly esteemed pharmacist at Goeppingen. According to their testimony none of the accused had any inkling of 'what Auschwitz was for'; with one exception they all showed open contempt for the court.

The trials continue (though most Germans would like to see them end) – and so does the controversy about the role of the SS. Paul Hausser, the elder statesman of HIAG has of late (1966) published the self-explanatory *Soldaten wie andere auch, Der Weg der Waffen SS* – (*Soldiers like the others – the path of the Waffen SS*); in earlier books Hausser acclaimed the soldierly virtues of Oskar Dirlewanger (an executed war criminal) and Gottlob Berger (serving twenty-five years for wartime murder of Jews) – and has described the Waffen SS as an early forerunner of NATO.

Adolf von Thadden and his co-founders of the NPD held the well-publicized inaugural meeting of their Party at the graveside of the Landsberg Seven – on the assumption that the 'blood of its martyrs will fructify the Church'. At the Federal elections of 1969 the National Democrats polled 4.3 per cent of the votes cast.

Elsewhere in the world there is unanimity about the role of the *Schutzstaffeln*. The initials SS are likely to remain symbols of abominable tyranny for generations to come. In Spring 1968 French youths born long after Oradour screamed them at the French special riot police – a few months later, on the other side of Europe, enraged Czechs born long after Lidice scrawled 'UϟϟR' on Soviet tanks.

The SS is a never-to-be-forgotten automaton that desolated Europe and left the world a poorer and darker place. Jewish legend tells of the Golem, a clay monster which a wonder-rabbi animated by placing the letter 'CHAI' (Hebrew for 'life') in its mouth.

The SS was no monster of clay but of flesh and blood. The letters animating it were 'TOD' (German for 'death'). But Hitler, though a worker of wonders, was no priest. His priestly power was derived from Nietzsche, who had written in *Thus Spake Zarathustra*: 'Ye say a good cause will hallow even war? I say unto you a good war halloweth every cause.'

# Notes on Further Reading

Hans Buchheim, *The Third Reich*, London 1961
Alan Bullock, *Hitler, A Study in Tyranny*, London 1952
Edward Crankshaw, *Gestapo – Instrument of Tyranny*, London 1965
Richard Grunberger, *Germany – 1918–1945*, London 1964
Gideon Hausner, *Justice in Jerusalem*, London 1967
Eugen Kogon, *The Theory and Practice of Hell*, London 1950
H. Krausnick, H. Buchheim, M. Broszat and H. A. Jacobsen, *Anatomy of the SS State*, London 1969
R. Manvell and H. Fraenkel, *Himmler*, London 1965
Bernard Naumann, *Auschwitz*, London 1966
Gerald Reitlinger, *The Final Solution*, London 1953
Gerald Reitlinger, *The SS – Alibi of a Nation*, London 1956
Hans Rothfels, *The German Opposition to Hitler*, London 1960
William Shirer, *The Rise and Fall of the Third Reich*, London 1960
J. Wheller-Bennett, *The Nemesis of Power*, London 1952

# Glossary

HIAG Mutual Help Association for SS soldiers
KZ Concentration-Camp
OKW Supreme Command of the Armed Forces
RSHA Reich Security Main Office
RUSHA Race and Settlement Main Office
SA Storm Troopers
SD SS Intelligence Service
WVHA Economic Administration Main Office
*Abwehr* Military Intelligence
*Ahnenerbe* SS foundation for research into Ancestral Heritage
*Asoziale* Anti-social (i.e. criminal or work-shy) concentration camp inmates
*Bildungsbürgertum* Middle class by virtue of education (as distinct from wealth)
*Braunes Haus* Nazi Party headquarters in Munich
*Eindeutschung* Germanization, i.e. turning foreign nationals into Germans
*Einsatzgruppe* Operational group carrying out liquidations in occupied territory
*Frauenlager* Concentration camp for women
*Freikorps* Right-wing para-military bands active after 1918
*Gauleiter* Highest Nazi Party leader in a Gau, or province of the Third Reich
*Gestapo* Secret State Police
*Gleichschaltung* Co-ordination or alignment with the Nazi state
*Gouvernement-Général* Nazi-occupied Poland
*Innenministerium* Reich Ministry of the Interior
*Iron Guard* Rumanian Fascist organization
*Judenrein* Cleared of Jews
*Judenreservat* A cluster of ghettoes
*Kamerad* Comrade – customary form of address within formations of the Nazi Party.

*Kleinbürger* Petty bourgeois
*Kristallnacht* Crystal Night, the pogrom of 10 November 1938, so-called on account of the shattered windows of Jewish shops
*Lager* Concentration (or prison) camp
*Lebensborn* Fountain of Life foundation – an SS adoption and child-kidnapping organization.
*Leibstandarte* Hitler's bodyguard
*Mischling* Person of mixed German-Jewish parentage
*Ostindustrie Ges.m.b.H.* Eastern Industry Ltd
*Protektorat* Nazi-occupied Bohemia and Moravia
*Putsch* Attempted *coup d'état*
*Reichstag* German Parliament
*Reichswehr* German Army; in 1935 its name was changed to Wehrmacht
*Reiter SS* Mounted SS
*Schutzstaffeln* Protective Squads
*Spartacists* Forerunners of the German Communist Party
'*Das Schwarze Korps*' Official weekly of the SS
*Sonderkommando* Special SS task force
*Stosstruppe* Shock troops
*Sturmabteilung* Stormtroopers
*Totenkopf* Death's Head
*Verfügungstruppe* Militarized formations of SS, renamed Waffen-SS in the winter of 1939–40
*Volksdeutsche* Germans living outside the Reich
*Volksgruppe* The body of Volksdeutsche within one specific country
*Volksgemeinschaft* The Folk community – the Nazi-projected image of a harmonious society
*Waffen SS* *see* Verfügungstruppe
*Wehrkreis* A Military District
*Wehrmacht* *see* Reichswehr
*Weimar Republic* The German democratic state constituted in 1919 and destroyed by the Nazis in 1933

# Table of Ranks

| SS | GERMAN ARMY | BRITISH ARMY |
|---|---|---|
| Reichsführer | Generalfeldmarschall | Field Marshal |
| Obergruppenführer | General | General |
| Gruppenführer | Generalleutnant | Lieutenant-General |
| Brigadeführer | Generalmajor | Major-General |
| Oberführer | Oberst | Brigadier |
| Standartenführer | Oberst | Colonel |
| Obersturmbannführer | Oberstleutnant | Lieutenant-Colonel |
| Sturmbannführer | Major | Major |
| Hauptsturmführer | Hauptmann | Captain |
| Obersturmführer | Oberleutnant | Lieutenant |
| Untersturmführer | Leutnant | Second Lieutenant |
| Sturmscharführer | Stabsfeldwebel | Regimental Sergeant-Major |
| Hauptscharführer | Oberfeldwebel | Sergeant-Major |
| Oberscharführer | Feldwebel | Quartermaster-Sergeant |
| Scharführer | Unterfeldwebel | Staff Sergeant |
| Unterscharführer | Unteroffizier | Sergeant |
| Rottenführer | Gefreiter | Corporal |
| Sturmann | Oberschütze | Lance-Corporal |
| SS-Mann | Schütze | Private |

# Index